KU-168-060

ABOUT THE AUTHOR

James Montague is an award-winning author and journalist from Chelmsford, Essex, who has reported from over 90 countries and unrecognised territories for the *New York Times*, CNN, BBC World Service, Bleacher Report and *Delayed Gratification*, among others. He is the author of four highly acclaimed books: *Thirty One Nil*, *The Billionaires Club* – both of which won Football Book of the Year at the British Sports Book of the Year Awards – *1312: Among the Ultras* and *When Friday Comes*. He lives in Istanbul.

ALSO BY THE AUTHOR:

Thirty-One Nil

The Billionaires Club

1312

JAMES MONTAGUE

When Friday Comes

Football revolution in the Middle East and the road to the Qatar World Cup

EBURY
PRESS

1 3 5 7 9 10 8 6 4 2

Ebury Press, an imprint of Ebury Publishing
20 Vauxhall Bridge Road
London SW1V 2SA

Ebury Press is part of the Penguin Random House group of companies
whose addresses can be found at global.penguinrandomhouse.com

Copyright © James Montague, 2008, 2013, 2022

James Montague has asserted his right to be identified as the author of this
Work in accordance with the Copyright, Designs and Patents Act 1988

First published by Mainstream Press in 2008
This revised edition first published by Ebury Press in 2022

www.penguin.co.uk

A CIP catalogue record for this book is available from the British Library

ISBN 9781529197167

Typeset in 10.5/14 pt SabonLTStd by Jouve UK, Milton Keynes
Printed and bound in Great Britain by Clays Ltd, Elcograf S.p.A.

The authorised representative in the EEA is Penguin Random House Ireland,
Morrison Chambers, 32 Nassau Street, Dublin D02 YH68

Penguin Random House is committed to a
sustainable future for our business, our readers
and our planet. This book is made from Forest
Stewardship Council® certified paper.

For Amr and the 74

'*After many years in which the world has afforded me many experiences, what I know most surely in the long run about morality and obligations, I owe to football.*'

Albert Camus

Contents

Author's Note

Back in 2004, when I first starting writing what would become *When Friday Comes*, I was a different person and the world was a different place. It was so long ago I used actual tapes in my Dictaphone. I had a film camera, not as some kind of retro fetish, but because digital cameras were the future. I could only send SMS from my Nokia. Facebook was still a pervy 'Hot or Not' website at Harvard. And I was writing most of it out by hand, in notebooks. It was before the Arab Spring. Before Yemen and Syria were destroyed. Before ISIS. And before Qatar won the right to host the 2022 World Cup finals.

It was strange looking at those notebooks now – and all the bus tickets and cigarette packets and political flags and obscure football shirts I collected along the way – nearly two decades later. As much as I can see my naivety and flaws, those years spent intensively traveling the Middle East to watch football left a lifelong affinity with the region and its people. I wrote other books, but they would always somehow find their way back to the region; the attempts by the Lebanese and Palestinian national teams to qualify for Brazil 2014 in *Thirty-One Nil*; the story of the Gulf's super-rich football club owners in *The Billionaires Club*; the revolutionary ultras of Egypt, Morocco and Algeria in *1312*. Somehow I could never forget the people I met and the places I visited whilst writing *When Friday Comes*.

When it came out in 2008 a book about Middle Eastern football was treated like an extreme niche, like an interest in Saxon pottery, or Soviet trains. But I decided to revisit and revise the book because so many people and teams I had met, and countries I had visited, had found themselves at the centre of world events and at the centre of the game. None more so than Qatar. In 2004, when I first went to Qatar, it felt like humans were more likely to colonise Mars before the Gulf would host a summer World Cup. But Qatar underwent an extraordinary transformation, whilst embroiled in controversy and a regional cold war, which I witnessed up close in real time.

There has perhaps never been a more controversial World Cup host. Qatar has been rightfully criticised for its human rights record, how it won the World Cup bid and especially its treatment of migrant workers. In 100 years from now, humans will looks back at *kafala* – in Saudi Arabia, the UAE, Qatar and beyond – as one of the great economic crimes of the twenty-first century. But that is only part of the story.

When Friday Comes is not an encyclopaedic history of football in the region, of the best players or the best goals. This book is made up of my experiences, some in my 20s, some in my 30s and some in my 40s, trying to watch football and understand the politics and culture of a place. A question I was often asked was why should Qatar be allowed to host a World Cup? Why should the Middle East, a region most people still stereotype as dangerous and unstable? If there was one thing I hope that *When Friday Comes* achieves, it is to show that the Middle East I witnessed is diverse, inspiring, full of contradictions but also full of hospitality and generosity of spirit. And that the Middle East has an obsessive love for football as deep and as profound as anywhere else on earth.

James Montague
İstanbul, April 2022

Introduction

DUBAI, UNITED ARAB EMIRATES, JULY 2006

The shisha café in the quiet, overlooked suburb of Hor al Anz in Dubai was the only sign of life on the street. It was late, past midnight, and the sticky humidity that always followed a searing Gulf summer's day coated everyone, and everything, in a thin layer of perspiration. My bed was enticing me home, but I still felt the pull of unfinished business. The lone yellow light along the concrete row of shops and shawarma stands threw itself enticingly onto the pavement in front. A distant clatter of cups and raised male voices in a foreign tongue wafted over. It was an alien sound, and an alien surrounding, but also immediately recognisable. I instinctively moved towards the light.

Inside, the harsh glow from the strip lighting mixed with the fog-thick fug of sweet apple tobacco and strong, dark cigarettes. It stung the eyes momentarily until a few moments of blinking acclimatised you to the toxic atmosphere. It was standing room only, the space tightly packed together by white-robed Emiratis wearing the traditional *kandura*. More stood in any available place they could find. I inched along the back wall and, to my surprise, found a solitary seat overlooked by the crush. A young Pakistani boy worked the cracks in the crowd, emptying ashtrays and refilling tiny thimbles full of thick Turkish coffee as his Egyptian colleague darted around the chairs with his metal ladle of hot coals, replacing the dying embers from atop each customer's billowing water pipe. The crowd was oblivious to their services. Tactics had to be discussed and players rated. All eyes were glued to the television in the corner of the room for the big match.

The appearance of white uniformity from the back of the room was a myth. Two tribes had emerged from Dubai's darkness to watch their respective teams do battle. An invisible line had been drawn in the sand, the room divided. To the right, the supporters of France, to the left, Brazil. The only way to differentiate the two was the hastily hung flags in each corner. It was the 2006 World Cup quarter-final and neither side could contemplate going home saddled with defeat. Arguments started to break out between the sets of fans over who was truly the greatest player in the world: Ronaldinho or Zidane. One Emirati supporting France had to be pulled back by his friends, so incensed was he that the great Zidane had been defamed. And the match hadn't even started yet.

Fights, devotion and obsession over faraway players and footballing nations was something I had quickly got used to when I accidentally stumbled into Dubai nearly two years previously. I hadn't even known for sure where Dubai was on the map when the email arrived advertising a job on the city's *Time Out* magazine. Two weeks later I was stepping out of an air-conditioned arrivals lounge into a brick wall of humidity. It was August and a hot, moist air had emptied my lungs the moment I stepped out of the controlled environment of the airport. Dubai was noisy, brash and hellishly hot. I had seen many new arrivals to Dubai react in different ways upon arriving in such an unforgiving environment. Some flew back home in a matter of days. Some were driven slowly mad by the heat. Relationships crumbled, vices fed. Most stayed, but stuck to their own in expat communities, replicating the life they had enjoyed back home oblivious to their surroundings and refusing to mix with the locals to acclimatise.

I had put my faith in football. In the beginning, to appease my longing for home, I would walk to my local shisha café late at night to watch English Premier League matches. More often than not the Egyptian manager would show only Tottenham games, no matter who else was on, given that the Egyptian international Mido was playing for them at the time. But soon I started to pick up the little threads of local football stories: a 2006 World Cup qualifier where the United Arab Emirates took on the mysterious North Korean national team; the struggles of the Palestinian national football team as they too tried, but ultimately failed, to qualify for the 2006 World

Cup; riots in the Lebanese league between supporters representing competing sectarian groups; footballers in Yemen struggling to kick the habit of their national drug qat. I devoured each and every story I could find. They were reported matter-of-factly, as if this kind of thing was perfectly normal in the Middle East. In a way, it was. But each story held something of wider significance. At its root football seemed to embody something about the country's psyche, its national character, its place in the world and where it was heading. I wanted to find out more about the Middle East and football seemed the perfect prism.

My catalyst was the news that French World Cup winner Marcel Desailly had signed to play in the Qatari league. Qatar was a barren, inoffensive country whose recent discoveries of gas had given it phenomenal wealth. A lot of this money was being pumped into sport, especially football, in an attempt to raise its international profile. Without thinking or having any particular plan I booked a flight to Doha. It seemed an absurd place with absurd ambitions to rule the world. How little I knew back then.

I then booked another flight to Egypt. And then another to Iran. It was the start of a journey that would take me to terraces and football pitches as far south as Sana'a, to Tehran in the east, to Tunis in the west and to Damascus in the north. In all these places I discovered the same thing: a deep and passionate love for the game and a window of wider understanding.

Talk of the globalisation of football isn't anything new but there is a reverence for the game in the Middle East that matches anything in Europe or South America. Yet, in theory, it shouldn't be like this. It isn't a place predisposed to successful Western interventions. Tragedy has stalked every corner of the region and when I first arrived the West's standing couldn't have been lower. Decades of nefarious interference in Iran, Lebanon, Saudi Arabia, Egypt, Israel and Jordan, to name a few, had created a toxic mix of corrupt regimes, Islamic fundamentalism, poverty, anger and disillusionment. The duplicity and betrayal reached its nadir after the disastrous Second Gulf War and the dismantling of Iraq. 'From the borders of Hindu Kush to the Mediterranean,' wrote the late Robert Fisk, 'we – we Westerners that is – are creating . . . a hell disaster.'

The chaos and the confusion had been a boon for Islamic fundamentalists seeking to paint the world in black and white, in us versus them rhetoric. It seemed – at least it did back in 2008 when I wrote the introduction to the first edition of *When Friday Comes* – that the diverse range of people who called the Middle East their home were rejecting the ideals that had once been heralded as the force of modernity. As a Westerner, an outsider trying to make sense of it all, taking the pulse of a region would be nigh-on impossible normally. Yet despite all this, one Western cultural export had achieved something that no amount of military intervention, aggressive foreign policy or attempted subjugation could. Football had won hearts and minds in the Middle East. Every country in the region was obsessed. A weekend of English Premier League or Serie A or La Liga football had the power to momentarily disable the most unforgiving jihadist. On the surface the apocryphal story of how Osama bin Laden would stand on the Highbury terraces of his beloved Arsenal in the 1980s sounded ridiculous. But it was a testament to the game's power and reach that it was almost believable. Almost.

How had the game conquered the land that one might expect to reject it the most? After all, the document that brought the game to life, one of the only documents that has universal and unwavering approval across the region and across sectarian lines, was set down in a smoke-filled room by English public school masters in the nineteenth century. In his *Twelve Books That Changed the World*, which included the *Rule Book of Association Football* among the dozen, Melvyn Bragg wrote that football '[h]as caused at least one war and many battles, often tragic, off the pitch. It has always triggered outbursts of local and national joy, pride and unity . . . and it all flowed from the meeting of a few Victorian Oxbridge graduates in a pub in Lincoln's Inn Fields in London 1863. Before the afternoon was out they had called themselves "the football association" and the *Rule Book* was on its way.'

It was perhaps one of the most successful imperialist documents ever written, allowing the British Empire to successfully spread the footballing gospel. When the British forces that helped colonise the game from land, sea and air retreated, momentum did the rest. Now, whether I was in Amman or Erbil, the first question I was asked in cafés and on street corners wasn't about George W. Bush or Tony Blair, or the war or Israel. I wasn't harangued for my country's complicity in very bad things. Rather, it was: 'Manchester United or Chelsea?' with the more sophisticated barracking me for supporting such a bunch of underachievers as West Ham United. One Lebanese international footballer in his late 20s even went as far as conceding that the 3–3 FA Cup final against Liverpool in 2006 was interesting to watch, but that West Ham were a shadow of the 1966 team, with Moore and Peters. I watched avowed Hezbollah members profess their undying love for Steven Gerrard, and spoke to Syrians who were livid – angrier than me, certainly – with Steve McClaren for not steering England to the finals of Euro 2008.

Simply put, football is one of the Middle East's great unifying threads. More so, you could argue, than Islam, divided as it is, sometimes violently, between Shia and Sunni, and certainly more than the failed forces of Arab nationalism. When I first wrote the introduction back in 2008, it was here that I said that *When Friday Comes* isn't a book with a happy ending, where football provided some kind of silver bullet to solve the region's seemingly intractable problems. Football doesn't change things by itself. A two-state solution won't be kick-started by the Palestinian national team playing Israel. Currently neither team would even dream of playing the other. And that still holds true. Football – thanks to its ubiquity and its closeness to the street, the beating heart of its society – is a mirror that reflects the Zeitgeist; a sponge that soaks up the tensions, the flaws, the frustrations and the hopes of society. For those involved it is one of the few forms of catharsis. Which might give another explanation as to why, every Friday from Aden to Aleppo, millions of fans leave the mosque and head straight for their local football club. In the absence of true democracy and a genuine public space, the terraces provide a forum for dissent. In Jordan, the songs for a free Palestine sung by the fans of the football team from Wihdat refugee camp wouldn't be accepted by the police on the street. In Iran, the frustrations of the women's rights movement are vented, not outside the Majlis, but outside the Azadi national football stadium before every home international. And in Egypt, it was the terraces that provided a space for young football fans to air grievances with Hosni Mubarak's dictatorship.

The power and the thought that the mosque has engendered have been well documented. But the terraces and stands of the football grounds of the region had been neglected for similar treatment, often because of a misguided idea that sport and politics are separate entities. Football is politics in the same way music is politics, or art, or film. It is an expression of the soul with a tribal beat. And it played its role – in some countries a vital role – in the greatest political upheaval to affect the region since the end of colonial rule.

When Mohamed Bouazizi, a poor, young Tunisian fruit and vegetable seller – blazing with injustice and frustration after having his meagre fruit cart impounded – set fire to himself in Tunisia in December 2010 it sparked a wave of uprisings and revolutions, the long-term effects of which are still only in their infancy. Tunisia, Egypt, Libya, Syria, Bahrain, Yemen; all saw their people rise up to depose leaders that had slowly constricted the life out of them. In the time before the Arab Spring, in the dark before the dawn, the atmosphere was hopeless and suffocating. Nowhere was this more true than in Egypt where Hosni Mubarak had crushed his opposition so completely that he almost succeeded in passing the mantle on to his son to continue his immorality. For three years the ultra groups of Egypt's biggest clubs grew more anti-regime with every beating and every arrest. Yet they couldn't be controlled. When the dam burst on 25 January 2011, the ultras were on the front line.

It was now more than simply using the game to hold a mirror to something that I wanted to understand better. The game itself had become part of the narrative. In Egypt, the ultras I had met by accident during a match in 2007 became the 'protectors of the revolution'. In Libya, the fledgling transitional government realised that the national team's qualification for the Africa Cup of Nations was worth more than a thousand show trials of Gaddafi apparatchiks. In Bahrain, the royal family realised the power of football too, but for the opposite effect. It was those involved in the game – national heroes – who were punished for their role in asking for greater freedoms. Their fame and their talent had been reversed, turned on them, bastardised to send a message to those that dared to question the status quo. Football didn't cause the Arab Spring. The neglect, humiliation and abuse of the poor and the young did. But in the game many found a voice that would not be heard by any other means, for good and sometimes for bad.

All the while, at its core, the fundamentals of the game and the passion it engenders remain the same: Indivisible, unchanging, sometimes ugly, always beautiful. The aftermath of the Arab Spring showed some of the game's power, as does the new oil wealth of the Gulf being channelled into football, through Manchester City, through PSG, most recently through the Saudi takeover of Newcastle United and, of course, through the 2022 World Cup, which will be held in Qatar. Football has now become a matter of state, with Gulf monarchies using the game to launder reputations and create a new reality.

When I think of that first trip to Qatar to meet Marcel Desailly in 2005, or that evening in Dubai, during the 2006 World Cup quarter-final, or watching a match in Damascus or Sana'a, they seem like a world away. And in some ways they are. But they still uphold the central tenet of what makes the game so fundamental to so many people in the Middle East and beyond: its power and its universality. In that café in Hor al Anz I watched France famously dispense with Brazil 1–0 thanks to a Thierry Henry goal. The French contingent of Emiratis celebrated as if the United Arab Emirates had themselves put the Brazilians out. They ran into the street and mounted a fleet of expensive, powerful 4x4s before driving them out onto a patch of sandy waste ground, spinning doughnuts and blaring their horns whilst hanging a French flag out of a blacked-out window. The Brazilian fans quickly walked away, heads down, in silence – the defeat tasting every bit as bitter as it did in Rio.

I
Qatar

DOHA, STATE OF QATAR, JANUARY 2005

Manfred Hoener was nowhere to be seen. The German football coach had agreed to meet me at Doha International Airport but, after running around the gleaming arrivals terminal, I had started to become desperate. By 9.30pm, and with the last stragglers from my inbound Dubai flight leaving the hall I still had no idea what Manfred Hoener looked like. I'd even begun to doubt his existence. Manfred had assumed something of a mythical status in my world. We had first made contact with each other when I came across an old story in the Scottish newspaper, the *Daily Record*. They had reported that legendary Dutch World Cup midfielder Ronald de Boer was close to signing a shock, big-money deal after falling out of favour at Glasgow Rangers. But rather than choose one of a host of ambitious mid-table English Premier League teams like Tottenham or Aston Villa, he had opted to decamp to the footballing powerhouse of Qatar on a whopping tax-free salary, with a nice villa and all-year-round sunshine. And he wasn't the first. Dozens of players, Gabriel Batistuta, Christophe Dugarry, Claudio Caniggia, Sonny Anderson and Romario, to name a few, had gone before him to play football in a country that few would be able to point to on a map. Qatar's population was under a million, its local football matches usually attracted a few hundred supporters at best and the country's nearest neighbours were Saudi Arabia, which was fighting an Al Qaeda-inspired insurgency, and Iran, which had been an international pariah since the 1979 Islamic Revolution. Iraq, on the verge of civil war after the Second Gulf War, was just down the road.

Still, Ronald de Boer didn't seem to mind. In fact, he had managed to talk his brother Frank into joining him in the ageing footballer exodus east. Or, more accurately, Manfred Hoener had convinced Ronald de Boer to convince his brother to join the ageing footballer exodus east. According to the *Daily Record*, Manfred Hoener was Qatar's 'Mr Fix it'. His real title was technical director for the Qatari Football Association and he was the man who worked on behalf of the Qatar FA to bring high-profile, big-name players nearing the end of their careers to the tiny Gulf state to play in their domestic Q League, no expense spared. His success had been legion, tempting players who could expect at least a season or two more in Spain's La Liga or the English Premier League to give up their plush cosmopolitan lifestyles in some of the world's greatest cities to move to Doha, a place of monumental dullness.

I had arranged to meet Manfred at the airport in the hope he could put me in touch with some of his success stories. But he clearly had more important things to do. As I sat on the deserted kerb outside the airport in the oppressive humidity, I wondered whether Ronald de Boer had been in the same position just weeks earlier, gently perspiring into his Armani suit as he stalked the arrivals lounge looking for the illusive Herr Hoener.

Manfred was supposed to escort me to a Q League match that night to see one of his charges in action. Pep Guardiola, the cultured Catalan midfielder who would soon become the world's best coach at Barcelona and later Manchester City, was, for now, playing for Al Ahli Doha. I could, Manfred reasoned, catch up with Pep after the game and interview him then. The interview was the last thing on my mind but in desperation I jumped into a shabby, orange and white Datsun taxi and took the short ride to where Al Ahli were playing.

It was immediately clear something was wrong. The floodlights were on but there was no sound. Inside, the main foyer was abuzz with tall Qatari teenagers who had just finished playing basketball. If any football had taken place here, I had missed it. But then, from behind the boys, came a man, striding towards me with a maniacal grin, arm outstretched. He was a big, perma-tanned, silver-haired fox with a handshake like a malfunctioning robot. 'Yes, yes, I'm sorry, but the interview is off,' he said in a manner that confusingly seemed to be both dismissive and friendly at the same time. 'The team was playing in Morocco and got caught in the worst snowstorms in 20 years. Never mind, I will drive you to a hotel.'

On the way downtown Manfred regaled me with his life story. In coaching terms he was something of a journeyman, a figure you often came across when at the coal face of international football. He had travelled three continents coaching football since he took his first job coaching kids deep in the Peruvian jungle in the 1960s. Although he was not without success. He was coach of the Nigeria team that reached the Africa Cup of Nations final in 1988 (they lost 1–0 to a Cameroon side led by Roger Milla, who was about to become a global star at Italia '90 two years later). That summer he took Nigeria to their first ever Olympics, in Seoul, but lost all three games. There was no shame in being ripped apart by a Brazil featuring a 22-year-old Romario. But the 1–0 loss to Australia meant Hoener was soon out of work. He spent most of the 1990s in Malawi building their national youth teams. Today he was arguably, *de facto*, the most important person in Qatari football. 'Yes, yes, it's all very good but the head, he doesn't want to talk to the press. But I don't tell him! Ha!'

'The head', Hoener's boss, was the president of the Qatari National Olympic Committee, Sheikh Tamim bin Hamad al Thani, the 24-year-old fourth son of the emir and his anointed heir. Between them, Manfred explained, they oversaw an odd transfer system where the committee directed Manfred to sign the players they wanted and then, in turn, doled them out to the clubs that bid for them. Manfred seemed to revel in his dissent, giving out a little whoop as we approached my shabby hotel. 'OK, OK. Call me tomorrow and we'll arrange something with Marcel.' Tomorrow I was to meet Manfred's greatest triumph thus far, the crowning glory of all his veteran baiting achievements: French World Cup winner Marcel Desailly.

Manfred had told me to go right at the mangled car on a podium. I hadn't a clue what he meant until my taxi dropped me off in front of a brand new shopping mall. Outside a large podium overlooked a roundabout. Atop sat a mangled car from a fatal car accident, a shock tactic to encourage young, wealthy Qataris to stop speeding in their powerful 4x4s. It was one of the unfortunate by-products of the Gulf's explosion of oil and gas wealth, a macabre metaphor reflecting one version of the region's own breakneck political, economic and social development over the past decade: too much, too young.

All I could see for miles around was flat, shimmering desert. Qatar didn't have much variety in terrain. The tiny Gulf state measures only 50 miles across, and almost all of it is desert. In summer, the thermometer rarely drops below 40°C during the day. Each road seemed to lead into a mirage of nothingness. I chose one and walked under the blazing midday sun. Soon a shining new building loomed into view – the sports complex of Al Gharafa. For one season at least it was to be Marcel Desailly's home. The facilities were magnificent, a steel-and-glass edifice that wouldn't have looked out of place in Manchester, Munich or Marseilles. But there was something of the *Mary Celeste* about it: a beautiful ship prepared for a sumptuous feast, in the middle of nowhere with no sign of life. The place was deserted but rather stranger was the fact that I could just walk into one of the biggest clubs in the country and poke around the changing rooms and offices totally unmolested. This despite the fact that Qatar was high up on the Foreign Office's list of places likely to experience a terrorist attack, in one of the most volatile regions of the world. In Europe I'd have been garrotted by a phalanx of security guards before I'd even got out of the taxi.

Eventually a curious secretary revealed that the players would be back from training any minute and that I should wait in the canteen. The players streamed in – largely young African men in their early 20s sprinkled with a few Arab players – for their buffet lunch of chicken and rice before the star attraction arrived. Quietly and without a word to the other players, Marcel filled his plate, retired to a table on his own and silently went about chewing on the meat. I watched for a while, too nervous to approach him at first. He looked lonely in his training ground tracksuit – stripped of fame – yet aesthetically appearing no different from the Desailly that had picked up the World Cup for France in 1998.

After staring at him for so long that other players were beginning to think I was some kind of infatuated stalker, I plucked up the courage to pick up a plate and invite myself for lunch with Desailly. 'Sit down. I don't mind if you eat with me.' I tried asking him politely why he had come out here, into the heat and the nothingness. 'Well, I would say it's no different from the second tier in a European league,' he replied, smiling. Clearly it was a question he was asked a lot. 'I was offered the chance to be coach of the Ghanaian national team but I could follow my passion, being paid what I was earning at Chelsea, and I said: "Yes, why not?" New experience, new people, new traditions, another mentality, a sunny place.'

And in Qatari terms, Marcel was thriving. Gharafa was top of the league and with Desailly being the most technically gifted player at the club, he had begun to loosen the defensive shackles and maraud upfield, playing almost as an attacking midfielder and scoring regularly. The Qataris loved him. As I was getting ready in the hotel, the local television station was replaying Desailly's two headed goals from the weekend over and over and over. But Desailly – a Christian who found himself in a staunchly Sunni Muslim emirate – was finding it a little hard to get used to.

'I am surprised when they go to pray,' he said. 'I never knew that Ramadan was so respected. It's the little details you discover. Training is at six o'clock and I am on the field ready to train and there's nobody – why? Because they are praying. Little things like that. But you have to accept it because it's their traditions and culture without judging them. We are not in Europe. I realised that they are not really lazy. I thought I was going to get into a country where, you know, maybe sometimes in Africa you get lazy and relaxed. But here they are still motivated to do things. And also they are really educated. I thought I was going to come to a country where they didn't really care. You are from Europe, you are stupid, they speak badly to you. But no.'

Despite Marcel's protestations something didn't sit right. He was shorn of that chin-thrusting arrogance he displayed at AC Milan and then Chelsea. But then it became clear why. Anywhere else but on the football pitch, things weren't going well. 'My family, they're in France,' he said. 'I had moved from England to France to settle down but then I signed for Qatar and thought about moving everybody here, the kids, wife, nanny. I have a great wife and my last-born is six months old. I wanted to enjoy it and be with him because with my career I really didn't have the time to give to my kids. But my wife saw that I needed to play on. She said: "Go on, we lose one year and we'll gain 20." People are working until they are 55 years old and I can give up after one year and start a new life.'

As I left the dinner table and thanked him for his hospitality, I asked about such a scenario: what if a European club came back in for you, as Bolton did when they signed former Real Madrid great Fernando Hierro from the Qatari wilderness after one season. Surely you'd give all this up in a shot? 'No, not at my age,' he replied. 'It's finished for me. I realised that I still wanted to play football and that's why I came here. But I would go back to Europe for what? I know everything from Europe. The crowd, the pressure. I did it for 20 years and it's enough. It's enough.'

Desailly, as club captain, led Gharafa to the 2004/5 title having lost just one game. He moved to league rivals Qatar Sports Club but his heart wasn't in it and he went home a few months later. 'I am a little homesick because of the distance from my family,' he said at the time. It wasn't surprising. He was here for the same reason that 80 per cent of Qatar's population – mostly labourers from the Indian subcontinent who build the country's stadiums, skyscrapers and hotels – were here: to put hardship away from your family to one side, save your wages and send them back in hope of a better future. He was in a much more privileged position than the exploited Asian workforce who built Qatar and kept it running but it showed what a transitory place Qatar was, whether you're a world-famous footballer or an Indian taxi driver.

Qatar has only existed as an independent country since 1971. When British prime minister Harold Wilson announced in 1967 that the country would be retreating from its military bases 'East of Suez' it left Qatar with a decision to make. The British had long guaranteed security for Qatar, Bahrain and the Trucial States, seven tribal emirates who would form the United Arab Emirates. Qatar chose independence over joining with its neighbours. The bulbous outcrop that juts out into the Gulf, dwarfing nearby Bahrain, wasn't the richest of Arab states as it didn't have the oil reserves of its neighbours in the newly formed United Arab Emirates or the economic and military might of Saudi Arabia. But whilst Saudi Arabia slowly decayed, thanks to corruption, autocracy and an over-reliance on oil, Qatar took a different route to development.

Post-independence the country's Emir was Sheikh Khalifa bin Hamad al Thani, a playboy who didn't rock the boat, centralised power, kept a tight lid on any dissent and spent most of his time in Switzerland. It was on one of his jaunts to the Swiss Alps in 1995 that his idealistic eldest son, Hamad bin Khalifa al Thani, seized control of the country in a bloodless palace coup. Palace intrigue within Gulf royal families is not new. But what was surprising was the path that the new Emir decided to take. One of Emir Hamad's first moves was to abolish the Ministry of Information – effectively ending direct censorship in the country. Not content with that, he decided to bankroll Al Jazeera, a new state-owned television network that wouldn't be hamstrung by the clumsy censorship and propaganda of TV channels in other Middle Eastern states, infuriating his neighbours – and later its allies in the West – with its uncompromising reporting. The money came from Qatar's newly found gas deposits, from perhaps the largest gas field in the world, which overnight thrust Qatar to the top of the world's GDP per capita chart. Even more surprising was his plan to introduce limited democracy to Qatar whilst hosting a US military base – CENTCOM, the US military's entire Asian command.

The Qataris had also formulated a cunning plan. Rather than pump billions into expensive advertising campaigns, allow sport to promote your country's brand for you instead. The UAE, and especially Dubai, had been particularly successful in doing this, hosting the world's most expensive horse race – the Dubai World Cup; a PGA tour event where Tiger Woods regularly appeared; and the Dubai Tennis Championship, where Roger Federer had won the past three titles. Thanks in no small part to celebrity sporting endorsements, Dubai had put itself on the map and, jealously coveting its success, Qatar decided to follow suit with its own tennis championship, the Qatar Open; golf tournament; and, most importantly of all, its star-packed football league. It even managed to win the bid to host the 2006 Asian Games, the smallest country ever to do so. So proud were they of their Asian Games achievement that they threw billions of gas dollars into developing sport in the country, building the dozen or so brand new, gleaming stadiums that each Doha-based football club now played in. The jewel in the crown was to be the Aspire academy, which – if the spin was to be believed – hoped to be the biggest, most comprehensive incubator for sporting talent in the world, all hosted in the state-of-the-art, Wembley-esque, 45,000-seater Khalifa Stadium.

The Qataris hoped to achieve global visibility and legitimacy, but also qualification for the World Cup. But the men's national team hovered around 100th place on the FIFA rankings and were struggling in their Asian qualifying group for Germany 2006. Manfred and the Qatari FA, however, reasoned that the influx of talented, experienced foreigners could only improve Qatar's national team players in their push towards the finals. And if that failed they could always attempt to buy players to play for the national team. After scoring for fun in the Bundesliga for Werder Bremen, Brazilian striker Ailton was approached by the Qatari FA to take up Qatari citizenship – taking advantage of FIFA's then relaxed rules on nationality – in exchange for a reported €1 million. After being shunned by the Brazilians, Ailton was seriously considering it. At 29, he didn't have many more shots at playing in the World Cup. Qatar's national coach at the time, Frenchman Philippe Troussier, was in favour. '[Naturalisation was] probably the only means to one day qualify Qatar for a World Cup,' he told French newspaper *L'Équipe*. 'Naturalisations are nothing new to Qatar, 80 per cent of my squad were not born in Qatar.' FIFA, appalled that a rudimentary transfer system was developing, stamped down on the practice – much to the embarrassment of the Qataris.

Given his expertise in this field, you sensed that if a forensic accountant went through the paperwork, Manfred's fingerprints might be found on the pages. The surreal meeting with Marcel Desailly in Al Gharafa's futuristic training complex had made me wonder about some of the other players who had come out to Qatar. Surely money wasn't the only thing that had persuaded them all to move themselves and their families to within a two-hour flight of Baghdad? I decided to phone Manfred and see if he could hook me up with anybody else. 'Yes, yes, I know Gabriel [Batistuta] is in the country, maybe you can call him. But be careful, he hates journalists,' he said helpfully before handing out Batistuta's mobile number anyway. 'You should speak to Ronald [de Boer] as well. He's very friendly.'

There's a strange slowness to Qatar that doesn't seem to affect the other Gulf states. Whilst the hyperactive capitalism of Dubai would appear in a neoliberal's wet dream, and with Bahrain racked with poverty and internal political struggles between the Sunni royal family and its restless Shia majority, life in Qatar is quieter, more spread out and far more relaxed. Certainly that's how Ronald de Boer had found it. 'There are some great golf courses here and I play with Batistuta, Guardiola, Frank Leboeuf, my brother, every week,' he said cheerfully. 'It's great fun. You feel safe in the country and there's no pressure. The papers aren't on you every day. And anyway, it's in Arabic, so you can't read what they say!'

Ronald de Boer chortled into his delicate porcelain cup at his last joke, that ignorance of the world's sixth most-spoken language was a foolproof way of avoiding bad press. With Batistuta's phone off, I'd speculatively called him and was surprised when he had agreed to meet me straight away for a cup of tea in the lobby of the Ritz Carlton hotel. But rather than seem glum and resigned like Marcel Desailly had earlier, Ronald had adjusted to the role of the rich, Western expat with too much time on his hands rather easily. 'The life here, I love it,' he said. 'Dubai is nearby and that's like New York. For me, if I could get another year and move to Dubai for another two I would love to do it.'

Ronald was happily playing for Rangers when the first call from Manfred came and, after agreeing to bring his brother Frank with him, they signed lucrative two-year contracts. The football, he explained, wasn't exactly La Liga standard but his team Al Rayyan could give most Scottish teams a run for their money. 'The standard is a little bit higher in Scotland but I don't think any of the lower teams would beat us. I must say, when I look at Rangers now, I think they might struggle against us,' he said. 'I mean, the last game we played to 12,000 people, and then you play some weak teams and only your wife and mother-in-law turn up. But they have some big rivalries like Al Rayyan versus Al Sadd. Al Sadd is like Ajax and Al Rayyan more Feyenoord, more with the working-class people, whilst Al Sadd is from the upper-class people. They don't have hooligans, though. They all want to make music.'

Ronald and Frank were loving their new surroundings, and the proximity of some of the most dangerous countries in the world didn't faze them. But Qatar offered them both something much more than money, although it clearly helped. It was a chance to play without the intense pressure they had known all their lives, from the media, from the fans and from their managers; pressure that had defined – sometimes for good, sometimes for ill – the most productive years of their careers.

'After all those years of pressure, it makes sense,' Ronald explained, finishing his tea and smoothing down his expensive jeans. 'Of course your level goes down at the end of your career. I've had six operations on my knee and can now only bend it halfway. I couldn't crouch down properly even when I was at Barcelona for the team photograph. Here you get well paid and do what you like, no stress. Of course it's a grave-yard of European footballers at the end of their careers. I don't want to make myself crazy with a second-ranked team [in Europe]. They expect so much from you because you are their big star and you probably can't do it. But why do that when you can come here and relax?'

Losing one's motivation through injury, time, or bitterness is an inevitable part of a footballer's evolutionary cycle. Gabriel Batistuta also seemed to be at the end of that road. Later that night I finally managed to get through to him.

'Hello Gabriel, Manfred Hoener has given me your number,' I said before being cut down. Batigol couldn't quite hide his anger.

'Manfred Hoener? Gragghh!'

With that strangled scream, somewhere between rage and incredu-lity, Batistuta hung up and turned his phone off. Later I discovered that he never played in Qatar, or anywhere else, again. Even though Batistuta had, in his first season with Al Arabi, broken Qatar's league scoring record with 25 goals in 21 games, his relationship with Man-fred soured. Manfred had earlier complained that Batistuta had missed numerous league games on trips back to Argentina for treat-ment on what he thought was a spurious 'injury'. Even the prospect of his weekly golf treat with Ronald, Frank and the boys wasn't enough to keep him there. Despite the money, privacy and the golf, Manfred Hoener had at least one unhappy customer.

NOVEMBER 2005

Diego Armando Maradona was standing on a football pitch looking short and sheepish. A ten-year-old Qatari boy lay prone on the floor in front of him clutching his ankle in agony with tears in his eyes.

Diego's curly mop of hair barely grazed the referee's nipples as he was given a telling off for his reckless and slightly inappropriate tackle. He was every bit as small as you imagined he was from those images of football tournaments in balmy, faraway lands. But his presence on the pitch was nothing short of a miracle. There are some things as a football fan you have resigned yourself to never seeing. Bobby Moore effortlessly ushering out an overhit through ball. Puskás tormenting a pack of defenders. Beckenbauer marauding across the pitch. But watching Maradona play football again was at the top, given that a few months earlier it appeared that the Argentine legend was not long for this earth.

His was the classic man-plays-game; man-conquers-game; man-takes-Herculean-quantities-of-drugs-shoots-journalists-and-balloons-to-the-size-of-an-ox footballing story. After being slung out of USA '94 for failing a drugs test, Maradona went into free fall, unable to deal with his addictions and his dwindling talent. He had tried his hand at management in Argentina, business ventures, even endorsements, but nothing stuck. By the turn of the twenty-first century, Maradona was morbidly obese, snorting lines of cocaine every morning. He had two heart attacks. Lying in the hospital and at his lowest ebb, salvation came from an unlikely source: Cuban dictator Fidel Castro.

The pair had been friends for years, both sharing a fiery brand of left-wing, anti-imperialist politics and a mutual loathing for what they saw as American imperialism in South America. Castro offered him the use of the La Pedrera clinic in Havana to try and beat his drug addictions. Eventually he was well enough to have a stomach-stapling operation in Colombia and, eight months later, Maradona was here, svelte, and once again looking like the tiny wizard that had lit up two World Cups and disgraced a third. It was the start of a new chapter in Maradona's life that would see him embrace the world of television, fronting his own hit talk show entitled *The Night of the Ten*, a reference to his famous number-ten shirt, which embraced hard-left politics. But the apex of his recovery was here, on a football pitch in Qatar, where he was once again kicking a ball, and young children, in anger.

At first I thought the email was a joke: Maradona and Pelé, it read, would both be present in Qatar to open a new sports academy. Usually such an honour would be reserved for government ministers, or even minor royalty. But somehow someone, somewhere, had persuaded two of the world's most famous sportsmen to come to a quiet, inoffensive country in the Middle East to open the Aspire academy, what seemed at the time to be a glorified leisure centre. The Qataris had pulled out all the stops to get them. Both were rumoured to have been paid half a million dollars just to turn up and the region's press would be flown in to witness the pair share a stage, putting their enmity behind them to discuss the footballing issues of the day. All this didn't seem to bother Maradona much as he careered around the Aspire training pitch, looking ten years younger than his 45, slide tackling boys a quarter of his age and still getting aerated enough to argue with the referee even though it was a kick around with kids.

It was a Damascene recovery. Some of his pace was gone, but that unmistakable, blurry-legged, barrel-chested gait was still there. He even had time to instinctively punch the ball into the net, much to the whooping delight of the English journalists assembled. I doubt they gave him the same honour when God intervened to score in the same manner against England in Mexico 20 years previously. Just as Fenwick and Butcher did back in 1986, the Qatari children looked on incredulously. Yet Maradona's impish charm beguiled all who encountered him – presidents, statesmen, royalty, even the English – which was never more evident than when, sweating from the 20-minute-long exertion, he decided to sign some autographs. The circle around him grew as Arab men in flowing white *dishdashas* and the previously restrained press corps literally threw children out of their path to get to their hero, to touch him, to feel his sweat on their hands. Eventually security guards had to intervene and hauled Maradona out of the ruck, beaming with the knowledge that – whatever FIFA thought – he was still the greatest of all time.

This issue had preoccupied him for some time. Maradona and Pelé first met in 1979 and were initially on friendly terms although that changed as Maradona's fame exploded and the comparisons began, rooted in a much deeper rivalry between Brazil and Argentina. In his autobiography *Yo Soy Diego* (I am Diego) Maradona placed Pelé top of his list of the 100 greatest players of all time, but also took a swipe at him over the fate of Garrincha, who had drunk himself to death once his playing career had finished. 'I'd like to have seen him [Pelé] look after Garrincha and not let him die in misery. I'd like to see him fight the rich and powerful that are damaging football.' And then, in 2000, FIFA threw petrol on the embers of the fire by announcing a new 'Player of the Century' award. It must have seemed like a good idea at the time. The winner would be decided by a public vote through FIFA.com, a relatively new concept in online democracy. It wasn't even close. Maradona won 53.6 per cent of the vote with Pelé a distant second, with 18.5 per cent. Portugal's Eusébio was third.

The result was a scandal in Brazil, who accused FIFA of choosing a voting system that would naturally skew the result towards younger voters who might never have seen Pele play, as well as bemoaning a campaign by the Argentina FA to get their vote out. The result didn't go down well at FIFA's headquarters in Zurich either. Maradona had only been retired three years after the drug scandals. Pelé, on the other hand, was a much more clean-cut ambassador for football who had even been appointed sports minister in Brazil. So, FIFA created a 'Football Family' award, voted for by committee and by readers of FIFA's in-house magazine, who overwhelmingly voted for Pelé. The award was, effectively, shared. Maradona was furious. 'The people voted for me,' he said, threatening not to attend the ceremony. 'Now they want me to share the prize with Pelé. I'm not going to share the prize with anybody.'

But attend he did. At the star-studded awards bash in Rome, Maradona picked up his award first and dedicated it to, among other people, his wife and his old friend Fidel Castro. And then he immediately left the hall, leaving Pelé to pick up the 'Football Family' award by himself. 'I would have liked to have had Maradona up here on stage with me,' said Pelé, Maradona's front-row seat now empty, 'but it looks like he's already gone.'

Five years later, in Qatar, Maradona is now sitting in front of us, slumped in a chair the same way a wayward schoolboy would confrontationally sit in the headmaster's office after he'd set fire to a classroom. 'Who is the greatest? My mother says it's me. And you should always believe your mother,' he joked. The crowd of a dozen or so journalists ignited into spontaneous, sycophantic laughter. He smiled at his ability to make a room of middle-aged men fawn at his feet and nonchalantly answered questions about football, drugs and his former life as a very fat man. Maradona was articulate in a rough, uncomplicated kind of way. After years of being barracked by the press, you would have thought that he would come across as guarded, even reticent. But he was the exact opposite, sitting for an hour talking about everything from Argentina's chances in the World Cup to how, despite all the money in the game, he would still choose to play for Napoli if he was 21 today. His most interesting moments came when he talked politics, openly criticising George W. Bush for the war in Iraq. '[Hugo] Chávez, Fidel [Castro] and Che Guevara, they fought for their people, to give them more equality [and] they fought against the United States and anyone who fights against the US is good for me,' he said when asked about the influence of his friend Fidel.

Maradona famously has a tattoo of Che on his right shoulder and Fidel on his left leg. Most thought it a pretty adornment rather than a deep affinity with left-wing politics. But they were wrong. 'I was at the Summit [of the Americas] in Argentina two weeks ago and I know Bush commanded the [Iraq] war from Qatar,' he said when asked about his antipathy towards America and the presence of a US military base in Qatar. 'But I support Qatar and an assassin is an assassin anywhere. Every country has the freedom to make its own laws and make a decision and you must respect that. So even if he leaves Qatar, an assassin can kill from everywhere.'

Pelé, on the other hand, had a strangely subdued reception. He arrived at the training pitch where Maradona had previously wowed hundreds of onlookers with his newfound fitness in an electrically powered golf cart. He wore a powder-blue 1970s safari suit which looked like an outfit he'd kept from his New York Cosmos days. We've got so used to seeing the replays of his magnificent career that you can forget that Brazil's greatest player is now a pensioner. He gingerly disembarked and wandered aimlessly around the pitch. He seemed too frail to kick a ball. Instead small crowds of middle-aged men politely queued for his autograph. Compared to the histrionics of the previous day, you'd have thought that the Qataris had wheeled out a minor character in world football, but Pelé had become strangely accustomed to indifference in recent years. Despite leading a near-exemplary life on and off the pitch as a clean-cut, family-loving ambassador for the game – and a flawless example to generations of footballers – even his countrymen hadn't been totally convinced by him. In Brazil he was mocked for not being very bright, lambasted for a disastrous but well-meaning tenure as Brazilian sports minister and derided for signing up to be the face of Viagra in Brazil. He quickly withdrew his support when the press began to question his virility. His press conference was half full, cut short after 15 minutes. Officially, the emir wanted to see the two of them for lunch. Unofficially, it provided a handy escape route.

Whilst Pelé inexplicably struggled to win hearts and minds, Maradona's failings were all but forgotten. Maybe it's because a flawed genius is someone who we can more easily empathise with. Maradona is one of us: flawed and fallible. Or maybe it's because his fallibility still leaves room for speculation. Pelé had become everything he could possibly have been. But for Maradona, the same question still lingered, even after his myriad successes in the game. What could he still have become?

The lights dimmed, the crowd already in their seats waiting for the main event. In the main hall of Qatar's Aspire Zone the local dignitaries in their white *dishdashas* chattered in animated Arabic at the front whilst journalists and photographers crowded around the hastily erected stage. Qatar's policy of sporting investment was about to reach its apex. First, Pelé modestly sauntered in. Polite applause followed. Then Maradona entered. Perhaps it was the rabid welcoming from the crowd, or the fact that the spotlight sparkled off his white suit jacket adorned with bright silver thread, but Maradona's entrance tasted like a coronation. And then the two shook hands. A thousand flashes followed, capturing the moment when Pelé and Diego buried the hatchet. Except this wasn't the moment they really buried the hatchet. Pelé had been Maradona's first guest on his talk-show debut earlier that year. There wasn't any real warmth in their reconciliation but the Pelé and Maradona show had become big business and useful for both men: a vehicle for Maradona's rehabilitation and an opportunity for Pelé to counter his detractors. Both were handsomely rewarded for their time.

Maradona admitted as much when the discussion started – a supposedly adversarial 'debate' on sportsmanship. Presumably the Qataris had hoped that Pelé would represent the fair-minded professional, with Maradona taking the role of the Machiavellian magician, willing to bend the rules and invoke God to get the right result. 'We just never clicked,' admitted Maradona, glancing over at Pelé. 'We always rubbed each other up the wrong way. We would see each other and sparks would fly.' He kicked out against the press that hounded him and the football authorities that doubted his ability. 'I was addicted … drugging myself. Then I would play football without sleeping, eating or even drinking water,' he said, getting increasingly irate. 'The media really only emphasised my drug addiction – they wanted a drugs story. All they wanted to do was publicise drugs. They wanted to kill Maradona and I make no apologies for my behaviour to the press.' His behaviour related to the time he tried to shoot a couple of Argentine journalists with an air rifle, who had been stationed outside his house. But then Maradona exceeded himself, comparing himself to the one person less popular than George W. Bush among the crowd. 'To defend my family I will become Bin Laden. And if that's what it takes I'll become the fiercest human being on the planet.'

Everyone took an intake of breath, Maradona looked at Pelé and they both laughed. The rest of the crowd laughed with them. The debate finished and, sensing that Qatar was unlikely to see the two greatest footballers of the twentieth century ever again, the crowd rushed the stage. The crush pressed in on Maradona. On the left of the stage Pelé stood on his own. The crowd clambered onto the stage and surrounded Maradona desperate for one last signature. A white-robed Qatari with a walkie-talkie manfully tried to hold back the hordes, screaming for the crowd to get back. The stage was buckling under the collective weight of the scrum. Diego's unkempt hair poked up from the mess, the rest buried in a sea of adoring fans. Pelé was being ushered away. Not for the first time in Pelé's life, not even for the first time in Qatar, Maradona had stolen the show.

Maradona would return to the Middle East twice for short, unsuccessful stints at Emirati clubs in the UAE as part of his erratic managerial career. He died of a heart attack in 2020, aged 60, outlived by Pelé, who was 20 years his senior.

At the time it was not clear what Qatar gained from this set piece. Some journalists wrote stories of the strangeness of it all, others used it to make tenuous comparisons between Diego and Wayne Rooney, whilst one journalist used the event as a Trojan horse to break a much larger story which appeared that weekend and made headlines across the world: that a leaked memo suggested that George W. Bush had allegedly contemplated bombing Qatar's meddlesome Al Jazeera television network to stop the bad news stories that had emerged out of Iraq. Whatever the benefit, it appeared slight and even the most enthusiastic of backers were now questioning whether Qatar's huge investment was a wise one. On my last day in Qatar, out on the training pitch, I spotted a familiar figure. A tall, silver-haired man. It was Manfred Hoener. Immediately he strode towards me and shook my hand, almost severing it at the wrist, whilst affectionately beating me on my back at the same time.

'I take it this is all your work then?' I asked, surveying the scene of journalists, PRs and world-famous footballers.

'What, this? No, I've given that all up now. It wasn't working out,' he replied. As if on cue, one of Manfred's last signings ambled past, the ex-Derby and West Ham striker Paulo Wanchope. As good a player as Wanchope was, he was no Desailly. Manfred had suffered from the law of diminishing returns. Each month it had been harder and harder to attract the big names. The old guard of Desailly, the De Boer brothers, Leboeuf and Batistuta were gone and whilst World Cup winners could once be persuaded to come, now only mid-table journeymen like Wanchope and Jay-Jay Okocha could be talked into the moneyed pilgrimage east. The Qatari government had even begun to lose patience. The whole point of the exercise was to raise the level of the league and its domestic players so that Qatar might qualify for the World Cup for the first time in its history. That dream, for Germany 2006, was over long before when the national team succumbed meekly to Iran in Doha. The Asian Games didn't quite go to plan either.

Firstly there was a diplomatic row with Iran. The country had just elected the firebrand, populist ex-mayor of Tehran Mahmoud Ahmadinejad – who proclaimed that, much like George W. Bush, God had guided him to the presidency – and had agitated to restart Iran's nuclear power programme. But Iran threatened to boycott the games over a more modest slight. The event's promotional material called the stretch of water that separates Iran from the Arab Middle East, the Arabian Gulf, and not the Persian Gulf, as everyone else does. 'If

Arab countries fall for the traps and tricks of Zionists, who aim to create discord among the region's Muslims,' said Mohsen Mehr-Alizadeh, head of Iran's sports ministry, 'it might also negatively affect political relations of the Islamic Republic of Iran to the Persian Gulf's states.' But the Iran team did eventually turn up.

When the tournament started it was hit by unseasonable torrential rain and a series of bizarre, and tragic, incidents. The authorities had incorrectly calculated the number of beds needed for visiting athletes and officials by as many as 3,000 – leading to the unedifying sight of three cruise ships having to be towed in to make up the numbers. The games were also marred by the deaths of seven spectators and a sportsman due to the conditions. A South Korean equestrian rider, Kim Hyung-chil, was killed after his horse slipped on the mud and fell, crushing him to death. 'The Death Games', as one regional newspaper referred to them, had been a publicity disaster. Qatar's expensive experiment in footballing immigration and sporting PR seemed to have failed. I felt sorry for Qatar. Like a teenager who had unexpectedly won the lottery, Qatar had spent big on expensive, flashy accessories but to little reward or seemingly any long-term benefit. It was a shame because, as a young country, some of its other, more enlightened investments had paid off. As the veteran BBC journalist Tim Sebastian pointed out, when asked why he had moved to Doha to host a regular series of televised debates: 'Qatar is building institutions. Places like Dubai are building malls.' But that was cold comfort for the emir when you compared the name recognition of Qatar's glitzy neighbour, which had neither democracy nor a free media. Seeing the writing on the wall, Manfred left the Q League and the FA before he was pushed.

'So what are you still doing here then, Manfred?' I asked, confused. He pointed over towards two nervous-looking Indian men, one holding a sound boom and wearing headphones, the other with a large camera strapped to his shoulder. It was his film crew. 'I'm in television now, a football talk show. I talk, they listen. Ha!'

I had taken it as an indelible sign of Qatar's sporting failure. And in a way, right then, in that moment, it was. But in a few years the seeds of Qatar's master plan – planted initially with mixed success – would begin to flourish.

2

Iran

Outside Tehran's hulking, grey Azadi national football stadium a riot
was fermenting. A mob, 70 strong, with whistles, drums and banners,
pushed on the crush barriers and screamed slogans in strangulated
Farsi. I hadn't expected my first taste of Iran to involve a loud and
angry protest. Iran, we are led to believe, isn't a place where dissent is
tolerated. Equally, I hadn't expected my first taste of Iran to involve a
loud and angry protest exclusively made up of abaya-clad women,
faces painted the colour of the Iranian flag and one and all clutching
a national football team scarf. They berated the hundred or so riot
officers who had constructed a Kevlar wall between themselves and
the stadium, as dozens of men – only men – streamed past unmolested
towards the stadium's huge gates and that afternoon's main event: a
2006 World Cup warm-up match between Iran and Costa Rica. None
of the passing spectators looked surprised and none looked back. But
the riot police looked on, perplexed, a dilemma etched into their faces.
At riot police school, presumably, they were taught how to deal with
enemies of the state. Wade in first and ask questions later. Instead they
were frozen, stuck between a conservative culture where women were
revered and protected from the wicked mores of the modern world
and the demands of the state. Paralysis broke out. They looked impo-
tently on as the women's angry cries broke on their body armour.

'They come here before every game to protest in their scarves,'
sighed Amir, my guide, of the familiar sight. I wanted to go and speak
to them, ask them about their protest, but the doors were locked.

Amir didn't think it was a good idea to try and talk to the women with police around. 'It's dangerous,' he said. I pulled the handle. The doors stayed firmly shut as we glided past. 'It's not a religion thing why they can't come to a football match,' Amir hastily tried to explain. 'They can go to a cinema with a man. But it's the atmosphere in the ground: the swearing, the bad language. It's just not suitable.' Three hours before every home game the female fans of Team Melli – as the Iranian national football team is affectionately known – trudge to the Azadi Stadium in the western suburbs of Tehran. And every game they are denied entry and trudge back to whence they came, past a huge motivational sign that mockingly adorns the entrance. It reads: 'The Most Powerful Person is That That Can Keep Their Hunger'.

It was a hopeless, unrewarding task. But the protests – along with my arrival at Sharjah Airport in the United Arab Emirates for my flight to Tehran – gave me a glimpse that Iran was very different to the image that had been promoted back home. I had been denied a visa but had been told I might be able to get in anyway. The trip was certainly worth the risk. The 2006 World Cup was a few months away and Iran had assembled arguably the best team in their history. For only the second time a team in the region had a good chance of actually making it to the knockout stages.

But first I had to get in, which is where Amir came in. Amir was an Iranian who worked for the airline, who had promised to get me in one way or the other. We agreed to meet at the check-in desk. Amir claimed to have connections in the upper reaches of pretty much every Iranian institution: the Iranian FA, the police, even, it seemed, Iranian airport immigration. 'Don't worry, get on the flight and we'll sort out your visa at the other end,' he assured me confidently over the phone. 'Don't worry,' he repeated, sensing my fear. Given the Iranian government's hostile attitudes towards my homeland (Great Britain), the place where I lived (UAE) and my profession (journalism) it was not a place I wanted to be stranded. 'My father used to be a minister in the government,' he said finally. I wasn't entirely convinced.

We met the next day at the check-in desk. Amir was young, in his mid-20s, and handsome. He used his charm to check-in a long, suspicious-looking package into the hold. 'Oh, it's a bumper for my BMW,' he said nonchalantly. 'I went a little too fast in the snow and hit a kerb. It's cheaper if I buy it here.' Even in an Islamic theocracy the appetite for luxury cars couldn't be suppressed.

As we flew the short journey from the UAE to Iran, Amir put the record straight on a few things, particularly when we discussed Mahmoud Ahmadinejad, Iran's recently elected president, who had called for Israel to be pushed into the sea and questioned whether the Holocaust happened. The West, Amir thought, had the wrong idea about Iran and it was his responsibility as a proud Iranian to make sure I had the correct version of events. 'I'm not anti-Jewish, I'm anti-Zionist, which is what he [Ahmadinejad] was trying to say,' Amir explained. I had the feeling that Amir had to account for the president's behaviour on more than one occasion since his election eight months previously, which he won with a little help from Iran's Guardian Council. The body of 12 hard-line clerics and jurists – appointed by Iran's supreme leader Ayatollah Ali Khamenei – played a crucial role in Iran's political system. They had the power to veto everything from legislation to presidential candidates, which they did during the 2005 presidential election, barring dozens of reformist candidates from standing. The council also ignored claims of vote rigging, appearing to favour Ahmadinejad's populist Islamic message. Ahmadinejad, an ultra-conservative former mayor of Tehran, was voted in on a low turnout by Iran's recent standards. Only 59 per cent of voters turned out for the second round of voting. The bearded, modest-looking, lounge-suit-wearing president quickly made a name for himself in the West thanks to his anti-Israel pronouncements and his quest for nuclear power. Now Amir and the rest of the population were waiting for Israel, who not unreasonably saw a nuclear Iran as an existential threat, to respond. 'If they [Israel] try to bomb us,' said Amir as he fiddled with the straw in his Coke can, 'It will be the spark that lit a room full of gas. It will explode. I truly believe that it would be the end of the world.'

Few in the West had heard of Ahmadinejad before his shock election. The Americans initially accused him (falsely) of being the mastermind behind the 1979 American Embassy siege. Although several of the American hostages still maintained he was present. What we did know was that his one luxury (officially anyway) was a 1977 Peugeot 504, he held revisionist views on the Holocaust and he didn't wear ties, which, like the George Michael songs he banned from the nation's airwaves, he saw as a tool of Western cultural imperialism. His one weakness was football and Ahmadinejad sought to use it for his own means. Iran had qualified strongly for the 2006 World Cup in Germany and were preparing for the biggest tournament in their sporting history. But the preparations weren't going well. I had come to Iran to watch one of their final home warm-up games: a mid-afternoon clash with fellow qualifiers Costa Rica. It was one of the few times a non-Asian team had made the trip to Tehran. It was sup-posed to be Ukraine but they pulled out, citing the spurious excuse that Iran were too good for a friendly. Amir was livid. 'They said we should go to Ukraine, but why? There really is no problem here,' he said angrily as the plane began its descent. All around, women stood and fixed on their head scarves, covering the long dark hair that had been tolerated in the UAE but would be tolerated no longer.

Given the political situation Tehran hadn't been a favoured destin-ation for international friendlies and after failing to entice Italy, Germany and England, the Iranian football federation persuaded Costa Rica to play the greatest crop of players the country had ever seen: Ali Karimi – Iran's cultured midfielder – had become the latest Iranian player to sign for a German Bundesliga club after signing a contract with Bayern Munich whilst Ali Daei, their 38-year-old centre-forward, held the world's international goal-scoring record. The team's popularity and imminent appearance on the world's biggest stage hadn't escaped Ahmadinejad. After landing at Imam Khomeini International Airport I picked up a copy of Tehran's only English-language newspaper. On the front page was a picture of Ahmadinejad, meeting the players before training. Initially it looked like your standard statesman-meets-the-team picture. But closer inspection revealed a telling difference. The squad, including the talismanic Daei, was rapt, sitting legs crossed and as if they were intently soaking up the president's motivational words.

'Excuse me, can you step forward?'

A border guard politely beckoned me towards passport control in English. As Amir pontificated with the man holding the stamp, I waited. A colleague watched nearby before leaning forward. Looking down, I feared the worst – handcuffs; a fist; an open palm demanding to be filled with a bribe? Instead, I saw a polystyrene plate full of meat and rice. He offered me some with a smile on his face. Not wanting to appear rude, I agreed, grabbed a fork and gobbled a mouthful. Lamb and gravy with sultanas. His colleague cheerily stamped my passport whilst a glass of cold water was pushed in front of me before being genially waved off. Confronted by arguably the most hostile border police in the world, I was offered dinner, pleasantries and a drink.

Even the most fervently nationalistic Iranian would admit that Tehran is not a beautiful city. As our battered Paykan taxi veered around other battered Paykans towards Tehran city proper, we were hit by monochrome blandness: rows and rows of stumpy, identikit, grey concrete tower blocks. The bleak urban cityscape is only broken by the huge, colourful murals that cover the sides of whole tower blocks, eulogising the martyrs from the Iran–Iraq War – images of young, handsome soldiers standing in wheat fields, handing poppies to care-free, patriotic children. A large network of channels – full of melting snow water from the nearby Alborz Mountains – laces the city. But Tehran's roads are some of the most dangerous in the world and are constantly jammed by state-made Paykans and Sepands, essentially copies of the Hillman Hunter and the Renault 5. Traffic accidents were so frequent that Tehran's drivers had given up caring about the dings and scratches and thought nothing of bumping or scraping you accidentally before driving off without a second thought.

Whilst Tehran lacks the aesthetics of Shiraz, or the cultural riches of Isfahan, the capital is at the centre of every political and social fad, its delayed ripples inevitably reaching its vast borders. It is Iran's beating heart and a microcosm of a huge country that holds 69 million ethnically diverse people, stretching from Afghanistan to Turkey with, it claims, the world's oldest continuously existing borders. The north of the city is dominated by the rich, middle-class intelligentsia who hate Ahmadinejad with a passion. The south is Ahmadinejad territory; working class and deeply devout, the electorate that carried him to the presidency. The physical division between reformists and traditionalists that bisects Tehran has shaped modern Iranian society. But it wasn't until a liberal cleric called Mohammad Khatami snuck past the Guardian Council censors and won a landslide election in 1997 that the reformist movement really had a voice. Preaching moderation, economic liberalisation and greater individual freedom for its people,

Khatami rose to office on a wave of optimism from Iran's young population, winning 70 per cent of the vote on an 80 per cent turnout. Iran has one of the youngest populations in the world: nearly 70 per cent are under the age of 30. The theocrats in the Guardian Council – never for a moment thinking that such a man was electable – were red-faced. The powers that kept the spirit of the Islamic revolution alive vowed never to allow such a mistake to happen again, and at every turn, Khatami was met with obstruction and hurdles, including vetoing a law that would have reformed the electoral system. In the end his government was so paralysed by inaction and bureaucracy, and the people so weary of big promises that were never met, that his popularity collapsed, laying the foundations for Ahmadinejad's form of populist Islam.

It's no surprise then, given this schism and the political sensitivity that his post possessed, that Branko Ivanković – Iran's national team coach – chose to live neither north or south but in the centre of Tehran. The Croatian had arrived in Iran in 2001 as the assistant to then national coach Miroslav Blažević. Ivanković was Blažević's number two when he took Croatia to third place at France '98. But when Iran failed to qualify for the finals in South Korea and Japan, Blažević was sacked and Ivanković promoted with the express aim of making it to the 2006 finals. He had fulfilled his obligation, qualifying with a game to spare after drawing against Japan in front of 100,000 fans at the Azadi – officially the highest attendance of any World Cup qualifier in that campaign, although most Iranians I spoke to suspected as many as 120,000 were crammed inside. He was now one of the most popular men in the country. Dressed in a preppy outfit of jumper, shirt and slacks and sporting expensive glasses, 51-year-old Branko looked more like a university don than a national coach and seemed much younger, remarkable given the pressure and the average career expectancy of a coach in Asia. 'With my job, you don't know what's going to happen the next morning, especially in the Middle East,' he grinned as we sat down in the lobby of his plush hotel apartment. 'In the World Cup in France Brazilian coach Carlos Alberto Parreira was sacked by Saudi Arabia. This is the destiny of our job and we can't make plans for our future. Sometimes one centimetre is all that matters. The ball might go one centimetre left, go out and I'm terrible, but it goes one centimetre right into the goal, I am a hero. Just one centimetre defines my destiny.'

Qualification for Germany 2006 had been made easier by the footballing riches bestowed upon him. Iran had produced something of a golden generation in footballing terms and a number of their key players had already got used to playing in Germany for a number of Bundesliga clubs – Karimi as Michael Ballack's successor at Bayern Munich; Mehdi Mahdavikia at Hamburger; Vahid Hashemian at Hannover 96; and Ferydoon Zandi at 1. FC Kaiserslautern. 'We can beat any side in the world,' Branko declared confidently when I asked about his team's chances. But after the draw against Japan, Branko's job became a little harder. With Ahmadinejad making trouble at the UN, foreign FAs stopped taking Iran's calls. Friendlies were called off and a tour of England's Championship clubs, held in the aftermath of the 7 July bombings, was cancelled by the Iranians halfway through over security fears. One match against Millwall, whose notorious fans have a long history of violence and racism, was cancelled after far-right extremists threatened to exact revenge for the terrorist attack on the London transport network a few weeks previously. After losing 3–0 to Queens Park Rangers, the Iranians returned home. As Ahmadinejad's rhetoric grew, so did the sanctions. Western politicians started calling for Iran to be thrown out of the World Cup. German and Israeli lawmakers tabled motions in their respective parliaments, calling for a ban after Ahmadinejad, in one of his fiery speeches, called for Israel to be 'wiped off the map'. There was also the issue of Iran's continuing uranium enrichment programme. Throwing Iran out of the World Cup, reasoned the British Conservative Party politician Michael Ancram, 'would give a very, very clear signal to Iran that the international community will not accept what they are doing'. Even the friendly against Costa Rica had attracted media attention, taking place as it did on the eve of a crucial International Atomic Energy Agency report on Iran's nuclear programme. If Iran was deemed to have shown sufficient doubt that its programme was anything but peaceful, it would set Iran on the road towards sanctions, further isolation and possibly war.

Branko wasn't too concerned. 'One of the very important rules of football is that politics is one side and sport is the other side so I'm sure we will go to the World Cup,' he said when asked about coping under the political pressures. Branko may have rejected the link between sport and politics in Iran, but few politicians in Tehran, Washington or London saw the difference, not least Ahmadinejad, whose visit to the squad was loaded with 'us versus them' symbolism. The national team provided an opportunity for Iran to be seen as equals on the international stage and to prove that, despite the privations and isolation of the past 25 years, the country was strong. The 11 men on the pitch represented what Iran really was, not the fiction peddled by the West's media lies. This nationalism held common currency in Iran. Ahmadinejad was not liked by all in the country, but he had tapped into a strong emotion that resonated with many Iranians, one which he saw embodied in the national team – resilience, independence and national, if not political, pride. Branko was just happy to be taking care of football matters, even if his meeting with one of the world's most reviled politicians gave him a somewhat dubious honour: he became one of the few Westerners to warmly shake the hand of the Iranian president. 'He's a big supporter of the team,' Branko explained, proud of the memory. 'He told us that football is very important to the country, especially at the moment because the image of Iran is not too good. He expects the players to do their best but that this is sport and everything can happen. He's happy with the players and that we won't have any problems going anywhere in the world.'

The inside of the Azadi Stadium is dominated by two, equal-sized portraits hoisted high up on the west stand. One shows Iran's future, the other its past. To the left was Ayatollah Khomeini, the cleric who shattered Western complacency towards Iran when he assumed control after the 1979 revolution and irrevocably changed the way his country would be viewed by the rest of the world. To the right, Ayatollah Khamenei, his replacement at the apex of Iran's spiritual hierarchy. The stadium was a third full with 40,000 spectators, a remarkable number given that the match was being played mid-afternoon on a Wednesday. After driving past the doomed all-women protests we parked and entered through large metal doors into the east stand. Amir thrust a bib and a pass into my hand, a hastily constructed piece of laminated plastic with a black-and-white photograph cribbed from my passport. It read: 'Photographer.' Amir shrugged apologetically. 'At short notice, it was the best I could do.' I had never been pitchside for a football match before. Making the most of my chance brush with privilege, and using my old-fashioned camera to try and achieve a modicum of professionalism, I walked around the pitch taking pictures. The crowd opposite the murals of the two ayatollahs banged on drums and chanted the name of Imam Hussein, grandson of the Prophet Mohammed and whose contested status as his true heir is at the root of the region's Shia–Sunni schism. Placards were waved in a language I didn't understand. One, on brightly coloured paper, had been written (and only slightly mistranslated) in English and was cheerily waved by two smiling teenagers. It read: 'Don't With the US [sic]'.

Just before the match started, a television crew approached. 'Can we speak to you, on camera?' I couldn't work out why the opinion of a fake photographer would mean anything to anyone, but foreign visitors were a rarity. He turned to the cameraman, nodded, and began filming.

'How are you liking Iran?' he asked.

'It's very nice and the people are very friendly,' I replied.

The next was trickier.

'Why does George Bush want to invade us?'

Ahh. 'Well, erm, I'm not sure . . .'

I couldn't find an answer. Why did George W. Bush want to invade? I wasn't sure that he did, although the press had speculated that the White House had been putting together contingency plans for an attack. Sensing that the dead air time of me lost in thought didn't make good television, the presenter changed tack.

'How do you rate Iran's chances in the World Cup?'

This was slightly easier to answer. The Iranians had pulled a hard group – Portugal, Mexico and Angola – but if they beat Angola and drew against Mexico, I offered, they might finish second. The presenter beamed, thanked me and walked off. It was what he wanted to hear. The interview, though, had only sparked the curiosity of other television crews, who rushed over just to make sure their rival hadn't scooped them. By the time the two teams came on the pitch for the national anthems, I was on my fourth interview, and had become an expert on Iranian football, firing off clichés and platitudes that would have made John Motson weep with pride.

'Of course, it all depends on the form of Ali Karimi.'

'If Branko can keep his team injury free, they have a great chance.'

'You know there are no easy games in international football any more, Mohammed, but . . .'

Iran were sublime. Within ten minutes they were ahead thanks to the best player on the pitch. Ali Karimi scored with a deft shot across the keeper from the outside of his left boot, and set up the next two, including Ali Daei's 109th international goal. The team tore their Central American rivals apart, who were just four places below them in the FIFA rankings, with Ali Karimi pulling the strings. You could see why the former Asian Player of the Year, dubbed the Asian Maradona, had been snapped up by Bayern Munich. They had a perfectly good fourth goal disallowed before Costa Rica scored against the run of play. Half-time arrived and the Costa Ricans couldn't get off the pitch quick enough. The Iranian media were ecstatic and jumped towards me, one by one, pointing at the empty pitch as if it were proof of Iran's inevitable World Cup success. Arash, a young French-Iranian journalist who lived in Tehran and wrote for L'Équipe, was a little more circumspect. 'Yes, it was a good half. But they have a small squad. Any injuries and we would really be in trouble,' he said. Arash was a dual citizen who had lived in Tehran for the best part of a year. 'I still need a permit,' he explained. 'But it helps that I write stories for France. They couldn't be published here.'

Arash's pessimism proved correct. Ali Karimi had picked up an injury and was taken off at half-time, whilst Daei and the Bundesliga contingent were rested as a precautionary measure. Branko patrolled his dugout studiously throughout, his assistant shouting his instructions onto the pitch in Farsi. The crowd chanted his name. The most popular foreigner in Iran smiled and waved back. With a weakened team, Costa Rica fought back strongly, and could have grabbed a draw. In the end it finished 3–2 to Iran.

As Arash and I left the stadium we talked about football's importance in Iranian society. Much like Catholicism in 1970s communist Poland, football was one area of Iranian life that even the religious establishment couldn't interfere with, although it did try. The league was suspended in the wake of the revolution, but the clubs quickly set up their own city leagues. Iran had just flown the country's flag for the first time in the 1978 World Cup in Argentina, securing a historic draw with Scotland. Yet six months later that team was dead. Many of those players fled to the US, including defender Andranik Eskandarian, who found himself playing in the same New York Cosmos side as Carlos Alberto and Franz Beckenbauer and eventually became an American citizen. 'I was travelling with the Cosmos on a tour in Brazil when the revolution took place,' he says when we speak on the phone. 'I am a soccer player not a politician. I don't like any of them. But that was a sad moment. I was too far away and couldn't picture it. All the papers and TV pictures were in Portuguese. I didn't know what was going on.' He opened a sportswear shop in New Jersey, and never returned home. Some went into politics. Hassan Nayebagha and Bahram Mavaddat became leading figures in the People's Mojahedin Organization of Iran (MEK), a leftist anti-Islamic Republic movement that was considered a terrorist organisation by the US until 2012. The captain of the national team, Habib Khabiri, was arrested, tortured and executed in 1984 for supporting them. Goalkeeper Nasser Hejazi tried to run for president in 2005 but the Guardian Council rejected his candidacy due to a lack of political experience.

After surviving the dissolution of the league, the clubs were then faced with another challenge. The Iran–Iraq War saw the availability of healthy young men collapse, meaning the football league couldn't continue. But the clubs soldiered on with an annual cup competition that drew huge attendances until the war ended and a national league could start up again in 1989, although it didn't fully return until 1993. Football boomed in the 1990s, mainly because the terraces of clubs like Pas, a team traditionally funded by the police; Persepolis, Iran's most popular team; and Esteghlal FC, formerly known until the revolution as Taj (which means crown in Farsi) but which had to change its name to Esteghlal FC to break its previous connections with the shah, were the only places where a frustrated (male) population, tired of the revolution's economic failure, could let off steam.

The climax came in 1997. Buoyed by the success of the reformist movement, Iran qualified for France '98 on a wave of euphoria and a million people took to the streets. It was the first time in 18 years that women had been seen in Tehran uncovered. And whilst now the Iranian government looked to football to give it a shred of

international legitimacy whilst securing support at home, the authorities had paradoxically always feared its power. 'Football is the only
place where people let go and those in power fear the power football
has,' explained Arash before we said our goodbyes. 'Football is a
threat to their authority. When a million people took to the streets,
women were dancing and throwing off their hijabs. The authorities
are scared of that, scared of losing control.'

That night I met Arash at Vanak Square, the Piccadilly Circus of
northern Tehran where handsome 20-somethings with duck-fin haircuts and turned-up jeans strolled the streets hand-in-hand with
girlfriends sporting hijabs so far back they only stayed on by virtue of
a stiff ponytail, making them almost redundant. 'The youth are so
bored, they don't have anywhere to go,' he said as we walked down to
a local restaurant he had recommended. 'Especially the middle class.
They have money, but nothing to do. So they sit around and take
drugs.' It's hard to imagine somewhere like Iran having a drug problem, but all the vices that are open to the youth of the West also seem
to be prevalent in Tehran. 'There are no nightclubs but people have
parties at home and drink or take drugs. Tehran has a really big crystal
meth problem. You have to remember, Iran has some of the best scien-
tists in the world! Last year, the city was full of heroin and everyone
would go to "ex parties". They would give you ecstasy at the door and
let you loose.'

Arash didn't take drugs, and I got the impression he didn't overly
approve. But I secretly wished an opportunity to attend an impromptu
'ex party' would present itself. We arrived at the restaurant, a small,
strip-lit café that sold Iranian staples like lamb with rice and sultanas
and iced vermicelli, where Pegah was waiting for us. She was studying
art at Tehran University and wore a brown hijab adorned with intricate stitching at the edges. Again, it hung off the back of her head, as
if wearing it was little more than fulfilling a technicality. 'Most would
probably say they'd rather not,' she admitted when I asked whether
Iranian women resented having to cover up all the time. 'It's just
the fashion, the way people wear it a little further back every year.'
The incremental inching back of the hijab could be a metaphor for the
increasing social freedoms that Iran's under-30s have surreptitiously
gained. Even under Ahmadinejad and an increasingly conservative

political culture, the small gains make a young person's life tolerable. 'They [the police] know that they can't turn things back,' agreed Arash.

One area where this had been put to the test on a nightly basis was in the field of dating. Although Bluetooth technology had helped people to flirt more easily, explained Pegah, there was an automotive version going on up and down Jordan Street every night. Known as the 'Jordan Game', cars full of single men and women would cruise up and down looking for prospective partners whilst the police sat in their patrol cars and did nothing. We climbed into Pegah's small car to take the short drive to Jordan Street. 'I like this a lot,' she smiled, as she pulled out a well-used tape and jammed it into the dusty car radio. Chris Rea replied back. 'Do you like it?' I didn't have the heart to tell the truth. 'I love him.'

With 'Road to Hell' blaring, we hit Jordan Street and the throng of Iranians looking for a date. Dozens of cars inched slowly up the hill full of expectant cargo: groups of men hoping to catch an eye streamed by and shouted bawdy slogans in Farsi. One group, spotting me, shouted something in unison in their mother tongue before the entire car collapsed in laughter.

'What did he say?' I asked Arash.

'He said: "Nuclear energy is our right." It is supposed to be a joke.'

Ahmadinejad's much-used slogan of nuclear self-determination and defiance might have struck a chord with his core vote, but to the youth of Tehran, the phrase was something to be mocked, an illogical rant that their elders had bought into but which should be viewed with disdain by their children. A second car passed slowly by us, this time containing a pair of heavily made-up girls smiling ferociously. I smiled back and waved before they laughed and sped off. Finally, a lone patrol car glided up the strip. The cars disappeared down side roads as quickly as they had arrived, like in a scene from *The Truman Show*. The Jordan Game was over, for tonight at least. I said my goodbyes, climbed into my taxi and looked out of the back window as it pulled away. Behind me Arash and Pegah flirted openly whilst considering where to go next. I got the feeling that out of everyone I'd seen that night, I was one of the few people going to bed alone.

*

As it turned out, I didn't have to go far to interview Ali Daei. I was staying at the Azadi's Olympic Hotel and his room was four doors down from mine. Daei had stayed in Tehran after the Costa Rica game to meet up with his Saba Battery teammates, a club ultimately owned by the Ministry of Defence. They were due to play a league match in the Azadi in what used to be called the Iranian Premier League. Now they call it the Persian Gulf Cup, to preserve, the Iranians say, the true name of the waterway that has been appropriated by Arab encroachment. On top of the recent fallout over the Qataris referring to the 'Arabian Gulf' in its 2006 Asian Games literature, there was also the thorny issue of the biennial Arabian Gulf Cup, involving every Gulf nation from Iraq to Oman. Iran hadn't been invited. Even Yemen, which is closer to Africa than the Gulf – be it Persian or Arabian – was allowed to play.

For Ali Daei, the league match was a long way from his glory days in the late 1990s when he was considered one of the best strikers in Germany. After playing for Arminia Bielefeld and Bayern Munich, he went to Hertha Berlin and spearheaded their Champions League charge in 2000. Daei excelled and scored twice in Germany against Chelsea – becoming the first Asian footballer to score in the Champions League group stage – and once against AC Milan in Milan. But even as age advanced and Daei went lower and lower to get a game (first Hertha Berlin, then to Dubai, then back to Iran), he continued to be first choice for the national team and had racked up an astonishing 109 goals, including his well-taken strike against Costa Rica. Sure, four of them came in a 7–0 drubbing of Laos, but a world record was still a world record. His exploits on the pitch in flying the Iranian flag abroad had made Daei phenomenally successful in his home country. He was the closest thing Iran had to David Beckham: he was handsome, owned a sprawling business empire (the Daei Sportswear & Equipment company) and was good-naturedly mocked for his gentle, lisping voice. Even his wedding was broadcast on public television. Also like Beckham, some fans had begun to wonder whether Daei was now redundant at the national level.

'A lot of fans think he's past his best,' admitted Arash at the Costa Rica game. 'But the coach won't drop him, he's too important to the team.' Branko had admitted as much in our interview. 'There aren't many in the world like Ali Daei but he's more than a footballer,' he said admiringly of his captain. 'He is a leader, a national hero and a symbol of the country.'

Ali Daei was lying on the floor of his hotel room, naked save for a pair of tight briefs that barely contained his modesty, being vigorously oiled up by his balding masseur. Daei welcomed me in and offered me an oily hand before we were interrupted by a string of excitable children, with equally awestruck parents in tow and totally nonplussed by their host's almost-nakedness. He signed autographs, gave words of encouragement and posed for semi-naked pictures with the kids. Germany 2006 was Ali Daei's last chance of international glory. Having missed the 2002 finals, France '98 was his only World Cup appearance so far, but it brought Iranian football its greatest achievement. Early on, the group fixture against the USA – who had reached the second round four years previously – was marked for its symbolism. It was one of the first public meetings between the two nations in 19 years. Bill Clinton recorded a message before the match preaching reconciliation and Iran's European fans tried to smuggle opposition T-shirts against the Islamic regime into the ground. The world waited for the two countries' political antipathy to spill out onto the pitch. Instead the world watched as the Iranian players showered their American opponents with symbolic white flowers followed by warm, smiling embraces. It resembled a first date more than the opening salvos of a proxy political battle. Iran's goalkeeper – Ahmad Reza Abedzadeh – shook hands with his American counterpart Thomas Dooley and handed over a large silver shield bigger than a small child to show conciliation and friendship towards their American foes. Dooley sheepishly handed over a tiny pennant in reply, too embarrassed to make eye contact with his adversary. It was singularly one of the funniest moments in international football, and the Americans were visibly stunned. So much so they conspired to lose 2–1, provoking the biggest gathering on Tehran's streets since Ayatollah Khomeini's funeral in 1989. Whilst the Americans gracefully took the defeat in the spirit of international fraternity, Ayatollah Khamenei back in Tehran was eager to make political capital. 'Tonight again,' he sternly extolled in an address to the national team on state television, 'the strong and arrogant opponents felt the bitter taste of defeat at your hands. Be happy that you have made the Iranian nation happy.' In the end, the only enmity that night was in France, as fights broke out between pro and anti-regime fans after the game.

Daei smiled at the memory of that June night. 'All we cared about, our only goal was to win against the USA,' he grinned. 'But we didn't take it seriously for the last match against Germany so that we could qualify for the second round. But this time around it will be different.' It wasn't just Daei who was convinced of Iran's impending footballing glory. If Team Melli's performance in France '98 was all about showing the world that Iran could hold their own at the highest level, the team at Germany 2006 wanted to prove what many fans in Iran – and Branko – sincerely believed: that they could beat anybody on their day and that in Ali Karimi they had arguably one of the finest players in world football. As the squad's spiritual leader the burden of expectation – from fans and politicians alike – had fallen on Daei's shoulders. After shaking hands with Branko, there was no question as to whom Ahmadinejad turned to next. 'The people of Iran, they're living with football so any good result has a big effect on the society and the country,' he explained as he started to get dressed.

Ahmadinejad's words of encouragement and earlier meeting with the squad hadn't convinced him that the team was being used as a political pawn in the West or at home. 'No, politics and football are completely different, totally separate,' he replied when I brought it up. 'We play football and that's what's important for us. We leave the politics to other people.' But Daei could, like the rest of the country, see that Iran's stock was at its lowest ebb for a quarter of a century. And even if the politicians wanted to hijack football for its own ends, he – as a proud Iranian – would do everything in his power to prove that Iran and Iranians were a world away from the cartoon baddies caricatured in the West. 'We'd like to go to Germany and prove that Iranians are completely different from the way the media show us. We have a high culture and our people work hard. The facts are totally different from the way the Western media are trying to show. It's very important for us to show the world exactly who we are.'

The next day's papers proved just how hard that task would be. The IAEA's report was delivered and it wasn't good reading for Ahmadinejad. There was sufficient doubt that Iran was seeking to enrich uranium to make a nuclear bomb, giving the US valuable ammunition in seeking sanctions, and possibly war, in the UN Security Council. Even winning the World Cup couldn't nullify that. Ali Daei and the rest of Team Melli had the hardest PR job in the world.

DUBAI, UAE, JULY 2006

From a distance it looked like the Iranian Club was under siege. It was three and a half months since I had seen Iran beat Costa Rica in Tehran. All their preparations had led to this day. Dusk was falling on another humid July day in Dubai and the upmarket district through which Oud Metha Road ran was stationary. Irate drivers held their horns down in vain to try and clear the road, but it was no use. Streams of disparate people – groups of teenage girls; pensioners hobbling on sticks; young men wearing expensive suits with mobile phones pressed to their ears – were making their way across the four-lane highway, creating a human river that turned the straight and true highway into a temporary crossroads. All were frantic to reach the heavily guarded compound on the other side. The ornate front gates were inundated with last-minute arrivals. Women argued with the guards whilst expertly fixing on head scarves, never breaking eye contact. The lone guard tried to hold the crowd back, but he was fighting a losing battle. The crowd simply pushed past. Others scaled the tall metal fences that surrounded the compound.

The Iranian Club wasn't used to this many visitors. It was meant to be the conservative social club for Dubai's huge Iranian diaspora, but Iran's conservatism didn't travel well abroad. It was a little taste of home, and they enacted Tehran rules. No booze, and women were expected to cover. Socially liberal Iranians preferred drinking in the city's bars or dancing at the many Persian nightclubs instead. The only people the Iranian Club expected to see were devout families and ex-military types in retirement. But today was a national occasion and, like the BBC being the British comfort blanket in times of crisis or celebration, Iranians from all walks of life put their politics to one side and flocked to the only place they could be sure everyone was on the same side. For many, even for those who rejected the regime, it was the only place in town to watch Iran versus Mexico, the country's first game at the 2006 World Cup in Germany.

The guards shut the gate closed, leaving hundreds locked out. One covered, middle-aged woman even tried to hitch her leg up on the sturdy fence to try and climb over, but gave up knowing that age would be the ultimate barrier to her entry. Hopes were rightly high inside. After visiting Tehran a few months previously I had witnessed a self-confidence that hadn't been translated by the world media, both in its football team and its youth. This World Cup, Iranians reasoned, was when Iran took a serious step to being one of the world's footballing powers. They had a good case too. The tournament had come with Iran's 'Golden Generation' at its peak: Mahdavikia, Zandi, Andranik Teymourian and, of course, Ali Karimi. There was also the figure of Ali Daei to contend with. It was surely to be his last World Cup as a player. But as he had told me back in Tehran, when he was sitting semi-naked in his hotel room, this was a vitally important World Cup for Iran for different reasons.

As the tournament drew closer, President Mahmoud Ahmadinejad's behaviour on the world stage had become increasingly divisive. The country's nuclear programme was almost universally suspected of being for anything but peaceful purposes, the prospect of an American invasion was now being openly mooted by hawkish commentators on domestic US news networks and the calls for the Iranian national team to be banned from the World Cup had become even more vociferous.

The focus now was on the Iran versus Mexico fixture to see whether the president, as promised, would turn up in Germany to cheer on Team Melli. Protests had been arranged in Nuremberg by Jewish groups livid at Ahmadinejad's potential presence, pointing out that his views on the Holocaust meant that if these pronouncements had been uttered in Germany he would have broken the country's strict Holocaust denial laws. If the protests didn't keep him away, then they would call for him to be arrested when – if – he landed in Germany. Even worse, neo-Nazi groups had planned on holding a counter demonstration to support the Iranian president. It wasn't exactly the kind of endorsement he or Iran needed.

Only one country from the region had made it past the group stage of a World Cup before; Saudi Arabia in USA '94. But this was probably the best chance for Iran to at least match that, having gained a top-15 place in the FIFA rankings that year. History wasn't exactly on the region's side, though. In fact, most World Cup appearances by Middle Eastern countries had been best remembered for catastrophic failure or embarrassing footnotes. Israel had acquitted themselves admirably when they qualified for Mexico '70, drawing twice and losing once. Iran, too, didn't do too badly in their first appearance in a World Cup finals, in Argentina in 1978, where the team famously drew against a Scottish team that had declared it would return home with winners' medals.

The appearance of Kuwait at Spain '82, however, was remembered for all the wrong reasons. With a creditable draw against Czechoslovakia already in the bag, Kuwait took on France. The French were too good for the Kuwaitis, who went 4–1 down. Or so the French thought. By the time the fourth goal went in, the Kuwaitis were standing stock still after hearing a shrill whistle. Assuming the referee had blown it, they had stopped playing. The French played on and scored anyway. The Kuwaitis were livid but the referee had made his decision; it was a goal. The ball had even been placed back on the centre spot. But from the stands a man wearing traditional Gulf Arab dress waved towards the disgusted Kuwaiti players, urging them to leave the pitch in protest. Cue one of the strangest moments in World Cup history, as the white-robed figure of Sheikh Fahad al Ahmed al Sabah – brother of the emir, head of Kuwait's National Olympic Committee – strode onto the pitch with his red-and-white chequered headscarf and black-and-gold cloak and calmly questioned the referee's wisdom. Amazingly, the referee backed down and called a drop ball. It was the last time he would referee an international match. The sheikh was fined $10,000, although would go on to be elected a FIFA vice president. In August 1990 he was shot dead on the steps of the royal palace, and then run over by a tank, resisting the Iraqi invasion.

Mexico '86 saw Iraq qualify. They narrowly lost every game but it wasn't until afterwards that it emerged that the players had been subjected to beatings and forced head shavings as motivation to qualify for the tournament. In Italia '90, the UAE and Egypt made it to the finals, the former making their debut just 19 years after the country was formed. Whilst Egypt narrowly failed to qualify out of a tough group, the UAE's president Sheikh Zayed bin Sultan al Nahyan, perhaps knowing the limitations of his team, promised each player a brand new Rolls-Royce, not if they won a game, but merely for scoring a goal. Sure enough, the UAE lost every game, conceding 11 goals. But two players, Khalid Ismail and Ali Thani, scored. They would later claim they never received their cars.

USA '94 was perhaps the region's finest triumph, when Saudi Arabia reached the second round thanks to arguably one of the finest goals in World Cup history. Saeed Al Owairan picked the ball up near his own penalty box and, in a carbon copy of Maradona's wonder goal against England in Mexico '86, slalomed past the entire Belgium team before slotting the ball home. But then Al Owairan experienced an extraordinary fall from grace. He was jailed after being caught partying during Ramadan with non-Muslim women. 'It wasn't like a jail, jail,' he told the *New York Times* before the start of France '98 as he was trying to break back into the Saudi national squad. 'It was a detention centre, and I was held for questioning for several weeks.' He later claimed he was locked up for six months.

France '98 was less successful for the Saudis – they lost their first two games against Denmark and France and conceded an injury-time goal to draw with South Africa – but the tournament did throw up the match between the US and Iran in one of the tournament's most politically charged games, which the Iranians ended up winning 2–1. After that it was downhill. The 2002 World Cup saw Saudi Arabia humiliated 8–0 by Germany in their first game. It could have been worse; the Germans had 26 shots on target. The Saudis went home without scoring a goal. The Iranians, meanwhile, hadn't even qualified. In total, the Middle East's record (not including Algeria, Morocco and Tunisia) wasn't something to boast about: played 30, won 3, drew 7, lost 20.

Inside the Iranian Club's packed lobby children cried and parents remonstrated at the doors to the club's huge cinema. They were too late. Inside, close to 700 people had already crammed into the two tiers of seating, with another 400 left outside. Eventually extra televisions were brought outside when the crowd refused to disperse. Dozens more crammed the walkways or sat at the front. The vast projected screen flickered into life, for a moment casting a green glow over the cheering crowd as the equipment corrected itself. The feed was from Iranian state television and as the commentators pored over the team selection – Ali Daei and Ali Karimi were both declared fit and were in the starting line-up – the club's manager stood in front of the crowd and urged everyone to be respectful. Clearly he was confident of a good result and didn't want a repeat of the last time Iran won a World Cup match in 1998, when women threw off their hijabs and danced in the streets of Tehran. Two young women walked past draped in Iran's flag with smaller, smudgy versions painted on their cheeks. 'We wore the flag and painted our faces to show everyone that we really love our country,' Shahrzad and Miadeh told a female reporter from a local paper standing nearby. The noise was deafening when the game kicked off; shouts of 'Iran! Iran!' rang out. Across town, one newspaper reported, several hundred Iranians watching the game in a pub began chanting: 'Nuclear Energy is our Right!' Given the setting, and what I had heard from the young people on Jordan Street in Tehran, I had no doubt it was chanted sarcastically.

On the pitch, at the stadium thousands of miles away in Nuremberg, all eyes were on the crowd. President Ahmadinejad had decided not to turn up, but had sent one of his vice presidents, Mohammad Aliabadi, instead. Which hadn't gone down well either. 'Aliabadi's presence means we could have a repeat of the 1936 Olympics, when they were hijacked by Hitler for his own political purposes and presentation,' Rene Pollak, chair of the Zionist Federation of Frankfurt, told the *Observer* before the game. 'We should have denied him entry to the country. Western leaders should know by now that appeasing fascist regimes does not work.' Hundreds of people representing Jewish groups and exiled Iranians attended the protest in Nuremberg. A smaller pro-Ahmadinejad protest by the far-right National Democratic Party was broken up when the police stopped a group of men marching towards Nuremberg's centre wearing Iranian jerseys and waving Iranian flags. Not that anybody in the Iranian Club watching state television knew anything about the protests as the match kicked off in a sunny Germany. The lights dimmed.

It was a tough start for Iran. Mexico was a team that had won three of their last four opening games at the World Cup, and they soon went ahead after some atrocious defending. But the crowd were soon back on their feet after the veteran central defender Yahya Golmohammadi fired into an open net. The Iranian Club erupted as high-pitched screams from the children present added to the roar. Iran pushed on and dominated the rest of the first half but missed a slew of chances. Ali Daei was dire, giving the appearance he was wading through treacle rather than air. More worrying was the fitness of Iran's star man. Ali Karimi had been injured in the build up to the finals but Branko Ivanković knew that his team's bid for progress would be over without him. With 20 minutes to go he was shattered, having run the midfield superbly in the sweltering heat.

Within minutes of his removal Iran fell to pieces. Mexico scored a second, before adding a third a few minutes later. The mood had changed at the Iranian Club. Before there was hope, now it was turning ugly. Men stood to barrack Ali Daei, the person the crowd blamed for their defeat. People began trickling out even before the final whistle had blown. Mexico had won 3–1. Outside I had hoped to catch victorious Iranian fans running into the streets to celebrate their victory. When the Iranian Club last hosted a victorious World Cup match involving the national team – that famous match in 1998 against the USA – I was told that a crowd had rushed outside and ritually slaughtered a goat. Now a trickle mooched out sullenly, unwilling to talk. 'Daei should not be anywhere near the team,' proclaimed one man, who wouldn't give me his name as he walked back out of the gates that had been the scene of such hysteria two hours previously. He wasn't angry, more upset that he had believed the hype. 'Why do Iran let me believe?' he said. There was still hope though. Iran was to play Portugal in Frankfurt. Win and they were back in with a chance, lose and their World Cup dream was over.

FRANKFURT, GERMANY, JULY 2006

Ask any German and they will tell you that Frankfurt is the most British of German cities. It's the country's financial centre and – so the stereotype goes – full of yuppies and rapacious, money-hungry capitalists. But for a few days the city would be full of Iranian and Israeli flags. The World Cup circus that was following Team Melli – the fans, the politicians and the protests – had left the heartbreak of Nuremberg behind and moved on to Frankfurt instead. Branko Ivanković,

Iran's manager who I'd met back in Tehran, was in the lobby of the team's hotel. Suited security guards stood guard around the room, wires trailing from their ears into their pockets.

'We were very unlucky,' he said, when I asked about the defeat to Mexico. 'The heat was a factor but we will come back stronger for the next game against Portugal.' The previous day's papers had also made an issue out of some of Branko's comments regarding how his players would be happy to meet Ahmadinejad if he came to Germany. 'It would be no different from Jacques Chirac meeting the French team,' he said. Probably wisely, he didn't mention that he and the players had already met the president before the Costa Rica game back in February.

All the political intrigue was getting to him and he wasn't sure whether, come the end of the World Cup, he still wanted to be the Iranian manager after his five-year stint. For a region where a coach's tenure would typically be measured in months, five years was a lifetime. But if Branko lost against Portugal, he would have no choice. 'We don't talk about politics,' he said, when I asked him about the controversy that had surrounded his team. 'I am only concerned about football.' It was a sentiment echoed by the fans staying at the hotel. A mixed group of a dozen Iranian fans lounged on nearby sofas. They had flown here from Tehran. The women chose to remain covered throughout. I asked one fan whether the controversy over the president's possible appearance had been reported back home. 'I, er, no. I don't want to talk about politics,' she replied shakily. 'I am here just for the football.' Her brother-in-law jumped in instantly. 'There are maybe five, six thousand of us who have flown from Tehran, I think, but we are here for football only.' The players marched through the lobby towards the team bus that was waiting to take them to training. The fans had been hanging around to catch a glimpse of them and rushed to take pictures on their mobile phones. For Branko and Team Melli, tomorrow was make or break.

That evening every country was represented at the International Village, a compound where the fans of every nation could mingle, eat each other's food and drink each other's hooch. The Iranians, however, weren't there. Whilst the centre of Frankfurt was full of second-generation Germans of Iranian descent drinking the city's bars dry, the Iranian federation decided against having their stand anywhere near the alcoholic excess of the other nations. They were allowed to have their celebration of all things Iranian on the other side of the river, hidden away from the debauched revelry. It was early evening and the sun was still warm as a troupe of singers and dancers performed traditional songs in Farsi, only stopping when a prominent member of the federation stood and gave a short speech about 'the need for peace in the world'. Several hundred were clustered around the singers in a circle when a commotion began to break out. A group of European bodyguards had formed a circle around a short, bearded man wearing a Nehru shirt and brown jacket. The bodyguards looked around shiftily as he waved goodbye to the Iranians watching the show. A man barged past me as he ran to get a closer look.

'I'm sorry,' he apologised breathlessly.

'Who is that?' I asked, expecting to hear that he was maybe a diplomat, or a famous singer. A popular ex-player, even.

'That's the vice president.'

Vice President Mohammad Aliabadi – President Ahmadinejad's man in Germany and the man whose presence had sparked angry protests in Nuremberg – had turned up the night before the game to be around friends and have a little taste of home. It must have been a tough job, travelling from city to city, having abuse thrown at you for something someone else said. A few dozen well wishers had crowded around him as he walked, making his security detail look even jumpier.

'Mr Vice President,' I called out, not being sure what the protocol was for addressing a vice president. I was sure I had heard something similar on *The West Wing*. He remained passive; his eyes met mine. He had seen me, but ignored my shouts. Instead he looked in the opposite direction, waving at a group of confused German tourists who had stopped to see what the fuss was about. The question had also alerted his security detail to the presence of a possibly hostile entity. 'Mr Vice President?' I shouted again, holding up a camcorder that I'd brought on the trip.

I felt a blow to my neck before I had finished my question. One of his guards dived in the way of the camera, jumping up and down and waving his arms to make himself as big as possible to try and obscure the shot. Suddenly his security went into overdrive, as if they'd just heard the crack of a bullet emanating from a nearby book depository.

The guards nervously looked left and right, bundling the vice president up a nearby stone staircase out of the park and onto the main street. Ironically, he found himself standing in front of Frankfurt's Jewish Museum, which was holding a night of Jewish folk music. The security guard was still in front of me even as Aliabadi was out of sight, stepping left when I stepped left, moving right when I moved to the right.

The walk from the train station to Frankfurt's futuristic Commerzbank-Arena offered a contrasting view on the Iranian government. Whilst anyone who had to get back onto a plane to Tehran was rightly worried to mention anything about Ahmadinejad, Israel or whether he might turn up in Germany or not, the Iranians that had lived in Germany since fleeing the country after the fall of the shah in 1979, and their children, followed a different line. At the time Germany held the third largest Iranian expatriate population in the world, after Canada and the USA. The stream of fans walking the short distance from the station all flew the Iranian green, white and red. But it wasn't the flag of the revolution they carried, it was a flag from the past. It bore the golden lion, the pre-1979 Persian symbol appropriated by the shah. The flag was a protest against the post-revolution regime. 'I'm Iranian, I was born there, I love Iran but the way they treat women there, I can't believe it,' one young Iranian-British woman, holding the shah's flag, told me outside the stadium. 'One day I'll go back, but not with a headscarf.' She was also in the same predicament as me. Ticket-less. 'Have you got any tickets to sell?' she asked.

'No, I was going to ask you if you had any. How much are they?'

'Eight hundred euros,' she replied.

That was that. The next best place was the fan zone next to the Main river, where a crowd of roughly 50,000 would be watching the game. We walked back past the convoy of Iranian fans with their pre-1979 Iranian flags. It would be as close to a home match for Iran as it was possible to get without holding it in Tehran. I rushed back down town, back on the train and then the long walk along the river in searing heat towards the big screen where we should have watched the game. It was due to start any minute but already, half a mile from the screen, there was a pedestrian traffic jam. Tens of thousands of Iranian fans had turned up to see their team. So many, in fact, that the purpose-built stands were full. Not everyone wanted to be inside though. A gaggle of protesters stood under the shade of a line of trees, each one peddling a different dissident political platform: equal rights for Iranian women; an end to racism for non-Persians in Iran. At the end of the line stood Mansoor, a young student, eagerly handing out leaflets to anybody that passed. He was an Iranian Marxist, campaigning for a socialist revolution in Iran. 'In Iran now, you don't know what it's like, it's hopeless. The theocrats have taken away hope.' Just as he said that a distant, worrying silence emerged from behind the trees. Portugal had scored with 20 minutes left. Cristiano Ronaldo ended the contest a few minutes later. All hope that Iran would qualify was lost. For Team Melli the World Cup was effectively over.

Yet their presence was still provocative. Nearby an anti-Ahmadinejad protest was being held, but as I approached, another silence greeted me. The square on which the Alte Oper opera house resided was empty. A stage sat empty to the side, as security guards quickly cleared away the crash barriers. The floor was a mat of blue and white. Stars of David fluttered along the floor. Close to a thousand protesters had been standing in the spot I was in a few hours previously, waving placards that said: 'Israel has a Right to Exist' and 'Support Israel Now'. A former Holocaust survivor and renowned academic, Arno Lustiger, had taken to the stage and, to rapturous applause, told the rally that Ahmadinejad's presence would be a 'provocation to all German Jews'. Now a single, lone protester stood in the middle of the square, an Israeli flag on his back and a cardboard hat with a Star of David on it. Stars of David seemed to cover every single piece of his body.

'You can't trust the Arabs, you can't trust the Arabs,' he repeated.

'You mean the Persians?'

'You can't trust them,' he continued as if he hadn't heard me.

The scraps of blue-and-white paper swirled around the square, but the protester remained, standing stock still, awaiting the next battle.

Ahmadinejad didn't show his face in Germany. Protests were planned for the final group game in Leipzig against Angola: a 1–1 draw. But it didn't take place under the president's watchful eye. The national team had been there to serve a purpose. Previously football had been a crucible of dissent. Ahmadinejad wanted to co-opt the national team for his own nationalistic ends, to prove Iran's strength in the face of adversity. But the campaign had been a PR disaster. On the pitch the glittering array of Iranian footballing talent had failed to live up to the hype. Off the pitch, Iran's position as the world's number one pariah state had been confirmed by the protests and vitriol that had spilled out in every German city they visited. Even the team couldn't escape that. Ali Daei was the chief scapegoat for many fans, and he quickly retired from the game along with a slew of other Iranian footballers. Branko quit too, his legacy in rebuilding Iran's footballing reputation tarnished by his team's failure to jump properly at the last hurdle. He would later emerge as manager of Dinamo Zagreb, where he would win the double. Back in Iran the head of Iran's football federation was fired, allegedly by Ahmadinejad himself. The move led to FIFA briefly suspending the Iranian federation for political interference.

But Daei would make an unexpected comeback. A few months after Iran's World Cup debacle, Daei was hired as coach of Iranian side Saipa. It was his first coaching job yet six months later he was appointed coach of the Iranian national team, almost exactly a year since I had spoken to him, almost naked on his hotel room floor. But the doubts that had dogged the end of his career continued into his coaching. Daei was charged with getting Iran to the 2010 World Cup finals, and things began brightly, going unbeaten in the first group stage and finishing top. But a succession of draws in a tough final group that contained their arch rivals Saudi Arabia and eventual finalists North and South Korea saw Iran struggle. When the Saudis fought back from a goal down to beat Iran 2–1 in front of 100,000 fans at the Azadi in March 2009, the writing was on the wall. Daei was sacked with three games left, having lost just one game in qualification.

He was replaced by a popular but unusual choice. Afshin Ghotbi had arrived at Imam Khomeini Airport 18 months previously under a hail of flowers. Thousands had greeted him at the arrivals hall. Those that couldn't get in lined the road towards the airport instead. His arrival was big news. He had just been hired as coach of Persepolis. It was the first time he had taken a job in Iranian football. In fact, it was the first time he had set foot in the land of his birth for three decades. Ghotbi was an Iranian-American. He fled Iran in 1979 after the revolution with his teacher father, leaving his mother behind. He was 13 years old. But soccer remained in the blood. He cut his teeth first playing and then coaching in college whilst studying electrical engineering at UCLA. By the time France '98 came about, Ghotbi was on the US national team staff, briefing the US on the team of his birth. He then followed Guus Hiddink to the 2002 finals with South Korea, and worked as an assistant to Dick Advocaat, again with South Korea, at the 2006 World Cup.

He had built a solid international coaching reputation. But he was also an Iranian who had vital foreign experience. In Iran he was treated like a returning rock star. At the airport he saw his mother for the first time in 30 years, before being carried out of the terminal on the crowd's shoulders. Initially his time in charge of Persepolis was a success. Close to 90,000 people were turning up to the home games and he dramatically won the league title in his first season. But he was still seen as an outsider, a traitor – in some quarters – for fleeing the country. A whispering campaign began about his coaching methods. Former players criticised his choice of tactics as well as the people he hired for coaching jobs. Previously a star player would usually waltz into a well-paid coaching position. But Ghotbi had picked up American sports' love of stats and analysis, rather than the illogical hunch of the pro. There was unease at the Western suits he would wear on the touchline. The subtext was obvious. As an American raised, if not an American born, Ghotbi was viewed with suspicion, not by the public, but by the federation and its political allies. On one TV phone poll asking the question 'who should be the next national team coach?' he racked up 85 per cent of the vote. He was overlooked, and Daei was hired. But in the spring of 2009, and with the national team in dire straits, Iranian football turned to him to save the day.

His contract lasted the length of the remaining qualification campaign: three games. His first was a 0–0 draw in Pyongyang before two crucial matches in quick succession: one against the UAE, the second a few days later against South Korea in Seoul. But the timing of the matches couldn't have been any worse. Iran's presidential election was being held, an election whose outcome was far from clear. Ahmadinejad faced a stiff challenge from Mir-Hossein Mousavi, a former prime minister, editor and artist who had campaigned on a reformist ticket.

Tensions were high. Corruption and squandered oil wealth had enraged the public as the economy crumbled under the weight of mismanagement and international sanctions. The timing of the UAE match in Tehran was such that the regime feared what effect a defeat might have on the election results two days later. An illuminating diplomatic cable sent from the US State Department's regional desk in Dubai on the eve of the election, and released by Wikileaks, entitled, IRAN'S FIRST FAN: DISSATISFACTION WITH AHMADINEJAD MAY EXTEND FROM THE SOCCER PITCH TO THE BALLOT BOX, highlighted just how worried the regime was that defeat against the UAE might swing the election against Ahmadinejad. Worse, it might start riots that could spread throughout the country. Yet equally interesting to Iranian football fans was the fact that Ahmadinejad's reverse Midas touch – which had so far ruined the economy and the country's international relations – had now spread to sport:

As a result of its enormous domestic fan base, soccer has become highly politicized in Iran. According to an IRPO contact closely involved with Iranian professional soccer, the Iranian government is well aware of the potential domestic unrest that can result from a Team Melli loss - or even win. Iran's successful World Cup qualifiers in 1997 and 2005 resulted in massive celebrations in the streets of Tehran, marked by public intoxication, dancing, and women removing their hijabs, while Team Melli's elimination from the 2001 World Cup qualifiers led to rioting. Contacts tell IRPO that the Iranian government worries that public unrest over a Team Melli loss could add fire to the increasingly volatile political demonstrations that have paralysed Tehran in recent nights.

President Ahmadinejad, in particular, has staked a great deal of political capital in Iranian soccer. A personal fan and former player, Ahmadinejad has made several press appearances practising with Team Melli. In an effort to capitalize on soccer's popularity with constituents, Ahmadinejad, a political conservative,

went so far as to call for the inclusion of women at
men's games in 2006, although he was overruled by
Supreme Leader Khamenei in a rare, but significant,
open disagreement between the two men.

The cable went on to allege that Ahmadinejad was involved in a string
of decisions in Iranian football, including personally sacking Ali Daei
before approving Afshin Ghotbi for the Iran job. He even lent Team
Melli his presidential jet, according to the cable, for the awkward
away trip to North Korea. Just like in 2006, Ahmadinejad understood
the political power of football. Except this time there was a presidential election at stake as well as World Cup qualification.

Through his decidedly public involvement with Team
Melli, Ahmadinejad has inextricably linked himself
to the outcome of Iran's bid to qualify for the 2010
World Cup. The presidential election, which has become
hotly contested over recent days as Ahmadinejad has
cast aspersions on his rivals and drawn other powerful elites into the fray by making sweeping allegations
of corruption, is increasingly turning into a referendum on Ahmadinejad himself. Though many serious
issues will draw Iranians to the polls on June 12, one
cannot overlook the effect that the result of the June
10 Iran-UAE match, especially an embarrassing loss,
could have on Ahmadinejad's electoral fortunes.

But football could be used both ways. As more people used the terraces to vent their opposition to Ahmadinejad's regime, the game also
became symbolic, reflective even of Iran's fall from grace.

To many, the state of soccer in Iran today reflects
the problems that Ahmadinejad's challengers claim the
country has suffered under his administration. Whereas
Iran achieved international prominence in the 1998
World Cup under Khatami, Ahmadinejad's politicization
of the sport has compromised Team Melli's standing on

the world stage, and in many Iranians' eyes, further
jeopardized the country's national pride.

Ali Karimi, now captain of the national team, scored the only goal
of the game as Iran beat the UAE 1–0, setting up a must-win clash
against Ghotbi's former team, South Korea. But as the team left the
country Iran descended into chaos. Just a few hours after the polls
closed for the 12 June presidential election, Ahmadinejad was
announced the winner, an impossibility according to the opposition
who alleged massive voter fraud. The result sparked huge
demonstrations – the start of the so-called Green Movement – that
saw millions of Iranians taking to the streets. It was the most serious
challenge the gatekeepers of the Iranian revolution had ever faced.
For a short time, it looked like the sheer weight of protest might bring
an end to Iran's three-decade-long theocratic experiment.

News of the protests – not to mention the reports of deaths and
brutality meted out by the police and militias in the aftermath of the
result – had reached Seoul too. Outside the stadium protesters held
aloft banners denouncing the Iranian government. 'Go to Hell, Dictator,' read one. As the Iranian team waited in the dressing room, Afshin
Ghotbi noticed that something was different about his players. Most
of his starting 11 were wearing green bands on their wrists. 'I asked
the players, but they were not going to tell me,' Ghotbi recalled when
I later asked him what happened at half-time. Karimi eventually told
Ghotbi that the green bands were in honour of a revered Shia cleric.
'He told me they were wearing it as a religious symbol. I thought,
"then why don't you wear the green every game?" It's the moment
that we stopped asking about it.'

But after the players had walked onto the pitch, their team photo
became an iconic symbol of protest. As they crouched seconds before
kick-off almost all of the players were clearly wearing the same green
bands that had become a symbol of protest against the election back
home. At the front Ali Karimi wore his green bracelet tightly around
his left wrist. At half-time – as news of the protest began to filter out –
Ghotbi insisted that no one was forced to take off their wristbands,
even though several did. The young up and coming midfielder Masoud
Shojaei scored and the team came within eight minutes of a poetic

victory. But, in the 82nd minute, Park Ji-sung equalised for South Korea. The match finished 1–1. Iran had failed, just as the Green Movement was due to fail too.

There were to be recriminations. Pro-government newspapers announced that the players – with Karimi in particular singled out – would be banned from the national team for life. Those that had foreign contracts would have their passports seized. Ghotbi, though, denied that any punishment was handed down. 'None of these players have been banned,' he said. Indeed, one spokesperson for the Bundesliga club VFL Bochum, where Vahid Hashemian played, explained that the player was returning to training in Germany as normal and that the whole story about passport seizures and international bans had been fabricated. 'I will speak to them both [Karimi and Mahdavikia] on a one to one basis,' Ghotbi said. 'The national team door is always, always, open to them.'

The defeat marked the last chance for many of the team to achieve their potential. Many players in that squad did retire. But Karimi, amazingly, would later return. Ghotbi had been good to his word, but it would mark the end of his honeymoon period with the Iranian public. He may have survived the scandal politically by claiming to not know anything about the green wristbands, but his failure to back the Green Movement and professing ignorance at his team's actions had damaged his popularity back in Iran. There would be no more jubilant crowds to meet him when he landed in Tehran. There would be no more flowers thrown at his feet. There would be no clamour to carry him out into the streets on the shoulders of men. Instead he would attend President Ahmadinejad's inauguration party two months later, even though dozens of reformist politicians had boycotted it. Ghotbi's Facebook account was inundated with abuse. But it wasn't all bad news. Ghotbi was rehired as coach of the Iranian national team and tasked with taking Team Melli to the 2011 Asian Cup in Qatar.

3

Israel

Oren hadn't seen business like it for years. The middle-aged Maccabi
Haifa fan, his face tanned and lined, hands rough from his chosen trade,
wore the green and white shirt of his team and stood in the long shadow
of Maccabi Netanya's crumbling stadium. He held open a large, flat
wooden suitcase of football merchandise, around which a crowd had
formed. Oren was used to being ignored by all but a few but today, the
first day of the 2006/7 Israeli football season, was different. The jumble
of cheap, polyester scarves and fake gold Star of David necklaces bearing his beloved team's name was being met with an unusually positive
reaction. The fans – usually so indifferent to Oren's mercantile
overtures – laughed, fingering and pulling his stock as if noticing him
for the first time before putting their hands in their pockets and dropping a few shekels into his palm. The source of this newfound interest
wasn't born in the sun and optimism that every football fan feels on the
back of their necks as the season starts; the equality of knowing that
everyone begins last, that everyone begins first. Nor was it based on
sympathy, as such, even though Maccabi Haifa had endured a torrid
time of late. The first game of the season was supposed to take place a
week earlier in Haifa, a mixed Jewish and Arab city in the north of the
country. But it was impossible to play games there now. For the moment
at least, Maccabi Haifa was homeless.

It was less than two weeks since the end of the Second Lebanon
War, a 34-day long conflict started by the Lebanese Shia militia Hezbollah and which claimed the lives of more than 2,000 people on

either side of the border. The majority of the dead were Lebanese civilians but the north of Israel had been bombarded by Hezbollah's arsenal of Katyusha rockets. Haifa, Israel's third city, had taken the brunt of Hezbollah's assault on northern Israel. They were due to play Ashdod at their Kiryat Eliezer stadium the week previously, but when a Katyusha narrowly missed the club's ground, the Israeli FA decided to ban games in the north of the country and put back the start of the season by a week, just in case hostilities resumed. The start of the football league, the return to normality, even a week later than planned, was still a symbolic moment, more so for Maccabi Haifa than perhaps anyone else. They had dominated Israeli football in recent years, winning four of the previous five championships in the Israeli Premier League, the Ligat Ha'Al. As Israel has been a member of UEFA since 1991 – thanks to a boycott by Arab teams in the Asian Football Confederation in the 1970s that effectively left the Israeli FA without a confederation to permanently call home for two decades – they had qualified for the UEFA Champions League.

It was ironic, too, that Haifa had taken such a heavy toll for Israel's incursions into southern Lebanon following the kidnapping of two of its soldiers. The city was often seen as a model of Jewish–Arab coexistence. Israel's Arabs make up close to 20 per cent of the population, and the football team had long championed the cause of Israel's Arab footballers who had found prejudice, like in wider society, within some of the country's clubs. It was one of a number of battles fought within the game; Jew versus Arab, left versus right, Likud versus Labor, rich versus poor.

But, today, fraternity was the answer to Oren's prayers. He thrust the key to his sale's boom into my hand; a small, green sticker. Drawn on it was a cartoon of a Maccabi Haifa fan urinating into Hezbollah leader Hassan Nasrallah's mouth. Crude, yes, but for only five shekels, it was a bargain. Oren had struck gold. 'It says: "Nasrallah you are garbage,"' he translated as he shifted another to a still-chuckling Maccabi Haifa fan. 'He's no good, he shoots rockets where there are civilians. They fire deliberately on civilians and when we retaliate they say we are bad. We have a chant for him today: "Yallah, yallah, Nasrallah, I kill you, I kill you, inshallah."' Shlomi, his fellow merchandise seller, part confidant, part turf rival, eyed Oren's booming trade with jealousy. 'If it was up to me I'd bomb every house in southern

Lebanon,' he spat through a mouthful of semi-digested sunflower seeds, as he sought a more valuable seam elsewhere. 'Give my regards to Nasrallah if you see him.'

Israeli football was some of, if not the, best in the region. But the league was also something of a microcosm of the divisions, hopes and fears of Israeli society. When most people think of Israeli society, they think of something monolithic; a Jewish homeland in constant conflict with the Palestinians. But football tells a more complicated story. Each club had its own distinct identity, rooted in different political cultures. 'Even before the state of Israel was founded, everything was very political and football was no different from that,' explained Uri Misgav, the sports editor of *Haaretz*, the country's liberal left-leaning newspaper, when we met at an Indian restaurant in Tel Aviv. 'Every big political group had its own team: Hapoel teams represented the big unions that were running the country – the workers and labourers; the teams of Maccabi represented the middle class; and the teams of Beitar were representing the right-wing nationalist minority.'

Uri was a supporter of Hapoel Tel Aviv, Israel's most famous socialist club. Hapoel means 'The Worker' in Hebrew and for 70 years the team was bankrolled by the Histadrut, the country's biggest trade union. The team badge still has a hammer and sickle on it. To their political and footballing opponents, they were simply and disparagingly known as 'The Communists'. Teams like Maccabi Tel Aviv, the grande dame of Israeli football, and Maccabi Haifa had always held the bourgeois centre ground. Beitar Jerusalem, on the other hand, has its roots in Ze'ev Jabotinsky's revisionist Zionist youth movement born in the 1920s. The club represented the political right and was closely aligned with the Likud party. Many of its past, present and no doubt future prime ministers were Beitar fans, the likes of Ariel Sharon, Ehud Olmert and Benjamin Netanyahu. Many Likud Knesset members had cut their administrative teeth on the board at Beitar. The two sides – Hapoel Tel Aviv and Beitar Jerusalem – had long hated each other for more than their competing styles of play. 'We had a cup final against Beitar in 1999 which was three days after the elections. Labor won and we took a huge banner to the game that read: "We fucked you in the elections, now we'll fuck you on the pitch,"' Uri recalled.

The rivalry existed on another level too. More than a century of Zionism had brought together groups of Jews from across the world, from Yemen to Ethiopia to Poland, united by a common cause. Israel in itself was the glue that held Israel together. But each community brought with it the essence of their homeland. In many areas – food in particular – this multiculturalism was a boon. In others it caused deep political tensions on and off the football pitch. For years Israeli society was dominated by the Ashkenazim, the white, European settlers that had fled Eastern and Central Europe's barbarism and largely coalesced around the leftist Labor party which dominated politics after the creation of Israel in 1948. The support of teams like Maccabi Tel Aviv and Hapoel Tel Aviv – the two teams along with Maccabi Haifa who have won the most league titles since 1948 – were drawn from the more affluent Ashkenazim. But things began to change in 1977. The Likud party broke Labor's hegemony and won its first general election, an earthquake in Israeli politics. They didn't count on white Europeans for their support. They looked to the Mizrahim and the Sephardim.

The Mizrahim were eastern Jews, those that had fled persecution in the Middle East, from Iraq, Iran, Egypt or anywhere else in the Near East, the majority arriving after being expelled by Arab governments in the wake of Israel's creation. Many spoke Arabic and came from marginalised working-class neighbourhoods. The Sephardim were Jews originally expelled from the Iberian peninsula who resettled in North Africa or elsewhere. They understood Israel's Arab neighbours better than their white, socialist countrymen. It was this changing ethnic mix that swept Likud, and Prime Minister Menachem Begin, to power in the 1977 election. It was the same ethnic mix – those that had claimed to know the true enemy best – that also made up Beitar Jerusalem's fan base. In 1976 Beitar won its first ever cup, beating the seemingly invincible Maccabi Tel Aviv. The two events are not seen as a coincidence by Beitar fans, nor its political rulers. The clash between the two – socialist Hapoel Tel Aviv, versus the religious, right-wing and nationalistic Beitar Jerusalem – was not just a clash between competing teams or ideologies but a fundamental struggle between two competing visions for Israel.

But a further dimension had come to define Israeli football in recent

years. Clubs like Bnei Sakhnin and Maccabi Ahi Nazareth hailed from
the poor Arab towns of the north, and had a resolutely Arab, largely
Muslim identity. The status, motivations and treatment of Israel's
Arabs, those who stayed behind after the creation of Israel rather than
be forced into exile, had become an increasingly fraught political
issue. Sympathetic to their Palestinian kin, but nonetheless Israeli citizens, Israel's Arabs faced discrimination in almost all walks of life.
Their towns were poorer than their Jewish neighbours, jobs harder to
come by. But for many they also represented an existential threat, a
growing non-Jewish minority that threatened Israel's Jewish demo-
graphics. Those on the right also viewed them as potential fifth
columnists, their allegiances to be found in the West Bank or Gaza
rather than Israel. Yet football was one area of life where race was
largely irrelevant. Bnei Sakhnin, a mixed team of Arabs and Jews, had
been promoted to the top division and had even won the State Cup.
The national team had Arab, Muslim players. Almost every team had
signed an Arab player. Except one. Beitar Jerusalem had never had
an Arab play for them. Their fans, notoriously right-wing ultra-
nationalists with a hardcore that held views that were out-and-out
racist, would simply not accept it.

It was an issue that came up in Netanya too. The stadium was built
before Israel existed. It was in poor shape, semi-affectionately known
as 'The Box' thanks to its enclosed atmosphere. It was also rumoured
to have been condemned years before. But Maccabi Netanya still
played here, and the fans still filled the terraces without the ground
collapsing around them. The crumbling walls and lack of an east
stand gave the place a neutered, dilapidated air of a 1970s English
ground on the brink of liquidation, like Millwall's Old Den, or Middlesbrough's Ayresome Park. There was little intimidating about The
Box, despite the profusion of barbed wire. Still, the inscription on the
front gates in Hebrew – 'Welcome to Hell' – seemed to be steeped in
irony. Although this was the first game for Maccabi Netanya, Maccabi Haifa's season had begun long before, in the north-west of
England. They had narrowly lost 2–1 to Liverpool in the first leg of
their qualification match for the Champions League group stage. But
with the city under siege and rockets getting worryingly close to the
pitch, UEFA ordered that their home match against Liverpool be

moved to a neutral location. Despite scoring first, Maccabi Haifa drew in a sub-zero Kyiv, narrowly ending their hopes of Champions League glory. They could take comfort from the fact that they lost to the eventual finalist.

Outside The Box, Nasrallah was everywhere. The fans angrily chanted his name and his image was desecrated and corrupted on hundreds of placards, posters, T-shirts and, yes, Oren's stickers. Which wasn't to say that Maccabi Haifa's fans were virulently anti-Arab or anti-Muslim – far from it. Whilst teams like Beitar Jerusalem refused to sign Arab players for fear of upsetting their hardcore right-wing fans, Maccabi Haifa could boast current Israeli international and the country's most famous Arab player, Abbas Suan. 'The fascists, like Lazio, they are Beitar Jerusalem,' explained Kornel, a 20-year-old soldier who fought in Lebanon and who was also a member of the Green Apes – the team's ultra group. 'We are less political like that because we have no problems with Arabs. The war hasn't caused any problems between us. We are from Israel, they are all Israelis too.'

The Green Apes were here en masse. Hanging around in the shadow of their crumbling host, drinking cans of Becks and singing 'I'm Forever Blowing Bubbles', West Ham United's famous song, in honour of Yossi Benayoun. The Israeli international had played four seasons at Maccabi Haifa, and had just moved to West Ham after a short spell in the Spanish league. In fact, he may have been the reason I was let into the country at all. As there were no direct flights between Israel and the UAE, I'd travelled overland from Jordan, over the Allenby Bridge that crosses what is left of the Jordan River, and into the West Bank. It was a metal and wire hellscape and the young female border guard was immediately suspicious of my passport's Iranian entry stamp. When I told her I was there to watch Maccabi Haifa, she immediately asked who my favourite player was.

'Yossi Benayoun,' I said.

It turned out that Maccabi Haifa was her hometown club. 'Israel's greatest player,' she replied with a smile, handing me back my passport.

The Green Apes all seemed a bit too nice to be considered hooligans – one part liberal integrationists; one part ultras – as they crowded around to show off their initiation tattoos: either a large green ape on the shoulder blade or the letters ACAB, an acronym for

All Cops Are Bastards, printed prominently on the forearm. They even had a huge ACAB poster – illustrated by a mean, American-looking cop – to hang on the hoardings during the match. They differentiated between 'their Arabs' and 'Nasrallah's Arabs' and insisted that war had only brought Maccabi Haifa's Jewish and Arab fans closer together. Except for Hezbollah, the only other organisation that united the fan base was Liverpool – or 'Chicken Pool' as they were known here. Liverpool's refusal to play their Champions League qualifier in Israel had made them public enemy number two. 'Rafa Benítez is a chicken. Sissoko is Nasrallah's cousin. He fights for Hezbollah!' shouted Tamar, a middle-aged woman escorting her son to the match. She angrily tapped at my notebook just to get the point across. 'Haifa is a safe place. Not even in England is it safe. What about your airports? And games were played after the bombs in London and Madrid, weren't they? You should write it in bold: Israel is safe.' I later wondered what they made of Benayoun after he signed for 'Chicken pool' in 2007.

With their Jewish brethren under attack and the opening game being something of a symbolic moment for the city of Haifa – a chance to show the world that it was bruised but unbowed – I'd expected Israel's footballing family to come together in a show of national unification. But the fraternity that helped Oren the merchandise seller secure a bumper pay day outside The Box didn't last long. Maccabi Netanya's fans, jealous from Haifa's near domination of Israeli football over the past half-decade, had a different plan: almost every fan wore Liverpool's yellow away kit. 'It's because we play in yellow as well, but it's to annoy Haifa,' explained Hagai, a 25-year-old Netanya fan who lived by the ground. 'We are glad they were kicked out [of the Champions League]. We hate Haifa because they think they're the best team in the world and take all our best players.'

Inside the stadium one stand was packed with thousands of Haifa fans wearing green and letting off red flares. Having started to watch football in England just before the dawn of the Premier League, when crowd violence could rear its head at any moment and the prospect of electrified fences to keep fleet-footed fans off the pitch was an all too real threat, it was still a shock to see Israeli police armed with machine guns patrol the perimeter fence through the badly observed minute's silence for the war dead. The favourites quickly went one down, then two, then three. Netanya's fans went crazy, scarcely able to believe that they were there to witness one of the great shocks of modern Israeli football. The game finished 3–1, the Green Apes rolled up their cop-baiting banner and left in silence without apportioning blame on players or management. They knew that the only person to blame for their team's poor preparations was a bearded ideologue, hidden in a bunker miles away somewhere north of the Lebanese border.

The Israeli landscape undergoes a subtle change as you drive north towards the Lebanese border. The industrial suburbs of the big cities gradually morph into plush, green olive groves, expansive valleys and signposts for flat, sand-yellow towns with names familiar from numerous past newsflashes: Afula, Jenin, Hebron. As the road north skirted the walled enclave of the West Bank an abundance of minarets gave away that more than just the terrain had changed. Most of Israel's Arab – mainly Muslim – community can be found on the fertile planes in the north of the country, although this wealth of natural resources hadn't translated into any economic or social parity. This was also Katyusha country, the southernmost point where Hezbollah's most advanced rockets landed.

After watching Maccabi Haifa's capitulation the previous night, albeit an understandable one given the team's preparations, Ahikam, an Israeli photographer, and I headed for the small Arab town of Sakhnin to speak to its most famous son, Maccabi Haifa's recent big-money signing and Israel's most prominent Arab footballer, Abbas Suan. His transfer to the country's most successful team was almost inevitable after his Herculean efforts of the past two years. Abbas came to the nation's attention after leading his hometown club Bnei Sakhnin to the Israeli cup in 2004, a success that shone a light internationally on a community viewed suspiciously both by their Jewish countrymen (for being pro-Palestinian fifth columnists) and by the wider Arab world (for being Zionist collaborators). His status as a poster boy for Israel's Arabs was cemented when he was called up for the Israeli national team. Suan came on late and scored a last-minute equaliser in a World Cup qualifier against Ireland in 2005. Now he was a national name. Everyone knew who Abbas Suan was, especially in his own backyard. Unable to find his house, Ahikam stopped to ask a child wearing Bnei Sakhnin's red kit whether he knew where Abbas Suan's house was. The child scrunched up his face in confusion before looking back incredulously, pointing up the road, to the left, as if the answer was so obvious it didn't merit a reply. Everybody in Sakhnin, it seemed, knew where Abbas Suan lived.

We pulled up at Abbas's modest stone town house and negotiated the large courtyard bustling with life: brothers, cousins, uncles – the entire Suan clan seemed to have decamped within his modest four walls. His father, whose face wore the deep creases of a man who had worked the land for half a century, shuttled back and forth to the kitchen, fetching tea, fruit and plates of dates for his guests, before sitting down and regaling us with stories from his childhood memories: his grandfather had bought land for farming from the Turks and moved to Sakhnin as a child before finally having all but a tiny plot seized during the *nakba* – or 'The Catastrophe' as it is known by Palestinians – when the local Arab population were expelled (or fled depending on your reading of history) in 1948 when the state of Israel was created. As Abbas arrived, his father tidied the empty plates and disappeared into the kitchen, offering the smallest glimpses into a past that was still fresh in at least one person's living memory.

'The Haifa fans accepted me very quickly,' yawned Abbas as he sat down, still rubbing his eyes after being awoken from a lie-in on his only day off. 'I know that in the beginning some kids wrote some slogans against me because I was an Arab but the club stamped down on this because they have so many Arab fans and they've had Arab stars playing for Haifa in the past.' The Maccabi Haifa fans might have greeted his signing positively, but it had been harder to convince the fans of other teams of the merits of playing an Arab in a largely Jewish team. 'Generally speaking, Israeli fans are wonderful, one of the best in the world. At the same time there are a few that behave shamefully and we're all shamed by them,' he said, referring to one team in particular. 'I'm speaking about the fans of Beitar Jerusalem which behave beneath an accepted conduct.'

Abbas had a somewhat fractured relationship with Beitar Jerusalem. After scoring his historic goal against Ireland, his next game was an away tie at Jerusalem's notorious Teddy Stadium. The home fans welcomed his achievement by unfurling a banner. It read: 'Abbas, You Are Not One of Us.' After one game, a group of fans managed to break into the stadium whilst he was giving a post-match interview and attacked him. Perhaps most surprising of all, Abbas very nearly became Beitar's first-ever Arab player. The club's newly installed billionaire owner Arcadi Gaydamak had close links with Bnei Sakhnin and donated millions of shekels to keep the club afloat. Then one day, on a visit to the club, Gaydamak decided he wanted to sign their star player for himself. 'I said I was ready, I could do it,' he said with an unexpected hint of disappointment. 'I believe he [Gaydamak] was trying to break the image of Beitar and say Arab players can play for them. But he got into trouble in Jerusalem. In the end he apologised and said he couldn't sign me.' The past three months hadn't gone well for Bnei Sakhnin. The club were relegated from Israel's top division, lost their captain and almost went bankrupt before Gaydamak came to the rescue. Then the Second Lebanon War came and the age-old suspicions levied against Israel's Arabs were once again raised.

'I don't take the Hatikvah,' he explained, as to why he doesn't sing Israel's national anthem. 'But I stand and respect it. It's the anthem of the Jewish people. So what can I do? I am Arab and Muslim.' Yet he was proud to fly the flag of the state, even before the country's media came to him when the war started. 'When the war broke, everybody asked me what I thought. A drop of blood from a Jewish or Arab child is the same, and the missiles don't distinguish between Jews and Arabs. So I was against the war, but I was worried for my family as rockets fell in Sakhnin. It was a big failure but politicians stick to their chairs. I wish politicians would enter Lebanon in a tank. Maybe then they wouldn't be so ready for a war.'

After we had finished talking, he agreed to drive us to his old home, Bnei Sakhnin's Doha Stadium – so called because the Qatari government paid for its renovation, a remarkable gesture given that Qatar didn't officially recognise Israel's existence. As he stood on the pitch and surveyed his former home, the parallels between the club's descent and the plight of his people during and after the war weren't lost on him. If anything, the role that had been foisted on him – of spokesman and role model for a whole community – had never been as important as now. 'When we won the national cup I was proud for the Arabs in Israel and the fact that we were narrowing the gaps between communities through football,' he said nostalgically. 'Now there are many symbols attached to me and many see me as an Arab symbol in Israel. I will always accept it.'

But times, and opinions, were changing. On the eve of Israel's 60th birthday, the *New York Times* reported that a majority of Israeli Jews now favoured the expulsion of some Israeli Arabs as part of a two-state solution. Transfer, as the policy was known, was once the preserve of the hard right. Now it had become mainstream. On the journey back to Tel Aviv we again passed the distant minarets of the West Bank, an area of extreme poverty ringed by what activists refer to as a new Berlin Wall, adjacent to an affluent Western democracy. Anywhere else in the world, such a juxtaposition of wealth and extreme privation would be considered vulgar. But for many Israelis, even Ahikam the photographer – a peacenik who agitated throughout his military service and was eventually given a dishonourable discharge – it's the price that the Palestinians have paid for years of terrorism and duplicity.

'I just can't understand these people like the International Solidarity Movement protesting here, what has it got to do with them?' he said when I asked him about the wall. Even calling it a wall caused offence. 'It's not even a wall in most places, just a fence. You don't see them [the ISM] protesting in China at human rights abuses.' But several activists had been killed in the West Bank and Gaza, including 23-year-old Rachel Corrie, protesting against the wall. 'Yes, but look at the reality. Since the fence we have had no attacks from suicide bombings. I was against it at first, too, but we feel safer because of it. If the Palestinians want their own state, fine. But it's crazy. How will they live? They could have been part of Israel and had a better quality of life and, if they were smart, they would have outnumbered Jews.' The fence has created a problem for Israeli liberals, who despised what it represented but had concluded that their country was safer because of it. That, plus the seeming failure of Israel's unilateral withdrawal from southern Lebanon in 2000 – a move which the Israeli right blamed for allowing Hezbollah to rearm – and Sharon's disengagement plan from the Gaza Strip had forced everyone to reassess their opinions rightwards.

*

The problems of war and racism seem a million miles away in Tel Aviv. With the north shaken after being on the front line for the past month, and with Jerusalem long used to tension for straddling both sides of the divide – the Jewish western half with its foot in the former, the Muslim eastern half seized from the Jordanians in 1967 in the latter – Tel Aviv gives a good impression of a city that hasn't read that day's newspapers. Israelis know the city as 'The Bubble', a reference to the fact that Hamas or Hezbollah still haven't yet been able to devise a rocket that can reach the country's financial capital. As a result Tel Aviv has remained relatively untouched from the rockets that have terrorised the north and the towns clustered around the Gaza Strip. It is famed for its 'life goes on as normal' detachment, its abundance of drugs and for being the party capital of the Middle East. Not to mention its vibrant gay community, a state of affairs that angers Israel's Orthodox Jewish community as much as the militant Islamists coveting their ancestral lands from afar.

I'd arranged to meet Amir, the editor of weekly listings magazine *Time Out Tel Aviv*. He had achieved a little notoriety in recent weeks after being interviewed by various American television networks along with his counterpart at *Time Out Beirut* during the bombings. Amir was in his late 30s, with salt-and-pepper hair and an interesting musical past. He used to be the guitarist in Israel's mid-1990s answer to REM. He had been troubled by the war, yet was annoyed by the lack of understanding internationally for Israel's position. 'I feel bad for what is happening in Lebanon, I really do,' he said whilst expertly rolling a joint in his modern, minimalist flat. 'But few people seem to be concerned by how we feel here, the fear of attack, the lives lost. Civilians have been killed on both sides.'

Amir supported one of Israel's left-wing clubs, Hapoel Haifa, designated by its distinctly political prefix. But the socialist clubs were changing these days. In recent years football had begun to become big business in Israel. Television deals were signed, stadiums spruced up and Israeli football experienced a new phenomenon: billionaire Jewish owners – some homegrown but many coming from abroad. Some were more welcome than others. Arcadi Gaydamak was one to make the headlines after buying Beitar Jerusalem. The Russian-born tycoon was beloved by his club's fans but his rivals were loath to forget his shadier business dealings – an international arrest warrant outstanding in France due to alleged gun running during the Angolan civil war, for one. Daniel Jammer was another, a German billionaire who bought Maccabi Netanya and straight away enquired of Real Madrid as to whether David Beckham would consider moving to the club (he wouldn't, unsurprisingly). But not every infusion of cash had been successful. Amir's Hapoel Haifa had a brush with infamy when Robi Shapira, a lifelong Hapoel fan whose dad used to be the club's kit man and who had made a fortune in African fishing concessions, bought the club and promised to bring the fans their first championship, which he duly delivered in 1999. The problem was that Shapira was so hell-bent on his dream he bankrupted himself in the process. In 2001 he flew to his home in Nigeria and shot himself in the head. They've been stuck in the second division ever since.

Nobody seems to go out before 2am in Tel Aviv. The bouncers stepped aside at one of Tel Aviv's best clubs – a grimy courtyard surrounding a split-level shed with a sunken dance floor. Its warehouse chic was more affected than it perhaps realised. But the city's nickname became abundantly clear the moment you entered. Despite being a few days after the end of hostilities, and with a relapse still very much a possibility, hundreds of people packed the bar, danced on the tables and kissed in corners. Perhaps this was what it was like during the Blitz in 1940s London: people throwing caution to the wind, shagging, taking copious amounts of drugs and generally acting as if the world would end tomorrow. Because, invariably, it could. But Amir was preoccupied with something far more serious. The war had exposed Israel to a greater threat than Lebanon or even Hezbollah: Iran. 'If they get the nuclear bomb,' he sighed through a bottle of beer, 'where do you think they'll hit? Here.' Behind him two beautiful skinhead boys kissed. 'This is everything they hate. Tel Aviv has a big red cross on it.'

Wearing a red T-shirt and admitting I was a journalist was looking like a bad idea. It was 24 hours after Maccabi Haifa's loss against Maccabi Netanya and the Israeli football circus had moved to the Bloomfield Stadium in Tel Aviv for one of the biggest matches of the season, and a replay of the 1976 State Cup final: Maccabi Tel Aviv versus Beitar Jerusalem. You couldn't guess it was a Maccabi

Tel Aviv home game, though. Outside the ground all you could see was the gold and black of Beitar. But some fans had taken exception to my choice of top. Red is the colour of arch rivals Hapoel Tel Aviv, the polar opposite of Beitar's right-wing terrace racism.

'We hate Arabs and Muslims!' screamed 19-year-old Eliran as I tried to explain that I was not a Hapoel agitator. 'If an Arab played for Beitar we'd burn their ass and burn the club. They are our enemy.' Eliran was a member of La Familia, Beitar's infamous, violent and highly strung ultra group renowned for being the most uncompromising in the land. 'Ten supporters went to meet Sakhnin and make peace with the Arabs,' he explained. 'But Beitar found out. They were beaten up and banned.'

They also don't have much time for journalists. 'Beitar have the best hooligans, we'd fuck the ICF [West Ham's infamous Inter City Firm],' boasted Itzick, a bare-chested fan who seemed a lot more intimidating than his 15 years should allow. 'And we hate journalists.' Now seemed to be a good time to tell him I supported West Ham, and by extension Yossi Benayoun. 'Yossi Benayoun!' yelped Itzick excitedly when I told him my allegiance. 'He should come and play for us. You seem OK for a journalist. The rest can go fuck themselves.' And with that he ran into his crew of bare-chested boys, as they sang 'I'm West Ham 'til I die' in perfectly accented English, a by-product, I was told, of the film *Green Street Hooligans*.

Beitar Jerusalem is not unique for sporting a fan base that holds some uncomfortable views. But what is unusual is the phenomenal amount of power the fans wielded both within the club and within the Israeli political system. Outside of its core activities of organising fights and making racist flags, La Familia also liaised with club officials on the issues that affected the fans, like high ticket prices and whether the management were planning to sign any Arab players. It was their virulent protests that eventually persuaded Gaydamak to abandon signing Abbas Suan. In perhaps no other football club in the world are its fans courted and favoured in such a way. '[Prime Minister Ehud] Olmert used to be here every game. But now he doesn't turn up any more, the police don't allow him to turn up as he's a security problem,' shrugged Nadav, a Beitar fan I met whilst hanging around in a nearby park waiting for the gates to open. It was perhaps wise.

Olmert's popularity had fared badly after what was widely seen as the disastrous Second Lebanon War. The only place he could call on much popular support, surprisingly, was at Beitar.

'He's popular because he introduced Gaydamak to the club. In Israel there are a lot of people who want to come to the government and they come to Beitar Jerusalem, they take pictures with the fans because there are lots of right-wing fans here, especially those that support Likud.' Yet many believed Gaydamak's acquisition of Beitar had more to do with his political ambitions than any great love for the club. By the sound of the fans who were singing 'I believe the Messiah is here, Arcadi, Arcadi' before the game started, he already had a few votes in the bag.

The Bloomfield Stadium was full two hours before kick-off and the 7,000-strong army of gold-and-black Beitar fans were deafening. In the large north terrace the Beitar faithful accepted me red T-shirt and all. I was offered cigarettes and sunflower seeds. This, I thought as another chant grew and filled the stadium, wasn't as bad as I thought it would be. It was only then I was told what they were singing. 'I know this one,' translated the only other Englishman in the ground, Jeremy Last, the sports editor of the *Jerusalem Post*. 'They are singing: "We Hate Nazareth, We Hate Sakhnin, I Swear on The Menorah There Will Be No Arabs Here".' Others followed, each darker than the last:

'War, War, War.'

'The Empire Will Return'

'Tel Aviv Will Be Sacrificed By Fire.'

Beitar thought they had taken the lead, but the goal was ruled offside. The fans were incandescent with rage and hurled missiles at the referee and linesman. A yellow smoke bomb, red flares and a volley of half-eaten pretzels rained down on the pitch. The decision stood although it made no difference to the final result: Beitar won 2–1 and the players were on their knees in front of their ecstatic fans as if they'd won the championship already. Unable to escape the heaving mass, I was carried along with the throng of Beitar fans that streamed out into Tel Aviv's southern suburbs. What began as a good-natured celebration started to degenerate into a riot. The fans let off red flares and climbed atop parked cars to get a better view. The police waded in to try and control the melee by charging the crowd, firstly with police horses and then by trying to drive a motorbike through the crowd at speed. We ran.

As we did, a Beitar supporter running in front of me was knocked to the ground by a fist to the face from an angry policeman. Another took a swing at me with his baton, but missed. The jubilant Beitar fans danced in the street, partially lit by the smoky glow of flares and firecrackers. For a brief moment it seemed that the fans' earlier promises to set Tel Aviv on fire were coming true. Even the police admitted defeat by falling back to defend a main junction whilst the party continued in the shops and car parks around them. Rarely do you get a chance to sit back and watch a bona fide riot. There was something frightening but exhilaratingly anarchic about it. For a fleeting few minutes, there were no rules, no government, only the pack and an internal dynamic being held together by a common passion. The downside of this was, as two skinheads grabbed me and tried to rip my T-shirt off, that if you appear to be off kilter with that internal dynamic, you're in trouble.

'Take off your Hapoel top, you fuck,' screamed one, mistaking me for a Hapoel fan. I begged for mercy, telling them they got it wrong. That I wasn't from Israel and I was only here to write about the match. They looked at each other, smiled and – convinced that I wasn't part of the 'local scum', as they called them, who were usually out to sully Beitar's good name – let me go. 'I wear this every day, to every game,' the smaller man said apologetically. 'It's special, and I give it to you. I'm sorry.' He patted me on the head and ran in to the smoke. A thick cotton Beitar scarf – embossed with the Star of David and a menorah – now coiled across my shoulders.

The next day, the Bloomfield looked like a very different place. The night before Beitar Jerusalem's fans were threatening to burn Tel Aviv to the ground and wishing death to the Arabs. Now the atmosphere was one, if not of conciliation, then certainly of tolerance: Hapoel's fans were singing the name of Walid Badir, an Arab player famous in Israel for playing for the national team (and, briefly, Wimbledon FC in the English Premier League). It was a Monday night and this was the final game of the season's opening weekend, a tricky tie against Tel Aviv's smallest but most right-wing team, Bnei Yehuda. The crowd was smaller than the previous evening, but given that the game was on television, it was understandable. The north stand was awash with red and black and socialist imagery: flags of Che Guevara, hammer and sickles, the large red banner of Ultras Hapoel and placards adorned with a bottle-green marijuana leaf. It was reminiscent of student protests from the early seventies, almost anachronistic compared to the prescient hatred of Beitar's travelling support. At the front a bald man surveyed the scene with a mixture of pride and apprehension.

'There is less politics than there used to be, the [political] parties are less important,' lamented Ronin, a wealthy-looking architect who moved from Argentina 15 years ago but quickly adopted Hapoel after being attracted to the club's left-wing roots. 'Most fans now come from the south of Tel Aviv, like Jaffa. They are poorer so they are a different type of fan, more right-wing. Usually you say that the left wing are poor people but not in Israel, it's the other way around. Rich people are on the left.' He introduced me to Faud, the leader of Hapoel's ultra group, a young skinhead in his early 20s. Faud was one of the new breed, a fan from the southern suburbs of Jaffa who still clung to Hapoel's left-wing imagery despite voting for Likud. 'The union may have been left wing, but the workers have always been right wing,' he announced.

Despite the shifting allegiances within the club, he denied there were any tensions between the fans that represented its past and those that represented its future, especially when it came to the issue that has divided Israeli football most in recent years. 'My deputy is Arab. We have two Arab players. Most have one but we have two. If we don't like [Bnei] Sakhnin it's because they beat us, not because they're Arabs. We love Hapoel, he is left, I am right, but we are all Hapoel.' But even Hapoel, for all their imagery, was not immune to the new commercial realities of Israeli football. As Uri, *Haaretz*'s Hapoel-supporting sports editor, had told me money had changed the nature of the club and its political identity had faded. 'All the teams now have private ownerships, have a very vague connection with the Labor party or the union and what are left are basically the fans,' he had explained. Money – in the form of billion-shekel takeovers from foreign and domestic donors, like Gaydamak at Beitar, and lucrative pay-per-view television contracts – had begun to flood the game in Israel. 'The only thing that stays the same is hatred – the level of hatred,' Uri said. 'You have 20 teams hating the other side and maybe two or three teams supporting their own side. Israeli society is so tense, there are so many conflicts: religious, political, economic, social. It can get really ugly. In Israel it's not a culture of supporting, it's a culture of hating.'

The match ended 1–1 and the fans trudged out into the balmy Tel Aviv night, all except around 40 members of Bnei Yehuda's ultra group that hung around waiting for the referee to emerge outside the ground. When he did they hurled abuse at him. After every game they would deconstruct the game in what they called 'The Parliament'. In the spirit of parliamentary democracy, they met, discussed and abused in the most rational of ways. They were also aligned to the far right and came from the same community that filled Beitar's fan base. 'We are Arab Jews,' explained Avi, one of the ultras. 'We understand the Arab culture, we speak their language, grew up in their countries. But the others, who came from Germany and Europe [the Ashkenazim] don't. We know the mentality which is why we are what we are.' Uncompromising as this 'know your enemy' maxim was, even Bnei Yehuda had taken the plunge and signed an Arab player. 'We didn't have any Arabs play for us until four years ago and he wasn't very good,' Avi said, although it hadn't dissuaded the ultras from considering another Arab player to play for Bnei Yehuda. 'As long as he's good we don't care now. Beitar hate the Arabs but we're a little bit more realistic,' he said as 'The Parliament' walked to a nearby falafel stand to continue dissecting the match long into the night. 'After all, if someone comes and fucks me in the ass, it hurts, sure. But the second time he does it, it doesn't hurt so much. We've had an Arab [Muslim] player once, next time won't be too painful. It'll hurt just a little bit less.'

As I walked past the stadium's main gate someone familiar was standing by the lamppost, illuminated by its yellow light. He wore Hapoel's red shirt, selling cheap polyester scarves and fake gold Star of David necklaces from a large, flat wooden suitcase. It was Oren, who only three days previously had been a passionate Maccabi Haifa fan, selling green and-white scarves and his popular Nasrallah stickers. Tonight, everything he sold was red and black. He cracked into a big smile and began laughing hysterically. He had been caught red-handed. 'I sell everything to everyone,' he replied, unable to contain the hilarity of his duplicitous allegiances. For at least one Israeli, religion, politics and tribalism didn't mean a damn thing.

JERUSALEM, NOVEMBER 2009

The Teddy Stadium in Jerusalem is named after the city's greatest mayor, himself named after Theodore Herzl, the founder of modern Zionism. Theodore Kollek, or Teddy as he was affectionately named, came to power in 1965 after running for office at the insistence of then prime minister David Ben-Gurion. He ruled over a poor, underdeveloped western half of the city but made his name when Israel captured the eastern, Arab half of Jerusalem during the 1967 War, and oversaw the city's modernisation. He was re-elected five times. Teddy was both a Zionist and a pragmatist, indelibly wedded to the idea of a united Jerusalem under Israeli rule but also sympathetic towards the plight of the city's newly disenfranchised Arab population. When he died in 2007 at the age of 95 the *New York Times*'s obituary described how Israel's assassinated Prime Minister Yitzhak Rabin called him 'the greatest builder of Jerusalem since Herod the Great'.

Today the vast, modern steel and brick edifice that bears Kollek's name – the colour of Jerusalem's famous, ubiquitous pale limestone – is home to Beitar Jerusalem. In recent years the stadium has seen little of the pragmatism or tolerance that saw Teddy demand that one of the Israeli military's first jobs after capturing East Jerusalem was to distribute free milk to Arab children.

La Familia were perhaps the most uncompromising fans in the world. I'd meet the founder and spiritual leader of La Familia, Guy Israel, outside the Teddy, handing out leaflets criticising efforts by the club to urge Beitar fans to inform the police of any racist chanting by La Familia. 'We have a little problem with the club, who wants to work with the police and get the fans out of the stadium,' explained Guy, who handed out his leaflets next to groups of children also handing leaflets urging the fans to denounce violence. 'This is not acceptable. This club is ours, it's our dreams and it's our life. I don't have a wife, I don't have children, all I have is Beitar. Why are they trying to take this away from me?'

I had friends who were both moderate and conservative who supported Beitar and over the following three years frequently attended games at the Teddy. They too deplored La Familia's behaviour. But something had changed over the course of the past few years. La Familia had once been ignored as an extremist irritant, kids cosplaying war. Now they had Israel's and the world's attention. Not because they had exploded in numbers, but because what they said, what they believed in, didn't appear to be that ugly any more. The club has been sanctioned many times for La Familia's racism: points deductions and heavy fines among them. The supporters had been regularly banned from the Teddy too, the team forced to play behind closed doors. Nothing seemed to chastise the hardcore. Nothing seemed able to change the culture at the club.

Yet Beitar exerted a strong pull on the rich and the powerful. With so many politically influential supporters, rich men lined up to help the club. It was often said that Beitar commanded one million supporters, and one million voters. Arcadi Gaydamak was one such man beguiled by the club. When I first visited Israel he had just begun to sink tens of millions of dollars into the club, bankrolling them to back-to-back championships in 2007 and 2008. But his efforts to try and make Beitar a club for everyone in Jerusalem was harder. When a minute's silence was held for the memory of assassinated former prime minister Yitzhak Rabin, La Familia sang songs in support of his ultra-nationalist murderer, Yigal Amir. The FA quickly banned Beitar's fans from the next game which, as fate would have it, was against Bnei Sakhnin. Gaydamak was the only supporter allowed in, iconically waving a huge flag from an empty terrace over the course of the 90 minutes. Bnei Sakhnin scored the winner at the death. The next day the Israeli FA's offices were firebombed. The title decider at the end of the season resulted in a pitch invasion that – until the intervention of the Israeli supreme court – very nearly saw Beitar's title rescinded. 'The idiot bastards can leave,' Gaydamak said of the hardcore troublemakers at his club after a particularly nasty pitch invasion. 'The fans that went wild yesterday are bastards, and I have no respect for them. While their numbers are in the thousands, they are not the majority.'

Gaydamak, of course, had his eyes on a bigger prize. He held political ambition and had become a thorn in the then prime minister Ehud Olmert's side, staging a series of deft publicity stunts. The finest was setting up a luxury tent village in Tel Aviv's HaYarkon Park for the residents of Sderot, an Israeli town under siege by rockets from Gaza in 2007. Olmert, who at the time had polled a zero per cent popularity rating in one national newspaper poll, had insisted that the residents of the towns near Gaza stay put, otherwise Hamas might view it as a surrender. But hundreds of terrified residents took up Gaydamak's offer. I had walked around the peaceful encampment. Each child was given a black and gold Beitar scarf, the menorah stitched at both ends, on arrival. Gourmet chefs were cooking internally displaced refugees dinner. Luxury tents were set up alongside booths with PlayStation 2s in them. It was a propaganda victory for Arcadi. Still, Gaydamak's popularity didn't translate into votes. After setting up his own political party, he announced in 2008 he would – like Teddy Kollek before him – run for mayor of Jerusalem. He was routed at the ballot box, coming a distant third. The humiliation, coupled with the financial crash which hit his business interests hard, saw Gaydamak withdraw from Beitar. His son, who owned Portsmouth FC, also sold his investment. Arcadi actively looked for a new buyer for the club. And then he found Guma Aguiar.

Aguiar was a young tycoon eager to make Jerusalem the capital of his world. His natural gas exploration company Leor Energy discovered and then sold a huge natural gas field in the US. He didn't always identify himself as Jewish. Born in Brazil to a Jewish mother, Aguiar was raised a Catholic but was brought back to Judaism by Rabbi Tovia Singer, the founder and director of Outreach Judaism. Outreach Judaism was a self-declared 'counter-missionary' organisation 'dedicated to countering the efforts of fundamentalist Christian groups and cults who specifically target Jews for conversion'. The controversial Rabbi had discovered Aguiar's roots and aggressively attempted to reconnect him to his heritage. Aguiar was 26 at the time. Three years later his stewardship of Leor had netted him an estimated fortune of $200 million. Reborn in his faith, Aguiar became enchanted with Jerusalem. He spent big to attract the attentions of the great and good in Israel, donating tens of millions of dollars to a host of Jewish organisations.

He may have grown up in Brazil but Aguiar wasn't much of a football fan. He was a basketball man through and through. But he had quickly gained a reputation for his acts of philanthropy in Israel since selling Leor Energy and his donations brought him to the attention of Israel's politicians – he could count the President Shimon Peres as a friend – and, eventually, Beitar. Without Gaydamak's backing, the club was on the verge of going under. Aguiar was persuaded to sink $4 million into the club, as well as a further $1.5 million into the city's basketball team Hapoel Jerusalem. That was in June 2009 and Aguiar agreed to a telephone interview where I asked him about how his decision to invest in Beitar and Hapoel came about. 'I love Jerusalem, it's special. You're not in Kansas any more, that's for sure,' Aguiar explained, sounding confident and erudite, as he did in the TV interviews he had conducted to woo the Israeli media. 'I was approached,' he said of how Beitar's predicament was brought to his attention. 'There are a lot of people here who feel strongly about their teams. It reminds me a lot of Brazil, going to the Maracanã. A lot of people here don't care about anything other than football. I can relate to that.'

Beitar was desperate for a new saviour and Aguiar seemed to be the perfect fit. He was young, rich and eager to please. Unlike Gaydamak, he didn't have any ambitions for elected office. 'I don't want to use football as a political tool because that's not fair, as an outsider, to come in and have a [political] agenda,' he said. In fact Aguiar, despite being married with four young children, had a reputation as something of a flamboyant playboy who liked to burn the candle at both ends. 'Like Madonna said the other night, this is the centre of the universe,' he told a local TV channel whilst trying to play tennis badly. He wore sunglasses, his head was bowed, voice hoarse. 'The only party I'm interested in forming is just a party.' But he understood Beitar's reputation in the world, and how it was beginning to harm, even define, the city's standing. 'The one thing I would like to see is more tolerance from the fans. In order for us to be competitive and to attract talent we want to play abroad and not be viewed as total hooligans. I certainly wouldn't want to go to Barcelona and hear them singing "Death to the Jews".'

Like Gaydamak, he wanted to improve Jerusalem's image. 'I want to see the flagship name of Jerusalem, bring some outsiders to Israel to visit [and] create awareness about this place,' he finished. 'Raising the profile of Jerusalem would be the most positive outcome. It's torn apart by a lot of conflict. But there are Christians, Jews and Muslims here that love the land they live in. I want Christian and Muslim fans here too.' Aguiar sounded sincere and knowledgeable. He agreed we should meet in Israel in a few weeks, after he had seen exactly what he had bought into. A few weeks later Guma Aguiar walked onto the pitch at the Teddy Stadium to rapturous applause. It was Beitar's first match of the Israeli football season, against arch rivals Hapoel Tel Aviv. Aguiar would later email me a link to a YouTube video from the Israeli TV station Channel 1, which aired an interview with him before kick-off.

It began with him blowing a shofar, a traditional ram's horn blown on some Jewish religious ceremonies. 'It's my first time in the Teddy Stadium,' he said to the camera. His shirt collar was open. Upon his chest lay a silver Star of David on a necklace. 'They say: "Are you some kind of Messiah?" I say no, I don't want to be associated with a word like that. I have no idea [about the outcome of the Hapoel game]. Only God knows. Maybe he's feeling extra sympathetic to Jerusalem tonight,' he said. 'And if not, perhaps he'll feel extra sympathetic later in the year.'

On the pitch a light and smoke show was underway. Dance music thumped out as beautiful Israeli girls danced in the centre circle. On the sidelines, Aguiar was jumping up and down to the beat, dancing with a man dressed in a dog suit. Aguiar moved into the centre circle and tried to wiggle his hips in sync with the music next to the singer. He closed his eyes, arms in the air, and stumbled through the choreography. The dancers didn't miss a beat. 'This is Aguiar's night,' intoned Danny Neuman, a Beitar legend commentating on the match for the evening. 'He has saved Beitar.'

It should have been a quiet midweek night in the Irish bar in the centre of Jerusalem but Guma Aguiar was gearing up for a party. Outside, on the quaint cobbled street, a hoard of expensive, blacked-out 4x4s sat clustered around the door, paying little heed to the city's parking law. Inside, the lights were low and the bar was almost empty. Dance music thumped around the vacuum. But, in one corner, up on a raised platform, stood the tall figure of Guma Aguiar. A ring of steel surrounded him; pumped, shaven-headed bodyguards wearing black jeans and black T-shirts. They stood firm as we approached. Aguiar was standing next to an identically dressed bodyguard, who was rolling him a cigarette. Around him several Beitar players, one an Israeli international, buzzed around, eager for his attention. 'Guma, can you get me a ticket to an NBA game,' one pleaded. Aguiar ignored him and lit his fat cigarette. The strong smell of marijuana filled the room.

It had been a few months since Aguiar and I had spoken on the phone. He had agreed to meet me in his favourite bar along with Jeremy, the sports editor of the *Jerusalem Post*, who I had met at my first Beitar game. Aguiar trusted Jeremy and was eager to curry favour with a paper that was widely read in North America. Aguiar spotted him, raised his arm, and the black sea parted. It was clear that not all was well. Aguiar seemed agitated. He couldn't focus on anyone for more than a few seconds before losing his trail of thought. Sometimes he would start the same conversation two, three, occasionally four times. The sycophants laughed. His personal bodyguard rolled him another joint, and then another. He had no recollection of our conversation a few months previously, nor of what he had said a few moments before. But his generosity remained intact. He bought round after round of drinks. Aguiar couldn't make eye contact when we talked. He hung his head, as if listening. He pressed the half-smoked cigarette between my fingers. I inhaled.

Stars.

A tunnel.

Silence.

White noise.

Time stopped.

Gradually the world returned.

Beitar's season had begun in mixed fashion. They drew the first two league matches of the season, against arguably their two biggest rivals Hapoel Tel Aviv and Bnei Sakhnin, 0–0. A handful of narrow victories against low-ranked opponents followed. But as the end of the year approached it was clear that Beitar would not be challenging for the league title, despite the early season optimism. Aguiar's life was taking an equally rocky path. As his profile rose, so did interest in his private life. A little-written-about court case between Aguiar and his uncle Thomas Kaplan – the man whom he had gone into business with a few years previously, making his fortune when they sold Leor – had suddenly become prescient, a taste of the familial litigation to come. In January 2009 Kaplan launched a legal action to remove Aguiar as a director of the Lillian Jean Kaplan Foundation, named in honour of Kaplan's mother. According to the *South Florida Sun Sentinel* Thomas Kaplan had given $40 million to the foundation, money used, among other things, to build drinking-water wells in Africa. But Kaplan had accused his nephew of miss-spending as much as $7 million in efforts to 'claim that he is the Messiah and to promote his messianic mission'. The lawsuit was the latest battle in a legal war with his uncle over the sale of Leor. Aguiar believed he was due $18 million more. Kaplan believed that Aguiar had misappropriated company funds – making inappropriate payments to himself and his family – and wanted Aguiar's share of the sale returned. The *Sentinel* dubbed it 'The Messiah lawsuit'. 'They are trying to distract and intimidate me from going on with my life,' Aguiar told them.

There was also the issue of Aguiar's arrest in Florida on drugs charges. He was arrested in June on counts of driving under the influence, possession of marijuana and 'drug paraphernalia', thought to be a bong. Aguiar had countered that he had been abused in custody and refused to pay the $536 court charges. 'When I got to the prison [a police officer] took my kippah off and then tried to convert me to Christianity,' he told the Israeli daily newspaper *Haaretz* in October 2009. 'I told him to leave me the fuck alone. He then took me – after blowing triple zeros on my breath test – to the Broward County Sheriff's Office where they arrested me and beat the shit out of me.' The Broward County Sheriff's office denied the accusations, saying that Aguiar was 'combative and verbally abusive' and that he had been 'controlled and restrained'.

But now, in an Irish bar in Jerusalem, he looked anything but combative. He looked lost as he swayed from side to side roughly in time with the music. I passed him back his cigarette as the world reformed around me. It was the single strongest thing I'd ever smoked.

'If you smoke that every day,' I advised through foggy eyes, 'you will go crazy.'

He didn't hear me. It was the last time I would hear from Guma Aguiar. On the morning of 14 January 2010, an ambulance and two police cars escorted him to the Abarbanel Mental Health Center in Bat Yam on the outskirts of Jerusalem. Under orders from his wife, he had been sectioned. Aguiar suffered with bipolar disorder and had suddenly taken a turn for the worse. A few days earlier he had given an interview with a local newspaper where he had claimed that he was in mobile phone contact with Gilad Shalit, the Israeli soldier kidnapped by Hamas and held incommunicado in the Gaza Strip since 2006. Aguiar claimed he had snuck into the Gaza Strip and freed Shalit, who was now holed up in one of his properties. 'I wanted to prove that I could enter Gaza and come out alive and that Shalit could come out alive as well,' he told the *Kol Ha'ir* newspaper. 'He [Shalit] said that he wants me to tell his family how much he loves them and Israel, and that he hopes this ends soon.' Within a few weeks it was announced that Aguiar would cease funding Beitar Jerusalem. As he hadn't yet taken full ownership, Arcadi Gaydamak was now back in charge again. His money had prevented Beitar from going out of business, but his philanthropic journey in Israel seemed to be over.

'He's an enigma,' explained Shlomi Barzel, the new sports editor of *Haaretz*. Barzel had met Aguiar shortly before he was sectioned. 'He was smoking [marijuana]. I met him at a Saturday game. The day before we had met and had an hour and a half meeting. He could not remember me at all. After a meeting he was coming out of the toilet with white powder all over his nose.' Barzel felt some sympathy for Aguiar. 'Was it Jerusalem Syndrome or was it too much powder in the nose?' he asked rhetorically, referencing the psychological condition where seemingly normal well-adjusted people, Muslims, Jews and Christians alike, fall into a religious psychosis when they arrive in the city. 'The man was a lunatic. I thought it was a question of conscience, how Gaydamak took the money. It was clear to me that Guma wasn't capable of taking one rational decision. You have to know that, after Gaydamak, there was a period when people [Beitar supporters] were not looking for the new king, they were looking for a rich man coming from nowhere.' It would not be the last owner that Beitar Jerusalem destroyed.

4

Yemen

The young, machine-gun-wielding soldier was the only man – well, boy – standing outside Sana'a's national football stadium. The imposing concrete bowl – ringed by faded walls of the red, black and white of Yemen's flag – was supposed to be filled with the voices of 20,000 Yemeni football fans, cheering on the country's biggest team, Al Ahli Sana'a. But the stadium was silent, and the vast car park was empty, save for the young soldier rhythmically chewing on the bulge in his left cheek as he gripped tightly onto his weapon. 'Football match?' I asked in broken Arabic, whirling around trying to catch sight of someone. Anyone. It had taken two days to get here, on borrowed money, to watch a match in Yemen. It made sense at the time, but with the grinning boy soldier and his AK-47 the only witness to my weeks of planning, it suddenly felt like madness. Silently he lifted his barrel and pointed it to his left, gesturing to me to follow its line. In the distance, in the corner of the car park, stood the headquarters of the Yemeni Football Association, an orphaned breeze-block box with an unnecessarily large sculpture of a football perched on its roof. The soldier grunted and I followed his cue to leave.

The nerve centre of Yemeni football was equally devoid of life, except for a caretaker who had been roused from his afternoon slumber after hearing me bang on the locked doors of the FA's entrance. I tried to explain my predicament as he sat in his room, on the floor, with two friends and half-a-dozen half-full bags of what looked like spinach. All the men had the same bulge in their cheeks. He pointed to his mobile: 'Hamid.' Hamid Shaibani was the only man he knew who might know what was going on. He was also the man in charge of Yemeni football, the FA's general secretary. The caretaker pressed the phone to his non-bulbous right cheek, rattled off an apology in Arabic and handed me his phone.

'The match was cancelled!' Hamid sang back enthusiastically. 'We had an Olympic qualifier to play in Sharjah, against the UAE, so we cancelled the match.' This, I later discovered, was not unusual in Yemen, where the fixture list for the First Division was often treated with the same amount of respect as a stray dog. The fans didn't know when, where or against whom a match would kick off until the day before the game.

When people think of Yemen, football isn't at the forefront of their minds. This, after all, is a country that was only second behind Saudi Arabia in providing the men who waged jihad on foreign battlefields in Iraq and Afghanistan. It was also the ancestral home of Osama bin Laden and the place where the American military received one of its pre-9/11 bloody noses, when the USS *Cole* was hit by a suicide bomber whilst moored in the southern Yemeni port of Aden killing 17 sailors. But I had come across a story, a football story, that encapsulated one of Yemen's most enduring problems:

YEMEN WITHDREW FOLLOWING DOPING CONCERNS: AFC
Yemen pulled out of the Asian Games soccer tournament because of a lack of cash to drug test their squad following reports that players were addicted to a banned substance, the Asian Football Confederation (AFC) said. Yemeni soccer chiefs withdrew the team on Thursday, citing insufficient funds to carry out dope tests ordered by the Yemen Olympic Council (YOC), the AFC said on its Web site. The YOC had advised the YFA to consider pulling out following media reports that a number of players were using the banned drug qat, a leaf which has a stimulant effect when chewed. (Reuters)

A whole squad of players pulling out of an international tournament for drug use was interesting enough, but the fact that the drug of choice was qat made it even more intriguing. Qat is the curse of the Horn of Africa, a drug that is only grown at high altitudes from Kenya all the way to Oman and which has, legally, weaved its way into

Yemeni culture. It's a small, innocuous-looking leaf that, when chewed over time, produces a mild euphoria and a heightened sense of awakening followed by lethargy. Depending on who you talked to it was either a mild stimulant that had the same giggle-inducing properties as weed or an aggressive cocaine-type high. Everyone I'd met at the stadium so far exhibited the tell-tale signs of qat use from the soldier to the caretaker to the youth-team players from local club Al Sha'ab Sana'a who had earlier arrived at the stadium and were milling around outside; the distended cheeks, watery eyes and thousand-yard stares. 'We all know what would happen if the coach caught me chewing qat,' replied Ali, a 16-year-old goalkeeper, whilst running his finger across his throat. 'I'd be cut, cut from the team. If he found out he would carry me out of the stadium himself.'

The other four kicked gravel around in a circle and avoided eye contact when I asked whether any of them still took the risk. The Asian Games debacle had been something of an eye opener for Yemen's sportsmen, and the young players were glad the team had been kicked out. 'It was embarrassing, yes,' admitted Naif, a 20-year-old striker. 'Because, if they had played and were on qat, they wouldn't have been very good. They were lucky because it would have been more embarrassing if they had gone on the pitch.'

Keeping the kids off the stuff long enough to play football was a big problem – even the Sha'ab youth team said there was pressure from family to chew at big events like weddings. Hamid Shaibani was the new general secretary of the FA, and had been drafted in to get tough on qat. 'There will be another game, we are not sure what game, but there will be one,' Hamid reassured me. 'I'll pick you up where you are standing now, on Thursday and we'll talk.' Hamid hung up, and I walked back to the front gate, past the soldier, and waved goodbye. He was too stoned to lift his arm in reply.

I wasn't that surprised to find Abdul, the hotel manager, worse for wear. I'd been warned a few days previously by a friend from Dubai to try and get to the towering, ancient hostel deep in the Yemeni capital's old city before 1pm, otherwise: 'The man behind the desk won't know what's going on.' Sure enough, by 2pm, Abdul was half-cut. Tall, with a receded hairline and a thin Nasser-esque moustache,

Abdul's glassy, unfocused eyes scoured his small manager's booth looking for my keys. His right cheek was bulging with matter, a thick green paste that could only be seen in cycles, when a periodic chew revealed his blackened teeth, one of its most common side effects. After falling over twice, bursting into a fit of hysterical laughter and giving me the keys to someone else's room, he finally, and with shaky hands, found the right set.

'Thank you,' he said with a half grin on his face, unable to look straight. 'What are you doing in Yemen?'

'I'm a journalist,' I replied.

'Ah, qat is very good for journalists,' he shouted, finding a common ground and pointing at his bulbous cheek.

'You chew and then you write. Later we go to the market and chew together.'

I thanked Abdul for his offer, before he stumbled into a backroom and collapsed onto a filthy mattress for his fitful afternoon nap.

There are three things you notice when you arrive in Sana'a. The first is the shear prevalence of qat. No one is quite sure when Yemenis started chewing it. One study suggested that Yemenis had been chewing qat before the discovery of coffee. But by all independent verification, qat had been a catastrophe for Yemen and the other states where it was grown, being blamed for the anarchic situation in Somalia, poverty in Sudan and massive unemployment in Kenya. For Yemen, the consequences have meant flatlining productivity, low economic growth, extreme poverty and water stress (given the amount of water it takes to grow qat, in an area where drought can occur), not to mention poor performances on the football pitch. The truly addicted would fund their habit to the detriment of food for their family, and the whole economy seemed to be moulded around its consumption. From sunrise until 1pm, life continued as normal. Then an estimated 80 per cent of the nation downed tools and headed to the qat market to buy a fresh plastic bag of the stuff. Midday is when the qat comes down from the mountain and most believe that it has to be chewed within a few hours or the active ingredient that gets you high is lost. President Ali Abdullah Saleh, the country's first – and only – elected leader since the unification of north and south in 1990, had tried to lead by example by stating that he would not chew qat, nor would his armed forces.

But he dared not ban it. There would be riots in the streets, as there were in Aden in the mid-1950s when a political party in South Yemen banned it. The issue destroyed the party and qat was back on the streets a year later. Even Islam was powerless to outlaw it. Whilst the devout and the intelligentsia frown on its consumption, and qat is banned in every other Middle Eastern country bar Israel (and only then because of its large Yemenite population), there are scholarly disagreements about whether it is prohibited by Islamic law.

The second thing you notice is that Yemen is awash with knives and guns. Every man, when he comes of age, is given a *jambiya*, a curved knife that sits in the front of his belt. The knife serves notice of your position in life: the more expensive the *jambiya*, the wealthier the man. But that's not all. Guns are everywhere, a hangover from the days before reunification when tribal loyalties and deep mistrust of central government meant that few threw down their Kalashnikovs. According to the 2007 Small Arms Survey, Yemen, with a population of around 24 million, had nearly 60 million guns in circulation. It is one of the world's most highly armed populations.

The third is Saddam Hussein's ubiquity. On nearly every street corner, wall, car and shop window, a picture of Saddam stared back at you. You could even buy 4x4 spare wheel covers bearing images of him in his pomp. He was revered by so many for being a symbol of Arab nationalism, for his financial support to the families of Palestinian suicide bombers and for his opposition to 'Zionist imperialism' during the First Gulf War. But Yemenis had another reason. The newly unified Yemen enjoyed good relations with Iraq and had backed an Arab solution to the First Gulf War, a stance which angered the Saudi royal family so much, fearful that Saddam's Middle Eastern tour would visit Riyadh after Kuwait, that they revoked the residency privileges of close to one million Yemenis working in Saudi Arabia. In 1991 Yemenis made up the largest proportion of foreign labour in Saudi yet 850,000 were forced home, depriving the country of hundreds of millions of dollars in remittances, and almost strangled the newly united country at birth. Saddam's execution a few months before my arrival had only deepened his status as a martyr.

The fourth, rather ironically given the third point, is the number of Stars of David carved on walls. The ancient Jewish symbol can be seen on many buildings in the UNESCO-listed old city, a legacy from the days when tens of thousands of Jews lived here. A small community still existed in the north, but most, around 50,000, were evacuated by Israel during Operation Magic Carpet in 1949.

Leaving Abdul to his rest, I traipsed up the seven flights to my room which overlooked the old city. Whilst the rest of Sana'a is littered with half-built concrete buildings and debris, as if an occupation force had recently left in a hurry, the walled, old city is a fragile, beautiful reminder of Yemen's wealthy past, when its abundance of natural resources – coffee and incense – made it one of the richest places in the world. Yemen's ancient architects had been credited with inventing the first form of skyscraper and this small section of Sana'a was packed with crooked, three and four-storey proto-high rises, all jostling for air and ringed with plaster. The whole district looked like it was carved from gingerbread. You suspected that one strong gust was all it would take to turn the city to dust, yet they had stood defiant since the second century and had seen Christianity, Judaism and finally Islam pass through.

The large key opened the door to my sparse room, its plain white walls only enlivened by the coloured light streaming through the stained-glass windows. On the roof a sandstorm blew through the old city's warren-like passageways, coating everything in dust and turning the air sepia. To help me get my bearings I had been trying to arrange an interview with Adel, a sports reporter at the English-language *Yemeni Times*, but our increasingly heated conversations over a crackly international line ended when it became clear that only a bribe would purloin any time with him. Still, his boss was more forthcoming and agreed to meet me at his offices near Hamdan Street, the Oxford Street of Sana'a. Outside their offices every parked car had a picture of Saddam prominently displayed.

Adel greeted me like I was a long-lost friend, forgetting our disagreement, and kissed me twice on both cheeks before leading me up to the *Times*'s modest office. Banks of old PCs were manned by silent journalists tapping out the next day's edition. Adel ushered me into the office of Raidan Abdulaziz al Saqqaf, the newspaper's managing editor. He was a big man with the face of an adolescent, Raidan had been working at the *Times*, which his sister edited, since he returned from studying in Nottingham and had spent most of his life outside of Yemen. The newspaper was set up by their father who was killed in a hit-and-run accident, which they both didn't think was an accident, back in 1999.

'Yes, he is quite popular,' Raidan sighed when I asked why so many people carried pictures of Saddam around with them. 'You see, we believe in the conspiracy theory here. It is deeply rooted in our culture. We . . .' he emphasised sarcastically, exonerating himself from the same view, '. . . think that what happened to Saddam is part of a conspiracy and he is a hero. He fought against America.'

Back then the perception in the West was that Yemen, and her imposing president, was an ally, a moderate bulwark against the spread of Islamic fundamentalism. The problem, Raidan explained, was that no one was telling young people that. 'Yemeni children are taught a subject called nationalism. It blames all the poverty and backwardness of Yemen on occupation and colonialism and the influence of foreign powers. So you grow up thinking that Israel has been taken away from the Arabs by America. If you see the news, you will see that they don't mention the most important news. It's a systematic brainwashing of our culture. If they say Israel, they say "Israeli enemy". If they say America, they say "the occupation forces in Iraq".'

Our conversation was halted when his phone rang. 'One minute,' he apologised, listening to the anonymous caller's tip, before holding his hand over the receiver. 'Four Ethiopian prisoners have died in Sana'a prison,' he said.

'How did they die?' I asked.

'Starvation,' he replied coolly. 'The guards didn't even know they were on hunger strike. We only found out when the embassy was called to pick up the bodies.'

After the next day's splash had been secured and a reporter dispatched, we continued talking, this time about qat. Raidan didn't chew, but he recognised how important the drug was for Yemeni society. 'In order to understand this problem, look at the Yemeni people. About 70 per cent are dependent on agriculture. We've had droughts, diseases and no subsidies. Ninety-two per cent of our wheat is imported. If you produce agri-products you can't compete so there's mass migration from rural to urban areas. Sana'a is expanding by 250,000 people per year, that's 3.5 per cent a year, the second highest [rate of urban growth] in the world.'

Which is how qat had gained its foothold. The only way people could survive was by planting a quickly grown, valuable crop. 'Qat is a plus and a minus. It's bad because of the damage to your health and people spend almost all their wages on it. But there is a benefit. Crop prices are down across the board. Except qat, so many people stop growing vegetables and grow qat. It's a cash crop, the same as poppy seeds in Afghanistan. There have been negative effects and anyone of sound mind would ban it as it's addictive. It's cheap, makes people money and it is sociable. That is why it is so popular in Yemen.' The drug was essential to the social fabric of Yemen. Like, Raidan told me, 'meeting friends in a pub in England'. Every house had its own *majlis*, a room designed for long qat-chewing bouts. Some had two, one for the men, one for the women. Female chewers, like Asian teenage smokers targeted by Western tobacco firms, were the qat industry's big growth area, the next big market to get hooked and to exploit. Even a rival newspaper had its own *majlis* for editors and journalists to chew and discuss stories.

I left the offices of the *Yemeni Times* and took a taxi back to my hostel. Abdul was waiting for me impatiently outside the hotel. It was early afternoon, just when the sweet leaves had been brought fresh from the mountains to market, and he didn't want to miss out on the good stuff. He took my hand and led me through the warren-like alleyways of Bab al Yemen, the walled ancient quarter. Shopkeepers sharpened their curved knives, or sold spices in huge, overpowering sacks that spilled out onto the tightly woven cobbled streets. Another polished frames in a shop that only sold pictures of Saddam Hussein. The impersonal bustle of market day gave way to a crush. There was no laid-out permanent stall or signs that directed you towards Bab al Yemen's qat market. Instead, the men headed towards a pre-programmed, long ago understood point, like homing pigeons returning to a coop. Abdul picked up the pace as others joined us, a half-run every six steps. The market was an unmarked arch guarding an alleyway full of qat sellers. They sat calmly, cross-legged, with their produce laid out in front of them on blankets, their steely demeanours contrasting with the frenzied bidding that was going on above and around them. I didn't have a clue what I was looking for. One bushel, which cost 5,000 rials (about £13), looked exactly the same as another that cost 8,000 rials. Buyers barged past as more men packed into the tiny alleyway.

'This is no good,' Abdul finally said after looking at a third, identical bag, with the squinting half-eye of a jeweller examining the veracity of a newly discovered diamond. Finally, Abdul was satisfied we had a good deal, and I handed over 1,000 rials for a bag. For the money, I would be getting some moderately swanky stuff, the kind of qat that the average Yemeni would take to a wedding. For their daily hit, a 500-rial bag of qat would do. Even then that represented half of Yemen's average daily wage of $6. The trick, Abdul said, noticeably more relaxed on the walk back to the hotel now that his daily fix had been secured, was to 'look for the red leaves. The more of them, the better it is.'

Back at the hotel Abdul collapsed back on his mattress and began to unravel the thin plastic doggie bag that held that afternoon's hit. I had read romantic descriptions about the rituals of Yemeni qat-chewing: the drinks, the conversation, the friends all gathered to catch up, as intricate and dainty as Victorian afternoon tea. I watched Abdul, on his haunches, greedily stuff leaves into his cheek in the dark corner of his office, the bright spring sunshine blotted out by the cool, medieval interior. It wasn't exactly what I had in mind. I said my goodbyes, went to my room and packed the qat into my bag for another day.

The taxi thumped through Sana'a, over potholed streets, back to the national stadium to meet Hamid, the general secretary of the Yemen Football Association. I was late and again no one was there. Even the qat-chewing boy soldier who had been patrolling the grounds had deserted his post. In the distance, a Honda Civic approached. It was Hamid, who hadn't forgotten about me after all. With dark hair and dressed in chinos and a jacket stretched over a large paunch, he took me upstairs into his large office. The walls were adorned with pictures of great Yemeni teams of the past, whilst the trophy cabinet was, understandably, given that Yemen was ranked 137th in the world, rather bare. Hamid eased himself behind his large desk, a Yemeni flag in one corner and a portrait of President Saleh hanging above him. As it turned out, the Yemeni FA had only really existed in its current form for the past year. FIFA suspended them in 2006 after the sports minister tried to install one of his cronies in the job, breaching FIFA's rule on political interference. Hamid was drafted in to bring a fresh approach to Yemen's seemingly intractable sporting malaise. He was one of the new breed, a liberal technocrat who had lived in New York, China and the Netherlands working for the UN. Now he was charged with modernising football in the country. His first job was dealing with the fallout from the Asian Games debacle and trying to kick qat out of the game. Even if the modernist had to resort to draconian methods to achieve it.

'We only started looking at this [the issue of qat abuse] last October,' he explained. 'We asked every player to sign a contract to say he won't chew qat and if any test result shows he chews qat he will go to jail.' Jail might be a tough option, given what I'd heard at the *Yemen Times*'s office, but for Hamid it was a necessary deterrent. 'Footballers earn $1,000 a month, even middle-class people here only earn $200, so they must look after themselves. We spend $50 a day on national team players, so imagine over six months. If we find he chews qat, he must compensate the association.' The problem was that, with the drug so ingrained in Yemen's culture, it was a hard, almost impossible sell. 'They [Yemen's footballers] were all using [qat for] a long time. We tried to educate them as qat destroys their energy. The next day you are dead [but] when you are chewing the qat you feel like a big man.'

It wasn't just the players whom Hamid was trying to forcibly wean off qat. The fans too had been banned from bringing the drug into the grounds, along with their knives and guns. 'We have security in the stadium to stop that, they cannot bring their knives in,' he added, walking to a window and absentmindedly looking at a woman wearing an all-enveloping black abaya as she slowly walked across the car park to the women's gymnasium opposite. 'We have tight security. Some people smuggle it in, but it's not like it was. Did you hear about last week? At a match the fans started throwing stones at the referee. The problem is that everyone in Yemen has weapons, Kalashnikovs mainly. We have to take them off them before they go into the grounds. Then they come out, get their weapons and fight. That happened twice here.'

The last time was in 2006, when the Yemeni national team unexpectedly lost 3–0 to Thailand at the same stadium. The crowd responded to the insipid display by rioting outside, smashing up windows, setting fire to cars and shooting up the stadium as the victorious

Thai team cowered inside. 'Unfortunately, it's a tradition,' Hamid sighed, grabbing his keys and pushing me out of the door to meet the national team doctor. 'No one trusts the government. The new generation, though, don't chew qat or carry weapons. I don't carry weapons, I never have. But they expect to beat teams like Indonesia and Thailand. We played India recently and it was 1–1. I was really worried. But we scored a second and there was no trouble, even if we didn't play well.'

The team doctor Mosleh Saleh Ali Salman was waiting for us at Hamid's local restaurant near downtown Sana'a. Outside, groups of smiling men slung themselves over the back of their Toyota pickups clutching Kalashnikovs. We settled down on a bench laden with what looked like 18 different varieties of lamb, before the doctor made a startling admission: qat wasn't that bad for you after all.

'We haven't done a study on this [but] there is some British study, I heard about it, about qat and they recommended that you should chew qat,' he shrugged, ignoring the well-researched evidence that qat can cause mouth cancer. 'We have prohibited players from chewing it. They can chew far away from the team but chewing qat reduces the training. They can't perform in the stadium to their best so chewing qat will reduce their promise.'

Hamid was making furious phone calls to find out which match was to be played tomorrow. The rumour was that Yarmouk would take on Al Ahli, a Sana'a derby. Yarmouk was a deeply Islamic club and had incorporated their religious doctrine into the club's constitution. The club would only sign Muslim players and only pick a player for the first team if they had proved their religious credentials by praying five times a day. Missing prayer, or having a Western-style haircut, were two foolproof ways of getting dropped from the team. Al Ahli, on the other hand, were Yemen's most popular team. The name derived from the Egyptian team Al Ahly, the Middle East's first Arab-run club. As it means 'The National', following the club has been seen as a way of supporting a more secular Arab self-determination.

The doctor continued to slowly chew on his meat. 'There are many clubs, like Yarmouk, that are very Islamic. Islamic men, but very political too,' he added. He liked the devout teams, mainly because they made his job easier as qat use in more religious households, much like smoking, had always been frowned on. So far the new regime's net had started to catch the odd intransigent player leading to a number being banned from playing. 'We have had to throw players out. We have found a player chewing qat in front of the team's official. Even if they are famous, it's no excuse, the rule is the same for everyone.' This, I was about to find out, wasn't exactly the case.

Hamid and I left to meet two of his best friends, both ex-Yemeni internationals who were now part of his new generation of officials trying to clean up football in the country. On the car journey north Hamid took the chance to rectify some of the misconceptions about Yemen: about how it actually pumped one million barrels of oil a day, the same as Iraq, but only declared 400,000, such was the corruption. That Yemen's Islam was actually far more relaxed than people assumed. That everyone had girlfriends and boyfriends. Drugs and booze were readily available and hip-hop was the soundtrack of choice for Yemen's 20-somethings.

The bustle of Sana'a soon left us behind as we climbed higher into the sparsely populated mountains that protected the city. Decrepit oil tankers inched slowly in the opposite direction, one misplaced tyre away from a fiery apocalypse. Parked cars littered the side of the road in front of a magnificent, panoramic view of the city. As it was 2pm, prime qat-chewing time, I'd assumed it was the view that had attracted so many visitors there. But no. 'We have a lot of gays in Yemen,' he said, jutting his head towards the line of silent cars. 'No one cares.'

Khaleed and Fayad were already there, a lay-by at the top of the hill, leaning against their 4x4s. Both players were stars from a bygone era, playing in a team that hated itself. Whilst East and West Germany were basking in the glory of the latter's triumph at Italia '90 and looking forward to a peaceful and prosperous future together under one flag, a more low-key, less successful version was taking place in Yemen. Unification between the warring north and south, the south under the influence of Soviet communism, the north by conservatives, had uneasily taken place in 1990. The reunification of the national team was equally fraught.

'There were two teams, I was with the north, then after 1990 we came together and there were big problems,' shrugged Khaleed, a tall, studious-looking man who, despite a protruding bald pate, still managed to exude youth. 'Politics has interfered with football too much here. A lot of political parties are involved. Some of the clubs have good relations with the regime and they support this club and some clubs follow the opposition and there are some problems. They are afraid but they support them through money. Ahli is the government team.'

The only thing that anyone in the newly united Yemen national team could agree on was qat, which was chewed mercilessly in an attempt to qualify for several World Cups. 'I was one who didn't chew qat,' Fayad stressed, 'but everybody did when I played. Some of them chewed one or two hours before the games, others after. They thought it would give them more energy, that it would make them strong.' Unsurprisingly, Yemen's performances on the national stage were abysmal. Even Khaleed, a baritone-voiced, bald-headed ex-striker once considered Yemen's most feared marksman, admitted that he chewed qat before a game. 'Sometimes,' he shrugged, as Hamid glared at him. 'Maybe once a year, in the last years before I retired.'

Khaleed pulled out a large plastic bag and handed me the reason why we had convened on top of a mountain. A can of Heineken. He cracked it open, shouted, 'Yallah, yallah, yallah' (Come on, come on, come on) and downed it in one. 'Heineken is the best beer in the world,' he grinned. 'You can't get it in the shops, but you can from the discos, everyone knows where.' It wasn't long before the subject of qat came up again. Khaleed asked me if I'd chewed, which I hadn't. 'Drink, and then fuck, haaaahahaha. Yes?' he said, banging his arm against the side of his car. Hamid jumped in to explain. 'Qat is like Viagra, if a woman takes qat, it is potent.' Everyone agreed whilst frowning about the effect it has had on Yemeni society. 'We could achieve much more economically without qat,' said Hamid. 'It takes so much money and time and we would have a big middle class with the power to buy commodities. It can take half your income. It's a curse.'

The group solemnly nodded in approval before, a few moments later, Hamid dropped a bombshell with unexpectedly brilliant comic timing. 'OK, we will go to a restaurant, get some beer and chew some qat. OK?'

I'd felt oddly subdued on the journey back to the mountain. Hamid and his gang were singing along to their favourite CD – Eminem – as if they were preparing for a big night on the town. With Hamid's zero-tolerance policy towards his players' use of qat and his explicit connection between Yemen's various failures and the drug, I was expecting a footballing Eliot Ness; a whiter-than-white enforcer, living by the same rules he implemented whilst shining the torch of justice under every last stone. We stopped at a nearby Chinese restaurant. The owner ran out, shiftily looked both ways, and handed Khaleed a black bin liner full of Chinese beer. Abdullah, a fourth friend who had joined us, wearing a red-and-white headscarf and a long flowing *kandoora*, was dispatched to the market to buy the qat whilst we went to Fayad's house. We entered into his specially designed qat-chewing room, his *majlis*. Fayad's was a large, open room, the edges skirted with cushions and the air full of sweet Yemeni incense, which before the discovery of oil, and the commodification of qat, was the country's most valued substance. Before the chewing could commence, we ate as much as we could as qat's main side effect is to suppress the appetite. Abdullah arrived from his qat run hot and bothered. He'd had to first go home to ask his wife's permission to come and chew. She was a doctor and, unlike the national team's medic, knew how harmful the drug was. With permission begrudgingly granted, he assumed his cross-legged position at the edge of the room.

The ritual began. First, tissues and a small bucket are laid out in front of each guest whilst the host empties the qat into five equally sized bags. Each large green stem looked like rocket, and the trick was to pick the right leaves. The best and most potent were the small and slightly red-dish ones. Each leaf was pulled, cleaned between the fingers and then jammed into the cheek, where it was chewed to a mush before more was added, and then more, and more, until a large ball of mush could be seen protruding from your cheek like a particularly nasty abscess. It tasted bad, like unwashed, bitter spinach, but once your mouth adjusted to the sourness it had a smoky, nearly pleasant after taste.

Then you felt it working its magic: the raised heart rate, the loss of inhibitions, the waves of pleasure that shook through you. It seemed to be one part cannabis, one part ecstasy, one part speed. Suddenly everyone in the room was my best friend; I was sitting with the wittiest people in the world. I felt invincible. After spitting some of the thick green juice into my bucket, we got down to the main reason why people chew qat: to talk. The four men in the room were all desperate to improve the image of Yemeni football. They couldn't have found it in a worse state. Yet Yemen was due to host the Gulf Cup in 2011, inviting the rest of the Middle East to view the steps it had made. It would be embarrassing if the rest of the region saw the current qat-addled mess. Although for Hamid, the problems were bigger than qat. We had only just got confirmation that Ahli and Yarmouk were to play at 3.45 tomorrow afternoon, less than 24 hours before the game. None of the teams had its own stadium. There was no such thing as a match ticket in Yemen: fans just rolled up if they heard about a match on the grapevine and watched it for free. Violence, guns, knives and qat were commonplace. The government owned almost all of the teams. And to make matters worse, unless you were at the game, no one would ever see it or have a record of it. Yemen's (one) state-owned television station got angry when the FA asked them to pay for the rights and had refused to show any more matches since.

More qat was stuffed into our cheeks and as the night drew on we made an action plan. Hamid would rebrand the league, like the English Premier League, and privatise the clubs. He would bypass the local television network and sell the rights directly to a pan-Arab satellite network. That would show them! Season tickets would be sold and for those that missed the game, no fear, a highlights show, an Arabic *Match of the Day*, would be the centrepiece of Yemen's Friday-night television schedule. It would be a ratings hit! Fayad and Abdullah shouted ideas as the room felt the frenzied white heat of footballing revolution. 'That's what I've been saying!' they shouted over each other. 'Why don't we bring over big-name foreign players, like in Qatar?' another asked hopefully. Someone else suggested Sami al Jaber, the legendary Saudi striker who had appeared in four World Cup finals. Why not? Why the hell wouldn't he want to play in Yemen?! 'How much would we have to pay him?' Hamid shouted excitedly. In the spirit of change, I made my own suggestion. 'How about allowing women into the stadium?!'

The other four looked at each other quizzically. 'No,' Hamid eventually responded. 'This would not work.' But still, great work had been accomplished. At last, Yemen's footballing problems weren't as intractable as we first thought. In ten years Yemen would have the best league in the Middle East! No, in Asia! Everyone laughed, and slapped thighs, and clinked glasses of beer. With these guys together we could save Yemeni football! The shout went up: 'Yallah, yallah, yallah.' All was great in the world.

Then the qat ran out.

Almost as soon as the last sweet leaf had been chewed, the euphoria ebbed away and the depressing inertia that suffocated almost every single good idea descended over the room. Sami al Jaber wouldn't come here. What a stupid idea. Which pan-Arab network would want to pay to show Yemeni football anyway? If the government were so riddled with corruption, how the hell would we buy the football clubs off them? Where would the money come from? Everyone sat in silence, the same questions washing around our temples. What comes up, must come down. I felt utterly hopeless and desperate for more leaves to stave off the inevitable. But there was none left. The gang cleared up their stalks and shuffled outside into the cool Yemeni night. We said our goodbyes and retreated to our respective beds, spent. I suspected that Hamid, Khaleed, Abdullah and Fayad had the same conversation every time they chewed.

It was Friday and the big match was less than an hour away. As 3.45pm approached there wasn't a bushel of qat in sight at the small football stadium on the outskirts of the old city. I'd had a fitful night's sleep, one of the drug's other side-effects, but I didn't have to walk far out of the old city to find the squat, condemnable wreck that passed for the testing ground for Yemen's new policy on cleaning up football. Soldiers with machine guns patrolled the front gates, taking guns and qat off anyone trying to smuggle them inside. But the main weapon against fan-on-fan violence was the jambiya, and the police had a plan. Rather than impound the knives, they set up a free cloakroom so the spectators could retrieve their knives after the games. The cloakroom was an engine-less Toyota Corona. Men queued by the back window as, Inside, two policemen poked their hands through a small crack to receive each spectator's knife. In return they received a small plastic ticket. The system seemed to make sense, until I realised that each ticket was exactly the same. Piled all around the policemen, the curved knives looked indistinguishable from one another.

After being frisked by a soldier I took my position pitchside as the terraces filled green and red – the green of Yarmouk, the red of Ahli. Minarets protruded from the nearby neighbourhoods like gleaming white skyscrapers as the basalt mountains watched over in the distance. Suddenly, the call to prayer wafted over the pitch from every direction. Most Gulf countries have employed a system whereby the call to prayer is called at exactly the same time. Some use a single recorded voice for uniformity. Others, like the UAE, make sure that it's not just the times and the voices that are in unison. Imams are picked and vetted by the government, which also controls what can, and can't, be said during Friday sermons. In Yemen, each mosque still had its own muezzin, prayer caller, and each kept its own time. Some calls to prayer start as early as 3.30am. The result is a glorious, deafening, jumbled cacophony that had not changed for a hundred years. As the two teams warmed up a tall, balding man with glasses, wearing a long white *kandoora* and sporting a huge *jambiya*, stalked around the Yarmouk players. Abdul Aziz was still allowed to carry his knife because he was the vice president of the club. The Sudanese manager Mohammad Mahdawi circled the seated players in the other direction. Aziz spotted me watching his team talk, straightened his back and walked over.

'We established this club in 1978 with a group of people who had the same idea,' he explained, before spreading his arms and pointing to both sets of fans. 'We are all Muslims, but Yarmouk is more strict. We pray before matches and we are more strict with our values. We don't allow players to chew qat or smoke. Their behaviour is more important than the way they play. So we choose players on that basis.' It seemed incredible that a team could exist that was chosen not on ability, but on a player's degree of religious devoutness. But Yarmouk hadn't been doing too badly. They sat mid-table and had a reputation for playing fluid, attacking football without ever challenging for the championship, a bit like an Islamic Tottenham Hotspur. Abdul still seemed suspicious and was overly eager to point out that his team wasn't filled with extremists or corrupted by fundamentalist ideology.

'Since the beginning it was like this, not as fanatics but to respect the values [of Islam],' he replied when I asked whether a non-Muslim could play for the team. 'We have a Nigerian, but they are Muslim too. [But] we would have a non-Muslim.'

'Don't you mind playing on a Friday?' I asked.

'It is no problem at all,' he laughed, patting me on the back and walking back towards the players. 'Look,' he said, pointing back to the crowd. 'It will be full today.'

He was right. Despite the short notice, the addictive draw of an afternoon's qat chewing and the demands of the mosque, 7,000 fans had packed into the stadium. It all seemed rather cordial as the players kissed each other's cheeks and rubbed each other's noses. Hamid finally arrived and we took our seats with the Yarmouk fans, who sang and shouted at the Ahli players, targeting those that had ponytails. 'You'll see a good game today and a good crowd,' Hamid assured me as the officials sorted out the paperwork. The linesmen sat atop the only three balls in the stadium as if they were rare and valuable eggs. Another official polished the brand new, $500 electronic substitutes board, Hamid's most recent attempt at modernisation. The referee blew and the crowd erupted. The Yarmouk fans flew the green flags of Islam and mocked any Ahli player who went down too easily. 'You're not hurt!' the 3,000-strong all-male Yarmouk contingent shouted. 'You have spoiled yourself!'

Then, against the run of play, Ahli broke away with their star player Ali al Nono. 'Nono' translates as 'baby' and Ali was once the great hope of Yemeni football. He had moved to more lucrative and better organised leagues, first in the star-studded Qatari league, then in the less glamorous Syrian first division. It hadn't worked out for him in either place, but in Yemen he was the closest thing they had to Ronaldinho, as he exhibited a curling shot from all of 25 yards into the top corner just before half-time. The red half of the crowd celebrated, the green half fell silent.

With half-time approaching the third official struggled with the electronic board. Two more officials came to his aid, none able to get the requisite number of added minutes to be played displayed on its electronic face. Soon, a whole crowd gathered around, pressing buttons randomly and shaking the lifeless board before giving up and resorting to the numbered cards that had done them just fine for the past few decades. Hamid shook his head before bowing into his cupped hands and leaving the ground. In the second half, Yarmouk fought back and equalised, the goal sparking a riot in the Ahli stand behind the goal. Police with sticks waded in hitting anyone who dared show a lack of immediate respect. With order restored, the game wound down to a 1-1 draw, just as dark clouds rolled over the stadium and the first spots of a cold, early spring rain started to fall.

Back in the changing room, Yarmouk captain Usman Salihu was happy with the result. Usman was Nigerian but had played in the region for almost a decade in Lebanon, Saudi Arabia and Syria for the army club Al Jaish – which literally means 'The Army' – before coming to Yemen and seeing the country's qat addiction first-hand. 'The players are not treated like professionals,' he said as we sat down in a large changing room, our voices echoing around the four peeling walls. 'The qat contributes a lot to the lack of performance in the team. I don't take it but from the people I know who take it, it absorbs their strength. They can't train. This is their main problem here.'

His manager, who had earlier been stomping around his squad like a recently promoted army general, was equally clear on Yemen's problem. Madawi was a former assistant coach to the Sudanese national team but had been in Yemen managing Yarmouk for two years. 'Every year they say it will change but it doesn't,' he said, slumping slightly as he delivered the news. 'Even the [FA] committee get together to chew.' I shook my head and offered a faked look of shock in response. For the outsiders, it was obvious who was chewing and if the FA really wanted to make examples of players they could. 'I don't want to name any names, but I see those who chew. We know who they are. This is not something that is hidden. It is not like cocaine. It is allowed so they chew. And it is available everywhere.'

Both Usman and Madawi hoped that Yarmouk's example would be the best way to exact change. One of the big advantages of only signing players that adhere to a purer form of Islam is that they would be fitter than the rest of the league. 'Every player prays before and after training and everything that religion doesn't allow, Yarmouk doesn't allow,' Usman explained proudly. 'Of course we are fitter because we stick to our religious obligations. We are seventh now but we hope to have a good position this season and maybe win the championship next year.'

This was arguably Yemen's best hope, that non-qat chewers lead by example, excel and are rewarded in whatever field it is they find themselves in, be it farming, journalism or football. I said goodbye to

Usman and Madawi. Outside was anarchy. The crowd was still leaving the stands and heading for the exit, but an almost reverential clamour had come over them. Ninety minutes of qat denial was more than most men could stand. Almost every single man I could see was filling his cheeks with the drug, secret stores that had somehow eluded detection from the armed guards outside. The pavement was dotted in the green effluence of Yemen's addiction. The crowd swirled around the engine-less Toyota Corona that doubled up as a knife depository like an unstable storm. Fans from both sides thrust their tickets through the window as the harassed policemen matched them to homeless ornate steel. The chaotic scenes sat in contrast to the lone man standing back from the pavement, watching from afar. Murat had been at the game, even though he was an Ahli Ta'izz fan from the south. Yet he didn't seem the slightest bit interested in joining in the melee. Was he not desperate for any qat too? I asked him. 'I gave up months ago, it broke my teeth,' he replied, before breaking into a bellicose laugh, his huge open mouth empty of teeth. Murat had accidentally stumbled across a foolproof way to kick his habit.

My time in Yemen had come to an end. I checked out of the hostel, said goodbye to Abdul, who was already on his first bag of the day, and hailed a cab on the Wadi Road towards the airport. Mujid picked me up in his ancient Toyota Corona, wearing the Yemeni uniform of white *kandoora*, blazer, headscarf and knife. 'Five hundred rials,' he asked solemnly. Seeing as it was a third of what I was being offered elsewhere, I agreed. The car lurched into life and spun off just before the other marauding taxi drivers could cut in and take his fare. Although, as I later discovered, they may have simply been trying to impart a warning.

Mujid's car, like almost every other car I'd seen in Yemen, was on the brink of extinction. You'd see cars cut out suddenly while driving down highways. Each driver seemed to have such a union with his automobile that he could sense the exact moment he was about to run out of petrol, ensuring that, as Mujid did, he glided into the petrol station on nothing but the most cursory of fumes. Mujid's luck had run out, though, as the car wouldn't start.

'Push,' he implored, poking me out of the car. I took my position behind a passer-by on the right, and grunted. The car came back to life just as I trampled through a stinking, overflowing gutter, and jumped into the passenger side, Mujid speeding up as if he hadn't really wanted me to get back into his cab at all. He laughed, before narrowly avoiding a truck and asking me to give him all my Yemeni money, using warped but impeccable logic.

'You will not need your money now because you are leaving Yemen,' he said. Stuck in a traffic jam, Mujid attempted to veer onto the pavement but slammed his brakes on, screeching to a halt in front of two Yemenis casually talking. This was clearly a provocation. Although the *jambiya* is a cultural accessory, it can be, and is, still used as a weapon to settle scores in Yemeni disputes under certain circumstances. I was pretty sure road rage wasn't one of them, but Mujid screamed at the two men before pulling out his *jambiya*, waving it inches in front of my face and stabbing it at the human roadblock. The two men responded, drawing their knives and thrusting them through the passenger window before they clumsily jousted in front of me. I wedged myself back into the seat as far as I could and prayed to the God I had long ago forsaken to let me live. Being outnumbered, Mujid sped off, his knife narrowly missing my throat in the recoil, his cab narrowly missing a lorry as he veered away. Behind us the men continued chasing after the car. Somehow, no one had been stabbed and my face had remained unslashed. I had witnessed, a little too close for comfort, my first Yemeni knife fight.

An angry silence fell over us.

'Have you ever stabbed anyone before?' I eventually asked, still rooted as far back in my seat as possible. Mujid looked back blankly.

'Stabbed someone,' I repeated, making a stabbing motion with my arm at the same time.

'Yes,' he replied. 'Many people. Now, give me a cigarette.'

Without hesitation I passed over a cheap Yemeni Kamaran Light and sat back in silence as Mujid swerved and shouted his way towards the airport, drawing his knife once more at another driver in a Land Cruiser that cut him up. The shell of a taxi careered into Sana'a International Airport. I handed over a 1,000-rial note and bolted, dragging my bag out of the back seat. I didn't look back, and I didn't ask for the change.

5

West Bank

The protest was already in full swing. Walking towards Bethlehem University, the low rumble of faraway raised voices could be felt, if not exactly heard, until the tall sandstone walls broke at the main gate to reveal the crowd inside. Dozens of young men danced in circles to distorted Arabic pop music, spinning their black-and-white *keffiyeh* scarves in the air. Those that didn't shook yellow flags. The flag depicted two fists crossing machine guns above a grenade. Behind the men, banks of women, some covered, some not, stood silently unmoved, as a demonstrator with a megaphone began to shout 'Allahu Akbar!' God is great.

The men mirrored his call. 'It was the student elections yesterday,' came a voice to my side, by way of explanation. It was one of the university's Christian Brothers, who administered the campus. This was a victory parade for Fatah, who had vanquished the likes of Islamic Jihad and Hamas to control the university's student body politic. It was some much needed good news for Fatah – the nationalist party of Yasser Arafat and now the Palestinian President Mahmoud Abbas; the party that had dominated Palestinian politics had squandered the goodwill of their people through corruption and mismanagement. Amidst the discontent Hamas, the Islamic fundamentalist party considered a terrorist movement in the West and by Israel, had moved in and was in the ascendancy after winning the 2006 parliamentary election. Hamas and Fatah had long rubbed each other up the wrong way and had been fighting for hearts and minds in the West Bank and Gaza, sometimes metaphorically, mostly literally, one espousing a secular version of

Palestinian statehood alongside Israel, the other promoting a vision of Islamic resistance and Palestinian statehood on top of it. It might have only been a student election, but Fatah needed all the victories it could get.

'I voted for Fatah,' said Jasmine, a 20-year-old studying computer science, as she watched the rapturous scene unfold. 'Muslims and Christians vote for them, only Muslims voted for Islamic Jihad and Hamas. In other universities they have won, but not here. It's supported by the Vatican and Hamas would make us cover.'

The screams from the victory parade couldn't be heard down in a basement office on the other side of campus. Samar Mousa was oblivious to the goings on in the main square as she shuffled important paperwork and fielded excuses from her students as to why they didn't have any kit with them for that day's physical education class. Short, with dark hair and piercingly friendly kohl-ringed eyes, Samar welcomed me into her tiny office out of which she ran the university women's athletics department. But that was merely a day job that helped her to build a subtler, but no less important, form of defiance: organising the Palestinian women's national football team.

Football had long been a man's game in the Middle East. Whilst women's football had grown in popularity in Asia and the West, women in the Middle East still had to fight just to get a game. Not a single Arab team qualified for the Women's World Cup in 2007. In fact no team from the Middle East or North Africa had ever qualified for the finals, which was no surprise given the reticence of governments and governing bodies towards the women's game. In Iran the authorities insisted that women covered themselves completely, only showing their hands and face. What's more, men were banned from watching them play. In Saudi, the authorities banned the national women's team from playing football completely. In Egypt, one high-ranking FA official I asked didn't even know there was an Egyptian women's team, even though they were arguably the best in the region and were ranked 85th in the world by FIFA. Kuwait's women footballers looked to have made a breakthrough when a member of the royal family, Sheikha Naima al Sabah, announced that a national football team would be set up. Fans on message boards joked that it was probably the best chance Kuwait had of qualifying for a football

World Cup again. The plan was quietly dropped when Waleed al Tab-tabae, a leading Islamist MP in the Kuwaiti parliament who ran a committee that monitored 'phenomena alien to society', forced the team to be banned by arguing that women's football was 'un-Islamic'. But even these barriers paled in comparison to those faced by the Palestinians, who have to fight not just their own communities, but also restrictions of occupation to play.

The seed of the Palestinian national women's team was planted over two decades ago, in Amman, Jordan, out of an injustice. 'I was studying there and they told me that I couldn't play football,' explained Samar cheerily as she showed me around her windowless office. Framed photos of her proudly standing next to the women's team littered the shelves along with old black and white prints of her family. 'They said I had to do aerobic dance, it made me mad so I made sure that when I was in charge, girls could play football.' It was difficult to imagine Samar getting mad; such was her disarming demeanour. Yet her experience of being slighted as a young, football-loving student wasn't exorcised until four years ago. It was whilst teaching physical education at the university that Samar's dream came to fruition. And that was only when she met 23-year-old Honey Thaljieh – the team's captain and star striker.

Samar opened her door and invited two girls into the room. 'We started with Honey,' she said, smiling at the brown-haired captain as she found her seat. 'Then we had three players, then five from the university, and then we spread the idea to other towns, in Ramallah, Jericho and Gaza. Now we have 20 players in all.' Honey and Jackline Jazwari, the team's left winger, had come to football from different places: Honey had played (and beaten) the neighbourhood boys in practice matches on the narrow streets of Bethlehem almost as soon as she could walk. She was blessed with a powerful right foot and natural leadership skills, and Samar decided to build the whole team around her. Jackie, on the other hand, had never kicked a football before she met Samar. 'For me it was a strange thing to play football,' Jackline recalled. 'But when I saw Miss Samar I was in the first year in university and I was playing in the basketball team and she said why don't you join our team? She said you'd love it and pushed me into it. I love her like my mother so I went to training, saw the girls and the spirit in the team and wanted to play.'

Despite having a strong nucleus of dedicated players, the practical-ities of living in the West Bank made it almost impossible for them to actually play any football. To start with the only grass pitch was ten miles away in Jericho, which was largely inaccessible thanks to the ring of Israeli checkpoints that surrounded Bethlehem. Instead they practised on a nearby concrete court. No women's club teams existed, which meant no league, no cup and no competitive games. It was also impossible for the girls from Gaza to train with their counterparts in the West Bank without leaving the country because of Israeli move-ment restrictions. 'We went to Egypt to meet the Gaza girls before a tournament last year. It was the first time I had even met them,' Samar said. 'We didn't know their names. It's strange playing together as a national team as we met the girls for the first time two days before our match. It was also the first time we ever played on a full-sized pitch once in Egypt. The girls didn't know their positions but they played with enthusiasm. We lost, but we didn't lose by that much.'

Yet one of the biggest obstacles to progress had nothing to do with Israell. Many in Palestinian society itself hadn't exactly welcomed the women's team with open arms. 'At first it seemed weird, women playing soccer in our society because it has such a male mentality,' admitted Honey as we all sipped tea in the cramped office. 'Some families had problems sending their daughters to play football, some still face prob-lems.' The resistance came from a mixture of conservative social mores and a creeping religiosity that has spread from Gaza to the West Bank. Although five players were Muslim, most were drawn from the West Bank's small Christian community centred on Bethlehem. Some towns were so conservative they were totally off-limits for recruitment. 'We don't go to Nablus, Jenin and Tulkarem,' Honey lamented. 'We've had some difficulties. One player – her uncles said she shouldn't play. Then they said she had to wear the veil and kept putting barriers up. But they eventually accepted the idea. Step by step they saw what we were doing.' Then there's the issue of marriage. The team has already lost two first-team players to husbands who demanded their wives give up football for duties in the home, a fact that meant that Honey was the oldest of the team. She had vowed not to get married unless her future husband accepted her love of football. 'I'm single, but if I get engaged and get married I will still play. If he loves me he will love what I am doing.'

Marriage wasn't the only barrier either. The team's kit had become somewhat of an issue. Sepp Blatter may have wanted to 'sex up' the women's game with a new kit that mirrors beach volleyball, but in the West Bank long shorts and over-sized shirts were still considered too risqué, especially for some families who regarded them as indecent. 'In the north of the West Bank and Gaza they are a little stricter,' Samar said diplomatically, but with a wry smile. 'The problem is that they do not respect us if we don't dress honestly. We wear shorts near the knee. This is the biggest problem. But our coach is Muslim, a strict Muslim, yet he still coaches us.'

As if on cue Raed Ayyad, the team's 37-year-old coach, introduced himself. Quietly spoken and with a large barrel chest upon which his whistle lay, he smiled and stroked his thick beard when I asked whether his religious beliefs had been conflicted at all by coaching a team of footballers that some, according to Samar, thought were not dressed 'honestly'. He was new to the job. The vacancy had only arisen after the last coach quit when the Israelis detained him as he tried to leave the West Bank for a match overseas. It wasn't the inconvenience that made him leave, Samar explained, but rather the unfairness that his presence might hamper the team's attendance at tournaments. The new coach wasn't there for the financial benefits either, as the position was unpaid. Worse, he had to combat a whispering campaign as to his intentions in taking the job.

'It was difficult for me because all the people were gossiping that I was training girls,' he admitted, the fourth person in the small room making it feel like a sauna. 'They would say: "Why is he training girls? Football is rough, it's not good for them," things like that. I tell them, from a religious point of view, Muslim or Christian, no one has said that it is forbidden, that women can't play soccer. Islam says that sport is good for the body and if [the players] wear long clothes then it would not be forbidden among the Muslim community.' Raed's moderate voice of reason had become more and more isolated in the previous months. Hamas's parliamentary election win had sent a signal that Palestinian society was perhaps becoming more religious, more conservative and more radical. Honey, for one, had noticed the difference, both as a footballer and as a Christian. 'Things are becoming more conservative under Hamas but not all women are the same,' she asserted. 'Some women believe that they can do something and won't just wait for their husbands to come along and make children. They believe that they can change something and I'm one of them, the rest of the girls too. It's one of the most difficult things we face. Sometimes we feel like we are fighting alone. We need some encouragement but you can't find it here. So it's about courage. If we have courage we can achieve anything we want.'

Honey's articulate call to arms heralded the end of our interview. Samar had to get on with her athletics training and Coach Raed was preoccupied with training the university men's team that afternoon. Honey, Jackline and I went for a kickabout on the basketball court outside. The basketball players stopped what they were doing and stared as Jackline teed up the ball and expertly transferred it from foot to foot, occasionally striking the ball higher only to control it back down to earth with her chest. Even within the university the team was considered something of an oddity. The ball passed to Honey who struck it with her ferocious right foot, the ball flying straight into my face. Holding my throbbing nose I climbed back up to the university's now empty main square. The detritus of the victory rally blew across the concrete floor. A yellow Fatah flag lay crumpled and unloved on the floor. I picked it up, put it in my bag and left through the front gate.

It was a short walk down a steep hill to Manger Square. If there's one thing that defines the West Bank it is an inequality of altitude. The West Bank's uniquely coloured, yellow-white hills are the most coveted in the world, with the incremental battle for supremacy between Palestinian and Israel settlements taking place at their zenith. Each hilltop has its own urban snowcap, clinging precariously to its summit lest anyone replaced it when they weren't looking. Bethlehem's ancient foundations meant it could be confident of continuity, but others had not been so lucky. Silver-walled Israeli settlements rise up on nearby hills, all steel and superiority. At its base, the previous occupants scratched a living in houses made from discarded wood and corrugated iron, waiting for the day they would once again claim the higher ground. Bethlehem will always be fixed in the mind as a place of worship for Christians and, sure enough, Palestine's shrinking Christian minority almost all live here.

In one small back alley Mike tended to his customer-free trinket shop, St Johns. 'Things here are bad,' he told me, lighting up a cigarette on the shop's step, revealing the large cross he wore around his neck buried in thick silver chest hair. 'Most Palestinian towns are industrial but we rely on tourism. The war in Lebanon really hurt us.' In fact, any bad news – suicide bombings, border restrictions, flareups in Gaza – was felt more keenly here than anywhere else. Once Bethlehem thrived on thousands of foreign tourists flocking here to see the Church of the Nativity, the site where Christians claim Jesus was born. Few were coming any more. Bethlehem's nadir came in 2002 when a bloody siege between the Israeli military and suspected Palestinian militants took place, flashing images across the world of bloodshed on the doorstep of one of Christianity's holiest sites.

'It hasn't been the same since,' shrugged Mike, handing me a small wooden cross as a present. Sure enough the square was empty, the small door to the church clear apart from two Palestinian Authority policemen patrolling nearby. The only other life was a gaggle of American preachers dragging a large wooden cross with a wheel on it. Arthur and Joshua, a father-and-son preaching team from California, had been dragging the cross around the world since the 1970s trying to break the world record for the longest walk – feeling Jesus' pain before the crucifixion whilst spreading the word of God. Almost everyone had been photographed with him; even Arafat and Gaddafi featured in the black-and-white prints Arthur proudly showed me. I was half-expecting a grinning photo of him shaking hands with Saddam. Everything they talked about seemed to point to a bigger, higher question. 'I've never felt alone on my journey because the Lord has always been with me,' replied Arthur when I asked whether he missed a settled life. 'Jesus knows where I have been.' I could only think of glib questions – 'Shouldn't you take the wheel off to really feel Jesus' pain?' or 'Do you ever get stopped at customs with that?'

'Here,' Joshua offered. 'Try the cross on for size.' He passed me the six-foot-long timber cross, so heavy it pinned me to the spot. I was a captive audience as Arthur gathered his disciples around in a circle: 'Let's pray.' His sermon was interjected by meaty shouts of 'Yeah!' from his followers every time he mentioned Jesus. 'Let Jesus into your heart,' Arthur intoned, holding my hand. 'You will never feel alone, amen.' Under my shades, my eyes were closed. Involuntarily I replied

'Amen.' Arthur took his cross, thanked me for my time and skipped into the Church of the Nativity, continuing on his journey. I shook my head, laughed and continued on mine.

JERICHO, WEST BANK

An Israeli told me a joke about Jericho. Three Palestinians are stopped at a checkpoint. The Israeli soldier asks where they are from. 'Jenin,' says the first. 'Get down and spread 'em!' shouts the soldier. The second says: 'Ramallah.' The soldier shouts at him to get down too. The third says: 'Jericho.' The soldier hands him his gun. 'Hold this whilst I arrest the other two, won't you?'

The road from Jerusalem is littered with crumbling towns and villages. Once you pass the Israeli checkpoint, a different West Bank emerges, one that Jericho seems to be the only representative of. The streets were wide and clean. Grass and palm trees lined the roads. A swanky hotel and casino could be found on the outskirts. Whilst the rest of the West Bank was racked by poverty, Jericho had the air of a thriving oasis town. After visiting the Palestinian women's team I had been told that one of Bethlehem's local men's teams was due to play a cup match in Jericho the next afternoon, a rare occurrence in the West Bank. Since the so-called al Aqsa intifada flared in 2000, movement restrictions between Palestinian towns had slowly strangled the life out of the Palestinian football league. With fans, teams and referees struggling to make it to matches, it was impossible to fulfil the league's fixtures. The FA eventually gave up, concentrating on smaller cup competitions to keep the clubs afloat until the day arrived when the league could return.

The quarter-finals were due to be played between two of the West Bank's best teams; Thaqafi Tulkarem, from the devout town of Tulkarem in the north, and Taraji Wadi al Nes, a small village on the outskirts of Bethlehem. Whilst the women's game had struggled to have its voice heard, the men's game in Palestine made international headlines after it tried, and tragically failed, to qualify for the 2006 World Cup. The national team had a higher purpose than most as it is in the unusual position of being a national team without an internationally recognised nation. So when FIFA recognised Palestine in 1998, one of Sepp Blatter's first acts as president, it was a cause for massive celebration in the West Bank and Gaza. Blatter flew to Rafah in the Gaza Strip, along with Michel Platini, and was greeted as a hero. FIFA was, after all, one of the few international bodies to recognise Palestine's existence. Reaching the World Cup finals, the Palestinians reasoned, would ensure that the world couldn't ignore their claims for statehood any longer. With the UN refusing to grant it full membership, it was the next best hope.

It all started so well too. FIFA had relaxed its rules on citizenship, allowing the team's Austrian coach Alfred Riedl to call on its huge diaspora to fill its team sheet. Adverts were put into magazines in Germany, Chile and the United States to attract players. A multinational squad was assembled, followed by an 8–0 thumping of Chinese Taipei (itself a political expedient name used for Taiwan) and a respectable 1–1 draw with Iraq, two teams that had to play their home games in exile, on foreign grounds. Then the wheels fell off. Movement restrictions between Gaza and the West Bank, not to mention the restrictions within them, meant the team could hardly train together. Training camps were set up in Egypt, but the players from Gaza would rarely get through the border. The coaching staff, realising that nine-man training sessions probably weren't the best sort of preparation, started picking more players from the West Bank, breeding resentment among the two groups of players and effectively creating two different national teams. The game was up when some of the team were denied permission to leave Palestine to play Uzbekistan. Five Gaza-based players had been held at the border in the aftermath of a suicide bombing in Be'er Sheva. The Palestinians could barely scrape together 11 players. It was a miracle they only lost 3–0. The campaign was over.

The national team had never really recovered after that, nor had local football. Back in the West Bank, the restrictions remained and a league was a distant memory and a forlorn hope. The quarter-final was due to be played at the rather hopefully named Jericho International Stadium. Covered in smashed windows and looking little more than a derelict car park with a rectangle of grass and sand at its centre, it was hard to imagine the stadium having ever seen better days. Faded posters of Yasser Arafat still adorned the low walls that led to the stadium.

Fans crushed through the single turnstile to pay their seven shekels for a ticket. Once inside they took their position in the one functioning stand at the side of the pitch, the Taraji Wadi al Nes and Thaqafi Tulkarem fans separated by a thick line of Palestinian Authority policemen carrying clubs. A few left their seats to take their positions towards Mecca and pray in the bright, late-afternoon sunshine.

'This competition is a little like, how do you have, the Milk Cup,' Khaldun, a Tulkarem fan, told me whilst sitting in the stands chewing on a bag of sunflower seeds and showing an incredible grasp of mid-1980s English football. The stadium looked half-empty but Khaldun wasn't that surprised. 'It's a long journey and there are three checkpoints to get through. Luckily it wasn't too difficult for me and only took an hour.' The referee, on the other hand, wasn't so lucky. Half an hour after the planned kick-off he still hadn't arrived. A few minutes later the rotund man in black came puffing onto the pitch to a wall of jeers. 'He got held up at a checkpoint,' Khaldun offered. 'But they are more free here in Jericho. In Tulkarem the police cannot work after 10pm, then the Israelis take over. But here they are everywhere all the time.'

Tulkarem were clear favourites. The team consisted of a number of Palestinian internationals and were coached by the current national team manager Mohammed Sabah. With the stadium not having any functional changing rooms, both teams received their last-minute instruction behind the steel fence that separated them from the fans. Finally the referee blew his whistle. Tackles flew in, players rolled around on the floor as if they had been garrotted and yellow cards were brandished like confetti. Seeing that it could be months before the loser got another game, both teams were desperate not to lose. Off the pitch the situation was worse. One journalist sent to cover the match from Tulkarem was escorted from the stadium after he jumped on the pitch in a rage at one of the referee's many dodgy decisions, clawing at the air between him and the man in the middle as he was dragged away by the police. The armed police had to wade in to beat back a crowd of Tulkarem fans after the perimeter fence protecting the players from the terraces was stormed. Their flailing nightsticks carved through the mass until they stopped, confused. At its centre a supporter in a wheelchair was repeatedly wheeling himself into the perimeter fence and hurling abuse at a Wadi al Nes player taking a throw.

'Of course, some of these players are for Hamas, others are Fatah,' Ahmad, a Palestinian journalist from *Al Hayat*, told me as the match unfolded. 'But there isn't one team that is for Fatah, the other for Hamas. We are all Palestinians.' That might have been the case for the West Bank but I had originally wanted to visit Gaza to see how Hamas and Fatah rivalries were being played out in the football league there. One of the few benefits for Gazans in the chaos that had followed Israel's pull out from the tiny strip in 2005 was the absence of movement restrictions, which meant that the football league could go on. The Israelis occasionally still bombed the odd match – the main football stadium in Gaza had been hit by a mortar a few months earlier as a team trained on it – but other than that, the games and the league went on as planned. But Gaza had become totally inaccessible to Westerners thanks to the continued power struggle between the forces of Mahmoud Abbas's Fatah and Hamas. Lawlessness had gripped Gaza as the two forces fought to exert what they saw as their mandate to fulfil the will of the people; the former presidential, the latter parliamentary. Matters were made worse since the BBC journalist Alan Johnston had been seized a month earlier and was still being held captive. I'd hoped that the Palestinian FA could have given me safe passage to the last game of the season, a title decider in the Rafah refugee camp. 'Not even the FA could protect you there,' Ahmad explained.

The game itself reached a frenzied conclusion, 1–1, extra time and then penalties. The two teams chose radically different ways to prepare. Tulkarem huddled, discussed the order of the kicks and took some last-minute instruction from the manager. The Wadi al Nes players and staff, even a few of the fans, put their preparations into the hands of God. They knelt in a line and prayed in the near darkness, hoping for divine intervention. Football fans may talk about how unfair a penalty shootout is, but for the neutral penalties are the most exciting part of any match, like squeezing a whole tournament into ten kicks. But if it's your team, it's hell on earth. For one Wadi al Nes player the tension was too much, and he sparked up a cigarette, smoking it surreptitiously in the cup of his hand so his coach didn't see. The goals, the saves and the misses ebbed and flowed. Finally, Wadi al Nes scored the winning penalty to go into the semi-finals. The players bundled into one another on the floodlit pitch as the Tulkarem players sprinted away and jumped into a waiting bus, before speeding off minutes after the end. 'We played better,' explained midfielder Kader Youssef, grinning wildly as his teammates celebrated around him. 'It is important to own the cup and it's great for our village and great for our people. *Inshallah* we will play Al Islam [next]. It's a derby.' Wadi al Nes's prayers had been answered.

BETHLEHEM, WEST BANK

It would be a month before I made good on the promise I gave Honey and Jackline to return. In the short time I had been away Hamas had broken its short-lived ceasefire with Israel and its feud with Fatah was veering out of control in Gaza. The Palestinian movement was in the throes of a civil war. Gaza was tearing itself apart as forces loyal to Fatah and Hamas fought for control. With Hamas enjoying popular support, Fatah were taking a beating. In both the West Bank and Gaza, the organisations had killed or expelled members of the opposite political party and their respective armed militias as Fatah officials fled to the West Bank. Extrajudicial killings and revenge attacks were reported across both territories, even in Bethlehem. In return, the Israelis had cracked down on movement through the wall. You could gauge just how 'hot' a situation was – as the Israelis refer to it – by the number and thoroughness of Israeli checkpoints. During my last visit our blue-and-white bus had left East Jerusalem and climbed the steep hill to the walls of Bethlehem unmolested. Now the bus stopped on the Israeli side and everyone passed through a security checkpoint before the wall.

I emerged on the Palestinian side, in Bethlehem, just a few hundred metres from the university. It was Thursday, training day. Coach Raed stood alone in the middle of Bethlehem University's concrete tennis court, a brush in his left hand, methodically sweeping broken glass bottles of soft drink into the dustpan in his right whilst muttering to himself. 'The boys,' he intoned despairingly of the teenagers who had smashed their drinks on the floor overnight. 'Sometimes they get a little crazy.' The girls arrived just as the sun began to dip behind the trees, casting long shadows over the hot gravelly surface. It wasn't an ideal place to give your national team a workout, but when you don't have a stadium or a full-sized pitch, this was better than nothing. Raed complained that the surface exacerbated his players' injuries, but there was nowhere else to go. All he could do was to arrive early for every training session and clear the court to make sure the players didn't cut themselves.

Dressed in her Palestine 'home' kit – coloured the red, black, green and white of the flag – Honey was the first to arrive, stretching and setting an example to the other girls, some of whom were as young as 12. They filed through the gates, one by one, some fixing their hijabs around their heads before smoothing down long-sleeved T-shirts over thick cotton tracksuit bottoms. It was prohibitively hot, even for late afternoon, but 22-year-old defender Nevine didn't see her veil as a hindrance. 'I played in the neighbourhood with the boys and they accepted me. Nothing is forbidden, the veil is a choice within my family,' she said, pointing out her uncovered 14-year-old sister Nadine, the second-choice goalkeeper, who was diving around on the hard surface as Coach Raed powered balls at her. 'It's the opposite to what people think,' Nevine said. 'Wearing the veil gives me power.'

Raed began to work the girls, but only lightly. He had told me earlier that he didn't want to scare any of them off by being a disciplinarian. They didn't have enough players. 'You can't be so rough with the girls, like the men's team, telling them: "don't stop here, don't walk here",' he said. 'We give them recreational training, not like hard training for the boys.' Only seven girls could make it to the training session. It was late spring and exams were in full swing, but there were enough present for a four-a-side game if I played as well. 'Come on,' Honey implored, dragging my arm. 'You can come on my side.' This was something of a dilemma. I hadn't brought any kit with me and my jeans had a large hole in the crotch. I was one lunging tackle away from exposing myself to a devout Muslim man and half-a-dozen teenage girls. But the main problem was my complete lack of any discernible footballing talent. The Palestinian team may have been one of the lowest-ranked women's national team in the world, but I still wouldn't have made the cut. Within minutes it became clear just how outclassed I was. Nevine nutmegged me and Jackline sprinted past, leaving me for dead. Fida, Palestine's 21-year-old midfield general, feinted. I responded by theatrically falling over. She skipped around my prone, humiliated figure and powered the ball into the top left-hand corner of the small goal. Raed had a smirk on his face as Nevine held out a hand and helped me to my feet. Honey looked on disapprovingly from the halfway line, perhaps wishing I'd stayed on the bench.

Predictably, my team lost, and with the sun fading from view the girls walked back to the bank of waiting parents and their cars. The silhouettes could have been anywhere else in the world, of proud parents picking up their kids from football training in Colorado, Tel Aviv or Madrid. That was until the huge UN-marked 4x4 came into view. It belonged to Sami Mshasha, whose daughter Sarona was the youngest member of the team. Sami worked for the UN agency that dealt with Palestinian refugees, the UNRWA. He too had seen Hamas's effect on the sport, but from a different angle. 'The prime minister [Ismail Haniyeh of Hamas] has done more than any other minister [for football],' he said, lighting a cigarette as we pulled away from the other girls. 'He used to play in his youth. He was a nasty defender too. He used to call them after every game, even now.'

The prime minister's help hadn't stretched to women's football. Sami had taken a keen interest in his daughter's dreams of footballing stardom, mainly by helping Samar to secure funding for the team. Few, he said, within the Palestinian Football Association or the government seemed that bothered. 'It's basically not their priority,' he shrugged as the Israelis waved us through the checkpoint. Travelling in a UN car certainly had its benefits. 'When I meet them [the FA] you can almost hear them snickering. FIFA allocate 20 per cent of their money for the team but they give Samar no money. You can't have an open-ended pro bono coach or rely on NGOs.'

He also sensed the pressures that are on some of the other girls to give up the game. 'Palestine was always religious, but never conservative,' he said as he drove back towards Jerusalem's old city. 'Now the society is becoming more conservative, which is dangerous, but that tends to happen under occupation. You tend to become fatalistic and things can become violent. The interest is so high in football among the girls. And the commitment is there among the players. But most of them are over 20 so marriage will be knocking on their door whether they like it or not. The family pressure will start now, even among the Christian players.'

The future, as he saw it, was in articulate, intelligent and determined players like Honey, to take on the next generation of players. 'Honey's the future leader of the team. She has to be smart and know the situation, know the politics. Unfortunately, the politics here in sport are as nasty as in national politics.'

I had agreed to meet Honey and her family at their home. I had used the blue-and-white Palestinian buses that spread through the West Bank from East Jerusalem dozens of times, but I had yet to hear anyone talk. A silence enveloped the bus as we trundled towards the wall, carrying students, workers and mothers between the two different worlds. But these were the lucky ones, the people who held Jerusalem ID and had permission to travel or work outside of the West Bank. With the World Bank estimating that unemployment in the West Bank was running at 47 per cent with 44 per cent living below the poverty line, any job, even in the home of the Zionist enemy, was a job worth having. It is one of the great tragedies of the ongoing impasse between Israelis and Palestinians. The Israeli economy needs cheap Palestinian labour to thrive; Palestinians need remittance cheques from Israel to survive.

Honey wasn't one of the lucky ones. Her home was a short distance from Manger Square, where she met me. We walked the short distance to her modest maisonette where she lived with her brother, sister and parents. Outside the walls were covered in Arabic graffiti. Life had been tough for the Thaljiehs in recent years. Honey's father had been unemployed since the intifada and Honey and her brother Eissa were the only breadwinners. Being a Christian had also got harder, according to Honey's mother Nahada. 'The [Palestinian] authorities treat us differently,' she told me as we sat in her comfortable, immaculately kept front room. 'Two of our neighbours were caught speeding by the police. They brought them to the prison for one night and shaved their heads and asked them: "Why are you Christians? It's easy, the life for you, being Christian." And they beat them.' Eissa agreed that there is an unspoken tension between the groups that is forcing many Christians to flee. 'Day by day the Christians are leaving, emigrating. In 50 years you will not see any Christians in Bethlehem.'

Since graduating in Business Administration from the town's university Honey had worked for the sports charity PACE, whilst Eissa had the unenviable task of trying to attract tourists to the West Bank as a travel agent. But Honey's football had given the family hope of a better future. 'We used to play football together in the street,' Eissa recollected in the family's front room. On his arm he sported a large tattoo of a soldier of Christ carrying a cross. 'It wasn't strange for me, but other people thought it was as they were thinking that Arab girls shouldn't play. They got used to it because she was a lot better than everybody else.' Her mother had also got used to her footballing exploits from a young age. 'She started playing at nine but we thought she'd grow out of it,' she said. 'But she didn't. [What Honey] is doing is good for the women of Palestine. It's necessary to have football for women, especially outside America and Europe. It's good to have this team here.'

Honey's own aspirations were like those of any young footballer. She wanted to travel. She had a training camp in Germany and a tournament in Jordan to prepare for. But deep down, despite the huge differences between the problems faced by the Palestinian men's and women's teams, their goals were remarkably similar. For Honey the big prize was one day reaching the World Cup and showing the world, and Palestine's fractured society, that football could triumph where politics had failed. 'The World Cup, that's what I'm aiming for. I was the first woman playing football in Palestine. There was no girl that knew how to play football before, even that women *could* play football.' She put down her mint tea. 'It will be the next generation that will make it but hopefully I will be the coach then. I won't let the team die. *Inshallah*.'

Outside it was getting dark, my cue to leave. Honey walked me back through the flickering street lights and tightly wound alleyways back to the main road and my lift back to Jerusalem. As we said goodbye I noticed the same wall covered in graffiti that I'd passed when it was still daylight.

'What does it say?' I asked.

Honey stopped to read the message, as if it was the first time she had noticed it.

'A Hamas member was killed by Fatah here,' she explained, her face blank. 'It says: "We will never forget. We will have our revenge."'

6

Egypt

CAIRO, ARAB REPUBLIC OF EGYPT,
MAY 2007

After all his planning and high expectations, Amr looked like a man broken by the unforeseen. He sat, along with 40,000 fellow Al Ahly fans, with his face in his hands. The vast stretch of red shirts and flags were motionless in their half of the Cairo International Stadium. The silence was stunted and awkward before a brooding malevolence rose, making me feel uncomfortable for the first time. In the distance, the white half of the stadium was a violent sea of celebration. Furrowed faces darted for explanation between friends and strangers alike. Al Ahly were 2–0 down thanks to a stunning goal worked by Mahmoud 'Shikabala' Abdelrazek Fadlallah. This was a bad thing for two reasons. Firstly, being 2–0 down to anyone was bad enough. Al Ahly weren't a team that lost often. They had once gone almost three years without losing, a streak that lasted for 71 games and had only finally come to an end a few months previously. But this was worse, for a second reason.

They were losing to Zamalek, their hated Cairo rivals, their bourgeois city foes. More people watched this match than any other in Africa, and for the six-figure crowd that turned up to see it in the flesh, the derby meant more than just football. It was about politics, history, identity, colonialism, escapism and pride. And for Amr, leader of Al Ahly's hardcore supporters group, the Al Ahly ultras, the battle was equally important on the terraces as it was on the pitch. For weeks he and his group of ultras had been planning for the game by devising the best way to taunt the opposition's fans. Their group had only been in existence for a few months but they were nothing if not ambitious. They opted for a huge flag, designed to cover most of the north stand, mocking the 6–1 defeat meted out by Ahly in 2002. It was proudly displayed before kick-off. Amr looked behind at it now, an impotent heap of plastic and paint crumpled at the back of the stand.

In Cairo you belong to one of two tribes, one red, one white: Ahly or Zamalek. There are other football teams in Egypt, of course. Ahly and Ismaily have a big rivalry; in Alexandria the biggest team is Ittihad. But nothing gets the blood pumping like Ahly versus Zamalek. Almost every Egyptian has their allegiance. On a taxi journey from Sharjah to Dubai four months previously my Egyptian driver had spilt his colours before he even told me his name. 'I am Ahly, of course,' he said proudly, before regaling me with stories of how 100,000 people would queue from the morning to get in, with another 100,000 stuck outside. Inevitably riots would break out. 'Do not go,' he imparted ominously as I handed over my fare. 'You will be killed.' His words came back to me as the plane landed at Cairo International Airport in the middle of the night. It was Friday, the day that Ahly and Zamalek should have played each other. But the authorities had got wise to the violence and moved it to an early kick-off on Monday, hoping that thousands would be put off by the awkward timing. 'Ahly or Zamalek?' I asked the taxi driver after our conversation in pidgin Arabic, and then pidgin English, had ground to a halt. 'Ahly,' he replied with a shrug, as if there could be only one answer.

The roots of the rivalry can be traced back to when the British army walked the streets of Cairo. Back then football was almost universally regarded as Britain's only popular cultural import. Al Ahly was started in 1907 as the first Egyptian-run club. The name translates as 'The National' and Ahly, wearing the old red colours of the pre-colonial flag, was seen as a team for the nation, a bulwark against occupation and a chance for the average man on the street to come together for a common nationalistic cause. Zamalek, wearing white, was considered the team of the foreigner, the elite. The club was formed in 1911 by George Merzbach, a Belgian lawyer, and went through various iterations, at one point being named after the hated King Farouk before being changed to Zamalek post abdication in 1952. The team was open to anyone and attracted not just the royalists and foreign 'occupiers' but also Cairo's awkward squad: the authors, poets and intellectuals who were uneasy with Egypt's newfound nationalistic confidence.

As much as the Cairo derby was about nationalism, it was also about class: the truly loyal man on the street versus the detached elite. But it has always been bloody. The entire 1971/2 season was cancelled after one particularly bad tempered meeting between the two. Such was the ferocious hatred between the fans that since the 1990s no Ahly versus Zamalek match had been played in their home grounds. Instead, all games were played at Cairo's huge national stadium. The referees were not beyond suspicion either. Foreign officials were flown in to take charge of proceedings. Scottish referees versed in handling the Old Firm rivalry between Celtic and Rangers were particularly popular. Egypt's notoriously baton-happy riot police took the threat of disorder very seriously and swamped the matches any time the two played. In fact, Egypt's riot police had become even more proficient with their batons in recent months. Hosni Mubarak had recently won what opposition parties called a sham election and had fought off threats to his power, especially from the popular but banned Muslim Brotherhood, a well-organised Islamist movement with links to Hamas. Police prevented voters from reaching the polls, intimidation was rife and opposition candidates were either locked up or denied the chance to stand. Mubarak won 89 per cent of the vote. Cairo felt hopeless; intractably poor and squeezed between an authoritarian government and rising Islamic fundamentalism.

Ayman Younis knew a thing or two about the enmity between the two sides of Cairo. As Zamalek's star player in the late 1980s, and a regular in Egypt's national team, Ahly fans targeted him in ever more elaborate, vicious and sometimes hilarious ways. These days he was the main anchor for Egyptian and English Premier League football on state television whilst supplying 3-D advertising mats for sports pitches. He was also on the Egyptian FA's board. I called him from a public telephone in a grocery store near my hostel. He had some bad news. 'There is no training today,' he said. There could have been any number of reasons: the clubs had swapped venues or dates to flummox Egypt's vicious sports press; or worried about fan violence, training might have been cancelled. The answer was far more surprising. 'It's the FA Cup final, Chelsea versus Manchester United. All the players and the coaches want to watch it.' Ayman invited me over to watch the match at his place.

His villa was on the outskirts of Cairo, towards 6 October City. This was where the moneyed upper classes chose to live, away from the noise, poverty and pollution of Cairo in a newly built and rapidly expanding settlement. It derived its name from the date in 1973 which marked the start of the Arab-Israeli war. It was also the same date that President Anwar Sadat – the man who made peace with Israel – was assassinated in 1981. It was as if, rather than struggling to integrate into Cairo, the wealthy had instead decided to start again somewhere nearby.

Short and with tightly curled black hair, Ayman welcomed me into his huge house as if I were a long-lost family member. His three-storey home told me that, post-football, Ayman had not struggled. Back in the 1980s he was a fast, skilful attacking midfielder who had a reputation for raising his game for the big derby. 'I think I played maybe 11 derbies between 1983 and 1994,' he explained. 'I scored four times. I was lucky, I always played well in these matches.' Handily Ayman had set up his large entertainment room, which doubled up as his trophy cabinet, so that I could experience some of his magic on television. He sat me down, passed me a Pepsi and slid the first videotape in. The screen blinked to life, initially a distorted mess of popping feedback, Arabic and neon-green. It was a compilation of his best goals: a scissor kick against Ahly in 1988; goals in the Africa Cup of Nations; the final of the African Champions League. He looked on, engrossed, oblivious to my presence.

'Mubarak was there!' he shouted, pointing at the screen, lifting himself out of his seat at the same time. 'There, he was there!' The crackling Arabic on screen gave way to a Brazilian-esque surge from the overexcited commentator: 'Ayyyyyman Yyoooooooooooounis!' And there he was, with his tight retro-shorts and large Afro, wheeling away in celebration after volleying it into the top left-hand corner. The camera focused in on the mass of white celebrating the goal. Men were standing on the terraces holding their babies up in celebration. 'Ahly fans say this goal was offside,' he said, turning around, breaking his grin and taking on an air of seriousness. 'But it wasn't. That was

the goal of the season. But 1990 was my best season, I scored a horrible number of goals.'

Ayman's best form coincided with Egypt's World Cup appearance
at Italia '90, their first since a brief, one-match appearance at Italy
1934. The stage was set for Ayman's goal-scoring prowess. But he
never made it onto the plane. 'I was in Scotland for the last [warm-up]
game [before the World Cup] and the fucking number eight,' he spat,
still angry at the memory of Egypt's 3–1 victory in Aberdeen 18 years
later. 'The number eight [according to the Scottish FA that shirt was
worn by Aberdeen midfielder Jim Bett] had a problem with me, he
kicked me in the knee and *khalas*, finished, I had to go to Germany for
an operation.' Bett may never realise it but he might indirectly have
had a hand in what was then England's greatest World Cup performance since 1966. Egypt had a strong, defensive-minded team that
drew its opening two group games with the Netherlands and Ireland.
The crunch match came against England, which Egypt lost thanks to
a solitary Mark Wright goal. The group was so tight that if Egypt had
won 1–0 England would have finished bottom. But Egypt had struggled to score goals without Ayman and, as one of Egypt's most creative
forces, he would almost certainly have played in the final game. A 1–1
draw would have created a first in World Cup history: every team
finishing on the same points, with the same goals scored and the same
goals against. England, Egypt, the Netherlands and Ireland's World
Cup future would have been decided on the drawing of lots. Instead
England made it to the semi-finals, Gazza cried and the course of English football changed forever.

The next season Younis went back to being a thorn in Ahly's side,
but he paid a price off the pitch. 'If I go to the stadium I have to go
without my car as they break everything,' he said of Ahly's fans who,
to this day, still hound him in the street. 'When I was playing I had a
lot of problems with Ahly fans. In 1990 I found my BMW car on its
side and they signed it: "Ahly fans". And that was when we lost, 2–0,
but they remembered that I scored in the first game earlier in the season.' That, however, wasn't the worst of it. 'Then there was the time
they attacked me in my home. I had to phone the police. Five thousand Ahly fans came to my street and shouted against me, my wife
and kids, throwing things at us.'

The FA Cup final turned out to be turgid and, with the game instantly forgotten, Ayman offered to drive me back to Cairo. For Ayman, his love of Zamalek, along with its fans, transcended nearly every other impulse in his life, even religion. 'Ask a Zamalek fan, can you change religion?' he said as his sleek black BMW pulled away down the empty highway. 'He wouldn't answer. But you ask them: "Can you change Zamalek?" They'd say "No!" And if you see a policeman, they won't ask you whether you are Muslim or a Christian, they'll ask you whether you are Ahly or Zamalek. It's true.' But there was a historical demarcation when it came to religion. 'Fifty years ago Ahly became the team of the devout [but] Zamalek was the team of the middle classes,' he said.

The car's average speed dropped as we neared Cairo and the conversation turned to Israel. Ayman sucked air sharply through his teeth. 'If you have been to Israel, trust me, someone is following you here.'

'What, even now?' I asked, looking around for any suspicious black cars keeping a steady distance behind us.

'I hate Israel,' Ayman continued. 'Not Israelis, but Israeli politicians and the wars. We've had three of them and lost something like 15,000 people. Everyone has lost someone.' Ayman's BMW pulled to the kerb when we reached Zamalek Island. He offered me his business card and pulled out a fat wedge of Egyptian notes, counting them out in front of me.

'Do you need any money?' he asked. 'I can give you money.'

'I'm OK, Ayman, I have money.'

'Are you sure?' He looked a little offended. 'OK, but if you need anything, ANYTHING, call me. If you need something, tell the person you're a friend of Ayman Younis. Exactly that.'

Ayman was a useful person to know given his status as the Egyptian Gary Lineker. On Monday he would be giving his thoughts in front of the biggest television audience of the year. As much as he was a White Knight to his marrow, he begrudgingly recognised the hold Ahly had on Cairo. They had already wrapped up their fourth consecutive title long before the game. 'Ahly already own the championship,' he conceded through his car window. 'So whatever happens tomorrow, Cairo will already be red.' He pulled away into the stream of traffic and left me on my own, on the pavement, checking over my shoulder for spies.

Zamalek's training ground looked like it was about to collapse. With Ayman as my golden ticket I'd arrived at their huge grey complex on Zamalek Island, by far the most run-down structure in an upmarket and aspirational part of town. Outside, a couple of hundred Zamalek fans had turned up to catch a glimpse of the players as they arrived. They could afford to be more optimistic than Ayman about the derby. Rumours had surfaced in that day's papers that Ahly, who were fighting for honours on four fronts, were to rest the majority of their first team. Even more encouragingly, Manuel José – their eccentric Portuguese manager who had won them their four successive championships and back-to-back African Champions League titles, and regularly boasted he was a better manager than his compatriot José Mourinho – was out of the country. He was on holiday, apparently, although most fans believed he had been asked to step down for a few weeks after infuriating Egypt's religious conservatives by stripping off on the touchline during a league game in protest at a poor refereeing decision.

Still, Manuel claimed that his players were 'bored of success', which had in equal parts infuriated Zamalek and given them a glimpse of their first derby victory in over three years. But they didn't want to look overconfident and their recently appointed and notoriously secretive manager, Frenchman Henri Michel, had banned his players from talking to the press. Michel was one of those managers that stalked the leagues and national teams of Africa, taking one generation to the heights of World Cup qualification before dumping them (or being dumped) and moving on to the next African job. His last job was taking the Ivory Coast to Germany in 2006, where they were knocked out in the first round. At the training ground the only player who would talk to me was Shikabala, Zamalek's best player who was in his second spell at the club after playing briefly for PAOK in Greece. 'I came back because I played with Zamalek since I was very young and Zamalek is my home,' he explained outside the dank, damp changing room. 'The derby is like a championship in itself: if you win it you win the biggest trophy since football started in Egypt. The players will do their best to win tomorrow, inshallah.'

On the other side of Zamalek Island, things were equally tense at Ahly's purpose-built 25,000-seater training ground. Security wouldn't let me in until I lied and said I was from the BBC. But that was just the first layer. Inside three separate flanks of security guards were on hand to keep the press away from Ahly's players whilst they trained. The closest I got was when the team boarded the bus to leave. Even Ahly's genial vice-captain Osama Hosny, famed for his strict adherence to Islam, impeccable manners and beautiful singing voice, looked guiltily at the floor as he appeared, mumbled an apology and climbed onto the coach.

Hosny had recently become one of the most famous voices in Egypt after embarking on a second career as a pop star. He had combined his love of Islam and his magnificent voice into one package and released a bestselling CD singing passages from the Quran. 'He always speaks to me [but] the press get so crazy that the players have stopped talking to us before the match,' sighed Usama, a journalist for an Ahly news website who had hung around for the past three hours just to get a few scraps of gossip. With any hope of a quote gone, we walked to a nearby café to talk about tomorrow's game. 'Ahly and Zamalek hate each other,' he told me over a mud-thick Turkish coffee.

'Is there much trouble at the games?' I asked.

Usama grinned. 'Ahly has an ultras group, they're crazy and they hate Zamalek. I can't tell you how much they hate Zamalek! At the Ahly versus Sfaxien African Champions League final in 2006 they had a lot of bombs and flares and entered with them into the stadium. When Ahly scored . . . the ultras, the only fans who had travelled to the game, let off the bombs.' It was the first time I'd heard of Ahly's ultras but their reputation seemed to be legion. 'The ultras are everywhere,' continued Usama. 'Cairo, Alexandria, 200km away, everywhere. There are maybe 200 officially but a lot of fans want to go with them when they travel so it's a lot more. You have to see them.'

Amr readily agreed to meet me. After a few phone calls I'd managed to get through to the ultra's leader. But it all seemed a little civilised. 'Of course, you can come with us, it will be a pleasure. Do you need a lift? We'll pick you up at Tahrir Square, you know where that is? Five-thirty pm.' He didn't look like how I expected him to. Amr, tall, rake thin and wearing thick-rimmed glasses, jumped out of the car and shook my hand before we squeezed into the car with Mohammed and Ishmail for the short drive to the stadium. 'We are very unique, we are the only club who have several Ahlys named after it in Jeddah, in Yemen, Libya, in the Emirates, Qatar. But Ahly is *the* Ahly, it was the first ever in the whole region to be the first 100 per cent Egyptian so it is very nationalistic,' he explained. 'Zamalek have changed their name so many times we sing: "You used to be half-British, you guys are the rejects".'

Amr started organising Ahly's ultras after spending time studying in England and Milan, immersing himself into the Italian supporter culture where ultra culture was born. It was time, he reasoned, that Ahly had its own fan movement that was separate from the sycophantic organisations that tried as hard as possible to 'suck up to the board'. They had a lot of things to rail against, but Zamalek was at the top of the list. 'In the past Zamalek used to be the bourgeois club, and Ahly the people's club, although that's changed a little these days,' explained Amr. As we neared the ground, I asked Amr why Ahly were so popular today. 'The two biggest political parties in Egypt are Ahly and Zamalek,' he said. 'It's bigger than politics. It's more about escapism. The average Ahly fan is a guy who lives in a one-bedroom flat with his wife, mother-in-law and five kids. And he is getting paid minimum wage and his life sucks. The only good thing about his life is that for two hours on a Friday he goes to the stadium to watch Ahly. That's why it is such an obligation to win every game. It makes people's lives happy. We are probably the only club in the world where we [the fans] expect to win every single game. Ahly is the only thing that makes people happy.'

And with the frustrations of modern life comes the inevitable violence. 'Between Ahly and Zamalek the stadium is segregated now so we don't meet and with so many police it's difficult,' he said. 'The violence happens in all sports. They attack each other's buses or go to the basketball derby between Ahly and Zamalek.' Mohammed, who with his large beard, baggy fatigues and baseball cap, looked like a Californian skater, agreed. 'Egypt is like a police state, they [the police] are the most powerful institution in Egypt without doubt,' he said as we got out of the car. 'So you can't even reach a Zamalek fan, but you can be as open as you like and say what you like in the stadium.'

It became clear as we pulled into the stadium what he meant. Thousands of black uniformed riot officers stood menacingly as a deterrent from the main road up to the stadium entrance. Plain-clothed security officers in dark glasses darted between them, asking suspicious-looking fans for their ID papers and tickets. Twenty thousand fans were already inside Cairo's national stadium chanting songs against their hated rivals: 'You are the white bitches', and 'Come on, come on, come on, fuck the mother of Zamalek'.

The ultras took their usual place at the back of the lower stand and discussed the best way of unwrapping their vast flag, the highlight of their achievements thus far. The stadium's huge electronic screen fluttered into life. There was Ayman Younis, his face now the size of a bus, talking the audience and the crowd through great moments from Ahly–Zamalek derbies of old, many concerning his input as a player. The Ahly fans jeered and whistled when they saw him appear. 'He was good, but he was always fat,' said Mohammed as the rest of the ultras, now 50-strong and rapidly growing, broke into hysterics. The reverie was broken by the piercing sound of the call to prayer. The more devout rushed to the nearest piece of flat ground next to the popcorn sellers. In the absence of a prayer mat, they used their Ahly flags instead.

The ultras launched their flag. It was vast, far bigger than anything else at the ground, and provoked rapturous applause from the Ahly fans. Amr looked on proudly at his creation, his little piece of Milano that he'd brought to Ahly's terraces. It was the last time I saw him smiling. From the minute the whistle was blown, it was clear that Ahly was in trouble, playing like a team that had made nine changes and had no coach. Shikabala was everywhere, first to every ball, no doubt spurred on by the abuse hurled down on him. By the time he had helped Zamalek take a two-goal lead, he was on his knees, bowing in front of Ahly's fans, infuriating the ultras.

'Why do Ahly hate him so much?' I managed to ask amid the uproar.

'He is pure Zamalek,' Amr replied.

The second goal had started to divide a fan base unaccustomed to losing. 'It's only one loss,' a man in a suit offered. 'One loss!' shouted Amr, before admonishing him for his low standards. A Nubian

Egyptian, a head scarf piled high on his head, shrugged and pointed at the sky: 'I hate Ahly, but what can I do?' The game ended 2–0. Ahly was vanquished for only the second time in three years. Yet the fans didn't recognise the defeat. As Zamalek paraded in a lap of honour, Ahly's fans refused to leave, screaming out their chants louder than before, over and over again: 'One, two, three, four, five, six, Ahly!', a reference to their 6-1 victory in 2002 that featured on Amr's banner.

Bottles and cans rained down onto the pitch and onto the thin black line of police keeping the ultras from the pitch. A bottle fizzed past my nose and cracked on the shield of a policeman cowering under the barrage. The jeering, seething mass, thousands strong, rolled out of the stadium. Momentarily, I was on my own. Fights broke out between police and fans. Fists flew and blood was spilt, but still the fans marched on, chanting: 'Ahly, Ahly.'

For a moment I had lost everyone as the mob carried us out of the stadium towards the main road, too big even for the phalanx of near-by riot policemen to contain. But then I spotted a gap in the crowd where Amr and the ultras were waiting, panting. The human river of red rumbled defiantly, and noisily, on. Ayman Younis was right. What-ever the result, Cairo was always going to be painted red.

We stood in the sand car park until the last of the crowd passed by and the ultras packed their banner back into the car. They had lost, but claimed an immoral victory by deciding to celebrate by getting some beer and weed. 'Until the 1980s it was virtually legal,' laughed Mohammed. 'Everyone smoked it, Muslims, Christians; but even now the police don't care as long as you don't make trouble. My last dealer? Man, he was a sheikh from a local mosque.' We drove back through Cairo's thick, polluted air to Amr's flat. Rather than arriving at a modest apartment, the car pulled up in front of a walled com-pound, complete with guards. It turned out that Amr came from a storied family. His father was the general secretary of the Confeder-ation of African Football (CAF). We were all sworn to secrecy.

We sat in Amr's flat watching famous Egyptian movies from the 1960s. 'You look at any Arab television channel at 7pm,' explained Amr. 'Eighty per cent of the films or programmes are from Egypt. We've been making films for 100 years. All the musicians are Egyptian too.' The Saudis had an authority bequeathed by Mecca and Medina; the other Gulf states have fabulous oil wealth; the Iranians have the legacy of the Persian Empire, of poetry and literature; the catchphrase of the tourist board of Syria was 'The Cradle of Civilisation'; the Iraqis had Baghdad and its history of advances in astrology, maths and medicine. The Egyptians too had a glorious past. A common refrain, as Ayman had told me, was: 'I'm not African, I'm not Arab, I'm Pharaonic.' Modern Egypt had suffered under the weight of poverty, nepotism and dictatorship, but at 7pm every night proof of the country's cultural greatness was there for everyone to see.

By 3am it was time to leave the ultras and head home. Outside I stood on the pavement and tried to hail a cab. The bookshop behind me was covered in posters of Osama Hosny. His almost-handsome face and ginger hair was advertising his latest CD singing the passages from the Quran that had made him even more famous. I got into a taxi and left Cairo. I had presumed that it was the last time I would hear of Amr and his ultras. But no. The young men I had met that day would play their part in one of the most seismic shifts in the modern history of the region, and help reshape a new Egypt.

But I didn't know that yet as the driver smoothly drove his way around Cairo's dead streets. We both sat in silence.

'Ahly or Zamalek?' I finally asked him.

'Ahly,' the driver replied.

Of course he was.

7

Iraq

AMMAN, HASHEMITE KINGDOM OF JORDAN, JUNE 2007

It was the hottest day in Amman in 90 years and Jorvan Vieira had taken refuge in the shadow thrown by the main stand of the King Abdullah stadium. Around him his squad of young footballers joked and chattered in accelerated Arabic, stretching on the sidelines in the green and white colours worn by the Lions of Mesopotamia. They didn't know Jorvan well; he wasn't too familiar with them either. It was only the second time he had met his players, a few weeks after the thin, stubbly faced, small-framed man with bookish glasses had landed himself the most difficult job in world football, as coach of the Iraqi national football team. 'This is the hardest job in the world, definitely,' Jorvan agreed earlier as we stood pitchside – waiting for the Jordanian national team to finish training. The Jordanians were running late after insisting that they prayed in their dressing room, as they did before every training session and match. The Iraqis didn't want to pray. Or rather, they had agreed not to pray. It had been decided long ago that religion, such a divisive force in their homeland, should be kept out of the team's pre-match preparations.

'These boys,' began Jorvan absentmindedly as the Jordanians stretched in front of us, 'I have to deal with many, many problems: social, political, internal. Most of these players don't know where they are. Every minute the situation changes.' Jorvan wasn't new to Middle Eastern football politics. A Brazilian Muslim, he had spent most of his career coaching in Saudi Arabia, Oman, Egypt and Morocco. He was fourth choice for the job and was only given a two-month contract. Jorvan was brought in to guide the team at the Asian Cup being held in Indonesia, Thailand, Malaysia and Vietnam. It was the region's top tournament, Asia's equivalent of the European Championship or the Copa America, and second only to the World Cup in importance. The Iraqi FA didn't have high hopes for the tournament and Jorvan was soon given a reminder as to the huge obstacles that faced him and his team. 'We lost our physio, two days before we got here,' he explained as his players finally trotted onto the field. 'A bomb exploded in Baghdad and he was passing by. He was on his way to the travel agent to buy his ticket to come here.'

The Iraqi national team had eluded me until now. For six months I had been chasing an audience with them through three countries: first in Kurdish northern Iraq, then the UAE, before finally catching up with them in Jordan. Earlier in the year, in the UAE capital of Abu Dhabi, I had watched the Iraqi team take part in the Gulf Cup, a biennial tournament that involved all the Gulf states minus Iran. The veteran coach Akram Salman was in his third spell in charge of the national team. Actually, it was technically his fourth. After being threatened by insurgents five months previously he quit his post and fled to the safety of the Kurdish north, which had remained stable as the rest of the country burned. The FA refused to accept his resignation and he was talked into coming back.

Iraq's team was still highly regarded but managed to lose to Saudi Arabia in its final group game and was eliminated. After a forensic investigation of the Gulf Cup performance, Salman was fired four months later without taking charge of another game, proving that, even after you put your life on the line for your country, there's no sentimentality in football. It made more sense to bypass Iraq and the UAE and head straight for Amman. Since the Second Gulf War as many as one million Iraqis, fleeing the anarchy in their homeland, were now living in Jordan, an island of peace in a sea of instability. To its east, Iraq slowly imploded. To the west, the West Bank crumbled under the weight of internecine warfare between Hamas and Fatah, agitating Jordan's already sizeable Palestinian-descended majority. Israel, Syria, Lebanon and Saudi Arabia – all with their own internal problems – surrounded it. Yet somehow Jordan had gone about its business, made deals, played countries off against each other and generally done anything it could to survive. Much of the credit sat with the wily King Hussein, father of the current monarch, King Abdullah II, who could keep all the diplomatic balls in the air at the same time; making peace with Israel, keeping the Americans onside and staying cordial with Saddam Hussein. Jordan had long been thought of as the quiet man of the Middle East. Huge portraits of father and son erected over one stand peered down as the Iraqis trained below.

To make the Iraqi diaspora feel even more at home their national football team had decamped there as well, meeting up for training and playing its competitive matches in Amman, waiting for the unlikely event that peace would take hold so they could return to Baghdad, Erbil or Basra and once again enjoy home advantage. Before leaving for the Asian Cup they were preparing for the West Asian Championship, a biennial tournament that brought together the Middle East's best teams for a knockout tournament. It had been due to take place in Beirut the previous year but the war with Israel made that impossible. Instead it was postponed and moved to Jordan. The problem was that the teams competing all had colourful histories off the pitch: Iran, Iraq, Syria, Lebanon, Jordan and Palestine. Almost every single permutation was charged with political significance. Iran and Iraq had fought a bloody war in the 1980s, a war that claimed as many as a million lives. And with Iraq degenerating into an inter-sect civil war, the country's Sunni minority feared the influence of Iran – who they suspected had more influence over Iraq's Shia majority than the government – more than the Americans. Syria had long had a hand in Lebanese politics, occupying the country from 1976 until 2005, and only pulling out after the assassination of ex-Lebanese prime minister Rafik Hariri, which triggered a series of protests dubbed the Cedar Revolution. One of the UN's investigations into Hariri's assassination put the blame on the shoulders of the Syrian secret service, whose influence many in Lebanon believed still loomed large. The Syrians, of course, denied any wrongdoing.

The Jordanians and the Palestinians also have a turbulent history. The creation of Israel saw hundreds of thousands flee to what was then called Transjordan, on the East Bank of the River Jordan. The many wars and conflicts that had arisen since 1948 had seen a steady trickle of Palestinians enter Jordan, changing its ethnic mix. Now, depending on who you listened to, Palestinians make up anywhere between 50 and 80 per cent of Jordan's population. Fearing being overrun, political power consolidated in the hands of ethnic Hashemite Jordanians whilst Palestinians struggled against discrimination – as in many other Arab states – to get work, housing or education. Instead, the Palestinians excelled in making their own future and were known for their successful business interests. Still, Palestinians could at least be fully naturalised in Jordan, something that was impossible almost everywhere else in the Arab world.

If the potential for a feisty tournament was already there, several developments had made the tournament potentially even more volatile. Two players from one of Lebanon's top clubs, Nejmeh, a Shia-supported but Sunni-owned club, were killed in a car bombing targeting one of Lebanon's Christian opposition MPs. In Gaza, open warfare had broken out between Fatah and Hamas, the lonely, overpopulated strip having been cut off from the rest of the world. But Jorvan was preparing for his next game, a must-win match against Palestine for a place in the semi-finals, with by far the most difficult set of circumstances to overcome. Almost every single player in the national team had now left Iraq. The league was only operating in the northern Kurdish city of Erbil, where the Kurdish Regional Government could ensure relative safety. Every player had been touched by tragedy, threatened by insurgents or feared being kidnapped by criminal gangs.

'How can they come through? Where can they train?' replied Jorvan when I asked how the next generation of players could emerge under such anarchy. 'Iraq will miss one or two generations because of the war. How can they develop sports in Iraq? Did you hear about the boys from taekwondo? It could happen with any player here.'

Hours before Iraq kicked off the tournament against Iran, news reached the squad of the fate of the 'boys from taekwondo', illustrating just how dangerous it was to be a sportsman or woman in Iraq. In 2006, 15 athletes aged between 18 and 26 were kidnapped in western Iraq on their way to a training camp in Jordan. A year later, their remains were found in a ditch near Ramadi. All had been shot in the head. The Iraqi national team wore black armbands during a diplomatic 0–0 draw with Iran.

The dangers were such that most players chose not to return home and those who did soon regretted it. Goalkeeper Noor Sabri had seen his brother-in-law killed a few weeks previously. Midfielder Haitham Kadhim watched as gunmen stormed onto the pitch during a match in Baghdad to execute one of his teammates. 'I'd lost two members of my family,' explained Hawar Mulla Mohammed, the team's Kurdish striker. The executions, bombings and insecurity had got so bad he left his home in Baghdad and signed for Al Ain, a club in the middle of the UAE, to ensure his safety. 'It's difficult when you have no safety. Cars explode all the time. I had to pick up my two guns before going to practice, because I'd been threatened,' he said nonchalantly as he was warming up. 'You can buy guns anywhere in Baghdad. You need them. I don't go back any more.'

With the Jordanians finally departed, Jorvan started running the team through its paces. It wasn't lost on him just what a potential powder keg the tournament was. 'All it takes is one match,' he said grinning before rejoining the squad on the pitch. 'And then, BOOM!'

The Iraqi team's coach moved quietly past the Wihdat refugee camp, over the still-intact tracks of the old, defunct Hejaz railway – the great, crazy Ottoman project designed to link Istanbul to Mecca which T.E. Lawrence regularly bombed during the Arab Revolt – and into the centre of Amman towards the Iraqi team hotel. The players and coaching staff, exhausted by training in the heat, dozed as the bus rocked and bucked through the traffic and badly tarmacked roads. The only man awake was first-team coach Ahmed-Rahim Hamed. Captain Rahim, as the players referred to him, was a legend of Iraqi football. He had played in the great Iraqi team of the 1980s, considered to be Iraq's finest crop of players after they reached the World Cup finals in 1986. Back then he was a 23-year-old striker and one of the youngest in the squad, playing alongside the current head of the Iraqi FA, Hussein Saeed Mohammed. The team narrowly lost all three games by a single goal against Paraguay, Belgium and hosts Mexico. To the outsider this was a respectable result for a team from Asia, which received just two World Cup spots in Mexico. But the players knew that anything less than silverware would upset the man who had been put in charge of Iraqi football: Uday Hussein.

Saddam's psychopathic eldest son had a myriad of interests – torture, extortion and football. After proving that he wasn't quite yet ready to take the mantle as Saddam's chosen successor by beating his father's valet to death in front of horrified guests at a party hosted in honour of the wife of the Egyptian President Hosni Mubarak, Uday was imprisoned before being sent to Switzerland to lie low. When he returned, however, he was handed the keys to Iraq's sporting empire, which he used to enrich himself as head of Iraq's National Olympic Committee. He also used some of his unique motivational skills on Iraqi footballers. On the journey to central Amman Rahim recalled one incident that still upset him, mainly because Uday ended his homage to his favourite player. 'You knew that if you didn't play well, Uday would do something bad,' said Rahim, running his hands through his dark hair. 'I loved Kevin Keegan, he was my best player, and I had a perm like him. After one game [that Iraq lost] Uday shaved everybody's hair. That's when I lost my perm.' Uday may now be dead, killed in a hail of American bullets four years earlier, but Rahim and the rest of Iraq's football community were still being punished for their involvement with the national team. Rahim had to move to Erbil after he received one death threat too many. 'I got a letter that said we will kill your children and . . . make something . . . with my daughter. They fired at my house twice. So I moved to Erbil. I'm Shia. I don't care, I'm Muslim and Iraqi. But now I sit in a small flat in a dirty area. It's expensive. My rent is more than my brother's rent in Holland.'

Others were less keen to talk about their time under Uday. Hussein Saeed Mohammed, the president of the Iraqi Football Association, was apparently Saddam Hussein's favourite player. He held Iraq's international goal-scoring record – scoring 78 times in 137 appearances – and was the team's captain, scoring the goals that secured Iraq's only World Cup qualification in 1986. His goal-scoring prowess had alerted the world's best clubs but he never got a sniff at playing for any of them. 'I had many teams that wanted me to play for them. Real Madrid wanted to know about me,' he said when we sat down to talk. But his dream move was scuppered. 'The government refused and wouldn't let me go and be professional.' The Iraqi regime's pathological hatred of foreign, Western influences was one reason for it. The other was Uday, who demanded a huge cut from any contracts players signed for foreign clubs. Former Iraqi captain Habib Jaffar – who told the *Guardian* how he'd been beaten with cables and forced to jump into vats of raw sewage following bad results – had to hand over 40 per cent of his earnings to Uday when he signed a contract with a Qatari club. Hussein would have been expected to do the same. Despite the hardships he had faced, he didn't want to talk about his time under Uday. 'We don't want to speak about the past,' he replied tetchily when I asked about the influence Uday had over the dressing room. 'I am the president for three years and we have had many difficulties now. No players have suffered like Iraqi players have suffered. All our teams qualify for all the tournaments. And we are proud that we have united our people under the umbrella of sport. There is no violence in Iraq when our team is playing. Everyone is watching television.'

Sportsmen and women had increasingly paid a high price for their visibility post-Saddam, along with the fans. 'They have kidnapped my driver and my bodyguard. For what reason? What do they need? Last year we had a match in Baghdad, a semi-final, 50,000 people were in the stadium and they fired many rockets at them. Why kill people who want to come and watch?' he asked incredulously. 'The cycling coach was killed; the wrestling coach was killed; the captain of the volleyball team was killed; many killings. But we don't stop because sportsmen are part of the people in Iraq. When the people suffer, we suffer with them.' The list he left out was even bigger: there was, of course, the boys from taekwondo; Iraq's head tennis coach murdered along with two players; the majority of the Olympic Committee, plus 30 staff, seized in one raid by kidnappers wearing army uniforms. To literally survive in his post for three years was an achievement in itself for Hussein. His aim was to get back to the glory years, to the team that excelled in the 1980s even with the constant fear of mutilation and imprisonment. 'I am proud of our players and our coach. We put it here on our logo, on our jersey.' He pointed at the breast of his brown sports jacket – 'I am Iraqi. In the future we will be a great team again.'

Thousands of Iraqi fans sat in the afternoon sun on a working day waiting for their team to take on Palestine. Amman's International Stadium looked like it had once been futuristic, with its plastic-looking cladding hiding an ugly concrete and iron frame. But it was busy for a mid-afternoon kick-off on a working day with Iraqi fans milling around outside. 'Jordan is good,' said Nasir, an Iraqi Christian, with the kind of intonation that you knew would be followed by a 'but'. 'But the government doesn't let us work. I brought my savings because if the government catches us working they send us back. It's a hard life, but at least it's safe.' Another spectator with time on his hands had brought his entire family along for a rare taste of Iraqi pride. 'I've been here a year. I had to come here when my brother was kidnapped,' said Essam, a Sunni sewing-machine salesman who was there with his wife and two kids. 'When we see our team we feel like it's home.' Given the huge Palestinian diaspora, I had expected thousands of fans supporting the old country. But the only Palestine fans I could find were a group of pissed off young men who couldn't afford to get a ticket. 'We can't watch because they doubled the prices because the Iraqis are here and they are very rich. It's not fair, it's like 6 JDs [Jordanian Dinars, about $9, a ticket], we have no oil, the Palestinians don't even have money to buy cigarettes,' said Salman, a Palestinian student living in Amman, who wanted to show solidarity. 'This team is important because it brings us together, Hamas and Fatah. This team is unity, this team will give us attention.'

It was an important time for unity. The civil war between Fatah and Hamas, between the West Bank and Gaza, had created an almost intractable separation between the two groups and two territories. Salman, who spoke in a strong North American accent from his days studying in Canada, knew who was to blame.

'Israel and America,' he said.

'Not Hamas?' I asked.

'Not Hamas, my friend,' he replied. 'When you have poverty and unemployment anything can happen. They [Israel and America] have deprived the Palestinian people of everything.' The football team, though, seemed to be functioning OK despite the chaos back home. The team's Gaza contingent, 13 players in all, managed to make it out before the border was shut.

'Why can they share a football team but not a government?' I asked.

'Why?' repeated Salman. 'Because the football team is from the people. Fatah and Hamas are made from the Israelis and the Americans and we know who they are. Trust me. The solution is for the refugees to go home. I'm a refugee. I was born a refugee, my father was born a refugee, my grandfather was born a refugee and I would not give up a single piece of my land. The UN can sort out Jerusalem, but I just want to go back home. I would die for it.'

Salman was 23 and had never set foot in Palestine. He wouldn't tell me which side he supported although he was clearly no fan of the Palestinian President Mahmoud Abbas. 'I wish he was dead,' he replied deadpan. 'He is a faulty sperm. He shook hands with the invaders. The South Africans didn't shake hands with the whites, the Vietnamese didn't shake hands with the Americans. He is a disgrace to us. So was Arafat.'

The game itself was a scrappy affair. Even though the Iraqi side of the stadium was full, compared to the 12 Palestinian fans who could afford the steep entry price, the Lions of Mesopotamia were devoid of creativity and had no idea how to get through a Palestinian side that put 10 men behind the ball in searing temperatures. By half-time the fans had had enough and started shouting for their favourite player: Hawar Mulla Mohammad. Hawar had been on the bench resting an injury, Jorvan had told me. But an Iraqi journalist covering the match for an Australian newspaper had revealed that he had thrown a tantrum when he wasn't made captain and was dropped as punishment. With things going badly Jorvan didn't have a choice. Hawar came on and swiftly dispatched an 86th-minute – twice taken – penalty to break Palestine's resistance 1–0. Later, Hawar was mobbed by more than a hundred fans who had waited for him to appear by the team coach, a swirling pack of Iraqi flags, digital cameras and mobile phones preventing him from leaving. Hawar didn't mind. The adulation was probably vindication for being upset about the captaincy. It took the police to eventually drag him out. He reluctantly stepped onto the team bus.

Each national team clustered in groups in the lobby of the Arena Hotel. Every group of footballers was demarcated by what was embossed onto the back of their tracksuits – the Syrians sticking together in one corner, the Palestinians in another, the Iranians in yet another. The gangs didn't mingle, only giving a cursory nod as they swaggered past one another in twos or threes.

Sitting down sipping on a thimble of Arabic coffee, with a shining bald pate and a moustache that made him look a little like Mussolini, was Emile Rustom. Emile was the head coach of the Lebanese national team, a Maronite Christian. This usually wouldn't warrant a mention but in Lebanese football, the demarcation between religious and political groups was arguably more pronounced than even in Iraq. 'Anywhere we go to play everybody says: "are you still playing football in Lebanon?"' he laughed. 'We are living day by day in Lebanon, we don't know what will happen tomorrow. Every day is a dramatic event.' The problem, Emile told me, was that each team had a strong link to each of the country's competing communities. And when Sunni, Shia, Druze and Christian teams met one another, it tended to end in fighting on the terraces. The authorities had banned fans from attending games, such was the fear that inter-religious fighting could spark wider instability at a time when Lebanon was still weak internally, both politically and economically, and vulnerable. 'There are teams for Hezbollah like Al Ahed. But it's a good thing if Hezbollah gives money for a club to help football. Mr Hariri [Saad, former prime minister Rafik Hariri's son] is giving money to Ansar and Nejmeh. We don't have the basics. We don't have sponsors, no money. If this political party is giving money then that is good.'

But Emile insisted that, within the national team, there were no differences. To prove his point he called over three players: Paul Rustom, his young son who was a striker for the Maronite Catholic team Sagesse, Ali Yaakoub from the Hezbollah-supported Al Ahed, and Bilal el Najjarine from the Sunni-owned team Nejmeh. 'When we play against each other, me and Bilal make trash talk against each other in the game, but we are best of friends afterwards,' explained Paul, the three chatting easily together. 'Our teams are a symbol for the community. Sagesse is a Christian team [but] we [Christians] are eight out of thirty. There are six or seven Sunnis, one or two Druze and the rest are Shia. We all go out with each other.' The problem was that this fraternity hadn't transferred onto the terraces. 'It is because of Nejmeh versus Ansar,' said Bilal. 'Forty-five thousand would attend the game and half of them would be Shia, half of them Sunni. They would fight.'

'The political problems are reflected between the fans,' continued Paul. 'If the Sunni and Shia leaders have a disagreement, there's trouble. This season the fans were forbidden but next season they will hopefully be back.' Ali, whose team was supported by Hezbollah, agreed but played down the role of the political organisation. 'The club is for Hezbollah, yes, but they do not interfere too much. They give money but they let the club spend it on players.'

'Does Hassan Nasrallah go to the games?' I asked.

'No!' shrieked Ali, the others laughing at the thought of Hassan Nasrallah on the terraces. 'The Israelis will get him!'

Things hadn't started well for the Lebanese at the West Asian Championship. The death of two Nejmeh players – teammates of Bilal's – after training two weeks before in a car bombing had dampened the mood. Worse, with Syrian involvement being blamed for the spate of targeted assassinations against politicians, who all happened to be from the anti-Syria political bloc, the fixture list had thrown up their eastern neighbour in the first game. They promptly lost 1–0, which didn't go down well back in Beirut. 'The fans were blaming us,' said Paul. 'They said: "Why did you lose? You could have lost to anyone by 100 goals, but not against Syria."' But there was, according to Emile, little animosity between the players. 'This is a political problem,' he stressed, finishing up his coffee and gathering his players for their early afternoon rest. Tomorrow they had to win the game against hosts Jordan. A victory was the only chance they had of making the semis. 'It's true that the Syrian army in Lebanon made many mistakes against the Lebanese people. They were abusing their power to have money, to kill people, to jail people. It happens during the occupation of any country, 30 years of occupation [but] we met the players before and it was a clean game. Many people back home wanted us to win against Syria. Sports people don't think in the same way.'

With that, the four got up, hugged me one by one, and left. 'Call me the moment you get to Beirut,' Emile insisted, giving me his phone number and promising to show me around. 'The season will start in September, hopefully, and the fans will be back too.' His son was less sure. 'September? With Lebanon you never know,' Paul added mischievously. 'There will probably be another war in Lebanon in September.'

Another coach with off-the-field worries was Palestine's Mohammed Sabah, who I had met in Jericho during the West Bank cup match earlier in the year. His Palestine side had narrowly been beaten by Iraq the day before but his players had other things on their minds. 'The main problem is the situation in Gaza as we have 13 players from there,' he told me. Mohammed was in the lobby reading the paper, trying to devour as much information as possible on what was going on in Gaza. It seemed that finding out about the political turmoil was equally important a job for the coach of the Palestinian national team as keeping tabs on training. 'What has happened in the past week means they are very worried, stressed.' The tensions between Hamas and Fatah that had simmered since the former's parliamentary victory in 2006 had finally come to a head. Hamas was, after weeks of bloody fighting that had killed several hundred Palestinians, in total control of the Gaza Strip. The Israelis responded by closing all the borders and isolating Gaza. Effectively, there were now two Palestinian governments. 'It's very difficult at the moment as some of the players and coaches wanted to go back as their minds and their hearts are with their families in Gaza but they can't because the border at Rafah is closed,' Mohammed explained.

The schism had long existed for the Palestinian national football team. Unable to travel between Gaza and the West Bank, there were essentially two national teams, one set of players training in Gaza, the other in the West Bank. They only met together a few days before a match in a third country, usually Egypt. Yet Mohammed was positive that within the camp there was no Fatah–Hamas rivalry. 'I think that a Palestinian team makes a unit for the Palestinian people,' he said when I asked whether any disagreements had broken out. 'The players are close, they are sharing rooms, training. Every player here is an ambassador. When you represent your country you must be good in every way. No players say I am Hamas, I am Fatah. Yes, some are members, but they are friends. If the people were like the Palestinian team there would be no problems.'

He brought out his captain, Saeb Jendeya, who played for Ittihad Shajeya in Gaza City, to prove his point. 'Every second I am thinking about my family,' he said. 'Every time I'm here I'm calling them in Gaza asking about the border, when they are going to open it and whether my family has food or not. In the past two days it has been difficult for them to get food and I have five very young kids. And my salary from the government hasn't been paid for ten months.' Oddly, as the West Bank and Gaza were on the brink of a civil war, a star-studded Real Madrid side fresh from winning La Liga was making its way to Israel for a peace match against a mixed Israeli–Palestinian side, hosted by Israeli president Shimon Peres and his Peres Center for Peace in Tel Aviv the next day. It was odd because Mohammed didn't seem to know any of the Palestinian players taking part in the match. Stranger still, the official press release with biographies of the Palestinian players taking part stated that they were Palestinian national team players playing in the Palestinian First Division – which was abandoned several years previously due to Israeli movement restrictions. I emailed the Peres Center and Roni Kresner gave an explanation:

> None of the players were from Gaza. Due to the present situation in the Gaza Strip, we were unable to include players from Gaza. That is, had they participated, they would have been severely punished for taking part in such a match. [Due to the dominance of Hamas in the Gaza Strip.]
>
> As for the players being part of the national team, there is a Palestinian national squad, and the coach selects players from the squad for each game. You are correct in stating that there was a match in Amman the same day. Players from the national squad played in that match. Similarly, players from the national squad took part in our match at Ramat Gan stadium. The coach, who is linked to the Palestinian Football Association, is looking for a way to punish these players for participating in a mixed Israeli–Palestinian team (a sad state of affairs!).

For Mohammed, though, the issue was cut and dried. 'No, I'm not sharing [a pitch with] the occupation,' he said when I asked why none of his squad was in Tel Aviv. 'The Israelis must know that when we have our rights we can play. But when we are killed and they make checkpoints so we can't play like in other countries? In my club [Thaqafi Tulkarem], many times they stop us going to the match, turn us away and arrest some players. It's very difficult to play and want peace when they won't give us our rights. I want peace, two states, but until now we cannot move freely, we cannot go from city to city. It's difficult to share a team over here, when over there they arrest my brother.'

Mohammed's sentiment summed up what I had heard from virtually everyone I had spoken to who was connected to Palestinian football. For them, football was about attaining international recognition and achieving internal unity. Football wouldn't be used to attain peace with Israel. In fact, the Iraq, Lebanon and Palestine national teams all had very different problems to deal with, but had one thing in common. All represented a forlorn, distant hope for unity in their homelands. In Lebanon and Iraq's case, the national football team was a rare chance to build some form of nationalistic pride by bringing together disparate, competing sectarian groups under one flag, something that a weak central government had singularly failed to do. For Palestine, the national team had always given the illusion of that elusive prize: statehood. But now, more than ever, it had to also try and engender its own form of common cause, bridging the ever widening gap between the supporters of Fatah and Hamas which had threatened to drive a permanent wedge between the West Bank and Gaza.

That night another group of Palestinian footballers also had to deal with the grim reality of division back home. I'd received an email from Honey, the captain of the Palestinian women's national team. After we had said our goodbyes in Bethlehem a few months previously, Honey and the rest of the squad had been in Germany to take part in a three-week-long training camp in anticipation of the women's West Asian Championship taking place in September. Now, however, they were stuck in Amman on their way home. The players' floor at the Sandy Palace Hotel was buzzing with activity, girls darting in and out of the different rooms as Coach Raed struggled to calm the excited players down. He nodded his head in recognition and disappeared into his room, unable or unwilling to control his hyperactive players.

Samar Mousa, the matriarchal team manager, and Honey sat in a large, modest suite on their own, eating a fast-food meal served in a polystyrene tray. They both looked worn-out after 20 days of intensive training and media attention. After such a high, Amman proved somewhat of an anti-climax. None of the players knew if they would be allowed back home. In Bethlehem, Samar told me, armed Fatah militias were roaming the streets rounding up Hamas members in retaliation for the latter's coup in Gaza. Not only that, two players and one coach from Gaza had been affected in different ways. One player had been refused permission to leave in the first place thanks to an overprotective father who disapproved of her playing football. A second didn't know how to get home as Israel had closed the border. One coach had to leave early after hearing that a rocket had destroyed her home. Now, all the players crossed their fingers and hoped they even had homes to go back to. Honey soon perked up when we talked about Germany. 'What was the best part of it?' I asked, before leaving them to try and negotiate safe passage home. 'To taste freedom,' she replied quickly. 'To not have to carry my passport wherever you go.' I left her sitting on the floor, deep in thought, staring at a faraway spot on the opposite wall.

The Iraqi team bus pulled through Amman's city limits, rocking to ear-splitting Arabic music. Training had been light this time, and with good reason. The team were recovering from their best performance of the tournament so far, a 3–0 victory over Syria. The game was held on a Friday yet, unlike every other single Middle Eastern football crowd that gathered on Islam's holy day, nobody prayed. The fans had taken on board the same mantra as their football team: religion was a private matter.

I had sat through the drills, patiently waiting to talk to more of the players. But on the bus, I was expected to dance. As soon as the bus had started, music from the famous Iraqi singer Husam al Rassam crackled through speakers that couldn't handle the volume. Drums rattled like gunfire as the players danced and shouted in delight, occasionally getting thrown into the lap of a teammate as the coach driver veered around a corner. Younis Mahmoud, the team's star striker and captain, and Nashat Akram, looked at me strangely. 'Come on,' Nashat implored, taking my hand and leading me to the centre of the bus. 'You can dance.' It didn't seem like a bad idea to be part of the team-bonding ritual. The whole team circled around as best they could and clapped me in. Defender Jassim Ghulam took the lead, hauling his shirt off over his bald head, bowing slightly, circling his fingers and jutting his neck from side to side. Every few beats he would slap an arm across his chest. I tried to mimic his actions. The whole coach descended into mocking laughter as the players started to mimic my rigid movements. Those that weren't dancing were filming it on their mobile phones. Jassim took things a step forward, pulling at my T-shirt and slapping his chest whilst urging me to join him in his semi-naked revelry. I slowly peeled off my top, revealing painfully white skin, and stumbled along to the beat as we slapped each other's backs. The two minutes seemed to go on for hours. The only thing you could hear over the sound of the music was the sound of laughter. Nashat slapped me on the back and walked me back to the seat. Behind me a group of players were watching the video back – me, pasty white, red neck from sunburn, dancing like a middle-aged woman.

Jorvan watched and gave a wry smile. 'We have to give the Iraqi people a good mirror. Inside the national team there are no differences between Shia and Sunni. I was asked, how can you coach Iraq? I said, "I don't have ammo, no grenades, no M45, no axe." I'd like victory to bring peace to Iraq. They don't have to pay me if I can help bring peace.'

Mohammad Nasser and Nashat talked business as we trundled through Amman's darkening early evening. Both had negotiated their way out of Iraq: Mohammed to Apollon Limassol in Cyprus, Nashat to Al Shabab in Saudi Arabia. The key, they said, was getting an agent. 'Most Iraqis don't have one but it's crucial because he can drop you in any country,' said Nashat. He had grounds to be more optimistic than most on the team. Nashat had been promised a top-four club in Europe. What he got was a visit from Sunderland, which was stretching the definition of top-four somewhat, but it at least meant that he was on the Premier League's radar. Nashat had even heard rumours that a Sunderland scout was at the first Iraq–Iran match. 'Iraqis can play anywhere in the world, but it would be a dream to play for [then coach] Roy Keane,' he said. 'I sent them my DVD and, *inshallah*, I'll hear something.' Mohammed had also been given some grand promises. He was promised Europe, and he got it, sort of. 'No one can see me play in Cyprus,' he complained. 'So I sacked my agent. I have one at the moment, an Iranian, and he's promised me a top-four club in Greece, England or Spain.' Still, life was preferable to back home for Mohammed, a Shiite who had lived in the southern port city of Basra. As a footballer who earned a handsome wage in Europe, albeit in one of the continent's lower leagues, he was a target for criminal gangs looking to kidnap players and make a handsome profit. The average ransom in 2006, according to the *New York Times*, was $30,000. But for a high-profile hostage that figure could rise to ten times that figure. 'When I go home,' he said, 'I just stay indoors. It's safer that way.'

After forcing me to dance, captain Younis Mahmoud now sat at the front of the coach on his own. Younis was arguably Iraq's greatest hope for the European stage. He was top scorer in the star-filled Qatari league and scorer of 30 goals in 49 internationals. French clubs had come in for him yet it was unlikely he was going to arrive in Europe soon. 'Of course I want to play in England or France,' he said, 'but my family is my priority and if I sign for a club in Europe, I can't take my family. In Qatar, it's no problem: they say, "Bring everyone!"' The EU's strict work permit rules meant that if Younis signed for an English or French club, his family would stay behind. Worse, with no reason to stay in Qatar, it might mean they had to move back to Iraq. It wouldn't be the last time an Iraqi player had been stung in this way.

For the players left behind in Iraq not lucky enough to get a move or well-connected enough to get a decent agent, there was a different set of priorities. Second-choice goalkeeper Ahmed Ali was one of only four players in the Iraqi squad for the Asian Cup who still played in Iraq, for Al Zawraa in Baghdad, founded by the Ministry of Transport. His day went something like this: 'I wake up at 9am, I go to practice at 3pm, go home at 6pm, lock the door and don't go out.' I ask what the security is like at the games. The players around him howl with laughter. 'I earn $100, a bodyguard gets $1000. I'm not David Beckham! My friend was shot dead during a game once, and they also dropped bombs, five of them, mortars I think, onto the field. It's very dangerous.' The bombs, the revenge and the war were a long way away now, though. The victory against Syria meant that the tournament was going to end as it had begun, a final against arch rivals Iran. This time there had to be a loser. The Lions of Mesopotamia were ready.

*

The noise from Iraq's fans could be heard nearly two kilometres away. From the outskirts of the sprawling, wooded Sports City complex, where the Amman International Stadium sat at its centre, the distant sound of drums and chanting grew louder and louder as I approached the front of the stadium. It was still two hours before Iraq was due to take on Iran but as many as 8,000 were already in the ground. Outside hundreds of men crushed at the single ticket booth desperate to snap up the last of the tickets. Their wives, daughters and young sons, holding miniature Iraqi flags, stood respectfully back, away from the unedifying scene. It was as if the Iraqi flag had been grafted onto almost every single available surface; on large pieces of cloth; on handheld banners; on hats; dresses; children's faces.

Back home large-scale pride in the national flag was a distant memory, from a time five years previously when hope and idealism of a new post-Saddam Iraq still existed. But here, in Amman, for the Lions of Mesopotamia, Iraqis picked up their flags once again in the biggest outpouring of nationalist sentiment since American bombs stopped falling on Baghdad. The terrace inside the stadium was frightening, a deafening noise that hadn't been articulated into any single song or chant. The years of frustration and isolation, of living in their own private hells of repression, humiliation and poverty, poured out. Twenty Iranian fans, the only ones who had made the trip from Tehran, looked on from beyond the wire fence that separated them in awe. A young boy, wrapped in the Iranian flag, stood at the front with tears in his eyes. In the Iraqi section a group of men hoisted a different flag high up on a pole they had somehow smuggled into the ground. It was red, white and green and blazed with a golden sun at its centre. It was the flag of Kurdistan.

'We fly this because we are Kurds and Iraqis, we fly it for Hawar [Mulla Mohammad, Iraq's best Kurdish player],' the young man responded when I asked about it. The Kurds had experienced less of the problems that had cursed the rest of the country in the past few years. After the First Gulf War a no-fly zone was forced on Saddam, making it impossible for him to revert to his genocidal ways. During the 1980s he had instigated the Anfal Programme, a policy aimed at wiping out Kurdish identity by destroying thousands of villages, banning the language and gassing its people. The programme saw thousands of Kurdish villages destroyed, killing some 182,000 people. Saddam feared the Kurds' long-standing desire for independence and also wanted to punish them for their support for Iran during the bloody Iran–Iraq War. He was the architect of the Halabja massacre, where as many as 5,000 men, women and children were gassed to death.

Yet in the freedom created by the no-fly zone, Kurdish nationalism had flourished. When the Second Gulf War arrived the Kurds were already in charge of much of their own affairs, with their own army. Now they had their own government and long-term ambitions for independence. They had their own unrecognised national football team too and had ambitions to one day join FIFA. Their confidence sat at odds with how the rest of Iraq, and the rest of the crowd, felt.

I didn't get a chance to ask the flag bearer's name. The smiling Kurd's face turned as, out of nowhere, a sick-looking middle-aged bald man – his face deeply etched and mean like a caricature of an officer in the Republican Guard – defied his frailty to leap down two rows of seats and lunge at him, knocking me out of the way. With one hand he had the Kurdish fan by the throat. With the other he had ripped down the flag. The Jordanian riot police quickly waded in and forced the old man outside, still bucking and screaming at the indignity. The Kurdish flag wasn't seen again that night.

The teams emerged to a one-sided roar. Hundreds of fans were still outside when the national anthems were sung. Iran's was booed mercilessly. The music was drowned out, causing the Iraqi bench to turn around appalled at the spectacle. On the pitch the Iranian players looked at each other as they struggled through the din, shocked by the outpouring of vitriol. They put their indignation to good use. Within two minutes they had sliced open Iraq's defence, one that hadn't conceded a goal all tournament, and taken the lead at the opposite end of the pitch. There were so few Iranian fans, and with the large LCD screen broken – from which a sign hung that pointed out it had been 'Donated by the People's Republic of China' – no one was sure what had happened. By the time the screen fluttered into life, Iran were two up after a mistake by the goalkeeper Noor Sabri. The crowd began to turn on their heroes, raining plastic bottles down on Mohammed Nasser, who wasn't having his best game, when he came near to the fence to pick up the ball. The second half pacified Iraq's fans somewhat and even gave them false hope of a victory with an 86th-minute penalty. But Iran had done enough and when the final whistle blew they ran to Iraq's fans to bow in mock appreciation, sparking a fight between them and some of the Iraqi players who ran to intervene. Nashat consoled his devastated teammates while Younis – topless and bearing a tattoo of Iraq on his left arm – harried the players to thank the fans, who had stayed in the stadium even as the Iranians collected their trophy, soaking up every last minute of pride.

Mohammed Nasser was distraught, standing on his own by the dugout, his white tracksuit limply hanging off his shoulders. Tears mingled with salty white beads of sweat that streamed down his face.

'Are you OK?' I asked.

Mohammed opened his mouth, but was unable to respond. Finally he choked out what he wanted to say: 'The Asian Cup. We . . . we still have the Asian Cup.'

And he was right, they did still have the Asian Cup. A month later Jorvan and the Iraq squad flew economy to the tournament. Iraq's 1–1 draw with Thailand in Bangkok on 7 July in the opening game didn't give a hint of the glory and the tragedy that would follow. But Iraq pulled off the shock of the tournament, beating favourites Australia 3–1 in the next game. Vietnam fell in the quarters. They were to meet South Korea in the semi-finals. The game finished 0–0 and went to penalties. No sooner had keeper Noor Sabri saved the deciding penalty than, back home, tens of thousands of fans poured out into the stifling Iraqi summer to dance and sing. For a brief, all too fleeting moment, Iraq was united, celebratory bullets being fired high into the late afternoon sky, the tracer fire from Kurd, Shia and Sunni indistinguishable from one another. Which is exactly what the insurgents feared. As the revellers rejoiced, a suicide bomber quietly approached an ice-cream stand in the well-heeled Mansour district of Baghdad, destroying himself and 30 football fans with him. That night 20 more fans were killed across town in suicide attacks, as were 5 more, accidentally, when gravity reasserted its will and the bullets of victory fell back to earth. The Iraqi team, ecstatic in the aftermath of triumph, were shattered by the news that their victory had indirectly led to the deaths of dozens of their compatriots. The team held a meeting to discuss pulling out of the tournament, but the players, spurred on by a bereaved mother who had begged the team to continue in memory of her murdered son, chose to play on.

On 29 July 2007, the Lions of Mesopotamia proudly marched out into the Bukit Jalil National Stadium in Jakarta to face Saudi Arabia. Younis was the hero, heading the game's only goal, sparking joyous scenes. Suddenly the intractable differences that had blighted Iraq didn't seem that intractable any more. Back home, the fear of attack wasn't enough to dampen the mood. The team and their remarkable achievement were suddenly the biggest story in the world. Television crews from Japan to Brazil wanted their story. Crowds celebrated on the streets from Erbil to Basra. Increased security measures meant just seven people were killed by insurgents, but it would have been many more had police not averted an attempted suicide bombing in Baghdad. The risk of such activity meant that celebrations on the team's return home were subdued. The prime minister's reception had to be held in the heavily fortified Green Zone in the centre of Iraq, away from most civilians. One person who wasn't there was the hero, Younis. 'I wish I could go back to Baghdad to celebrate, but who will secure my life?' asked the captain.

Typically, every silver lining has a cloud. Jorvan quit after the match as he had promised, despite pleas from fans, players and even the prime minister. 'If my contract was for six months and not for two, they would have had to take me to the hospital for crazy people,' he explained. For some of the players it would be the making of them. Some were signed to regional teams in the Gulf on lucrative contracts. European teams courted others, like Younis, after he had been nominated for FIFA's prestigious World Player of the Year award. One player, Nashat Akram, almost went one step further. Sven-Göran Eriksson's big-spending Manchester City side had offered him a lucrative contract to become Iraq's first English Premier League player. The significance of the move couldn't have been overstated. At a time when Britain's standing in the Middle East was at its lowest ebb, huge numbers of Iraqis would watch their hero gracing the grounds of some of the world's most popular football clubs week in, week out. Or they would have if the British government hadn't refused Nashat a work permit on the grounds that the Iraq national team wasn't good enough. Despite just picking up the Asian Cup and surviving against all the odds, Iraq sat below 70th place on FIFA's ranking, the minimum required by the British government to award a visa.

But as Younis, Nashat, Jorvan and the rest of Iraq's national football team walked off the pitch at Amman's International Stadium, no one could have predicted what they would achieve in a few weeks' time. Outside the ground, the procession of fans who had gathered in Amman in their thousands for every match had pushed into the streets, singing once more. This time, the incoherent noise had morphed into a single song, sung over and over. 'Do you know what they are saying?' shouted Salif, a 16-year-old who had fled Baghdad with his family. 'They are singing against Iran. "The Sunni and Shia and brothers. We will never sell Iraq."' I stood on a concrete bank, high above the crowd and the police below, and watched as Amman's street filled with red, white and black, the drums beating victoriously in defeat long into the night.

8

Lebanon

I awoke when the wheels of the plane hit the tarmac. It was 3am and, out of my window, I could feel the presence of dark mountains lit up by a patchwork of crisscrossing lights. It felt like I had been here before. Almost a year ago I had sat in my flat in Dubai, watching CNN as Israeli planes unloaded their missiles into the very same tarmac I was currently taxiing on at Rafik Hariri International Airport. Like twentieth-century Poland, Lebanon was coveted, fought over and taken by the neighbours that surrounded it. Lebanon was a place other people went to fight their wars. But for me, living in the UAE with its large Lebanese population, I had heard only of the boom times, of the economic revival of the post-civil war 1990s, of tourists from the West flocking to witness its café charm. The Paris of the Middle East, they called it, and it was surely about to return to its former glory. Then the Israelis came again and reset the clock to 1982, the last time their forces had headed that far north. A year on, Beirut was still trying to get back on its feet. The flight was empty. Not many people wanted to come to Lebanon right now. Even the weary-looking border guard happily stamped my passport despite the fact I had an overland exit visa from Egypt into Israel.

After watching the final of the West Asian Championship, and the aftermath of Iraq's stunning, against-all-odds victory in the Asian Cup a few weeks later, I thought of Emile Rustom, the head coach of the Lebanese national football team. We'd met in the hotel in Amman where all the national teams were staying and he explained just how divided Lebanese football was. It seemed emblematic of the political crises that had afflicted the country over the years. Each football team represented a different sectarian group, funded by politicians. The country's biggest club and current champions, Al Ansar, had traditionally been a Sunni club, bankrolled by ex-prime minister Rafik Hariri. After his assassination in 2005 his son, Saad, continued to give money to them, as well as Nejmeh, a team that was Sunni-owned with a Shia fanbase, although that was changing. Saad also helped fund the Orthodox Christian team Racing Beirut.

Hezbollah had got into the game too, supporting their team Al Ahed. The Druze community had Al Safa whilst the Maronite Catholics backed Sagesse. Every Saturday was derby day in Lebanon, where Sunni met Shia, Shia met Druze, Muslim met Christian. With the dust still settling after Israel's 2006 bombardment of the country, Lebanon was jittery. The central government and its army had been humiliated by its impotence both in the face of the Israeli onslaught but also by the power and organisation of Hezbollah's guerrilla army. The West demanded that Prime Minister Fouad Siniora reined in what they saw, essentially, as a state within a state. The problem was that Hezbollah's stock – both within the Shia and some non-Shia communities – had never been higher after what they had spun as a successful act of resistance. They were also a legitimate political party, with elected members of the Lebanese parliament. Siniora's hands were tied. The only thing he could do was tinker around the edges. So he banned all football fans from attending football matches.

This year it was supposed to be different. I was there for the first weekend of the Lebanese season and this time, I had been told by Emile, the fans would be back. The problem was another political crisis, one of a regular cycle of crises Lebanese people endure every year thanks to their dysfunctional and rapacious political class. But this one seemed different. Ever since Rafik Hariri's 2005 assassination two political groups had formed and vied for political supremacy. On one side was the anti-Syrian March 14 group – who had blamed much of the country's instability as well as Rafik Hariri's assassination on the Syrians that had occupied the country for years. It was made up mainly of Sunnis like Rafik Hariri's son Saad and his Future Movement political party, the Druze and some Christian groups. On the other stood the pro-Syrian March 8 group, an alliance of convenience between President General Michel Aoun, a Maronite Catholic who had formed the Free Patriotic Movement, and the Shia militia Hezbollah led by Hassan Nasrallah. Lebanon's constitution had been drawn up on sectarian lines, a confessional system where each community was given a slice of the political pie. Aoun's Free Patriotic Movement, who had fought against Lebanon's Muslims and Syria in the civil war, had now jumped into bed with the pro-Syria camp. Although the Maronites constitutionally hold the post of president, no one could agree on a suitable candidate, fearing it gave Hezbollah and the pro-Syrians too much power. An agreement between the political parties was due in September but it was postponed and a new date set. It had created the last thing that Lebanon needed: a power vacuum.

The football season was due to start on Saturday, but the presidential vote was on the following Tuesday. I got into a taxi and headed for the Christian area of Achrafieh, home to two of Lebanon's most bitter footballing rivals, Racing Beirut and Sagesse, who were to kick off the season against each other. Paul Rustom, Emile's son and Lebanon's international striker, had told me back in Amman it was Lebanon's answer to Scotland's 'Old Firm'. Only this time the Christian rivalry was between Racing Beirut, which had an Orthodox Christian identity, and Sagesse, backed by Maronite Catholics. Like the Glaswegian version, from an outsider's perspective at least, both teams seemed to have more in common then they cared to admit: both were from the same small hill in northern Beirut, both were on the same side during large swathes of the country's bloody civil war, both were Christian. The crucial difference was that the Maronites were an Eastern sect of Catholicism allied with Rome whilst the Orthodox Church broke links with the Pope in the eleventh century. Both now celebrated different Christmases and Easters and, in Lebanon at least, supported different football teams.

Beirut by daylight is a beautiful thing. The small narrow streets of Achrafieh were filled with stylish old Mercedes-Benzs. The buildings – French and Ottoman style with little iron balcony railings and wooden shutters – were magisterial; turn of the twentieth-century concrete palaces that had only been enhanced by their corruption over time. They wore the scars of civil war well. It wasn't until I walked outside into the hot autumnal morning that I realised that the facade of the hostel I was staying in was riddled with bullet holes. The tell-tale dimples seemed to be clustered around the window of the dorm I was staying in, as if my room was once the workplace of a hard-to-dislodge sniper, methodically picking off his prey whilst his increasingly desperate enemies indiscriminately sprayed bullets back in return. The main street of Gemmayzeh is quiet in the morning. This wasn't its time. The idle bars and clubs that are packed on either side tell you that life doesn't truly fill its streets until somewhere around midnight. During the civil war it had a very different reputation: a sniper's alley. Walking down it would mean almost certain death. But even for Hassan, who worked in a mobile phone shop on the street, and Nader, a club singer – or so he told me – it was still unusually quiet. 'Watch what you say, everybody is tense,' warned Nader, a Sagesse fan, when I asked for directions. 'Tuesday is an important day for the country, maybe after Tuesday, no one will be safe.'

Eventually I found my rendezvous point on a dual carriageway near the hostel. Emile pulled up in a brand-new black 4x4 wearing a Lebanese national team training top, tracksuit bottoms and trainers. There hadn't been training that day but Emile was evidently a man who was always ready to kick a ball, no matter where he was. Emile was a Sagesse man, an ex-player who still coached and helped out at the club, but the financial hardships – no fans, after all, means no revenue for the turnstiles – meant that for the first time in his adult life Emile would be starting a football season with no domestic football club, which made his full training-ground attire all the stranger. 'It is still not decided [about the fans] as we are waiting to hear from the Ministry of the Interior,' Emile declared as we drove up through Achrafieh. He didn't seem to think it was that bad a thing. 'Because of the bad political situation the fans are fighting . So the FA was ordered not to create more problems. I think they will not change this decision. They will make the clubs wait.'

Emile lived in the tallest building in north-east Beirut, a huge tower block that dominated all around it. Out on the balcony, the Mediterranean stretched out before us. The Rustom family didn't leave here during the 2006 Israeli war, Emile said, looking out towards the horizon. 'We just watched as the planes came and bombed over there.' He pointed towards the port. 'That was the closest they got.' He continued to storyboard Lebanon's bloody recent history across the panorama: in front, where Israeli planes unloaded their missiles into Beirut's dock; over there, to the left, where Rafik Hariri was assassinated; over here, slightly closer now, the huge blue-domed Mohammad al Amin mosque which Hariri helped build. He never saw it finished, but he was buried next to it. Over the past 30 years Emile had seen it all. He'd played through the civil war. 'I played in 14 Sagesse versus Racing derbies – the first in 1966,' he said as we drank cold water on his balcony. Emile had been a centre-back who had played for the national team at a time when there was scarcely a nation. 'We lost many players at that time, five were killed. Once during practice a bomb went off injuring several of us. We were targeted because we were Christians.'

Between 1975 and 1990 Lebanon's civil war saw Christian and Muslim communities fight against each other as outside powers – in particular Syria, Israel, the USA and the Palestinian Liberation Organisation (PLO) – tried to manipulate the situation for their own ends. An estimated 150,000 people were killed by the time a ceasefire was brokered, leaving Syria as its de facto occupier. The war saw Beirut divided into two by the Green Line, the east controlled by a Christian forces, the west by Muslim militias. Lebanon's football league also split, with Sagesse and Racing competing in exponentially fiercer derbies. Even though they were both Christian teams that should have been united by a common enemy, the rivalry between Maronite and Orthodox remained fierce. 'There was no solidarity between us, even in the war. We hated each other more when there was a war between Muslims and Christians,' said Emile. Even those involved in the game were puzzled by the hatred. 'I don't understand it,' Emile admitted, shaking his head. 'It's the twenty-first century and we still make a difference between Maronite and Orthodox. It's a shame to have two Easters. What, Christ died twice? We make the sign of the cross with a hand, they make it with three fingers. That's it.'

Emile had agreed to make some calls and arrange for me to meet some of the players. With Emile and Sagesse parting ways, he arranged that we visit Racing Beirut. Racing didn't have a training ground. Instead they trained on a rented sand pitch at a local school. The closer we got to the sand pitch, the higher the density of bullet holes in the buildings. Just behind the pitch was Damascus Street, which separated us from the Shia area on the other side of the road. This, for a time, was the frontline during the civil war and some derelict wrecks still stood here, missing chunks of concrete blasted by artillery shells. One building closest to the road looked little more than a shell, with front rooms that once housed life hanging through the blown-off facade. The building looked derelict until you realised that, up on the third floor, a line of children's clothes hung between two concrete pillars.

Racing Beirut's pitch looked like it had taken a few hits itself. With no nets and large holes gouged in its surface it was virtually unusable for football. If Saad Hariri was funding Racing, he wasn't giving them very much. In the penalty area, a used hypodermic needle stuck out of the sand. What looked like a sewage truck rumbled onto the pitch in an attempt to make it playable, spraying water to dampen the coarse surface. Bahaa Salem Hanoun, the team's Iraqi coach, stood by waiting for his team to arrive. He was used to working with this sort of privation. 'We have gifted players but the situation is ruined here by politics,' he said as the truck bounced through the uneven pitch, leaving wet tyre prints in its wake. 'But they keep going. The players and coaches of both sides serve the country better than the politicians.' The team's captain, Tony Rahi, was the first player to arrive. Unsurprisingly given the political problems that had surrounded the first weekend of the season, he tried to take the sting out of the weekend's biggest potential flash point. 'We must not look at this game as a rivalry, simply as three points,' he said before the rest of the squad arrived and began stretching on the potholed surface. 'We play football because we love it. You don't get a good salary but I thought, when the war finished, the whole country will be good, and football too. But there was too much fighting so if the fans are there, it will make problems for the country.'

The comparison with the champions Al Ansar couldn't have been starker. We drove south, past the Shatila and Sabra Palestinian refugee camps – famous for the 1982 massacre of as many as 3,000 innocent civilians by the Lebanese Forces Christian militia, with at the very least the complicity of Israel – and around a broken-backed bridge that was still to be rebuilt one year after it had been destroyed. 'Nothing rebuilt by the government has finished yet,' lamented Emile. Anything that had been finished had been organised by Hezbollah, using money either from prominent local businessmen or outside sources. Sure enough, we passed under a brand new pedestrian bridge with a sign hanging from it: 'Donated by Tehran Municipality'. Emile pulled into a car park surrounded by rubble. Expensive cars juxtaposed sharply with the blackened concrete and rocks that surrounded them: BMWs, convertible Mercedes, blacked-out 4x4s. In front of us sat a pristine football pitch, floodlights and a stand full of well-dressed spectators in expensive suits smoking expensive cigarettes. From the podium we watched as the players below were run through training, including Emile's son Paul. When I had last met him at the West Asian Championship the previous June he was playing for Emile's now former team Sagesse. Now he played for the champions, for Rafik and now Saad Hariri's favourite team. 'Football is a reflection on society, definitely [and] I can't deny that we are a Sunni club,' explained Mahmoud Natour, a member of Ansar's board who was there to check on his team's progress before the first game of the season. 'But we have mixed players, especially here in Ansar. Our board members are Shia, Sunni, one is even Jewish. We care more about football. It doesn't mean [because we are a Sunni club] we are doing anything for politics. We are trying to build a professional club.' Without the Hariri family's money, half the league would go to the wall. Even Ansar, Lebanon's most supported club, would struggle without the fans being allowed in. But the fans had become a problem for the authorities. 'We did have a problem with the national team when the fans fought in a game [against Kuwait] because of the political tension,' Mahmoud admitted. 'The government aren't happy with that. It's whether football fans [use] the political tensions on the field to start a fire, that's why the government is doing this. You never know who will use it.'

The club that had fascinated me most, however, was Al Ahed, a club that I had heard was heavily subsidised by Hezbollah. Hezbollah translates as 'Party of God' in Arabic and was formed – with Iranian patronage – as a consolidation of militias to protect Lebanon's poor and socially marginalised Shia population after the Israelis invaded Lebanon in 1982. The Shia had good reason to seek protection. For them, the threat was four-fold – the Israelis; the Americans; the Christian north; and the Sunnis. For 1,500 years the two major branches of Islam had bristled against each other. The split revolved around an issue of succession over who really embodied the true spirit of Islam when the Prophet Mohammed died in AD 632. Without a son to take the mantle as a natural successor, two sides emerged: those who believed that the line should pass through Mohammed's son-in-law and cousin Ali and those who believed that the lead should be taken by the most suitable person chosen from the Prophet Mohammed's close personal cadre. The former were referred to as Shia (which comes from Shiat Ali, which roughly translates as 'followers of Ali'); the latter Sunni (which comes from 'one who follows the Sunnah' or the words and deeds of Mohammed). The two took different paths, creating an Islamic schism, and had been at odds ever since.

Today, Hezbollah was the best-known and best-organised Shia militia. Western nations consider it a terrorist organisation. The Americans had a particular animus. In 1983 suicide bombers struck two blows against the US presence in Lebanon. In April, 63 people, including the entire CIA Lebanon desk, were killed when the US embassy was bombed. A few months later, 307 US and French soldiers, part of a multinational peacekeeping force there to oversee a ceasefire between Israel and the PLO, were killed in the Beirut barrack bombings. An unknown organisation called Islamic Jihad claimed responsibility. But, over time, US intelligence believed it to be Hezbollah's first major operations, directed by Iran. The multinational peacekeepers left Beirut after those and other bombings and, as the insecurity and anarchy grew in Lebanon during the 1980s, Hezbollah started to achieve a form of legitimacy among its core constituency, winning hearts and minds among the poor and downtrodden Shia communities by providing essential services the central government couldn't (or wouldn't): water, healthcare, education and other social and sporting projects. And despite still holding on to its arsenal – the 1989 Taif Agreement that ended the civil war allowed for them to keep their weapons – Hezbollah had an important presence in the Lebanese parliament too after entering politics in the 1990s. Blue-and-yellow signs that sit on street corners in Beirut's southern suburbs – two yellow hands enveloping a small, blue collection box asking for donations – summed up Hezbollah's raison d'être: 'The hand that fights, the hand that builds.' Al Ahed's training complex wasn't far from Al Ansar's training ground, just across the main highway south out of Lebanon, on the edge of the

Shia suburb of Dahiyeh. To the left of the entrance a large banner hung with Nasrallah superimposed onto a Hezbollah flag. Inside, Mohamad Assi, the club's general secretary, sat in his large office. It was harshly lit, the strong strip lighting bouncing off the white tiles and abundance of silverware on show. Behind his large, brown wooden desk hung two flags; the Lebanese flag, and Hezbollah's distinctive yellow flag, with a raised fist brandishing a machine gun. But Mohamad wouldn't be drawn at first about his club's connection. 'We are a team of all Beirut,' he replied when I asked him to describe Ahed's catchment. 'This is the Shia area. But the fans of Ahed are not just Shia; they are from all the political parties. But here we don't talk about politics. This is a club of football, and a good club.'

Yet all around him more subtle evidence of Hezbollah's connection presented itself. Next to his desk a table was clustered with photographs in wooden frames. From where I was sitting it looked like a picture of a football dinner of some kind, with a visiting foreign dignitary. It was only on closer inspection I realised who it was: Hassan Nasrallah. 'Yes, the leader of the resistance. This is after the war with Israel,' explained Mohamad. Two large portraits hung on the far wall, one of Ayatollah Khomeini, who led Iran's 1979 Islamic Revolution, the other of his successor Ayatollah Khamenei. Nasrallah's face suddenly jumped out from every corner, on every wall.

'I take it he's a big fan of the club,' I asked.

Mohamad led me outside his office and pointed proudly at the large team photo that hung at its entrance. It showed Al Ahed's victorious Lebanese FA Cup-winning squad of 2005. In the middle Mohamad pointed to a picture of himself, standing next to the grinning face of Nasrallah who had dropped in to congratulate the team. 'This isn't an office for the football club, though, I would not be able to hang all these pictures,' Mohamad admitted, looking slightly sheepish. He had been cautious about Hezbollah's involvement in the club ever since I had arrived. 'This is the club office.' He pointed to the lobby outside his office. It was pretty unconvincing, although not entirely surprising. Hezbollah had always been cagey about the scale of its social projects to outsiders and worked hard to present itself as the party of resistance for the whole of

Lebanon, not just the country's Shia community. Anything that seemed too sectarian from the party's members – and Mohamad was a sports officer for Hezbollah after all – was decidedly off message. And there were few things in Lebanon more sectarian than football.

'Hezbollah doesn't give money to us, not like Hariri gives to Ansar and Nejmeh,' Mohamad continued, trying to distance himself and Hezbollah further. 'He gives money and those in the club are now for him. [Walid] Jumblatt [the long-standing leader of Lebanon's Druze faction] and his party is the same, giving money to Safa. When Nejmeh get money they send a communiqué to all the media that they [the Hariris] are backing this club. In this team we have many forces within the team. The players are free to believe in what they believe. Hezbollah is backing the team.' He paused, perhaps realising the futility of arguing away Hezbollah's involvement in front of a picture of him with his arms around Nasrallah. 'When we need help, Hezbollah is backing us,' he clarified.

'In what way?' I asked.

'I am the sports officer for the Hezbollah party. I am taking care of it,' he replied.

'But what kind of help?'

'If we need any help, administrative help, to push people to back the team with money. They know that the team gets help from the party, and they respect the party, so they come and help the club.'

Despite the obvious discomfort about the link between Ahed and Hezbollah, Mohamad and the team were still excited about the prospect of Nasrallah dropping in to see them. The problem was that, with Hezbollah's secretary general under constant threat of assassination, he couldn't give forewarning. 'Everyone can expect Mr Nasrallah, but we don't know when or where!' Mohamad laughed when I asked whether he'd be there for the first game of the season. 'It is very dangerous. He would love to be here. He is very normal. He supports the team and gives orders to support them.' Still, even if he wasn't watching Ahed's opening-day fixture, he would still no doubt be getting his footballing fix, although it would be from an unlikely source. 'He likes English football too, the Premier League is on Al Manar every weekend.' Al Manar, 'The Lighthouse', is Hezbollah's own television network, itself listed as a terrorist entity by the USA, and which boasts 10 million viewers worldwide. It was also Al Ahed's main shirt sponsor.

But like most things with the mysterious Nasrallah, no one was sure what he was thinking. 'I think maybe Liverpool,' one of the club's members interjected when I asked who Nasrallah liked to watch in England. 'I like Steven Gerrard. My father likes Michael Owen but I don't like Wayne Rooney. He is Manchester.' Even in Beirut there was no escape from the Liverpool and Manchester rivalry. Most of the big four have their own pariah supporter. Famously, it was alleged that Osama bin Laden was a keen follower of Arsenal. There is an apocryphal tale that he watched four games at Highbury in 1994 when he was briefly studying in Oxford. Arsenal fans had even come up with a chant, to the tune of 'Volare', made famous by Dean Martin:

Osama, woah-oh,
Osama, woah-oh-oh-oh,
He's hiding in Kabul,
He loves the Arsenal.

'Do you think Nasrallah could be a West Ham fan?' Mohamad smiled a sympathetic smile. 'I will ask him. But it is unlikely to be West Ham. He will need a lot of persuading.' I never did find out who Nasrallah supported. Instead West Ham had to make do with the endorsement of another powerful politician a year later when US president Barack Obama declared his allegiance to the Irons.

The club agreed to allow me to see the rest of Ahed's ground. Outside the front gate I was confronted with a blond-haired man speaking in a German accent with a twang. He grabbed my hand with a Teutonic fervour I hadn't felt since Manfred Hoener almost ripped my arm from its socket back in Qatar. It turned out to be the team's manager, Robert Jaspert. Robert was an Australian-born German coach who had worked with the South Korean national team until, out of the blue, someone from Lebanon called. 'I got a call and was asked if I wanted to coach Ahed,' he explained happily as he slowly walked me around Ahed's vast training pitch. The complex was even more impressive than Ansar's, with two pitches, a stand and a fully equipped gym. There was even a heated swimming pool. Ahed had got his number after Lebanon had played South Korea and he had met some representatives from the club. Unbeknown to him when he accepted the offer, they were also representatives of Hezbollah. 'I'm not very political so I was on the plane on the way over here and I was sitting next to a Lebanese guy. He told me about Hezbollah and I thought: "What am I doing here?"'

Almost immediately Robert was immersed into Lebanon's complicated football politics when, back in March and after only a few days in the country, he was caught up in the car-bombing assassination of politician Walid Eido, which also killed two Nejmeh players, Hussein Naeem and Hussein Dokmak. 'Everyone talks politics, even on the football shows. It was in March and my hotel room was wrecked. There was glass everywhere. We all went to the funeral, which is something I will never forget. Now, with the presidency, we do not have spectators. We are artists and need to perform to people.' It wasn't the only difference that Robert noticed. Any ostentatious religious symbols were frowned upon. 'I have to keep this covered,' he told me, showing the silver cross he wears around his neck. And Nasrallah was everywhere and nowhere. 'We have a few Sunnis [in the team] but everyone in the club loves him so much. We have a television show that gives awards for the best players. They all dedicated their awards to Nasrallah.' If success followed on the pitch, Robert was even told he might meet the man himself. 'I was told: "If you get to the cup final again we are sure Nasrallah will meet you and shake your hand." In Germany they have the wrong journalism about Hezbollah. They think it's like Al Qaeda. It's not, they do a lot of social work, for orphans.' Robert disappeared to prepare his team for their first match and I was left to roam the grounds. It was inconceivable that the money for Lebanon's most advanced training facilities had come from anywhere other than Hezbollah. Through a metal door that was left ajar, I walked into a high-walled gym, itself bigger than Racing Beirut's small sand football pitch. On the back wall two more portraits of Iran's spiritual leaders looked down.

Al Ahed's main support came from Dahiyeh, the name given to a collection of working-class Shia districts and municipalities in the south of Beirut. It was Hezbollah country and allegedly the place where hostages like Terry Waite and American journalist Terry

Anderson had been taken and imprisoned during the civil war in the 1980s. Emile wasn't sure it was a good idea I went when I phoned him and asked for directions. 'Be very careful around there, they think everyone foreign is an Israeli spy,' he said. I took a service bus with Andrew, a young Hungarian student I had just met. He was a militant Arsenal fan. 'Who do you support?' he asked me. When I told him 'Fuck off' was his abrupt, but tongue in cheek, response.

He was headed for the same destination as me, an exhibition that had been organised by Hezbollah called House of Spider. It was an exhibition that celebrated the 'divine victory' of Hezbollah over Israel, so called because Nasrallah had said that Israel was 'weaker than a spider's web'. It didn't really deal with any heroic acts of bravery. Instead it exhibited pieces of captured Israeli hardware whilst showing pictures of children mutilated by Israeli munitions. Dahiyeh was also famous for bearing the brunt of the civil war and of Israel's 2006 bombardment. In both cases Dahiyeh was impossible to subdue, and as our taxi inched through the lunchtime traffic, it was easy to see why. With its identical, sand-coloured tower blocks and warren-like alleyways, it was almost impossible to navigate on foot, let alone in a tank – Dahiyeh seemed to have been designed with guerrilla warfare in mind. Compared to the excess and the revelry in Achrafieh, it felt like a different country: gone were the church steeples, gone were the countless impossibly beautiful women with long, tumbling dark hair, gone were the bars and the Parisian-style cafés. In their place stood minarets and shisha cafés. Every woman covered their heads. The unmistakable yellow flag of Hezbollah fluttered on every street corner. Down one road, every few metres, hung huge portraits of Hezbollah fighters martyred in the most recent conflict with Israel. The district, though, isn't as densely populated as it used to be. Every three or four buildings, a sudden gap appeared, the footprint of an Israeli rocket attack that destroyed the tower block that once stood there, a reminder that the majority of the 1,000 Lebanese killed perished in Dahiyeh. 'That was where Hassan Nasrallah lived.' The taxi driver pointed to his right. Two large tower blocks stood guard over a patch of twisted steel and sandstone blocks.

The exhibition itself was on a patch of rubble too. From the outside, the House of Spider had been arranged like a battlefield.

Green-and-brown military netting rose up on either side of the main path inside. To the right sat the broken propellers of a downed helicopter, to the left a trench full of boxes that once held ammunition. There was activity, but not as we expected. A group of men with beards had formed a line and were quickly passing broken pieces of military hardware down towards their truck. When it had first opened it had made international headlines for its lurid exhibitions and for its gift shop, where for just $10 you could buy a copy of a Hezbollah-developed computer game, a first-person *Call of Duty*-style shoot 'em up called Special Force 2: Tale of the Truthful Pledge where you played a Lebanese fighter resisting the Israeli invaders. Now they were less pleased to see tourists. One of the men spotted us surveying the scene and turned around.

'We are closed, *khalas*, it's finished,' he barked angrily before turning his back to us once again. We stood there for a few moments, hoping he would change his mind. Then Andrew had a brainwave.

'Allahu Akbar,' he shouted. 'Khomeini Rahbar!'

As if we had just said a secret password, the man turned around and welcomed us in.

'What did you say?' I asked Andrew incredulously.

'I learned it in Iran. It means: "God is great, Khomeini is the leader."'

Inside, men rushed past us with hastily packed boxes. 'You can't go there, only here,' the worker intoned, a little softer now that we were deemed friends of a sort. The centrepiece of the exhibition was a huge crater where a captured Israeli tank sat inside. Around it dismembered mannequins, each with its own Star of David painted on it, were scattered, as if they had been blown outwards by whatever force had stricken the prone tank. Its own Star of David was burned and forlorn, the blue only visible on one side. As I inched closer to the crater my right foot clanged on something metal. I knelt down and picked up a spent rocket launcher with instructions on the side written in Hebrew. Within seconds a guard snatched it off me and carried it outside. The room next door was off limits but I managed to creak the door open just enough to poke one eye through. The large white room was empty except for some large colour prints hanging on the walls. Each depicted a different scene of Israeli misery: a crowd of crying Israeli soldiers hunched over the body of a fallen comrade; a party of Israeli women crying in grief thanks to the destructive power of one of Hezbollah's Katyusha rockets. I had seen enough. Andrew and I left them to finish off their packing. It was obvious why they were leaving. If I could find my way here on the back of the press House of Spider had got, Mossad would have no problems. We walked through the district, past the new offices of Hezbollah's media office, until we found a local souvenir shop. The shop was a homage to Hezbollah – mugs, key rings, Nasrallah prayer mats. On the floor, in a big pile, I saw dozens of Lebanese flags. They weren't selling too well.

'We sell three times as many Hezbollah flags as Lebanon flags,' explained the young shopkeeper, not moving his eyes from the newspaper he was reading. That said everything about where Dahiyeh's heart was. I bought a Lebanese flag and a Nasrallah key ring before leaving.

Finally, on Saturday morning, the first day of the Lebanese football season, a decision was made. Rahif Alameh sat at his desk in the Lebanese FA's smart offices on Verdun Street with a face like thunder. The FA's general secretary had been forced to make a choice he didn't want to make, even if he understood why it had to be made. 'Football is a little dangerous,' he sighed as I sat in front of him to pick up my press pass and find out whether the fans would be let in or not. To illustrate the point he stood up, removed a photo from his wall and passed it to me. It was a picture of Beirut Sports City Stadium, the 60,000-capacity national stadium I would be heading for later to watch Nejmeh take on Shabab al Sahel, after the Israelis had destroyed it in 1982. There was no pitch. Any grass that had survived the bombing had been grazed to dust by the herds of cows that lived among the blackened concrete pillars. They belonged to the owners of the forlorn tents that surrounded it. In the aftermath of the attack it had been used as a makeshift camp housing refugees and displaced people. Rahif had only just learned that the fans would indeed be banned from attending matches for the foreseeable future. 'The prime minister [Fouad Siniora] directly interfered in this case. We said: "Every club should have to decide how many spectators they can accept on his responsibility, to help the government as the situation in Lebanon is not safe." But everyone is looking for the [presidential] election.'

The decision had far larger ramifications for Rahif. The game itself was under threat in Lebanon. Even in the darkest days of the civil war, matches would be organised and thousands would turn up for a distraction from the horror. Not anymore; the lack of fans had strengthened the hands of those seeking to fund football clubs for political gain. With no money coming in from the turnstiles, the clubs were even more dependent on patronage from political figures. 'It's not healthy. If the assistance is based on politics it's dangerous. Excluding maybe one team I think all of the clubs receive political money,' he said, signing press accreditations for the game. I told him of my visit to Al Ahed and how they had tried to deny that they received any help. He could barely hide his anger.

'Of course they get help from Hezbollah!' he said. 'Look at their ground: they have two pitches, a swimming pool and are building an indoor gymnasium for the winter. It's against the future of the game what we do now. If no one can come to the stadiums they will forget the football. Once there would be 40,000 to 60,000 at a game. They will choose another way, like drugs or fighting.' Or basketball. With the prospect of a second season of no football, many fans had started watching Sagesse's basketball team instead. It didn't help that they added a little bit more glamour than their football team thanks to being considered one of the finest teams in Asia. The Lebanese national team had enjoyed some success too, qualifying for the 2006 World Championship, the World Cup of Basketball, and only narrowly missing the knockout stages after beating France and Venezuela. Although many of the same sectarian rivalries existed in basketball, there was less trouble in the domestic league, and the authorities hadn't felt compelled to intervene. 'Basketball,' snorted Rahif handing me my pass. 'It's a big joke.'

It only took a few hours for the word to get out that the fans would be barred from entering football matches this season, but some fans already had a well-prepared plan. In a small, dusty building back in Achrafieh, the Sagesse Fan Club was holding their annual pre-season meeting. Like any fan meeting, the delegation discussed the basics of fan politics: from the crisis the club found itself in now that Emile had left the coaching side to the dilemma of who would play the drums in the supporters' band. The Sagesse fans had agreed they weren't going to let anything as trifling as a government ban, heavily armed troops or arrest deter them.

But that plan was further down the agenda and things had already started to get heated. An argument had broken out and swiftly been ended when a gun was pulled out and slammed onto the table. Samir, a board member who had produced the weapon, was forced to act.

'We thought we'd agreed 500 fans with the [Lebanese Football] federation,' screamed Bashir, a huge bear of a man who looked like he had slept rough the previous night. He possessed a voice so deep that oceanographers might have been able to pick up the growls. He was responsible for leading the terrace chants during games, which had pretty much made him surplus to requirements in recent months. Another season of inaction was unthinkable. 'It's not the federation, the government didn't allow it,' replied Patrick, the young, clean-cut president of the fan association. Joseph, Patrick's grey-haired deputy, tried to calm Bashir down by covering his mouth. The room descended into farce as clipped Arabic effortlessly segued into French and occasionally English. Six conversations rose at the same time, in three languages. It was chaos. The club's vice president, there to give 'The Management' perspective, gave up and walked out before Samir pulled out his gun and used it on the table as a makeshift gavel. He didn't need to say a word. Calm was restored.

'In Achrafieh, you're either a Sagesse fan or a Racing fan, there's nothing else and after the games there were too many problems, fights,' explained Patrick as the meeting continued. 'It was really a derby in every way, like Barça and Real. Look at how much this club means to us.' Patrick qualified the point by sweeping his arm in front of the packed table of arguing fans who were now filing out into Beirut's steaming Indian summer. But Patrick had a plan. 'This is a secret,' he said, lowering his voice, 'as we don't want any Racing fans to find out. At some grounds they have a motorway which is a little bit higher than the stadium so we are using guerrilla tactics. It would kill some people to know Sagesse are playing without them so we are going to watch it at the highway and if the army won't let them we will go to the roofs of tower blocks around the ground. We know the owners. Although we won't bring the band as we don't want to make noise and upset the residents.' I took a mobile phone number and was told to call his right-hand man Joseph when I got to the ground. Samir walked by, clutching his gun. He didn't usually turn up with a weapon

to football functions, apparently. He had just finished his shift working as a bodyguard at a foreign embassy. 'Here, you want to fire it?'
he asked, forcing the gun into my hand. It was heavy and powerful. I
felt weak holding it, as if it controlled me, not the other way around.

'Where shall I shoot it?' I asked, looking at the kids standing by the
entrance of the building unfazed, as if men swinging pistols was normal.

Samir looked over his shoulder, kicked open a shoddy-looking
white door in front of us and pointed at the cistern. 'Fire!' he shouted.
Nothing. I couldn't do it. It wouldn't have mattered if I had. Samir
laughed, taking the gun out of my sweaty grip, holding up an ammunition clip in his right hand.

The silence that followed Ali Nasseredine's goal covered the empty
Camille Chamoun Sports City Stadium in a dark melancholy. Ali
wasn't sure what to do at first. The pure, blind ecstasy of scoring had
led him to perform an act of gymnastic heroism, flipping backwards
in successive – perfect – arches. But then the silence caught him too.
His celebration was in vain. No one would ever see his backflips, his
team's initial adulation or his goal. Ali trudged back up the pitch,
shoulders hunched, head down, as if he'd just watched the opposition
score. The shouts of the few soldiers allowed into the ground – the
same stadium that had once been a shell housing broken refugees in
the mid-1980s, rebuilt into a new, all-seater stadium in time to host
the 2000 Asian Cup – were well-meaning but only provided relativity,
a benchmark with which to measure the stadium's vast echo.

It was Nejmeh's fourth goal against Shabab al Sahel, in the first game
of the season. Shabab had already had a player sent off early in the first
half for comically diving and handling the ball on the goal line. Nejmeh
missed the penalty but proceeded to destroy their opponents. There was
still half an hour left. The first day of the Lebanese season had started
with footballing fireworks. But it felt like a pyrrhic victory. After meeting with Sagesse's guerrilla fans, I hailed a cab and went south again, this
time to Beirut Sports City and the first game of the season between
Nejmeh and Shabab al Sahel. As soon as I approached the Roman-esque
facade of the national stadium, the troops loomed into view. APCs scut-
tled at its base, carrying troops brandishing automatic weapons. For the
first time at a football match I saw tanks, six of them, parked to one side.

The teams came out just as I had taken my seat on the press bench, the only place in the ground that exhibited any sign of life. The Nejmeh players carried on a long banner eulogising their fallen teammates who had lost their lives in a car bombing during pre-season. 'I think it's better now [the fans are banned] because you know it won't be a massacre,' argued Pauline Sahyoum, a reporter for the *An-Nahar* daily newspaper, who was sitting next to me. 'Before, the fans beat the fans. Even the army couldn't stop them, especially when Nejmeh played Ansar, there were too many of them. So the Ministry [of the Interior] had to make a decision.' The sun was setting now, and the minarets began their call by the time Ali had scored his goal. The game ended 5–0. I was used to a crush leaving a football ground but outside was dead, the troops still clustered around the entrance whilst the distant beeping of traffic heralded the Lebanese rush hour. At this game football had become everything and nothing. On the one hand, the fingerprints of the game's importance were there: the need for troops, the banner honouring the innocent bystanders of Lebanon's increasing anarchy. Yet on the other hand, it felt futile. Who was this game for if no one was there to see it?

Football for these two teams had been so removed from the terraces, the weight which tethers any club to reality, that soon you feared these teams would be playing on empty pitches in parks. A new generation had begun to desert the game, not knowing or understanding what it was to collectively love a team that you could actually breathe in and almost touch. The players too had begun to feel the disillusionment that this might be a permanent state of affairs for Lebanese football. As I was walking back to the main highway, a figure wearing Nejmeh's kit walked past, looking for his car in the dark. It was Ali Nasseredine, the player who had celebrated his goal in vain. 'Normally I score and I am so happy because everyone knows we have the most fans in the East,' he said ruefully when I asked about his celebration. 'But without the fans I score and it feels like I have died.' Ali continued to look fruitlessly for his lift home. Behind him the army stoically remained, as if not fully believing that Nejmeh's supporters weren't planning a final sneaky attack on the stadium's entrance.

*

Sunday was an appropriate day to hold Beirut's most prominent Christian derby. Like the previous day's match, the army was out in force outside the ground. An hour before kick-off heavily armed soldiers patrolled the Bourj Hammoud stadium, in the majority Armenian district that gives the stadium its name, lest any fan dared get near the ground. Inside, the tight, ageing concrete structure was alive with activity. Through a half-open door, I watched as the referee and his assistants prayed to Mecca in their office. A solitary Racing player did the same on the pitch. Meanwhile Christian players from both sides sporting large Jesus tattoos got dressed in their respective changing rooms. Sagesse's team manager stood guard at his team's door, refusing entry to anyone but players. He apologetically explained that the stakes were too high to risk letting outsiders in. 'Every year one of us would get relegated, so we haven't played each other for so long,' he said. 'The rivalry is still there, Maronite versus Orthodox, and fighting was normal. I used to be young and run from the police. This is football in Lebanon. We have to do it today, especially for the people of Achrafieh.'

The Racing management were less worried about their tactics being leaked to the opposition and let me sit with the players. The atmosphere was thick with Deep Heat, almost blinding, as captain Tony Rahi explained Racing's religious mix. 'There are maybe ten Christian players, ten Shia and four Sunni,' he said, although even this basic explanation sparked a political debate between the players. 'I'm with General Aoun,' the Maronite presidential candidate supported by Hezbollah, he said. 'The majority here is with him because we are Christian and we have a bond with the Shia.' Joseph Attieh, the team's long-haired left-back who wore a huge cross on his arm (although it's likely he gave me the name of a famous Lebanese singer who recently won *Star Academy* rather than his real name), agreed. 'I'm with the general too,' he admitted, just as other players walked in to admonish him. All mention of politics abruptly ended as the coach began the team talk, mapping out the 4–3–3 formation he hoped would bring Racing its first derby victory in close to a decade. There was just one last thing to do before kick-off. The Racing team huddled in the changing room, with the captain instructing the players to 'each pray to their own god'. For a brief few moments, the 11 men were tightly locked in a circle, three different prayers to three different creeds rising from the group. Finally they shouted together: 'Oh Mary, Oh Mohammed, Oh Ali, one, two, three, Racing!' and ran to the tunnel. Sagesse were waiting for them. 'We are all Achrafieh,' an anonymous Sagesse voice implored. 'Let's take it easy, OK?' The two sets of players got the nod and walked out into the empty stadium and to the faint, almost inaudible hum of applause.

High up on the nearby overpass, Joseph and his Sagesse supporters were there in force. Despite the government ban and the threat of arrest, hundreds had avoided the army directly outside the stadium and made it to the overpass that skirted the northern end of the stadium. The rooftops were dotted with more fans, all cheering on their team from their precarious vantage points. On the overpass cars flew past and swerved to avoid the growing crowd on the road. 'It's dangerous, there are mad drunk drivers driving past,' shouted Jeffrey, a Sagesse fan clinging onto the crash barrier. 'You can't blame the government. People are afraid of the fights, some people are crazy and mad [but] I've supported this team for 40 years. Can I stop now? How can I stop now?' Joseph, fiddling constantly with rosary beads, looked on proudly, smiling at the large contingent of support he'd brought. The vast majority were Sagesse, with a few Racing fans thrown in.

'Aren't you worried they'll fight?' I asked him.

'No, I don't fight here. I used to fight for real.' He lifted the sleeve on his right arm, revealing a tattoo of a skull, with a red beret and two swords: the insignia of the Lebanese Forces, the feared armed militia of the fascist-inspired Phalange political party. They were widely believed to be responsible for the brutal Shatila and Sabra massacres in 1982, one of the civil war's bloodiest atrocities. It gave a new, wholly unexpected meaning to the phrase 'guerrilla fan'. Perhaps the presence of a potentially genocidal maniac could explain the rather genial peace that had descended on the crowd although, as Jeffrey explained, just as Racing missed the first chance of a heated opening few minutes, there was a far more mundane reason. 'The truth is that neither of us, Sagesse or Racing fans, have anywhere else to go.' Sammy, a Racing fan, agreed that the government ban had forced the two groups of supporters to accept each other just so that they can watch their teams. 'I'm happy we are playing in the first division again, but I'm happier just to be watching. I don't care if there are any Sagesse fans here anymore.'

The game, though, descended into brutality. Players were stretch-ered off and yellow cards brandished. Ironically given the pre-match talk, there was far more animosity on the pitch than on the makeshift terraces. Finally the deadlock was broken by Racing's Sierra Leonean striker Donald Minter running through and coolly beating the keeper. Suddenly the Sagesse fans came to life, screaming at their own team for their inept display.

'You are playing like kids!'

'Your mother's cunt!'

'I'm too angry to swear at you!'

Things got worse when Sagesse went 2–0 down, Donald Minter again the scorer. It could have been four. The final whistle went and the Racing players celebrated like they'd just avoided relegation. Joseph flung his arms in the air and stormed off without saying another word as the rest of the Sagesse fans negotiated the perilous path back down the overpass, back to Achrafieh. There were no fights and no arguments. It had taken every ounce of effort just to be there, let alone rekindle decades-old antagonisms. But it also constituted a hope of sorts, that football wouldn't be forgotten, even if it took an underground resistance movement to keep the flame alive. And what of the presidential vote? The following Tuesday was tense but passed peacefully. The vote was postponed again, further deepening the coun-try's political crisis and leaving Lebanon in a precarious, rudderless position. By the time I had sat down to write this in 2008 it had been postponed 18 times and street-to-street fighting was being reported between Hezbollah's forces and pro-government militias in Beirut.

'It looks like it's going to be a long winter,' shrugged Jeffrey as he finally let go of the crash barrier that had kept him safe for the previ-ous two hours. He was right, in more ways than one.

APRIL 2009

The final call to prayer of the day crackled to life from the megaphone fixed to the roof of the nearby white concrete office block, washing over the mangled metal and broken glass that carpeted the street below. Armed Lebanese soldiers stood brandishing their machine guns on the perimeter of the carnage to keep the crowd – some curious, but most still angry – at bay. Passers-by pointed at the crushed, blacked-out BMW that sat at the centre of the crossroads, wondering loudly whether the street had been the target of another car bomb. Beirut, after all, is a city used to random acts of violence. Crushed cars, some compressed to half the size, littered the road towards the city's main highway, as if a monster from a Japanese horror movie had lurched down the road, indiscriminately squashing passing traffic. But this wasn't the scene of a bombing, but rather the aftermath of the final day of the 2008/9 Lebanese football season, which had just ended in a riot between the fans of Nejmeh and the Al Ahed team.

It was 18 months since I had left Lebanon with it on the brink of another violent crisis. The ongoing political stand-off between the anti-Syrian March 14 and pro-Syrian March 8 groups had been simmering under the surface. Many thought that the continued postponement of a parliamentary vote to elect a new president had the potential to plunge the country into another civil war. It was the reason why the country's sectarian football fans were banned from entering the stadiums. Instead the spark came from another source. Hezbollah had long been able to build its own state within a state but a key component of that was a shadow telecommunications network that the group viewed as an essential weapon in its war of resistance against Israel. But it was completely out of the control of the government. So when it emerged that the network was allegedly being used to spy on government figures flying in and out of Beirut airport, the government moved in May 2008 to shut it down and show Hezbollah who was in charge. Instead, Hezbollah took its guns to the streets and showed the government in no uncertain terms who really held the power in Lebanon. Dozens of people died in the clashes, no one knows how many for sure, until an agreement was reached in Doha to end the political impasse and allow a new president – Michel Suleiman – to be elected after the vote had been postponed an incredible 19 times. But Lebanon remained as politically divided as ever. Now there was a new flashpoint: parliamentary elections. The football league had again become the proxy battlefield for competing sectarian interests. Religion, politics and mistrust had combined to produce a flammable mix, culminating in the riot between Nejmeh fans and Al Ahed's players, which sounded a dark note of caution ahead of the election in a few months' time.

A week earlier I was sitting on the Nejmeh team bus, parked outside Beirut's fancy Commodore Hotel in downtown Hamra, with Emile Rustom. He exhaled loudly when I asked him about the last game of the Lebanese football season. Emile was now coach of Nejmeh. He had done well too, taking the team to within two matches of the championship. Like Al Ahed, Nejmeh traditionally had a Shia fanbase. But this had changed. Nejmeh was funded by the Sunni politician Saad Hariri, part of the March 14 alliance and the leading candidate to be prime minister. But even though Emile had landed one of Lebanese football's plum jobs he didn't look happy. The season had come to a dramatic conclusion with both Nejmeh and Al Ahed, the team supported by Hezbollah, taking the championship down to the wire. The fans were still banned from the stadiums but the latest round of political bloodletting seemed to have taken its toll on Emile. Nejmeh were hours away from taking on their arch rivals Al Ansar – a Sunni team that was also funded by Hariri – in the penultimate game of the season. Victory was vital to regain the top spot from Al Ahed, the reigning champions after winning their first ever championship the season before. The money I had seen poured into the club's superior training facilities had clearly worked. But it wasn't matters on the pitch that were causing him concern, or to lower his voice to a whisper as he spoke to me. '[There is a] man that pulls the strings everywhere and pays money for the games,' Emile hissed like a bad spy as the bus jolted through Hamra's tightly knit streets. 'When teams play us, the Shia players play like they have knives out. [In one game] Ahed offered to pay the opposition players $1,000 each to beat us. Ahed won the other day. Did you see it?'

'I hadn't,' I replied. Emile continued anyway.

'[The opposition's] Shia players were on the pitch, but didn't play. It was a very bad comedy.'

When we had met before in Beirut Emile had been a garrulous host, taking me to meet the movers and shakers at Lebanon's top football clubs irrespective of their religious or political affiliation. He had been greeted warmly by Mohamed Assi, Hezbollah's man in charge of Al Ahed, when he took me to the club. Now, things were different.

Tensions, always waiting for an anniversary, a constitutional crisis or an election, had returned and the football league, its empty terraces, mistrust and hidden violence, were once again merely an extension of Lebanon's fractured political life. And, like in politics, the footballing establishment could see Hezbollah's hand everywhere whilst also repeating an oft used criticism that was mostly, but not exclusively, aimed at Lebanon's Shia population: That they were fifth columnists with little interest in Lebanon or its flag. Its true devotion was to its Shia faith, to Hezbollah and to Tehran. That Shia players on other teams would tailor their performance according to the religious beliefs of their opponents found depressingly fertile ground.

'Next week Ahed play another Shia team,' Emile explained about the last weekend of the season, as the bus silently jolted towards the coastal town of Saida. This was true. Al Ahed was due to play Chabab Ghazieh, a Shia club from the south, whilst Nejmeh played Safa, a team from Beirut funded by the Druze community. 'So, of course, they [Ahed] will win,' Emile stated matter-of-factly. Emile didn't seem to think that the same logic, that Safa and the Druze were aligned with Nejmeh and Ansar's backer Saad Hariri, which might seem equally as suspicious, applied to his team. 'It is up to us to win fairly.'

Saida's beautiful seaside stadium deserved better than this. It was built at a different time, when the Lebanese had real hope that the sectarian problems of the past were behind them. Sat on a rocky peninsula jutting into the Mediterranean, the sea could be heard lapping on the shore from inside the stands. When the sun shone the awnings that covered the stands glistened brilliant white. It had been built for Lebanon's greatest moment in football, when it hosted the 2000 Asian Cup. They didn't make it out of the group stages but the national stadium had been filled with fans and flags. It had been ten years since the end of the civil war. The country was booming. But it was all an illusion, destroyed by the powerful car bomb that killed Rafik Hariri in 2005. Now armed police patrolled the concourses to prevent any fans from gaining access to the game. No one even tried. Once, the Nejmeh–Ansar derby would have attracted 40,000 people; now only a few of the club's dignitaries, and the press, could attend.

'I think football is dying, yes,' explained Bilal Arakji, a Nejmeh board member, as his team romped to a surprisingly easy 3–0 victory.

Even without the fans, this was still a heated derby. But Ansar was swatted to one side. So easy was their victory that Emile was surrounded by journalists demanding to know why the game (played between two teams funded by Hariri) was conducted at such a leisurely pace when so much was at stake. Despite the insinuations by the press, for Emile and the rest of the Nejmeh management, the conspiracy lay in Beirut's southern suburbs. They believed Al Ahed and its pro-Hezbollah hierarchy wanted to steal the championship as a publicity stunt ahead of the June election. 'Is it a conspiracy? Of course it is! Everyone knows it, it's as obvious as the sun,' Bilal told me as we drove back to Beirut, three points in the bag. 'Ahed and Hezbollah want to take the championship, by force if they have to.'

'Why by force?' I asked.

'What about Hitler and the 1936 Olympics? Why did he want to win that? Ahed won the league last season and presented Hassan Nasrallah the cup. They said it was another victory [for Hezbollah].'

Last season's championship was still a sore point for Nejmeh and Ansar. All three teams went into the last weekend with a chance to win the title. Whilst Nejmeh and Ansar drew against each other, Ahed scored in the last minute against a team from the south, pipping both to the post. Ahed protested their innocence but Bilal wasn't convinced. 'In Arabic we have a proverb,' he said, laughing, as the capital's city lights brightened into view. 'What a big scene to see a prostitute give lessons in etiquette.'

Bassem Marmar, Al Ahed's captain, wandered slowly around the pitch of Beirut's Municipality Stadium, in a Sunni district in West Beirut, an hour and a half before kick-off, counting his prayer beads and poking his boot at the shoddy turf under-foot. 'The pitch is very bad,' he lamented. 'But at least we are not playing in Tadamon Sour [a team from southern Lebanon]. There the pitch is like a farm!' The final round of the Lebanese football season had arrived. Nejmeh's match against Safa was to be played back at the seaside stadium in Saida. But Al Ahed were playing Chabab Ghazieh, a Shia team from the south. The equation appeared simple: Nejmeh led Ahed by one point. A win for Nejmeh was all that Emile needed. But all eyes were on the opposition to see whether the conspiracy theories were true. Bassem knew that he needed other teams to do Ahed a favour. He knew, too, of the accusations made against Al Ahed: that the club, with money from Hezbollah, had been paying Shia players in other teams to motivate them against Nejmeh.

'We will play a fair game, unlike Ansar and Nejmeh last week,' he smiled, referring to the accusation that Ansar had rolled over for Nejmeh, as the Hariri family funds both. 'You could see the coach [Emile Rustom] on the pitch telling his players not to score any more than three. Everything in Lebanon is political. We are supported by Hezbollah, we are with them. Not financially. It is good for them if we win the title. It shows the outside world that they are not just terrorists.' Hezbollah itself was cagey about the help it gives Ahed. But the club's yellow shirts were emblazoned with the logo of Al Manar, Hezbollah's TV network. A month before the match, a US court sentenced one man, who had his own satellite TV business, to six years in jail for providing material support for terrorists, simply for carrying Al Manar. The players and officials milled around the pitch, including Mohamed Assi whom I had met 18 months previously. He was less happy to see me now, complaining that I had written about the pictures of Nasrallah that had adorned the club's walls. But the big match was upon us and he soon retreated to the stands.

On the other side of the pitch Chabab Ghazieh, the alleged stooges in Hezbollah's league plot, warmed up. Not that the manager appeared to know anything about it, laughing at suggestions that his team would roll over. 'Here we will play,' Makram Ghaddar announced defiantly. 'We're the same religion, and we are from the south but, for us, we have to prove that we'll play. This match is on TV. We will not give Ahed the game. We will play for the shirt.' Jihad Habhab, a sports correspondent covering the match for Al Manar, was more annoyed by the insinuations. 'This is not true,' he said when asked about the $1,000 payments Hezbollah were alleged to have been making. 'This is designed to hurt Shia players in other teams. This is to humiliate Shia players, to say that they are loyal to their religion rather than their teams. I can assure you that Shia players are loyal to his shirt, and to themselves.'

The game began in front of empty stands and unfolded like typical, vital last days of the season do. A bearded man in a brown sports jacket pressed a radio against his ear to relay reports from the match in Saida as the championship seesawed between the two teams. Safa were playing well but it was Al Ahed who scored first, tipping the balance towards them before Nejmeh themselves scored, reclaiming the league table's higher ground. Rumours circulated that Safa had scored, causing the stand of dignitaries to erupt in cheering and laughter. The man with the radio sat in silence, knowing the truth. It had been disallowed. Then disaster. Chabab Ghazieh scored. It took the crowd a full 20 seconds to realise their Sierra Leonean striker Donald Wellington had just levelled the score. If there was any collusion Chabab Ghazieh hadn't been handed the script before kick-off. The match reached a frenzied conclusion, both teams determined to win until, in the last minute, Ahed forced themselves a lifeline when the captain Bassem Marmar bundled in what turned out to be the winner: 2–1. It wasn't enough. When the final whistle was blown, the Al Ahed players stood in the centre of the pitch, awaiting the news in their kits, their morose fug only broken by the growing celebratory moped horns blaring outside the ground: proof that Nejmeh were champions. Confirmation came when my phone rang. It was Bilal. 'We won, we are champions!' he shrieked with a touching, child-like abandon. In the background a similar noise of celebration could be heard, of shouting and horns. 'Safa played like they wanted to kill us, but we won. I will let you know where the party is.'

One place the party wouldn't be was Beirut Municipality Stadium. A different gathering had been planned. The noise outside changed from the distant tweeting of innocent celebration to a bad-tempered roar. Al Ahed's players and staff rushed from the pitch to see what had happened. A large group of men, numbering close to a hundred, had arrived. One was flying Nejmeh's red flag with its gold star. The crowd began to sing anti-Hezbollah songs before attacking Ahed's players. One young man, a boy really, pulled out a screwdriver, before trying to stab one of Ahed's management. Bassem had to be dragged away from the melee. 'I can't believe . . . what they are . . . singing,' he stuttered, heaving in big breaths, unable to talk because of the anger. 'What they say, about [Hassan] Nasrallah . . . I cannot repeat it.' The Ahed staff were trapped, the coach parked beyond the angry mob. A delegation from the club managed to broker a ceasefire, just enough time for the Ahed's players to sprint to safety. The players scrambled onto the bus. The last person through the door, still wearing his full kit and boots, was Bassem. The mob tried to drag him backwards through the closing glass doors. But he escaped just as the crowd attacked again, fists raining down on the door where Bassem had just stood, cracking the glass with the first thump, shattering it with the third. Hundreds stormed out of side streets to take up their positions as they once more peppered the coach with missiles – broken bottles, pieces of car, plant pots, lumps of concrete.

The driver tried to escape the storm. He was trapped as the crowd swarmed in, battering the windows all around. There was only one exit: over the dense traffic in front. The bus jerked forward, smashing through one car, crushing another, crumpling the side of a third. It pinballed down the street like violent drunk, before disappearing on to the highway and back towards the safety of Beirut's southern suburbs. The street was littered with the smouldering, smoking remnants of violence – at least half-a-dozen destroyed cars and a mat of oil and broken glass. A grey-haired taxi driver with a thin, grizzled face silently stood fixed to the spot by his destroyed old Mercedes, hands alternately clasping his face before pointing at his mangled livelihood in disbelief. Oddly for a football match in Lebanon, the army was nowhere to be seen. When the machine guns did finally arrive, all that was left was to order the young men off the partially crushed, blacked-out BMW they had started smashing to pieces in the mistaken belief an Ahed official owned it.

The next day different narratives would be pushed. Some newspapers and television stations reported the fighting, blaming the violence on Hezbollah or Future, depending on their political allegiance. Both sides tried to make political capital out of the incident. The reporters from Al Manar who I had stood next to at the game claimed that guns had been pulled on them and that they had been shot at by a group of Hariri supporters, a claim taken up by SKeyes, a press freedom group named in honour of the assassinated journalist Samir Kassir. 'Three journalists who had been with Al Ahed were attacked and the area where the attack took place is pro-Future,' explained Khaled Soubeih, a journalist himself who worked for SKeyes. 'The reporters from Al Manar said they were shot at. With the election close, tensions are very high. As long as tensions rise there will be many more of these incidents.' Soubeih admitted that eyewitnesses had yet to confirm that shots had been fired. I hadn't heard any either. Bassem, though, was convinced he had been shot at. I called him the next day to check if he was all right. The last time I'd seen him he was being kicked and punched on his way back onto the bus.

'We are all OK, the driver was a hero, but the coach was shot at. This happens only in Lebanon,' he said, an anger rising in his voice. 'I didn't think we were going to die, but some of the players did, they were afraid of death. The driver was not scared though because we are with Hezbollah and if anything happened to us, well, we are strong, and all of Lebanon will again be with us as if it was May 7.' The 'May 7' he referred to was the takeover of Beirut by Hezbollah the year before. It was a telling statement. Bassem's fallback, the place where he felt safest, was not under the protection of the police, or the army, but Hezbollah. Future TV, Bassem claimed, further inflamed matters by showing the damage that the bus had made escaping, without mentioning the rioters that had caused it to flee in the first place. 'It's a bad sign,' he said when I asked what this meant for the June parliamentary election. 'If anything else like this happens, there will not be an election, that is for sure. There will be civil war.'

The slim hope that fans would return next season had been all but extinguished and the Lebanese FA Cup final, which saw Ahed take on Shabab al Sahel, would take place outside Beirut, in Saida, under tight security. The cup was lifted by Ahed. For the third year in a row, the presentation took place in almost complete silence.

Back outside the stadium the army spread out over the road. The crowd of wired men, jumpily looking for somewhere to channel their adrenaline, disappeared back down the side streets they had appeared from. Nejmeh's seventh league title, just a few minutes old, was already a distant memory. Four middle-aged men standing on a street corner had watched the whole incident unfold. 'Ahed players had come out swearing,' said one certainly, although not certain enough to tell me his name. 'They [Ahed] are in our area and started saying things against the Sunni.' The other men nodded silently in agreement. Bassem and the rest of Beirut would hear the same story the next day. History, as ever, was being rewritten by the victors.

9

Syria

Colonel Hassan Swaidan wasn't best pleased and wanted to see me straight away. Outside the training complex of the Syrian football team Al Jaish, six armed soldiers had surrounded me, shifting awkwardly from foot to foot. They knew what the rules said, and the rules were the rules. This was the army after all. The taller of the six asked if I had taken a picture, as another went into the guard post to phone his superior. There was no use lying: I'd been caught red-handed. After being dropped off at the training ground I had walked past the heavily armed entrance to the club, the first time I'd ever seen a football club protected by such a show of force. But then Al Jaish weren't any normal football club. They were one of Syria's most decorated teams but they were also the team of Syria's huge and all-powerful army. Al Jaish literally means 'The Army', and the club had long dominated Syrian football, as the army had dominated Syrian society, winning ten league titles and at the beginning of the twentieth century winning the AFC Cup, a kind of second tier Asian Champions League, making them one of the best teams in Asia at the time.

They weren't run like other clubs either. Al Jaish was run by the Ministry of Defence, with a strict chain of command. A general sat at the top whilst 'The Colonel' took the role of technical director and oversaw the day-to-day running of the team. Every aspect of the team was run like a military operation, even player recruitment. It was a beautiful arrangement. As Syria still enforced national service, every 18-year-old had to complete two years in the military. So as soon as a good player hit 18, Al Jaish would force rival clubs to hand over their star man. It was no wonder they had enjoyed such dominance on the field.

The soldier repeated his question: had I taken a picture? A few scenarios ran through my mind. I could run and jump into a taxi. But I'd probably be shot dead before I got off the curb. Or I could lie. I had been desperate to get to Syria ever since one of Yarmouk's Sudanese players in Yemen had told me about his previous club, Al Jaish, and how it had used its position to recruit conscripts to its cause and sweep all before them in the Syrian league. It seemed to encapsulate something about a heavily militarised country that possessed an army numbering close to half a million, trained for its inevitable next conflict with Israel, a country with which it has already fought various conflicts over the past 60 years. That fact is made acutely aware to Syrians, not just by propaganda but by geography. The surprisingly short road from Jordan to Damascus is dominated by the eerie, snow-capped mountains of the Golan Heights, policed by the peak of Jebel Al Sheikh. Israel won the Golan Heights in the 1967 Six-Day War and, for Syrians at least, it's a line in the sand for any potential peace deal. You understand why it is so important when you reach the outskirts of Damascus. The city spills out before you whilst the mountains smile down at all those who pass.

It was when I reached the Al Jaish training ground that the real problems started. If they arrested me at the front gate and found out I was a journalist then my trip was over, at least. I could have offered a bribe. But I only had $3 and a few Syrian pounds in my pocket, about £2 worth. I would have been laughed at all the way to solitary confinement. I came clean. 'Yes, I took a photo.' They had me bang to rights. The soldiers had watched as I approached the entrance to the training ground, stopped to see whether I'd been seen, and took a photo of a sign that said: 'Military Zone, No Entry, No Cameras.'

'You can't do this!' the young soldier shouted, more out of exasperation and fear than anger. 'The Colonel, if he found out he would . . .' His voice trailed off as he crossed his wrists in an unambiguous sign that transcended any language barrier. Jail. 'Film,' the shortest soldier, carrying a chipped machine gun, demanded. I considered handing them a roll of unprocessed film, hoping they wouldn't know the difference. Instead, I pathetically blurted out the first thing that had come into my head. 'Please, I was just taking a picture of a kitten.'

'Film,' the soldier repeated, more menacingly than the first time.

Just as I was about to hand over my camera, a breathless young recruit with a sketchy teenage moustache ran into the crowd with new orders. The tallest soldier seemed relieved. 'The Colonel will see you now.' The gateway cleared and the young recruit led me into the complex, past the stone frieze dedicated to the president, Bashar al Assad; past the huge, Lenin-style bronze bust of his father, the late President Hafez al Assad; through a trophy room fit for a champion. He marched me up the stairs, along a dark corridor that stank of fresh detergent, the smell you imagine a windowless room deep in the bowels of a football stadium in Pinochet's Chile smelled like minutes after it had been cleansed of a recent and horrific torture. His shoes squeaked as they met the linoleum-covered floors. The walls were plastered with the Syrian flag. We walked past banks of troops as they sat at desks, craning their necks to see who the new arrival was.

This was it. The end. Deportation at least. If not more. The look of fear in the soldier's eyes at the gate told me The Colonel was not a man to be messed with. The soldier stopped abruptly, pivoted 90 degrees, knocked on a door and walked in. The Colonel was sitting behind a large desk, in a grey lounge suit. The soldier immediately stiffened his back and offered a salute. The Colonel rose and turned towards me. He was short, with white hair and a round cheery face. Out of uniform, he didn't look so intimidating.

'What are you doing here?' he asked in perfect English.

I was an English journalist, writing a book about football in the Middle East, I explained.

'English . . .' he replied, letting the nationality hang in the air for a few seconds. 'Where else have you been?'

'Oh, Lebanon, Egypt, I . . . Iraq,' I had almost said Israel.

'How did you go to Iraq?!' he laughed, guessing correctly that I obviously wasn't a man of military bent. 'The Americans and the English have made such a mess with their stupid war!' He nodded at the soldier to leave, who saluted and spun out of the room. 'Sit,' he ordered. The Colonel squeezed behind his desk. 'You shouldn't have just come here without a letter, without permission. And you cannot take pictures here. This is the army, there is discipline here.' He said the last sentence as if he wanted to smash his fist on the table to emphasise the point, but couldn't quite bring himself to do it.

Behind him a large portrait of President Assad loomed over us. His piercing blue eyes were hung forward so that they bore down on anyone sat below. The Colonel smirked and reached under his desk. He pulled out a small wooden box and placed it in front of him. About the same size as a revolver, I thought, as he lifted the lid and stared at its contents before looking up: 'Sweet?'

With the tension broken I brought out my notebook and turned on my Dictaphone, thinking I had crossed some kind of Rubicon with the man. 'Stop!' he shouted, picking up the phone. 'I have to verify who you are.' The Colonel made a call, and was quickly assured. Content that I wasn't a spy, he called the soldier back into the room. 'I will ask whether you can talk to the players, but there is a procedure, rules to follow' – he was a stickler for the rules. He left the room, leaving me alone with my babysitter.

The Colonel's room was adorned with dozens of pictures of the president. A large squad photo of Bashar with the famous Al Jaish side that won the AFC Cup in 2004 hung behind me. He assumed pride of place in the middle, where the manager should have been sitting. 'President Assad,' I said, pointing to his portrait in a futile attempt to make conversation with the soldier. He placed his right hand over his heart. 'I love him,' he instinctively responded in Arabic. The Colonel returned with a decision. 'The General will see you now.' 'The General'? I was to be shown into the office of a Syrian army general, with a voice recorder still whirling in my pocket. There was no way I could turn it off without The Colonel and the soldier realising my error. Taking photos of a military zone was bad enough, but recording the voice of a Syrian army general was bound to be some kind of criminal offence. The General's office was at the end of the corridor. Dressed in a green military uniform, his left breast sagging under the weight of military honours, he sat behind a large, expensive-looking desk as soldiers buzzed around, handing him pieces of paper for his perusal. Each was read and promptly dispatched into the shredder that sat next to him. Even sporting secrets were state secrets. Behind him were more photos of the president, several of The General shaking hands with the great man himself. He stopped midway through signing a letter when he realised I was in the room. Words weren't necessary. His well-fed jowl, grey side parting and red, important-looking epaulettes smacked of a man who had grown accustomed to privilege. He didn't like surprises any more than The Colonel. He merely went about his business as I sat there, with more soldiers buzzing in with more pieces of paper. They too met with the shredder. Eventually he stood up and walked around to the front of the desk.

'I'm not a big fan of football,' he declared. 'I am more of a track-and-field man. I used to run the marathon.' And that was it, my cue to leave. A decision had somehow been made. I wouldn't be allowed to visit the training ground or see the players. The day after tomorrow, maybe. If I got the right letter. Then we would see. No promises. Maybe. He shook my hand and I was bundled out. The Colonel walked me back to the offices, arranged for my escort to the front gate and made his own excuses to leave. 'How many generals are there in the Syrian army?' I asked.

'Ahh,' The Colonel winked. 'That is a state secret.' The soldier saluted, turned on his heel and walked me quickly back down the corridor, back down the stairs and through Al Jaish's trophy room. I stopped briefly to see what they were for. One seemed to be an unmarked plaque adorned with the Olympic rings with a bayonet and a rifle pushed through them. The soldier escorted me out into the spring sunshine and through the front gate. He saluted me before turning and disappearing back into the building. I didn't take out my voice recorder until I was safely in a taxi and well out of shooting range.

Damascus is a city that walks to a military beat. It is often said that the Syrian capital is the world's oldest continuously inhabited city, although pretty much every regional metropolis with a walled old city seems to lay the same claim. What can't be denied is its turbulent history; a merry-go-round of wars and owners from the Persians to Alexander the Great to the Ottomans, who ruled for 400 years. The forces of Arab nationalism, and the secrecy and authoritarianism that followed its failure, have moulded modern Damascus. Down every Damascene street you'll find soldiers on patrol. Whole districts of the city make their living from clothing the country's new conscripts. An inordinate number of amputees go about their daily business, selling newspapers or cigarettes or pushing a cart full of fruit with their one good arm – testament to Syria's past, unsuccessful, conflicts. You can imagine, however, that Damascus's ancient streets have always been filled with soldiers, its tailors drawing a wage from its warriors, whether sewing camouflage trousers or Roman tunics.

With the army so ubiquitous, it's no surprise that little dissent was tolerated in Syria, either of its political institutions or its armed forces. But then, five years ago, opposition came from an unlikely source: the Syrian Football Association. Al Jaish's player plundering had reached critical level. The league was still amateur, which meant there was no compensation when Al Jaish took a player. As it was the military doing the taking, there was no argument. By sucking up the league's talent they won honours and attracted huge crowds, whilst the other clubs had to keep a lid on their simmering discontent. The FA decided that enough was enough. Syrian football was turning professional and if Al Jaish wanted to take any club's players, then they'd have to bloody well pay for them.

'Before, they took all the players,' admitted Taj Addin Fares, a former referee who was now vice president of the Syrian Football Association, when I visited its headquarters a short walk down the road from Al Jaish's training ground. 'Any good players, they would just take them and if they played for Al Jaish they played for the national team too.' The military had successfully turned what should have been a partisan league club into a de facto national team, flying the flag for Syria at home and abroad. 'More than 80 per cent of Damascus used to support the army club,' said Toufik Sarhan, the FA's general secretary who, with his salt-and-pepper hair and thick-rimmed black glasses, looked like a Syrian Michael Caine. 'But now many of the clubs are as good as Al Jaish, if not better, because we made the league professional. Rich men started to support their clubs. Football is much better now.'

Just how much Al Jaish's stranglehold had been broken became clear the next day, Friday, match day. My taxi arrived at Damascus's biggest stadium, the Abbasiyyin Stadium. Hundreds of troops had been drafted in to police the match even though a paltry 1,000 Al Jaish fans had turned up for the Damascus derby against title-chasing Al Majd. Ten years ago, all 45,000 seats would have been taken. The

Colonel was out on the pitch early, dressed in his neat grey suit whilst keeping half an eye on his team warming up. Well-dressed men wearing sunglasses approached to kiss him on both cheeks. The coach was nowhere to be seen. With The Colonel otherwise disposed I had the freedom to roam. In Al Majd's dressing-room the players were raucously preparing to go out on the pitch. 'It always was a big rivalry,' explained Ali Rifai, a Syrian international, as he put his shin pads on. 'I was in the army for two years but the people don't like the army [team], so they see us or Al Wahda instead.'

In the Al Jaish dressing room, the atmosphere could not have been more different. The room was empty, except for the forlorn figure of Ahmad Refaat, Al Jaish's experienced Egyptian coach who a few months before had been in charge of the Syrian national team – before a vicious media campaign was launched to have him removed – and Egypt's Zamalek. Refaat had been conspicuously absent from his team's warm-up. After his sacking, for Syria not reaching the final stages of qualification for the 2006 World Cup finals, he was now with Al Jaish hoping to build a team capable of breaking the new monopoly of Al Karamah, the current Syrian champions. They were a team that hailed from Homs, a Sunni-dominated city that had an uneasy relationship with the minority Alawite regime of President Assad. Al Karamah had been the biggest beneficiary of Syrian football's privatisation, winning the past two championships and making it to the final of the 2006 Asian Champions League.

But now Refaat sat in the changing room as The Colonel strode around outside on the pitch sucking up the plaudits. Yet according to Refaat, it was he who had implemented the changes that the army had previously refused to admit needed to be made. 'When I got here last year Al Jaish's results were not good,' he said. 'I made a young team – only two players are above 30, the rest under 23. I'm here for two years and *inshallah* I hope that next year we will have a good team.' He insisted that he still picked the team and that The Colonel was the team manager off the pitch but he still found it something of a culture shock managing an army team after spending his managerial life looking after civilian outfits. 'It is very different. With the army team you have any facility you like. The only problem is the new rules for professional players,' he lamented. 'Before, Al Jaish would take all the competition. Now this is a different football. The other teams take good players and pay money for them. But the army doesn't buy because they have good facilities but a low budget. It's difficult for us because I see a player, I want this player, but I can't take this player any more.' The team had also lost something of its military identity. Only two players now split their time between military and football duty – although Ahmad claimed another five wanted to wear the uniform since playing at the club. 'Now the club is down,' he said as kick-off approached. '*Inshallah*, we will be big again.'

After the crowd, the players and the soldiers present had stood for the national anthem, in front of a huge Syrian flag, things went downhill for Al Jaish. They were dire and quickly went 2–0 behind. But then something unusual happened. Every decision, it seemed, went in Al Jaish's favour. The small band of Al Majd fans were livid as the full force of the apparatus of the state willed an Al Jaish comeback. When Al Jaish scored, the soldiers celebrated. And then they scored again, and again. The players knelt on the pitch and placing their foreheads on the grass after each goal as Al Majd tried to work out what had hit them. It was only when the fourth goal had gone in, courtesy of Zambian striker Zachariah Simukonda, that they finally gave in. It finished 4–3 to Al Jaish, and as the players walked off the pitch, the soldiers there to keep order shook their heroes' hands without any pretence of neutrality. Back in the dressing room Zachariah didn't find this odd in the slightest.

'I didn't know I was coming to the army team,' he explained, sitting in the dressing room in his jockstrap. 'There is no difference though between playing for a civilian team and an army team. They don't treat you like army, they are professional.' Outside the dressing room The Colonel was busy taking congratulations from a large, jubilant crowd that had gathered. 'It was a good game, no?' he shouted as I walked past just as yet another man grabbed him and kissed his face, first on the left cheek, and then three times on the right; a sign of true affection. Ahmad Refaat anonymously climbed onto the team bus, in silence, away from the melee and without fanfare. His work was done, even if no one had appreciated it.

In comparison to the next day's game, Al Jaish's unpopularity was only too evident. Al Wahda, Damascus's most popular team, were taking on bottom-of-the-table Al Horriya at the smaller Al Fayhaa stadium. Fans draped in the orange of Al Wahda's shirt hurriedly skipped towards the ticket booths cradling their 100 Syrian pounds (£1.10p) for a ticket. The anticipation was no different from a match in London or Turin; children excitedly dragging parents towards the stands, nervous teenagers singing Arabic songs outside the ground. Hope and expectation hung in the air. When watching Al Jaish all you felt was the heavy hand of the law, of conformity, of order. No one skipped to go and watch Al Jaish play anymore. The complete collapse of their crowd to a 45th of its past glory proved that, for all the cups and the league titles, Damascus's love was essentially bought by a tacit understanding that opposing the government and its powerful institutions was unpatriotic. Al Jaish may have stolen the league, but it could do nothing to steal its supporters' hearts and minds.

Walid, a young Syrian working security at one of the stands, explained it to me. 'Al Jaish is hated,' he said as the match kicked off. Twenty thousand had made the trip to watch the game, even though it had virtually no significance to the home team. 'They are hated because when you are 20 they bzzzzzz, shave your head. If they play for Al Jaish they don't shave your head, you don't have to serve. And then there's *wasta* . . .' *Wasta* is what oils the wheels of Middle Eastern society. It means influence, connections, money, clout. Those with *wasta* can expect to negotiate the Middle East's labyrinthine bureaucracies with ease, or secure a table at a fancy restaurant, or get off a parking ticket. Everybody else had to wade through a sea of forms and treacle-thick obduracy. No one can expect to get anywhere significant in the Middle East without *wasta*. 'They have more money,' Walid continued, 'and the referees always give them decisions.'

Almost every single football league in the world has its own successful team that its rivals suspect have curried favour with the authorities, but when you hear Arsène Wenger or José Mourinho or Sir Alex Ferguson complaining it sounds laughable. In Syria it seemed plausible. After the impeccably observed national anthem, the Al Wahda band – of three trumpets and a tabla – struck up and the fans sang, until Al Horriya took the lead. And they sang some more. 'Fuck your mother!' they screamed as the Al Horriya team, without any fans there of their own, bowed in front of the nearest Al Wahda stand. In Saudi I had been told that a popular football chant was: 'I shit in your father's beard'. Having found it virtually impossible to enter Saudi Arabia to see a game I had never heard it myself. Nor could I realistically find any trace of it. Largely because (a) how do you bring it up with a Saudi in polite conversation? And (b) putting the words 'father', 'shit' and 'beard' into Google returned some truly horrific results. Still, Walid and his groups of friends revelled in teaching me the phrases you wouldn't find in your standard Arabic phrase book. Omar, Luqmar, Imad and Aram were Al Wahda fans who detested Al Jaish and the army. 'I will not go to the army,' declared Omar. 'I'll pretend I am crazy.'

We talked about life in Syria as the match ebbed and flowed in front of us, about how, in their opinion, the West had a bad impression of Syria and Islam because of distortions in our media. 'You can see in Syria, we are not all terrorists,' said Assam, a wiry boyish-looking 23-year-old studying English. On the pitch players and coaches from Al Wahda were praying during half-time. 'What do you think of Islam?' Aram asked, before answering his own question. 'We are all Muslims,' he said, turning around and pointing his finger to lasso his group. 'We pray every day. But this is the true Islam, between me and Allah. It's personal. Anything else is not praying to Allah. It's for other people to see that you're praying for Allah.'

He was right; Syria appeared to be the least outwardly religious country I had been to in the Middle East. It seemed less hung up on public displays of faith, much at odds with Saudi Arabia or Kuwait or the UAE. Most women walking around the centre of Damascus had long ago dispensed with covering their heads and alcohol was easily available in the city. Damascus, like Tehran, seemed to have at its core a more liberal, laissez faire social attitude than its regional contemporaries. Yet a mixture of unbending Islamic fundamentalism and political strongmen with a knack of making bad tactical choices – both Assad and Ahmadinejad fall into the latter category – had soured their relationships with the rest of the world to the extent that war against both countries was talked of as a possibility at the highest level in Washington and London.

But whilst the Iranians were growing tired of Ahmadinejad's increasingly erratic behaviour, President Assad still seemed to enjoy some level of popular support if the terraces were to be believed. 'Yes, people love him,' Omar enthusiastically replied when I asked whether their dislike for the army stretched to the president. The rest of the group nodded in agreement. 'He stands up for Syria. Everyone wants us to get on our knees in front of Israel and America and England. But we won't.' The only thing they were prepared to kneel in front of the West for was the Premier League and the musical talents of former British *X Factor* winner Shayne Ward. 'Listen, listen!' Omar demanded, pressing headphones into my ear from his mobile. A saccharine sweet pop dirge blared into my skull. 'Shayne Ward, "No Promises". He is very popular here. But Backstreet Boys are the best.' Everyone in the group nodded: Backstreet Boys five, Shayne Ward nil.

The match had taken a turn for the worse for Al Wahda as they went two down before another remarkable comeback unfolded. Al Wahda hit back with three goals, one offside, one a foul on the keeper, the other a scuffed shot. Scuffles started breaking out between the Al Wahda faithful as the third goal went in and the clock hit 90 minutes. Al Horriya's players slumped to the floor knowing that another chance at clawing their way out of the relegation mire had gone begging. Al Wahda's fans didn't miss the opportunity to gloat. 'Horriya, go fuck your sister!' they sang.

As the victorious Al Wahda fans piled out of the stadium into Damascus's early evening, only briefly stopping by the exit to harass players as they came out, it became clear from the two games just how successful and vital the Syrian FA's challenge to the army had been. I'd originally planned on heading to Homs to watch Al Karamah play, but had decided to stick to Damascus and been rewarded with 12 goals and some of the best attacking football I had seen in the Middle East. Football had become more meritocratic. Players were reaping the rewards of their talent and had been cut free from Al Jaish's monopoly to gain freedom over whom they played for. The rewards were being reaped on the pitch too. The FA's overhaul had also heralded a policy of promoting youth. By beefing up its scouting and training structure, and encouraging league teams to play more young Syrian players, the FA has been able to identify and develop more talent. At the 2007 Under-17 World Cup, Syria surprised even themselves. After drawing with Argentina, beating Honduras and then losing by a stoppage-time goal to Spain, their tournament ended with a 3–1 defeat to England. At the 2005 Under-20s World Cup in Holland, Syria beat Italy before narrowly losing 1–0 to Brazil in the last 16. Many of these players had been groomed for the senior team and were now spearheading Syria's attempt to qualify for its first ever World Cup finals. An excellent draw with Iran in Tehran, followed by another against the UAE, had put them in a good position to make the final Asian qualifying round for the World Cup finals in South Africa in 2010. In the end, they missed out on goal difference. In the last game of qualifying they had to beat the UAE 3–0 in Al Ain. They fell just short, winning 3–1. But time was still on Syria's side, or so I thought back then. Theirs was a success story, I thought, other emerging leagues would have been advised to follow.

I still hadn't given up hope of gaining entry to Al Jaish's suspiciously fortified training complex. After the senior team had won its match The Colonel intimated that it might be possible for me to return with the blessings of The General, so long as I didn't bring my camera. I agreed and arrived back where I started, at the guard booth at the front gate. The soldiers recognised me but, fearing that The Colonel might throw them in jail if they let in an undesirable who had been ejected a few days previously, they barred my path. Remonstrating with the commanding officer didn't work either, until 50 metres away The Colonel's white head poked out of a brand-new VW hatchback. I was sure his head cocked slightly in irritation as he spotted me waving furiously from the gate before beckoning me with a cursory handshake. He avoided eye contact as he shook, as if he was about to engage in a highly illegal transaction of some sort. 'Please, please,' he begged, finally meeting my eyes. 'Don't take any photos. Off the field, OK. But anything else. No.'

I walked the short distance to the scrubby green field, where the players were waiting. The Colonel had been chauffeur-driven the short distance, before emerging onto the pitch with a large smile and a skip in his step. Ahmad Refaat was there too, but sank into the background as The Colonel took centre-stage and started giving the team talk. With his motivational words done, the players started warming up whilst The Colonel sauntered over to the rotting wooden stand I was sitting on and shuffled next to me.

'Who exactly is in charge?' I asked.

'I am the manager. The coach is involved with everything on the pitch.'

'So, who picks the team?'

A pause.

'He does.'

'Do you have any influence on it [matters on the pitch]?'

'Well . . . I might say before a big game that a player in the side is weak and that he should be replaced with someone who is a strong player, a player who won't be weak. Then after the season we talk and see which players we will take and which we leave out.'

It seemed that The Colonel was the true power behind the throne at Al Jaish, with Refaat merely a civilian figurehead: a Medvedev to The Colonel's Putin. Which is not to say he wasn't qualified for the role of de facto coach. He himself had been a promising player in Syria's lower leagues as well as an international referee. That was in between the 21 years he spent as a lieutenant in the army, which included a stint fighting with the infantry on the Golan front in 1967 and 1973. We sat watching the players circle the pitch as he ticked off his military career and many battles with the Israelis.

'Do you think Syria would play Israel if they ever both reached the World Cup finals?' I asked him.

The Colonel smiled a wry smile. This was a bit of a mean question. Iran, Syria and Saudi Arabia would be powerless in the face of the world's biggest, most prestigious football tournament. Qualifying was hard enough and if a Middle Eastern state forfeited its tie with Israel, not only would it push the country into the footballing wilderness, it would also spark riots in Damascus, Tehran and Riyadh. Pretending Israel didn't exist mattered to many in the Middle East, but playing in the World Cup finals mattered more. 'We'll make a decision when we get there. Israel has some of our land, the Golan. If they give it back we can have peace and we can play but every day they are killing women, children, babies, girls, men. How can they live like this? They need peace too. It's like France coming over and taking a piece of England. Would you play them after that?'

The Colonel knew he had gone further than he should and quickly changed the subject, charging off to fetch one of the players. Abdulrazak al Hussein was the team's star midfielder and one of the few players who still chose to join the army as well as playing for Al Jaish. The Colonel walked him to the rickety wooden stand to meet me. 'You only ask him about football. Not politics,' he instructed. In the end he decided to translate for me. 'How have you benefited from Al Jaish's new youth policy?' The Colonel sprang into action, collecting the response and offering a reply. 'Al Jaish has good facilities, two fields for practice, swimming pool, sauna, professional coach. I have a good chance to show off my technique and fitness. We have discipline here and it is serious. This is why he has come to Al Jaish. Al Jaish is the best in Syria, it is not just my opinion but of everyone, all the journalists.' It was clear that The Colonel had started to inject his own opinions into the replies.

'Syria will improve with football only if it follows the example of Al Jaish, with discipline, being serious, good training, good money.' Then The Colonel dispensed with the pretence of translation, answering the questions himself. 'Yes I think we have a good chance of qualifying for the World Cup if we win the four games, because two teams qualify,' he replied without even offering it to the confused-looking player.

'What does Abdulrazak think?' I asked again.

'Oh,' he said, relaying the message and garnering a long reply. 'Maybe,' The Colonel answered.

Despite the club's autocratic tendencies, The Colonel, Refaat, The General – whoever was truly responsible for what happened on the pitch – had started to turn Al Jaish's fortunes around. They had started their own youth programme, training talented kids as young as 13. If they didn't make the cut, it was but a short walk to the recruitment office. They won either way. Al Jaish had been forced to change and was starting to show signs that it was finding its feet in the bright new world of professional football. The Colonel offered to drive me back to my hotel. On the journey back he was convinced that Al Jaish would rise again, stronger than before and better adapted for the modern world of cash-rich football. 'We are number one in Syria. Number one in terms of facilities and number one in discipline,' he reiterated as we passed the old city before pulling up in front of my hotel. 'Other clubs will be following our lead.' The Colonel was right. Al Jaish won the Syrian league in 2010. The army did rise again but not in the way he had meant.

10

Jordan

Tareq Khoury greets his guests like any politician would, with a warm smile and a firm, over-friendly handshake. His office in a quiet suburb of Amman, the capital of Jordan, smelled of money. The desk was covered in rich, dark leather, as were the seats and the large bookcases that covered the walls. He was dressed in a dark designer suit, head shaved, a packet of expensive cigarettes open on the desk. 'There will be 20,000 fans at the stadium to celebrate,' he said excitedly, pulling his seat tightly behind his desk. 'They will all be for Wihdat.' Khoury had obviously done well in business, and he was now changing up that success for a political career. He'd recently been elected a deputy to the Jordanian parliament. But his most important job, and perhaps the root of his political popularity, was his role as president of Al Wihdat Football Club. And Tareq was preparing for a coronation.

The last game of the Jordanian season had thrown up a fixture between the country's two biggest clubs: the champions Al Wihdat and Al Faisaly, the team Wihdat had replaced as the dominant force in Jordanian football. There was no love lost between either of them, a rivalry that went to the heart of an unspoken enmity in Jordanian society. The roots of the schism were found on either side of the River Jordan, between the country's large Palestinian community and Jordan's self-declared 'indigenous' population, the East Bankers.

Both clubs had gone into the final few fixtures with one eye on this final match. It had been feverishly anticipated by the fans all year. Four months previously I had passed through Amman as it froze during a bitterly cold winter. In a bar at one of the city's hotels, the barman – a Wihdat fan – showed me some of the footage he had captured on his phone of the previous meeting between the two teams that season. The blurry video showed the intense celebrations as Wihdat triumphed 1–0. But this wasn't just a celebration. Faisaly's captain had been sent off. As he walked he swore at the crowd, causing pandemonium of a level considered a national security risk by the authorities. There were riots in the stands as the police stormed in to restore order.

That victory had given Wihdat the advantage in the championship but, week after week, Faisaly had matched their results, meaning that the title would almost certainly go to the last game of the season in a winner-takes-all battle. It was going to go right to the wire. Or so I and Tareq Khoury had thought. A few days before meeting him, Wihdat played Al Baqa'a in a late afternoon kick-off. Faisaly had drawn against Shabab al Ordon. It was the penultimate game of the season and it meant that if Wihdat beat Baqa'a, they would go into the final game champions and the finale everyone had been readying themselves for probably wouldn't be as tense any more , as none of the Faisaly fans would turn up. Wihdat won 1–0, and with it the championship.

The victory made things easier for Tareq. Previously he had made contingency plans for violence, the most likely outcome when Wihdat and Faisaly played. But now, it was to be a celebration. Tareq, a Christian of Palestinian descent, got involved with the club in the late 1980s, giving money to a community scheme that fed and educated Palestinian orphans. As his business interests grew – importing anything from Ralph Lauren shirts to oil – so did his influence until he was elected president of the club the previous year. 'Wihdat club was established in Al Wihdat refugee camp with Palestinian players, but to tell you the truth, there are a lot of Faisaly fans who are Palestinian and most of their players are Palestinian,' he explained when I asked about the background of the club. 'But because of the location it has the look of a Palestinian club. All Palestinians support it [Wihdat] as there is no good national team. People look at Wihdat as the national team of Palestine. All Palestinians in Jordan, the USA, West Bank, UAE, Saudi Arabia.'

The club was certainly a symbol of Palestinian identity, one of the few in Jordan. Yasser Arafat once even called Wihdat the national team of Palestine, long before it had one of its own. But overt symbols of Palestinian identity were in a short supply, a tacit agreement that many Palestinians had with the Jordanian government – citizenship and rights that few of their kin enjoyed elsewhere in the region in return for loyalty to the king. Tareq represented a new generation, one assimilated into Jordan but proud of his Palestinian heritage. 'I am originally Palestinian, my wife is Jordanian, my mother, brother-in-law are Jordanian,' he said. 'It's mixed now. Maybe 90 per cent of the Jordanian families are mixed. Now you can't tell that I'm Palestinian or Jordanian [but] I feel for Palestine. We say we are Palestinians so we can save our country so that all people can have Palestine. In Jordan it used to be in the past that there was tension between Palestinian and Jordanians. After the marriage of all families, education, people are more educated. There is no problem. Only with illiterate people and poor people. The poor people don't feel they have anything from this country and think of Palestine as if it could offer them something if they went back because here they have nothing.'

Things were different 30 years ago. Jordan became the battleground for a Palestinian homeland. 'It started in the 1970s and 1980s,' Tareq said, pinpointing the time when tensions between Jordanians and Palestinians intensified, 'when people had influence over Jordan from other countries.' That period in the early seventies was one of the darkest chapters in recent Jordanian history. By 1970 the country had taken in two huge waves of Palestinian immigration. The first, in 1948, when Israel was created. The second, in 1967, following the Six-Day War when Israel captured what is now the West Bank and East Jerusalem. After the second wave, the *fedayeen* (guerrilla fighters) of the Palestinian Liberation Organisation became more radical and formed a base in Jordan.

The PLO, headed by Arafat from 1969, was a resistance movement determined to fight the Israelis and create a Palestinian state. Unfortunately for King Hussein, the West-leaning monarch of Jordan, the PLO was also acting with impunity in his country, launching cross-border raids into Israel and ignoring the authority of his armed forces. The Palestinians now lived in refugee camps in squalid conditions across the country, which were no-go areas for his troops. Instead, camps like Wihdat had their own security, levying their own taxes and meting out their own form of local justice. The PLO had effectively created its own state-within-a-state. There were several attempts to assassinate King Hussein, who struggled to reassert the state's authority, as any action might antagonise what had become a huge proportion of his subjects. But in September 1970, the king had to act. The Popular Front for the Liberation of Palestine, a Marxist resistance force, had hijacked five planes en route to New York. Three were flown to Jordan, to the north-eastern city of Zarqa, emptied of hostages and symbolically blown up in front of the world's cameras. The provocation sparked Black September, an assault by the Jordanian army to rid the country of the PLO.

By October, and despite Syria sending tanks to help the PLO, King Hussein had been successful in reasserting his will, but not without its human costs. Thousands, perhaps tens of thousands, of fighters, soldiers and innocent civilians had been killed in running battles in Amman, Zarqa and Irbid. 'The Palestinian Wahdat [sic] camp in Amman, the PFLP's stronghold, is just a pile of smoking rubble,' the AFP reported in the aftermath of the operation. By July the following year the PLO were eventually forced to flee north, to Lebanon, where their presence added an extra dimension to an already unstable political mix. Behind them, though, King Hussein had to deal with a deeply divided population – the Hashemite Jordanians angry at the incursion of foreigners on their land, the Palestinians feeling like second-class citizens and burning with the injustice of Black September's heavy-handed assault on their camps. These resentments were rarely allowed to be discussed in public. But on the country's football terraces two teams represented the hopes and fears of each side: Wihdat the downtrodden Palestinians, Faisaly the embattled Jordanians. The Palestinians, who now make up anywhere between 50 and 80 per cent of the population, claim they face discrimination and are barred from positions in the army and the police, dominated by the 'true' Hashemite Jordanians. The Jordanians claim that their country is being overrun by people who have no loyalty to it. When Wihdat and Faisaly met, it provided twice-yearly catharsis.

'For Wihdat, 99 per cent of the fans are Palestinian. You won't find any Jordanian fans of Wihdat,' Tareq admitted. 'They [Jordanian Faisaly fans] feel that the Palestinians came to their country and control all the business and are well educated. Some illiterate people think this way. They should be proud that Palestinians are living here and have all their rights like the Jordanians. It's a plus to the country.' The rivalry usually led to anti-Palestinian chants and then riots after each game, so much so that some Palestinian players felt uncomfortable playing for Faisaly. 'My brother used to play for Faisaly but after he heard what the club and the fans said about the Palestinians, some cursing in the games, he is now with Wihdat,' he said. 'It's the same with Rangers and Celtic or Barcelona and [Real] Madrid. Here it is between two countries, Palestinians and Jordanians. Because it is between two nationalities it is becoming a big problem. Me, as the president [of Al Wihdat] and MP, I don't feel it is between people who are educated, or think right about the country.'

The match also represented something far deeper, beyond the confines of Jordan's borders. From Lebanon to the UAE, Palestine's diaspora had long been treated like second-class citizens. I had visited Lebanon's Palestinian camps, where it was illegal for refugees to work in most professions, to leave the country or get further education. In Egypt, employment restrictions were levied; in the UAE and Saudi, Palestinians could never become citizens. Their reticence was couched in the rhetoric of resistance: normalising each country's Palestinian population would destroy the raison d'être for future generations to fight Israel for their return. If the next generations felt, say, Lebanese rather than Palestinian, why would they fight for their homeland? Keeping the Palestinians in a perpetual state of flux was a necessary policy decision that kept them hungry for home. There was domestic political expediency at play too. If the largely Sunni Palestinians were given citizenship in Lebanon, it would change the religious mix in the country, giving one group the largest population. In the UAE, granting citizenship for the Palestinians would open the royal families up to awkward questions about the other 85 per cent of the country that were foreign-born residents.

The fact, Tareq said, that a Palestinian Christian could be elected to the Jordanian parliament – making him one of 15 Palestinians in the 110-strong legislature – was proof that differences were slowly being married out over generations. 'Palestinians have full rights and we are happy,' he said. 'I care about Jordan exactly like I care about Palestine, I have the same feeling towards both countries.' Of course, being elected president of the country's most popular team wouldn't exactly have been a hindrance to his elevation as an elected member of parliament. 'There are two million [supporters] just in Jordan,' he claimed, quite a boast for a country that has an official population of six million. 'It is the highest number of fans compared to population. We have millions around the world too, 10 to 15 million. When we played in Saudi against Al Nasr club, we had 10,000 fans there [who lived] in Saudi Arabia. More than the local team. In Egypt the same thing happened.' Tareq insisted that buying political popularity through Wihdat couldn't have been further from his mind, but when a third of the electorate sing your name every weekend it can't be bad for it either. 'I'll tell you the truth. What made me go to Wihdat is that if you accomplish anything in Wihdat club you make millions of people happy,' he said just as a board member from the club knocked on the door and let himself in. Tareq handed him an envelope with a cheque for $25,000 in it. A gift, Tareq said, to the players who had brought him the league in his first season. 'I love that. I love to make people happy. It has cost me a lot out of my own pocket. I love it. When I see people are happy and people call me from Korea, the States, Palestine, they are so happy we won the league. I can make millions happy.' Tareq got up to leave. He had important parliamentary business to attend to but wanted to just put me straight on one last thing. 'You know Wihdat isn't a refugee camp any more, it's part of the city.' He urged me to go there before heading for the game.

'You will be at the stadium?' I asked.

'Of course!' he replied.

'What will the score be?'

He laughed as we left through the front gate and shook hands goodbye. 'You know, now, I really don't care.'

I'd grown to love Amman after passing through it so many times. If Lebanon was the place aggrieved parties went to fight, Jordan was the place aggrieved parties went to decompress. Or spy. Anything but open conflict. They were all here. Israelis pretending they were American,

Americans pretending they were Israelis, Jordanians pretending they were Palestinian, Iraqis pretending to be Jordanian. It was a place of calm, if not peace; a place of refugees, tourists and those with enough money to buy a little temporary respite from the privations of Jenin or Riyadh or Baghdad – be they recreational or medicinal. It had the feel of a benign Casablanca. The landscape, too, was something addictive. Amman is often unfairly characterised as an ugly city, yet there was something beautiful about the shabby, identikit flat-topped buildings that stuck out of Amman's seven hills, and the deep valley that cuts through it, like a mouth of badly kept teeth. On street corners and atop hills, evidence of Amman's Roman past presented itself when you least expected it – a Roman amphitheatre wedged between modern buildings in downtown Amman; dissolving columns that once held the roof of a grand Roman palace left orphaned next to a set of traffic lights.

Tareq was right about the refugee camps that had sprung up six decades previously, put down roots and then grown into permanence. On the morning of the match the sun shone as it did on most days in Amman. The taxi cut through the quiet roads, emptied of traffic for Friday prayers. From the top of the hill Wihdat, or the Amman New Camp as it is known, sprawled in front of us. It was still, like the rest of the Middle East was at midday on a Friday. But today was different. As we drove into the camp the still-deserted streets gave signs of what was to come. Everything was green and red. Green-and-red ribbons hung from shop fronts. Green-and-red balloons were tied to signposts. Shop displays had been artfully arranged with green and red products, Wihdat FC's colours. No sooner had I noticed the colours than the taxi screeched to a halt. This was as far as he would go. In front of us the road was full of thousands of men blowing horns and boys waving posters adorned with their favourite players above their heads. Bunting of red and green crossed the street along with the bare electricity cables. Pickup trucks sat stationary in the sea of people, each draped in Wihdat flags, whilst the fans in the back improvised with their own costumes. One had made his own league cup out of foil, another wore a green sweatband with Wihdat written on it in Arabic. It was a scene of unbridled joy but somewhere in the centre of the chaos was the office for Wihdat football club, and I had to find it.

Tareq had told me to be here by 1pm so that I could meet the team and travel up on the team bus. A small boy wearing a Wihdat shirt took my hand and led me through the maze of stalls and shops and celebrating fans. We came to a long street. What looked like the team bus had been swamped by fans all waiting for a glimpse of the players before they left for the match against the old enemy.

'Come back here at seven or eight tonight and then you'll see a celebration,' Mohammad, a bald, dark-skinned 45-year-old smoking a cigarette told me as we both surveyed the scene. 'This is all they have in Wihdat,' he shrugged. 'They are poor people, poor Palestinians. For them it is always misery, but Wihdat winning can make them happy.'

This was no refugee camp in the stereotypical sense. This was a town with the population of Middlesbrough. The concrete buildings had lost their newly built lustre some time back in the 80s but they were stout. The roads were paved, the mosque minarets stood up like medieval castles, white and impenetrable, all-seeing watchtowers impervious to the sun, the wind and the rain. Where Wihdat ended and the rest of Amman began was now impossible to make out. It was progress, sure, but the camp's permanence was also a depressing reminder of just how intractable the Palestinian issue was. I managed to push through the crowd and into the club's front door. Just as I got through the doors a man thrust a wad of coloured paper into my hand: posters of last season's victorious title-winning side.

In the team manager's office, Wihdat's players had taken shelter from the crowds outside, sitting silently on the sofas that had lined the walls. They waited for the signal, so they could start their journey and plough through the maelstrom to the stadium. On the wall hung a long map of Palestine. In this alternative reality of geographical history Palestine stretched from the Red Sea all the way to Syria. There was no room for Israel. On the windows an incongruous collection of posters was displayed. Ronaldo in a Brazil shirt; King Abdullah and Queen Rania smiling; Ronaldinho holding an award in his Barcelona shirt; a baby wearing the black-and-white keffiyeh of Palestinian resistance; Raúl mid-celebration for Real Madrid; the Star of David superimposed on the Stars and Stripes, burning.

The call came from the bus. The players, all wearing their shirts, got up and silently walked through the dark corridor outside into the harsh sunlight and the deafening roar of the crowd. Car horns blared as their drivers finally got a glimpse of the team that would be leading their convoy to the stadium. The rickety team bus crawled through Wihdat as children jogged alongside, giving the two-finger victory salute and shouting '*Filastine*!'

It was to be a longer journey than normal. The match had been moved from Amman to Zarqa, 20 miles north-east. Zarqa was famous for a number of things. It was here that the PFLP blew up its hijacked planes in 1970, sparking Black September. It was also the birthplace of Abu Musab al Zarqawi, arguably the most notorious Jordanian citizen in recent times. The Islamist militant founded Al Qaeda in Iraq and was responsible for numerous beheadings, kidnappings and suicide bombings, including the last time suicide bombers targeted Amman when three of the city's hotels were attacked, killing 60 people. Our bus careered through the valleys of lower Amman as the busload of players cheered and sang:

> *Allah! Wihdat! Al Quds Arabi!*
> *God! Wihdat! Jerusalem [for the] Arabs!*

The driver, an old man with sunken cheeks whom one suspected had been driving the bus since the team's inception in 1956, kept his elbow on the horn, emitting a permanent high-pitch screech whilst singing along, adding his own 'Yallah, Wihdat!' ('Come on, Wihdat!') every few breaths. 'The championship gives something to the people of Wihdat,' explained Faisal Ibrahim, Wihdat's captain. He sat at the front of the bus with his young daughter on his lap, watching the trees pass by. 'It is very important for the Palestinians. We are one people, the Jordanians and the Palestinians, but we hope one day Palestine will be for the Palestinian people.'

Faisal summed up the difficulty that his generation of Palestinian-descended Jordanians felt. The two identities were being successfully assimilated, which was leading to a more stable Jordan, but was at the same time reducing the number of Palestinians who would seek the right to return to Israel. He felt kinship with the land of his father, his grandfather even. He captained a team heavily identified with the Palestinian diaspora. His shirt was the colour of the Palestinian flag, and his club's badge, worn proudly above his left breast, showed the Dome of the Rock. Yet he had a Jordanian identity too. His children would be even further removed from their Palestinian heritage. He was also part of something that was inescapably Jordanian: he was a first-choice defender for the Jordanian national football team. 'I would like to play for the Palestinian team, the national team,' he added cautiously. 'But I can't because I have a Jordanian passport.'

'You need the Palestinian ID,' the team's doctor, Mamoun, shouted through the puff of his strong cigarette. 'You can't have two passports here.' The bus slowed down suddenly. The police had pulled us over and wanted to see what the fuss was all about. 'They hate us for being Palestinian,' spat the doctor. 'Maybe they like Faisaly.' He had a point. As the team of the king, Faisaly were well supported by the police and military. We waited patiently as the team's manager remonstrated with the stony-faced officer. Eventually, he waved us on our way. Somehow, you knew that Faisaly's coach wouldn't meet the same fate.

We arrived at the stadium and already 10,000 Wihdat fans were inside. The stadium's tiny doors were inundated by a crush of fans wearing white, green and red, each man pressed up against the next one's back in the harsh, early afternoon sun. They began singing as soon as they saw their team arrive, going quiet as intimidatingly dressed riot police sauntered down the line. Only one set of fans would be in attendance, but the full force of the police had been drafted in just in case. They wore all black; huge pieces of Kevlar body armour surrounded their chests and backs whilst bulky arm guards and leg protectors made each policeman appear twice the breadth of normal men. They wore black helmets over black balaclavas, to keep their anonymity. Their gloved hands carried black nightsticks. A judicious thwack kept any stragglers in line. By their appearance they had arrived expecting war. Yet there was no one for the Wihdat fans to fight, even if they had wanted to. The Faisaly team bus arrived without fanfare, a gleaming, modern luxury coach with AC and blacked-out windows. It parked next to Wihdat's tiny Mitsubishi minibus, dwarfing it with its opulence. Only a handful of fans cheered the team's arrival.

This match wasn't for Faisaly. They knew it was a victory parade for Wihdat and only a few dozen of the die-hard fans bothered to turn up. By the sullen faces of the Faisaly players, they didn't want to be here either. Inside the stadium, one half was already full with fans jumping up and down and singing, shaking black-and-white headscarves. I asked one of Wihdat's entourage what they were singing.

'They are singing, "*Allahu Akbar! Al dawry ahdar!*"' answered Ahmad, who ran Wihdat's website. 'It means, "God is great, the league is green."' Oddly there wasn't a single Palestinian flag in sight. 'That's because the police won't let them bring them inside [the ground],' Ahmad explained. Wihdat's faithful sang it over and over again: '*Allahu Akbar! Al dawry ahdar!*'

The tiny, embattled minority of Faisaly fans looked on sullenly. Usually they would be in fine voice too, pledging allegiance to the king or singing: 'One, two, divorce her [Queen Rania] Abu Hussein [the King].' Queen Rania, whom King Abdullah – the son of King Hussein – married in 1993, is of Palestinian descent. But this time they kept their silence, only showing any anger when Wihdat's players unfurled a banner heralding their title-winning exploits in front of their small section of fans. Two police officers ran onto the pitch, ripped it out of their hands and escorted them back to the dressing room. The dressing room was surprisingly tense as the manager went through his last instructions. Most listened raptly whilst the goalkeeper chose instead to pray next to the tactics board. It being Friday, the fans prayed in the stands too. Officials kneeled on the side of the pitch, in the shade. The players emerged to a one-sided roar. There was no guard of honour for Wihdat; Faisaly were just going through the motions. Minutes before kick-off another roar went up. Tareq Khoury arrived to take his seat at the top of the VIP section. The fans chanted his name ecstatically. He gave a regal wave back, acknowledging his popularity.

The game, predictably, was absolutely dire. With neither team having anything left to play for, it degenerated into an attritional dirge. The fans couldn't have cared less. They weren't here to watch football. Not really. They were here to see their players lift the championship trophy. The sky got dark and the minarets sang as the game limped to its sorry conclusion. Only a missed penalty by Faisaly gave Wihdat anything to cheer on the pitch. Apart from the final whistle. The staff, substitutes and players' families rushed onto the pitch to celebrate. A makeshift stage was constructed and the players invited to accept their medals. Tareq was there in the centre. It was he who lifted the trophy first. The crowd screamed as he sucked in a few more precious votes. Looking round I realised that the police were hurriedly moving the Faisaly fans out of the ground.

At first it appeared to be a well-worn policing strategy. But then it turned more sinister. As Wihdat's die-hard fans sang the name of each player as he bowed in front of the main stand, I decided to sneak out. It was a long way back and I had no idea how I was going home. But, on the steps of the entrance, the riot police had gone berserk. A wave of well-dressed journalists and dignitaries fell back through the glass double doors. The men immediately scrambled past up the stairs to get away from the beatings. Outside, the men in black battered any-one who came near them. It wasn't immediately clear what the trouble was. After squeezing through the doors into the storm, I could see the prone bodies of green and red as the police went about trying to restore calm, screaming indiscriminately and waving their nightsticks at anyone in the crowd who looked at them. Within seconds, the crowd quietened, bruised and tired. A small boy stamped on a green balloon that had no doubt been proudly tied to the windscreen wiper of a Wihdat fan's car. It was all the provocation they needed, and they returned to beating fans indiscriminately as they passed. One police-men grabbed my arm, marching me to a 'safe spot' where I was ordered not to move.

Nearby a Wihdat fan protecting his wife and young son stood next to their car watching the chaos unfold. 'They do this because we are Palestinian,' the man told me, declining to tell me his name. 'All of the police, all of the army, they are with Faisaly.' I made a break for the front gates, past the unconscious figure of a topless teenage Wihdat fan, his friends splashing water in his face to rouse him whilst a police-man prodded the group with his truncheon, intimating that he'd prefer if they undertook their makeshift first aid elsewhere. Behind me the man and his family were being screamed at by another policeman for taking pictures.

Dusk had quickly given way to night. As 20,000 people moved away from the violence and the beatings, there seemed little hope of finding a route home. Stuck and desperate I spotted a man wearing a

Pixies T-shirt. I asked him where I could get a taxi. He glared suspiciously.

'Are you with Wihdat or Faisaly?' he asked, his crew of fellow Wihdat fans crowding around to listen for an answer. I pulled out the poster I'd been given whilst boarding the bus earlier that afternoon, of Wihdat's title-winning squad from last year, and held it aloft.

The crowd was satisfied.

'You can come with us!' he shouted, taking me by the arm.

Salah and his crew of Palestinian 'gangsters', as they referred to themselves, wriggled through the crowd, past a broken fence and over wasteland before emerging onto the main road gridlocked with Wihdat fans. Car horns and police sirens blared in the foreground. Salah's Nissan was parked in a ditch on the side of the road. We squeezed in, four of us on the back seat. The road ahead was full and stationary, but we were safe. Salah settled into the front seat and lit a joint, inhaling deeply and blowing the thick white smoke into the cabin, before passing it on, turning on the radio. Palestinian pop music crackled through the Nissan's speakers. We shunted along the celebratory motorcade, with the distorted tabla rattling through the speakers and the horns blaring around us. Green and red hung from every vehicle, except the car in front which had a poster of King Abdullah in the back window, a sure sign that the driver was a Faisaly fan.

'He's a son of a bitch!' Salah screamed, bouncing forward and chopping his arm towards the king.

'What about Queen Rania, she's Palestinian, right?' I asked.

Salah breathed in a lung's worth of thick smoke, leant his head back and blew it slowly out into the fabric of the roof.

'She,' he started, coughing through blurry, watery eyes, 'she is the biggest son of a bitch of them all.'

No one spoke for a few seconds, the nodding heads in the car giving their seal of approval. Wihdat football club was finished for them for another season. It was back to their jobs and their normal lives. For a few short, hot months football would be a distant memory. But soon enough August would be back and Fridays would envelop them once more.

The hostilities would soon resume. In 2010 Al Jazeera reported 250 Wihdat fans were injured when a metal fence collapsed after riot police used the same crowd control methods I'd witnessed after a game with Faisaly. Al Jazeera also reported that two fans were beaten to death by the police, although the police denied the allegations. More illuminating, however, was the release of a US diplomatic cable by Wikileaks. The classified cable entitled JORDANIAN SOCCER GAME HALTED AMIDST ANTI-REGIME CHANTS, HOOLI-GANISM TOWARDS PALESTINIANS, sent to the US State Department on 28 July 2009, details an incident a few weeks previously where a match between Faisaly and Wihdat had been called off because of chants against the king, his wife and the Palestinians in general. According to the cable:

```
Anti-Palestinian hooliganism and slogans denigrat-
ing the Palestinian origins of both the Queen and
the Crown Prince led to the cancellation of a July
17 soccer game between the rival Faisali [sic]and
Wahdat [sic] clubs, who traditionally represent the
East Banker and Palestinian communities, respect-
ively. Matches between the two teams have a long
history of violence, but the specific digs at the
royal family marked a new low. The clubs have been
fined and their fans publicly chastised, yet official
media reporting and commentary has been noticeably
thin. The game exposed the growing rift between East
Bankers and Palestinians in Jordan. The King's silence
on the event is noteworthy, as is a reluctance among
our contacts to discuss the issue.
```

That US Intelligence believed a football match was a worthy subject to help document the political and social undercurrents of a country is interesting enough. But equally as interesting are the names mentioned. Only one person's name appears in the cable who was not a member of the royal family.

```
The club's current president is Tareq Khoury, a suc-
cessful businessman who allegedly bought his seat
on the Wahdat [sic] board. He has since leveraged
```

that position into a political career, and was elected
to the Lower House of Parliament in 2007.

But, back on the highway from Zarqa after the game I had just
watched, the Wihdat fans travelling home to Amman could savour
another league title, their third in four seasons.

'Come on,' Salah shouted, breaking the silence. 'Sing!'

There was only one song left to sing. The six of us replied in unison,
through the smoke and over the drums, as the car sped down the
dark, unlit highway towards the capital.

Allahu Akbar! Al dawry ahdar!
Allahu Akbar! Al dawry ahdar!

God is great.

The league is green.

II

UAE

DUBAI, UNITED ARAB EMIRATES, SEPTEMBER 2008

It was apt that the biggest erection in the building belonged to Dr Sulaiman al Fahim. The Cityscape property exhibition was the largest real estate show in Dubai, which pretty much made it one of the largest real estate shows in the world. Heavily made-up models milled about the sea of identikit pods, towering in their heels over the short, alpha-male money men who had come for a slice of a modern-day gold rush. Dubai – one of the seven emirates in the United Arab Emirates – was deep in a decade-long property boom fuelled by what appeared to be unlimited funds and ambition. No project was too big to consider. The exhibition was proof enough of that. Off-plan villas were already being offered on a collection of new islands built in the shape of the continents of the world. Another, shaped like the fronds of a palm tree, was almost finished too. The men in suits talked of a global shortage of high-rise cranes thanks to the sheer number of developments under way. There were more cranes in Dubai, they said, than anywhere in the world. A jigsaw of flatscreen TVs showed off the next generation of futuristic tower blocks and malls that would soon join them. And, in the middle, jutting up like an East German observation tower, was the stand for Hydra Properties, owned by the new face of twenty-first-century English football.

Sulaiman al Fahim had recently, and briefly, become one of the most famous people in the world. A month earlier he fronted a takeover that would change the nature of football in England, and possibly the world. It would change the way that UEFA and FIFA governed the game. It would change Manchester too. Manchester City had been in the third tier of English football a few seasons before. Now they were the richest club in the world, owned by the Abu Dhabi United Group. They could outspend and outgun anyone thanks to the UAE's fabulous oil wealth. And it was Sulaiman al Fahim who appeared to have brokered the deal. When City's shellshocked fans arrived at Eastlands for their first home game as a newly knighted, genuine footballing super power, many wore tea towels on their head in homage to the Gulf's traditional male headdress. Some waved wads of freshly printed £20 notes, the Queen's face replaced by Al Fahim's, the number 20 replaced by 500 billion. In those crazy, whirlwind few days, Al Fahim was the embodiment of football's new world order; brash, arrogant, unstoppable.

'I always feel like I'm a kind of bulldozer, a fully insured bulldozer,' he'd said at the time. 'If nobody likes it, it starts moving – even if there are cars in its way, it has to crush the cars and move. I can't stop. If I have an idea, I have to do it.' The deal was struck between the previous owner, former Thai prime minister Thaksin Shinawatra who had been removed from power in a military coup and who had recently had his assets frozen by the military, and ADUG, an investment vehicle representing the interests of Sheikh Mansour bin Zayed al Nahyan, the deputy prime minister of the UAE. Grand pronouncements were made about future transfers. Cristiano Ronaldo would come. Manchester City, Al Fahim said, would become bigger than Real Madrid and Manchester United. For a few days it was as if Al Fahim was the owner. And then, he was gone, pulled away from the cameras before he could do any more PR damage. The ruling royal family of Abu Dhabi is one of the most opaque in the world, in charge of one of the least democratic nations on the planet. Bragging should be seen, and not heard.

'I like the British media when they exaggerate and add words,' laughed Al Fahim after arriving on to his stand with his entourage, wearing a blue *kandoora*, white headscarf and flashing a unanimous smile. One of his sycophantic underlings announced just how much money Al Fahim had made so far that year. Another handed me the first instalment of his autobiography which, even by the standards of modern football's pornographic obsession with player's autobiographies, seemed a little premature. 'This just covers the years when I set up my company,' he said. One suited woman cradled the book as if it was an album containing the only photos from her childhood. Dr Al Fahim was 31 years old.

He sat down to talk about his time at the centre of a global whirl-wind. 'I was the one who did the deal, I was the one who closed the deal,' he explained when I asked what his involvement was in the sale. 'I find myself as chairman, as owner, even our official press release said I was the owner. It was nice, I like it. I like it when they put my picture in the news!' That was certainly true. Al Fahim had a gift for self-promotion. Before he was 30 he was driving around in a Lamborghini, having made his first billion dollars heading up the fastest-growing real estate company in the UAE. He counted Hollywood actors among his friends. Piers Morgan would later glowingly profile him for a TV programme about Dubai, choosing him as the walking, physical embodiment of its upstart swagger.

He also fronted the Middle East's version of *The Apprentice*. *The Hydra Executives*, as the show was called, had to be seen to be believed. Imagine *The Apprentice* but set in the desert with added geopolitical competition. The first series saw eight Americans take on eight Brits for the chance to win $1 million and a share in a business venture. The second series was planned to have a team from Pakistan fight it out against eight contestants from India. Crying, screaming and idiocy followed. His catch line – 'impress me' – was delivered in the style of a camp Bond villain. He didn't even bother sacking any-one: he handed the winning team a 'pink slip' and got them to do it, *Lord of the Flies* style. Like a proper Bond villain would.

'TV is the best way to market your company so I tried to see if there was anything we could use for reality TV. When you see Trump, you see Piers Morgan, I see everyone is doing something to promote the company and the country,' he said. 'For me this is the best way to promote Hydra and Abu Dhabi. To give a good image to the people. When we started using American and British [contestants], we showed them this was a land of opportunity. Many Americans only know Dubai, this was an opportunity to show people the difference. It's not about Dubai . . . it's about the UAE.'

Al Fahim had encapsulated the raison d'être of the Manchester City deal. Promotion. Football – at least European football anyway – was passionately followed here. But it was the English Premier League's ability to convey a message into the homes and offices of billions across the world that really appealed to the Abu Dhabi royal family. It was advertising on a previously unimaginable scale. 'It's a very good opportunity for Abu Dhabi to be in the Premier League. Everyone here loves the Premier League,' Al Fahim said. 'Man City is one of those clubs that has real big fans in the UK. It's not just about buying the best club, most profitable club, football is passion but you have to buy a club people will really love. And then you need to make a plan to get it into the top five.'

Of course, Al Fahim's ubiquity was also part of the problem. The Abu Dhabi United Group grew annoyed at Al Fahim's increasingly bellicose announcements and, allegedly, pulled him from the spotlight once it had been done. Now Khaldoon al Mubarak, another young Emirati businessman who rarely spoke to the press and who could pass as an accountant, steered the Man City ship. Mubarak was one of the smartest and most powerful administrators in the country. It was felt a steadier pair of hands was needed, although Al Fahim denied he was moved on, insisting that he was only ever there 'to bring this opportunity and to bring it in on time, in less than three weeks.'

'In the UAE I am a supporter of Al Ain club, but in the UK I am Manchester City,' he said proudly. 'Honestly, after the buy-out of the club almost half the UAE nationals watch the match and follow the team. They are all watching as if it is like a UAE team in the Premier League.' He also wanted to see one player in particular come to Eastlands. 'I am a fan of [Cristiano] Ronaldo, he is handsome,' Al Fahim said, bursting into infectious, almost childlike laughter. 'But I don't like to interfere. [Khaldoon al] Mubarak, he knows the player. It depends on the management. They are focusing on the ten-year plan. They are looking for good, talented British players. I hope, what's his name, Mark Hughes and Gerry Cook [sic] and Mubarak pick good players.'

With the interview finished, Al Fahim got up to shake my hand. He had things to do. Piers Morgan, he said, was coming to town and wanted to ride horses on his farm. And he was looking after a very special Hollywood power couple, in town to help him with a new real estate venture that would, he hoped, bear their names. 'I have to go and pick up Antonio Banderas at 2pm,' said Al Fahim, 'in my Lamborghini.'

It was true that Al Fahim embodied one side of the UAE. But there was another side. For three years I'd lived here, among its contradictions; its wealth and hypocrisy; its opportunities and its venality; its prostitution and its religiosity. It was true that 180 different nationalities lived here, making up the vast majority of the country's population. Barely 10 per cent were UAE nationals. As much as this was a country where those with cut-throat ambition could get ahead quickly, it was also a country where most people could never break free of their circumstances. The vast majority of the population were construction workers, maids and service staff from Asia – India, Pakistan and Bangladesh – corralled in work camps with few rights and treated appallingly. I had visited one on the outskirts of Dubai, near the iconic Burj al Arab hotel. Men from India sobbed in front of me as they told how they were trapped here, earning $50 a month, working in 50°C heat. Human sewage ran through their camp where they slept in awful, cramped conditions, sometimes a dozen to a room. Suicide, they told me, was a credible option of last resort. They all knew someone who had thrown themselves in front of oncoming traffic on the glass skyscraper-lined Sheikh Zayed Road, not because its eight lanes offered the most certain of deaths. But because, they believed, the UAE's legal system allowed blood money to be paid by the driver to the family of the dead. A cost-benefit analysis had been made. The workers thought they were worth more to their families back home dead than alive.

Most stayed for decades, but not out of choice. They were often trapped after having their passport taken by their employers, and trapped by the loans they had taken out to pay an agent, usually after being given false promises, to get here in the hope of a better life in the first place. Occasionally the government would announce a new law to improve matters, but they were rarely enforced. Instead a form of economic apartheid had been accepted where your nationality dictated how much freedom you could enjoy. As Piers Morgan rode horses with Sulaiman al Fahim, indentured servitude was in rude health a few miles away. Open the door to virtually any bar and club in a five-star hotel on any night and you would see the faces of young women trafficked from Eastern Europe and Central Asia for prostitution; wearing looks both hopeful and disgusted at the same time.

There was little freedom of speech and there was virtually no democracy. The UAE had only existed since 1971 when seven emirates that had made up the Trucial States – a protectorate of the British Empire – won independence: Abu Dhabi, Dubai, Sharjah, Fujairah, Ajman, Umm al Quwain and Ras al Khaimah (which joined the UAE in 1972). But it was Abu Dhabi, the capital, and Dubai who shared the power and hogged the limelight. Dubai in particular, under the leadership of Sheikh Mohammed bin Rashid al Maktoum, had seared itself onto the world's consciousness with a string of high-profile sporting investments and events and increasingly ridiculous building projects. While Dubai got all the press, Abu Dhabi was quietly building one of the world's largest sovereign investment funds from the huge oil revenues it enjoyed (10 per cent of the world's oil in 2008 sat under the UAE, almost all of it in Abu Dhabi).

Yet Dubai was so good at marketing itself abroad – Dubai's airline Emirates sponsored Chelsea, PSG, co-sponsored the World Cup and gave Arsenal £250 million for naming rights over their new stadium until 2028 – that most foreigners assumed it, and not Abu Dhabi, was the UAE's capital. Sheikh Mohammed had previously deepened his connection with Britain's aristocracy, and the town of Newmarket, by investing huge sums over 40 years in his Godolphin horse racing empire. Football, though, offered a wider reach and Sheikh Mohammed's sovereign investment fund, DIC, aggressively pursued the purchase of Liverpool FC. They had got close to securing a deal, too, but the board chose an offer tabled by American businessmen Tom Hicks and George Gillett (and seemingly soon regretted it: a court ousted them from the club just three years later in 2010). There was even talk of Dubai bidding for the 2018 World Cup, even though it would be held in the middle of summer, at a time when the outside air temperature regularly nudged 50°C.

They were ambitious, but also in competition with their neighbours. Dubai and Abu Dhabi had a history of low-level antagonism, a state of affairs exacerbated by Dubai's current turn in the limelight even though the political power and the oil resided in Abu Dhabi. But with the UAE's media forbidden from discussing anything controversial about the intrigues of the UAE's royal families one of the few times this enmity was exhibited was when teams from the two emirates played each other in the local league. The first I knew of this was, when watching the local news on television in Dubai, I saw two stands full of men wearing the traditional *dishdashas* fighting during a league match. 'It's a changing relationship,' explained Professor Christopher Davidson, a Gulf expert whose book *Dubai: The Vulnerability of Success* was banned in the UAE. The ban was only overturned when the government was embarrassed into a U-turn after it came to light in the international press. 'Look at foreign policy. During the Iran–Iraq War Dubai backed Iran because of trade links, Abu Dhabi backed Iraq. We have the same issue in 2008, Condoleezza Rice putting pressure to sever money links into Iran. But Dubai's trade with Iran is $14 billion, compared with $2 billion with the US.'

Davidson agreed that Dubai and Abu Dhabi – as well as neighbouring Qatar – were building their own distinct brands through sport and especially football. Sport had been used in recent years as a marketing tool by many of the Gulf states as a form of nation building, announcing that they have arrived on the global stage. But football, at least domestic football, had another use. 'Football receives massive backing from the state as it's a replacement for tribalism as they want to limit powers of tribes and eliminate cronyism,' Davidson explained. 'Football is one very secular and easy way of engendering tribalism, it replaces one identity with another. The sheikhs are very visible in the stand, it brings the leaders into contact with your population in a benevolent way. It is an outlet for grievances that has nothing to do with the government. You can shout and scream and forget you can't even shout and scream on the street.'

Yet for all the money and all the glitzy, eye-catching projects, the local league was in a relatively poor state with low wages and an antiquated transfer structure that meant it was the clubs, and the powerful ruling families, that held the power. No UAE player had ever played in Europe, although there wasn't any shortage of talent. The country's best player was Ismail Matar, a diminutive, pacey striker who burst onto the world stage at the 2003 FIFA World Youth Championship, which was held in the UAE. Matar won the Golden Ball, only the second Asian player to win the award at an official FIFA tournament. Previous winners tended to have a big impact on the world stage – Diego Maradona, Robert Prosinečki and Lionel Messi had all had the honour bestowed on them (more recent winners have included Sergio Agüero and Paul Pogba). The interest of big European clubs was pricked. Inter Milan had been mooted as a possible destination. Yet, oddly, Matar chose to stay in the closeted confines of the UAE first division with Abu Dhabi's Al Wahda rather than seek fame and fortune abroad.

Why? The answer may be found in the bizarre case of his international strike partner Faisal Khalil. Faisal had attracted the attention of second division French club Châteauroux, who he signed for from Dubai's Al Ahli in early 2006. The saga played out in the UAE press. 'I am very happy with this first step towards a professional career with Châteauroux and I hope it will be successful,' Faisal happily told Dubai television once he'd made it to France. 'I know Châteauroux are a second division side. But I hope I can contribute with my teammates to win promotion to the first division. I will do my best.' Châteauroux's manager, Didier Ollé-Nicolle, was equally happy with the signing. 'I had visited the UAE and watched Faisal play against Al Wahda in the league and also with the UAE national team against Brazil,' he told the *Gulf News*, even though the friendly match between the UAE and Brazil had resulted in a humiliating 8–0 thumping. 'He is a talented player and we are sure he will succeed with us.'

Everyone was happy. Everyone, that was, except his old club Al Ahli who were livid they had lost a key player midway through the season. Instead of getting mad, they got even. The UAE FA mysteriously refused to issue the proper documentation to allow him to play in France. Even though Ahli were playing hard-ball, Faisal was still confident of fulfilling his dream. 'I think two weeks is a good time to get all these formalities out of the way and I should be in a position to play for Châteauroux after I get back to France [after international duty] in the first week of March,' he said. Al Ahli was demanding an apology from the striker and his immediate return. And then higher powers got involved. Dubai's crown prince, 25 year-old Sheikh Hamdan bin Mohammed al Maktoum, also happened to be Al Ahli's owner and intervened to solve the crisis. Whatever he said did the trick. Within days of the royal family's intervention Faisal was back to the UAE and ready to play for Ahli again. 'It's sad that players are so gullible and they have fallen prey to the empty promises,' said Jassem al Sayed, who represented Faisal, when his player had returned home. 'Faisal Khalil was lucky as his club has stood by him.'

The one area where foreign influence was tolerated was when recruiting the manager. The impressively toned figure of Bruno Metsu, who had memorably taken Senegal to the 2002 World Cup quarter-finals after beating world champions France in the first game of the tournament, was now in charge of the UAE national team. But he hadn't been the first choice. With much fanfare Dick Advocaat had been unveiled as the man to take the UAE on to great heights, and maybe even World Cup qualification in 2010. At the time I was working for *Time Out Dubai* and had planned to interview Dick until a better opportunity came about. Gordon Ramsay, who had opened a restaurant in the emirate, was guest editing the magazine for the week. Gordon and Dick had some form: Gordon had claimed to be a youth team player for Glasgow Rangers who made a few first-team appearances before injury caused him to retire and seek alternative employment in the catering industry (it later emerged that Ramsay had at best played a testimonial as a trialist); Dick had successfully managed Glasgow Rangers, famously winning the treble in his first season. Both still held a deep affection for the club, so they jumped at the chance to meet at Ramsay's smart restaurant and talk Scottish football.

Dick was very happy to see us. He had been living out of a hotel since his arrival a month previously and didn't have much to do as the UAE hadn't qualified for the 2006 World Cup. His next competitive tournament was the Gulf Cup 18 months or so away, which was to be held in Abu Dhabi. The UAE had never won it and Advocaat was brought in on big money to change that embarrassing fact. Every time the Old Firm was mentioned, he lit up, reeling off anecdotes about how he once throttled Fernando Ricksen after getting sent off in an Old Firm game. It was, Dick maintained, the finest derby in the world. It was also a long way away from the more sedate environs of international management. His whole demeanour dropped when asked about the World Cup.

'We can't qualify for the World Cup,' he said, looking deep into his plate. 'But we're getting ready for the next Gulf Cup.' It was added so half-heartedly you felt he was about to cry. Dick poked around his *salade niçoise* as he tried to summon up some excitement regarding the UAE's next friendly, against Benin. He seemed pretty unhappy to be stuck in the desert. But lunch was good and his spirits seemed lifted as Gordon shook his hand and we said goodbye. 'He won't stick around long,' declared Ramsay as Dick descended the futuristic staircase. I didn't realise just how soon he would be proved right. A week later the magazine and the interview with Advocaat had gone to print. On the way home from work, I picked up a copy of the *Gulf News* and read the headline:

ADVOCAAT'S SUDDEN DEPARTURE SHOCKS UAE

 The sudden departure of Dutch coach Dick Advocaat from the UAE to sign with the Korean FA has made the UAE football officials, media and supporters furious for many reasons. The first was the way Advocaat left UAE. He secretly went to Dubai Airport. He left the car keys with the reception of the hotel where he was staying after he arrived last month to start his job with the FA. Advocaat did not inform any FA officials about his departure. When the FA board members read about his signing with the KFA in a local newspaper, they tried to call him but his mobile was switched off.

Equally galling for the UAE FA, there was no clause to penalise Advocaat if he walked out. Although Yousuf al Serkal, the chairman of the UAE FA, seemed more upset he hadn't had the chance to fire Dick himself. 'Never in the past did any coach terminate his contract with the UAE FA,' he said. 'It was always the FA that had sacked coaches.' It was too late to retract the interview. The magazine had already gone to print. The next day I sat at my desk wondering whether this was a sackable offence when the phone rang.

'Hello James, it's Dick.'

'Dick, where are you?'

'I'm, ahh, in Holland.'

The lunch, it turned out, was the turning point. Dick had to get out and get out quickly. And with the South Korean FA offering the chance to guide the 2002 semi-finalists to Germany, it was an easy decision to make. A few phone calls later and he had hurriedly packed and fled the country. He'd lasted less than six weeks. 'I'm sorry,' he said as I tried to work out whether to feel angry or guilty. 'It was too good a chance to miss.' At least he had the good manners to call.

The man the UAE FA turned to next had no problems adapting to the job. Bruno Metsu was a footballing chameleon, a consensus seeker who soaked up his players' advice and acted accordingly. He also arrived in the UAE a Muslim after converting to Islam during his time in Senegal. When the 2007 Gulf Cup came around nine months later, the country had gone football crazy. Gone were the poorly attended league matches that would see a few dozen men in white dishdashas watch from the sidelines. The games had been packed and Metsu had steered the UAE into the semi-final and a tie against neighbours Saudi Arabia. If the nervous looking Saudi men sitting at the bar in the Madinat Jumeirah in Dubai, wearing their team's green football kit and sipping on large glasses of lager, were to be believed, victory for the Green Falcons was a foregone conclusion. 'We will win 2–0, for sure,' boasted one as he ordered a double whisky. '[Striker Yasser Al] Qahtani is the best.' The game was due to start at 8.15pm, but the Saudis were planning on getting there at 1pm, such was the expected rush for tickets.

I took a taxi down to Abu Dhabi's Al Nahyan Stadium a few hours before kick-off. I should have taken the Saudis' advice. Already, two-and-a-half hours before the match was due to start, every seat was taken. Thousands milled around outside whilst the police, arguably never having seen so many of their countrymen in one place before, struggled to control the crowds. Groups of Emirati teenagers in traditional outfits stormed one fence, half a dozen making it over the sharp metal prongs before the police could beat the rest back with their batons. I doubted I would ever make it over in time before getting a beating. I had to find another way. One stand seemed remarkably quieter than the others. With strict segregation between the fans being enforced, the only seats left were with the Saudis. I picked a green Saudi flag off the floor, waved it at the policeman guarding the gate and he let me in.

Inside, the stadium was deafening. Three stands in front of me were blanketed in the white of the UAE's national dress. A single area of black broke the monotony of colour – the women's section, filled with young female fans wearing the traditional abaya. Despite being out-numbered, the Saudis were louder, banging drums and singing religious songs, the UAE fans' weak replies only audible during the occasional lulls. The match was tense and tetchy, neither team making any clear-cut chances. At half-time some Saudi fans, along with the policemen charged with looking after them, found a quiet corner deep inside the stadium and prayed together. The second half wasn't much better and, with the game heading for extra time, the Saudi crowd relaxed slightly, allowing their gaze to be distracted from the tense stalemate.

The referee gave the UAE a ridiculous free-kick in a dangerous position. 'The referee!' exclaimed Mohammad, a young Saudi in traditional dress standing next to me. He rubbed his fingers together in an accusatory manner. 'Money.' With the game deep in injury-time Ismail Matar smashed the ball into the left-hand corner with virtually the last kick of the game. The stadium exploded from its torpor. Robed sheikhs ran onto the pitch towards the mound of bodies that had covered the tiny striker. The UAE bench joined them, as did one man in a wheelchair, determined to reach the pack, wheeling himself heavily over the grass towards his hero as fast as his arms could take him.

Matar emerged from the melee and sank to his knees as the stadium continued to celebrate. The Saudi section felt like the eye of a tornado: the barometric pressure of quiet violence bearing down around us. There was stillness and silence. Mohammad brushed past me whilst furiously shaking his head. Others simply sat, stunned, robed heads in hands. There were still people on the pitch when the match continued its last few pointless moments. Seconds later, it was over, Metsu and Matar were national heroes. It wasn't the end of the UAE's journey either. They went on to beat Oman in the final, Matar again proving the difference, scoring his fifth goal of the tournament to lift the country's first ever piece of major silverware in front of 60,000 fans at the Zayed Sports City Stadium. He never did get the move abroad his talents merited. But for his efforts at the Gulf Cup one prominent local awarded him two prized camels worth $109,000 each. Even Inter Milan couldn't match that.

For close to 18 months, that victory in Abu Dhabi – alongside the national team's qualification for Italia '90 – was the UAE's greatest claim to footballing fame. And then came Sulaiman al Fahim, Sheikh Mansour and the purchase of Manchester City. Little was known about Manchester City's new owner. Like most members of the Gulf's royal families, Sheikh Mansour didn't have to contend with a prying press nor divulge his accounts for public scrutiny. What was known was fairly typical for the heir to an absolute monarchy. He was a member of the Nahyan dynasty, the world's second richest royal family with access to an oil fortune that could be as much as $1 trillion. He was one of 19 sons sired by Sheikh Zayed, the country's revered first president who founded the nation and persuaded the heads of the six other royal families that would make up the UAE. He was half-brother to the next United Arab Emirates president, Sheikh Khalifa bin Zayed al Nahyan, and held the post of minister for presidential affairs in the UAE cabinet. More importantly he was one of the Bani Fatima. The Bani Fatima were the six sons of Sheikh Zayed's favourite wife. The six would go on to control every aspect of Abu Dhabi's economy, society and military. His brother was Sheikh Mohammed bin Zayed, Abu Dhabi's crown prince and the true power in the country.

Whilst Sheikh Mansour's money was being spent on the likes of Robinho and the talk was of City breaking into Champions League contention, back in Abu Dhabi a smaller but no less important football revolution was taking place. Manchester City wasn't Sheikh Mansour's first football love. That was Al Jazira, the Abu Dhabi-based club he owned. And as the UAE's money was being poured into the English game, it was decided that more had to be done about the embarrassing lack of fans and professionalism in the local league.

A long line of brand-new 4x4s queued to get into the car park that serviced Dubai's Al Maktoum Stadium in the quiet district of Oud Metha. The floodlights buzzed through the humid early evening in preparation for that night's entertainment, a Friday cup match between Dubai rivals Al Nasr and Al Ahli. Young boys in long white *dishdashas* walked past in groups as the call to prayer cried out. They were not talking to each other, but talking into the hands-free mics connected to their expensive mobile phones. The only thing that differentiated the groups was a slash of colour from their club scarves: blue for Nasr, red for Ahli. According to the UAE Pro League's new

CEO, Romy Gai, what happened here would provide a good indicator of what Man City fans could expect in the future. Gai was previously a commercial director at Juventus for 14 years but received a call out of the blue earlier in the year. Emirati teams were in danger of being slung out of the Asian Football Confederation's international tournaments, like the Asian Champions League, for being too amateur. 'I got the call telling me about what was happening so I joined them as there is little opportunity in the modern age for something like this,' Gai said as the teams warmed up on the pitch in front of us. His job was to essentially build a professional league from scratch. 'It was difficult at first, with the heat and then with Ramadan. But then the AFC came for an inspection and said we were the benchmarks for Asia.'

Even by the UAE's standards the turnaround was remarkable. In four months they had formed a professional league, refurbished all 12 stadiums and persuaded the television networks to go from paying nothing to 12 million euros a year – even if the Nahyan and Maktoum royal families agreed to split this cost after the Qatari TV network Al Jazeera threatened to win the rights. Some clubs even started flashing their cash in the transfer market. Sheikh Mansour spent tens of millions of pounds, sanctioning the purchase of Brazilian Rafael Sóbis from Real Betis for Al Jazira. But the change may have come too quickly for some. Only 100 fans lined the stands waiting for kick-off. 'Football is the country's sport,' Gai insisted. 'The locals love it. If a European club is bought [by a UAE royal family] then international football offers us lots of opportunities. This is a country that has told us that dreams can become reality.'

LONDON, UNITED KINGDOM, OCTOBER 2009

For once, Sulaiman al Fahim had successfully blended into the background. But these days – against every fibre of his being – the art of invisibility was a necessity. We had agreed to meet in the lobby of an exclusive five-star hotel in London. I had walked past him several times, expecting to see him in his trademark *kandora*, ordering the most expensive thing on the menu. But, no, Al Fahim looked anything but the cocksure tycoon presented to the world's media 12 months before. Now he wore a sports jacket and baggy jeans, mooching slowly along with prayer beads in hand. Without his Gulf attire his hair was thinning, making him look ten years older. He appeared demure, devout, contrite even. 'People say I am a playboy, but I am not,' he quickly explained as we sat down. 'That picture with Pamela Anderson was a normal picture. I was in LA and we had coffee with her mother and she came along. It's a wrong perception. The British media made me look like that.'

It was just over a year since I had first met Al Fahim, the face of the Manchester City takeover. In that time he had been busy, deciding that he too would own an English Premier League football club. But with a slightly different outcome. After his proximity to the Manchester City deal, he decided to buy Portsmouth FC, just as the world economy – including Dubai – was in full meltdown. His meteoric rise began when he returned to the UAE after studying abroad in 2003 and began buying up property and land that was being sold for £10 a square foot. Just 18 months later it was selling for £100 a square foot. In a few years he was head of one of the fastest-growing real estate companies in the world. But then the bubble burst. The Dubai property crash arrived on the ripples of the US subprime mortgage crisis, almost bankrupting the emirate. Dubai, far from being blessed with natural resources to fund its booming economy, had paid for it all on its proverbial credit card, running up debts of $109 billion. When one property company, Dubai World, announced it might default its debt payment the news sent stocks crashing around the world. In Dubai, people were laid off. As the non-payment of debt is a criminal offence in the UAE thousands would simply drive to the airport, leave the keys in the ignition and flee. Dubai had to ask for an embarrassing bailout from Abu Dhabi, inoculated from economic contagion thanks to its oil wealth. In return Sheikh Mohammed named Dubai's greatest achievement thus far – the tallest building in the world – after the UAE president (and head of the Abu Dhabi royal family) who saved him. The Burj Dubai would henceforth be known as the Burj Khalifa.

But Al Fahim said he hadn't been affected by the crash. He already cashed out his chips. 'I was lucky because [before the credit crunch] I pulled the plug,' he admitted. 'I sold most of my shares at the right time in 2006. I bought stock at Dhs1, but sold it for Dhs48. It was sixth sense. No one told me anything, I just felt it.' Bruised but un-deterred from his experiences with the English press, Al Fahim emerged six months later to buy Portsmouth, a move that once again captivated the UK media. The *Guardian* described his 42-day stint as the club's owner as 'not only the shortest but surely the most ill-fated tenure in Premier League history'. Portsmouth had been crippled thanks to big spending by previous owner Alexandre Gaydamak, the son of Beitar Jerusalem owner Arcadi Gaydamak. Sasha, as he was known, had always denied his father was the real owner of Ports-mouth, but just as the global financial crisis had prompted Arcadi to exit Beitar, Sasha Gaydamak followed the same path. An Israeli court case against Arcadi forced him to list all of his global assets. He included Portsmouth FC on the list. Sulaiman al Fahim stepped in but the money never seemed to appear. Portsmouth fans and the press had a field day. Al Fahim was, according to them, another 'Fake Sheikh', a fantasist who over-egged his net worth to play the Premier League game after getting a taste for it when fronting the Manchester City deal. Portsmouth began the season with seven straight defeats and were rock bottom of the table. But, much more worryingly, by Octo-ber the players and staff had stopped being paid.

'I believe Peter Storrie [then Portsmouth CEO] from day one wanted the consortium of [Saudi investor] Ali al Faraj. He brought them in,' he explained. It was only a few days since he'd sold most of his shares in the club to Ali al Faraj and the criticism, the protests, the threats from fans and internet trolls alike, had wounded him. If any-thing, Al Fahim believed, it was his financial diligence that counted against him. 'With me there would be no overpayment, everything would be at the right time with the right investment. Mine was £5 million as equity. But ... they wanted £10 million in two weeks. So I sold the club. But look how much the [Ali al Faraj] consortium has invested. It's only £1.8 million. So where is the money they [Storrie] were asking me for? I was getting 100 emails a day. Why do they not care now that the consortium hasn't paid this?'

As far as Al Fahim was concerned, he was put in an untenable position. 'I don't know why he [Storrie] thought I wasn't the right guy. He was pushing me out, using the media and website of Portsmouth.' Strangely, the controversy and the bad press that had constantly sur-rounded the Portsmouth deal hadn't been detrimental to Al Fahim. In fact, the opposite was the case. He insisted that the deal was a success for him personally. His involvement in Manchester City and Ports-mouth had meant that other foreign businessmen were now calling him to broker more Premiership takeovers. 'I get phone calls from the States, from Asia, saying "Mr Sulaiman, help us to buy a club,"' he revealed, prayer beads still tightly held in hands. 'Real businessmen don't ever look at my 90 per cent stake as a failure. Anybody, when they see the deal I have done, is really happy. People call me to buy and find opportunities in the Premier League. They also call me to open new football clubs in their own countries. My [new] company understands the football business.'

The traditionalists viewed Al Fahim as an example of everything that was going wrong with the English game. The English Premier League's incredible global success had meant that the game had slowly untethered from its local roots and attracted billionaires, royalty, politicos and criminals from across the world. '[People] should not criticise foreign owners,' he said. 'Whether I am the owner or the owner is Chinese or from Hong Kong or Saudi Arabia, the reality is we are not the owners. It is owned by the supporters and the com-munity. None of the owners are involved in the day-to-day management of the club. It's the foreign owners' job to secure finance, to expand the brand and help with cash flow, but not more than that.'

When we met he was still involved at Portsmouth as club chairman, and held a 10 per cent stake. He couldn't quite extricate himself from the role of Portsmouth's commander-in-chief. At one point during our interview he was approached by Nader Shawky, the Middle Eastern super agent, who was waving a telephone in his direction. On the other end was Amr Zaki, the Egyptian international who briefly took the English Premier League by storm with Wigan Athletic before falling out with manager Steve Bruce and moving back to Zamalek in Egypt. He wanted to speak to Al Fahim. 'I believe that Portsmouth needs someone like Zaki,' he sighed, after a brief chat. 'But seeing that I have sold 90 per cent of the shares I don't have much say. I have one vote though!'

The next day Al Fahim took his place at Fratton Park, assuming pride of place in a seat next to the club's new director of football, Avram Grant. It was one of the few areas of UAE life where an Emirati would openly sit next to an Israeli. 'You should come to the game against Wigan tomorrow,' he had offered. I politely declined, partially due to the distance, partially due to the fact that Portsmouth were bottom of the table and another loss could turn the combustible Fratton Park into an ugly bear pit, with Fahim as its sacrificial offering. Twenty-four hours later I turned on the TV to see Al Fahim, a huge smile on his face, applauding next to Grant and the rest of the board. Portsmouth had won 4–0. Al Fahim's famous sixth sense, one that had avoided catastrophe during the Dubai property crash, was still working. Yet football wasn't where Al Fahim's future lay. He had now moved into film, pumping millions of dollars into a production called *The Road to Darfur*, a gritty, political road movie directed by leading Arab filmmaker Said Hamed. 'I play Sulaiman himself, a philanthropist. I want people to see the real me, not what people like you have written about me!' he joked. At least I thought it was a joke. 'And not what people saw in *Hydra Executives*. You know, my only problem was the first season wasn't me. It showed someone with ego, ignorant, selfish. I want this [film] to show my real, honest lifestyle.' By the end of the 2009/10 season Portsmouth had been relegated, having also become the first club in Premier League history to enter financial administration. They were bottom every week of the season bar one: the first. Manchester City meanwhile hired Roberto Mancini, finished fifth in the league, and set the stage for an unprecedented period of success. And the film? It never saw the light of day.

12

Bahrain

Milan Máčala was a man with a very obvious dislike of the press. The 66-year-old coach of the Bahrain national team had – like any coach who had weighed the cash benefit of working in the region against the insane pressure that followed – good reason to be suspicious of the circus that had just enveloped him and his team. The Czech had spent the past 15 years hopping from one managerial job to the next in the Gulf, hounded by the Middle East's sclerotic, demanding football press whilst both being adored and pilloried by the all-powerful royal families that controlled every aspect of the game in the region. He had largely succeeded wherever he went, winning two Gulf Cups with Kuwait, for example. But sometimes he didn't, like the time he was brutally fired by the Saudis after his first match, a 4–1 defeat to eventual winners Japan at the 2000 Asian Cup in Lebanon, a common demise for most coaches of the Green Falcons. Since his sacking 13 years ago, eight more Saudi national team coaches had followed the same fate. Now he was on the verge of what would be one of the most remarkable achievements in world football. But the veil of secrecy and suspicion remained. 'I will speak to you for five minutes, but that's it,' he barked down the phone. Máčala was busy preparing for the first leg of an intercontinental World Cup play-off against New Zealand in the Bahraini capital of Manama. The winner would qualify for the 2010 World Cup in South Africa. 'The training session will be closed,' he added, 'so you won't be allowed in or to speak to the players, OK?' Somewhere in Bahrain, he slammed down the phone.

This was a problem. I had travelled to Bahrain in the hope of seeing one of the unlikeliest qualifications in World Cup history. By all measures Bahrain shouldn't have been anywhere near South Africa. The tiny Gulf kingdom was one of the smallest countries on earth, a tiny island next to Qatar and connected by a causeway to Saudi Arabia. Nonetheless it had geopolitical significance. The US military stationed its Fifth Fleet there. It had a population under a million where the local football league was semi-professional at best. Unlike its Gulf neighbours, Bahrain was poor but more democratic. Aside from brief periods of Persian, Saudi and British colonial rule, the country had been governed by the Khalifa family since 1783. The Khalifas were Sunni Muslims, the vast majority of their subjects Shia Muslims. Years of economic and political sectarianism – buttressed by a brutal security regime – eventually forced together a coalition of Shia groups, leftists and Islamist who rose up in the 1990s. They very nearly swept the Khalifas from power.

'The uprising began in 1994 when sections of the Shia community in Bahrain and several supporters among the Sunni community issued a petition for political reform,' explained Dr Kristian Ulrichsen, a Gulf expert and associate fellow at Chatham House. In 1994 Bahrain was still being ruled by emergency decree as it had been since 1973, two years after independence from the British. But, according to Dr Ulrichsen, there had been almost daily clashes between protesters and security services since then. Bahrain's internal security was, effectively, run by Ian Henderson, a former British police officer who had been awarded the CBE for brutally suppressing the Mau Mau uprising in Kenya in the late 1950s. He moved to Bahrain and in 1966 was put in charge of the General Directorate for State Security Investigations. For over 30 years, until Henderson stepped down in 1998, allegations of the torture of political opponents were rife. Henderson earned the nickname 'The Butcher of Bahrain'. 'Henderson was credibly implicated as being present at the torture of several detainees,' said Dr Ulrichsen. The Saudis sent a force over the causeway to help the Khalifas thwart the uprising, which Riyadh believed was part of an Iranian plot to spread its influence.

When King Hamad bin Isa al Khalifa came to the throne in 1999 it was seen as a clear step towards reform and reconciliation between the two communities. Hamad was a military man, educated at private schools in Surrey and Cambridge, and then at the Mons Officer Cadet School in Aldershot (the predecessor to the Royal Military Academy at Sandhurst), before graduating from the famed United States Army Command and General Staff College at Fort Leavenworth. He still picked the prime minister, but there was a parliament that gave voice to Bahrain's unusual sectarian mix. Shia politicians began to accumulate power. On the surface things improved. Living standards rose. Banks moved their headquarters to Bahrain. And the national team flourished, becoming one of the strongest in the region. In 2004 they reached only their second Asian Cup finals and shocked the continent when they made it to the semi-finals. Two brothers in that team accounted for over half of Bahrain's goals: Mohamed and A'ala Hubail. A'ala had finished joint top scorer in the tournament alongside Iranian midfielder Ali Karimi. He scored twice in Bahrain's quarter-final victory over Uzbekistan, as well as the winning kick in their victorious penalty shootout.

That was just the start. Both the Hubail brothers starred as Bahrain tried to reach the 2006 World Cup finals. A'ala scored six times, the second highest in Asian qualification, setting up a play-off match, again against Uzbekistan. After a bizarre scandal the first match between the two in September 2005, which the Uzbeks won 1–0, was annulled after FIFA judged that the Japanese referee had made a technical error. He had awarded Uzbekistan a penalty but, after spotting an Uzbek player encroaching in the box, blew for an indirect free-kick to Bahrain. FIFA said he should have ordered the penalty be retaken. The Uzbeks were incensed, especially as they won the game and should have had a retaken penalty anyway. Bahrain went on to draw the replay 1–1 in Tashkent before holding the Uzbeks 0–0 in Manama, going through to the final intercontinental play off against Trinidad and Tobago on away goals. If Bahrain had won that tie against Trinidad and Tobago, they would have been the smallest country ever to qualify for the finals. They almost made it too. After grabbing an away goal in a 1-1 draw in Port of Spain, they had hope for the return leg in Manama. Both the Hubail brothers started that match. They held out until the 49th minute when Dennis Lawrence scored for Trinidad and Tobago. It was they, and not Bahrain, that became the smallest ever nation to qualify for the finals, at least until Iceland later qualified for Russia 2018, a record that is unlikely to ever be broken.

Bahrain's journey towards the 2010 World Cup finals was full of drama. A'ala was again joint top scorer in qualification for the Bahrainis as a new star emerged. Sayed Mohamed Adnan was a tall, cultured central midfielder who could also play at centre back. His performances had caught the eye of European clubs as well as the Asian Football Confederation, who nominated him for their 2009 Player of the Year award. They, along with evergreen winger Salman Isa, helped set up a play-off against their Saudi neighbours. A historic dislike existed between the two, partly to do with history, partly due to Saudi forces invading a few years previously and partly due to the regular pilgrimage made by young Saudi men driving over the King Fahd Causeway every Thursday night to get drunk and start fights.

The first leg in September 2009, almost exactly four years after that Japanese refereeing debacle in Tashkent, ended 0–0. As the second leg, played just four days later, entered the 90th minute, the score was 1–1 and Bahrain was going through to the final round on away goals. The board went up showing three minutes as the 50,000 crowd started to get restless. The Saudi's pumped the ball forward. Yasser al Qahtani somehow volleyed a cross over from the right-hand by-line. Asian Player of the Year Hamad al Montashari rose to clatter the ball into the top left-hand corner. The game was over. The crowd exhaled into a state of what turned out to be premature ecstasy. With ten seconds left of injury time Salman Isa burst forward and won a corner. Isa swung in the ball in a last, desperate, seemingly futile attempt. Time seemed to stop as Sayed Mohamed Adnan and Ismail Abdulatif both rose for the ball. It glanced off Abdulatif's head. The ball looped goalwards, as if in slow motion, and nestled into the bottom right-hand corner: 2–2. It was one of the most incredible four minutes of football you could ever hope to see. The whistle blew a few seconds later. Máčala, his white hair and rotund frame giving him the air of young Boris Yeltsin, seemed shocked, conflicted even, hugging his players before they collapsed in tears around him.

'At 1–1, 90 minutes, the game was over,' Máčala said as we met after nightfall outside the offices of the Bahraini Football Association.

It was October but a late summer heatwave made the air feel like warm soup. Nearby his team was warming up for training as a dozen local journalists buzzed around, taking advantage to speak to the players as Máčala was looking the other way. 'I nearly had a heart attack,' he said. 'It was 30 seconds into injury time. But then we scored again. What can I say? It was luck!' Luck only gets a team so far. Unlike the UAE and Qatar – two Gulf countries now leveraging their wealth to change the shape of global sport – football in Bahrain was a street game. Rusty goalposts jutted out of spare patches of sand in the capital, where young children played until dusk. 'I don't know how to explain it, you compare the leagues in Bahrain to Kuwait and Qatar, they have much more money and better quality pitches,' explained Máčala, now much more amenable than he was on the phone. 'But spirit and desire is much more important. We have had many, many positive moments to help us dream the dream. They have talent and they have speed and flexibility. They [Bahrainis] are playing football every day, everywhere. It's a small place but they play football, it is in their nature. But now they need organisation to prepare, and to have a strong league.'

Much of the team had now moved to the better paid professional leagues in places like nearby Qatar. There was also Jaycee John, a naturalised Nigerian who played in Belgium. But the key dynamic was one of faith. Máčala believed that a mixed team of Sunni and Shia players sent an important message to the rest of the country that was still coming to terms with life after its uprising. 'It [qualification] is very important to them because this is a great moment for the country, because of football,' he said. 'Everybody on the street is talking about the Bahrain national team. The team is a representative of the country as a whole. This island is small, only 700,000 people [citizens], and everybody loves football.'

The match was also viewed by many in Bahrain as a last chance. The heartbreak against Trinidad and Tobago four years previously had left a mark. 'After what happened four years ago we are desperate,' said Sheikh Ali bin Khalifa al Khalifa. Sheikh Khalifa was the excessively genial vice president of the Bahraini FA and a member of the royal family, offering countless cups of tea as we talked. 'Every Bahraini is desperate to go to the World Cup for the first time. It's a dream for every Bahraini . . . we have been through hell.' Máčala had seen enough of football in the region to know that chances like these rarely come along once for a country the size of Bahrain, let alone twice. 'This is the moment for our players,' he said before heading back to the pitch and ordering the press off the pitch as if swatting away a swarm of flies. 'Fifty per cent of this team played in the game with Trinidad and Tobago. Everyone was crying . . . we need luck.' The large doors, covered in green tarpaulin, were shut and the press pack thrown outside.

By 3pm on the day of the match, the flags that adorned the walls and fences of Bahrain's National Stadium, in Riffa outside Manama, had already been meticulously hung. Usually the groundsmen on flag duty busied themselves in silence in front of empty stands but not this time. With three-and-a-half hours before kick-off thousands had already arrived in their seats in anticipation of Bahrain's first leg World Cup play-off against New Zealand, creating an incessant, deafening din that didn't stop until the final whistle. The red and white of the Bahrain flag didn't flutter alone. Portraits of King Hamad had been tied to the hoardings. Flags from Sudan, Palestine, Kuwait and Saudi Arabia, among others, flew in solidarity. The message of Arab fraternity was clear. If Bahrain were to be the region's sole representative at the 2010 World Cup finals, then the Middle East would rally behind it. 'They play good football and Bahrain is like a second country to us,' said 24-year-old Abdulatif Hamed, a Kuwaiti who had flown to the game with a group of friends. 'The whole of the Arab world will be behind Bahrain, *inshallah*.'

By kick-off the stadium had far exceeded its 25,000 limit as hundreds of supporters filled each spare walkway in the main stand. As it was Friday, many prayed before the game, including one supporter I saw in a red Manchester United top with 'ROONEY' on the back. The conditions were so humid you could almost see the air. But the atmosphere was perfect for Bahrain. A few hours previously the New Zealand team appeared so hot they struggled to get off the team bus and walk the few metres to the stadium. But the All Whites were made of sterner stuff. Sayed Mohamed Adnan controlled the game but Bahrain just couldn't score. The pivotal moment came when Salman Isa was put through on goal and, after rounding the keeper, contrived to smash the ball against the post with the goal at his mercy. It finished 0–0. At the full-time whistle the Bahraini players left the pitch grim-faced, knowing a wonderful opportunity had been lost. Isa lay shattered and motionless on the floor by the bench. For the All Whites it tasted like victory. The players ran to their jubilant section in the corner of the stadium, 1,000 supporters strong, mainly expats from the region, to link arms and acknowledge what must count as one of the longest away trips in the history of international football.

'Any team that has beaten Saudi Arabia back to back will be tough. Australia found it hard too,' said Kiwi coach Ricki Herbert, a veteran of the All Whites team that had qualified for their only other appearance at the World Cup in 1982, as his staff celebrated pitchside. 'We wanted to take the tie back home to have a chance and we did that.' He was less circumspect when he thought he was out of earshot. 'We've done it!' he shouted whilst bear-hugging members of the New Zealand delegation. 'We're going all the way now. We've fucking done it!'

Outside the ground the crowd trickled home, muted but unbowed, dragging their multinational flags behind them in the sand. 'Nil–nil is not a bad score and it's not a good score but there is a saying in Bahrain that we play better outside of Bahrain than in it,' shrugged Mohammed Alwadhi, a 17-year-old student making the long trek back to Manama. 'We just couldn't find the goal. Even if we put a goal above the goal we wouldn't have found it.'

Ricki Herbert's confidence wasn't misplaced. Back in Wellington New Zealand took a first-half lead before conceding a second-half penalty. It was Sayed Mohamed Adnan, the beating heart of Bahrain's qualification campaign, that stepped forward to take it. He hit it low to the goalkeeper's right, but it was too weak and too close to Mark Paston, who saved it. Adnan still had his hands on his head in disbelief a few minutes later. New Zealand won 1–0 and would go on to draw all three of their group games in South Africa. They were the only team in the tournament to go unbeaten.

The Bahrainis knew they wouldn't have another chance like this, especially A'ala Hubail, the team's top scorer for the past six years. He wasn't in Wellington. The striker had snapped a cruciate ligament in his knee playing for Al Ahli in the Bahraini league a few days before the tie. He would be out for six months. But he sent a message to his teammates before they embarked on their long and ultimately fruitless flight down under. 'We don't know what will happen in the next four or five years, and it is difficult to know who will still be playing with the national team at that time,' Hubail had told the *Gulf Daily News* of his fear that, after coming within one match, and one goal, on two occasions, he would never play in a World Cup finals. 'I think this will be the last chance for at least four of our national team players, and I hope they can grab this opportunity for all of us ... the national team is more than just one player. If I am out, there will be someone there who can play for me.' His words were both prophetic and cruel.

13
Gaza

GAZA CITY, OCTOBER 2009

The metal walls of the Erez Crossing sizzled under the midday sun. Around its heavily guarded entrance stood a group of angry, desperate people, mainly women, their heads covered. They shouted and swore at the Israeli guards standing between them and the only entrance to the terminal, pointing to imaginary wristwatches. The guards shrugged indifferently before they turned and slowly marched away, machine guns in hand. Israel's only crossing into the Gaza Strip was about to close. Once this had been an important entry point between the two, but the stream of visitors and businessmen had been constricted to a tiny trickle in recent years. Israel has been blockading Gaza with various degrees of severity since the turn of the twenty-first century. But after the 2006 kidnapping of Gilad Shalit, a young Israeli soldier seized by the armed wing of Hamas, and Hamas's violent takeover from Fatah in 2007, Israel and Egypt had virtually sealed off the entire Strip. This was the only way in or out. The restrictions had continued, through Operation Cast Lead, the Israeli assault on Gaza in 2008 – designed, they said, to stop cross-border rocket attacks aimed into Israel – that led to anywhere between 300 and 1,000 civilian deaths. That was ten months ago. Now nothing went in or out of the Strip, except the barest of essentials, NGOs, journalists, the sick and the dead. There was the Rafah crossing bordering Egypt in the south. But Hosni Mubarak's border police seemed gleefully efficient in maintaining a blockade there too. The only way of getting many goods into Gaza – from generators to car parts – was through Rafah's network of illegal tunnels, piece by piece.

But, today, for some reason, the Erez Crossing had yet to be opened. There was a problem, one of the soldiers told me. I was headed for Gaza City where, the next day, the biggest football match of the year was taking place, the Gaza Cup final between Al Shati, a team from the largest of Gaza's eight refugee camps, the Beach Camp, and the team from the Hamas-affiliated Al Salah Islamic Organisation. The internecine warfare between Hamas and Fatah had ended. Hamas had won and some stability had returned. Yet football was now in chaos with no league and just a short cup competition for sustenance. This was, I would later discover, as much to do with the Palestinian civil war as the Israeli blockade. With the Jewish sabbath fast approaching, the border would be closed for two days. Once in, you would be stuck in Gaza until the border opened again. Just as the impatient had begun to drift away, the guards gestured to the crowd to come forward. Whatever had gone wrong had been resolved. We walked into the gleaming metal edifice.

Entering the Erez Crossing was like walking into a hellish, disembodied theme-park ride. It stank of efficiency. The crossing is a series of chambers, each with automatic metal sliding doors that hissed as they opened and closed behind you. In one room a metal table was all that greeted you. A voice from above delivered instructions to empty your bag for inspection by an unseen eye. More chambers followed. More disembodied voices. More metal. Until the final door lifted. The final room was covered with dozens of spent bullet casings, spread like shattered teeth across the floor. There was no voice. No instruction. No explanation. Just a silent, metal room, the smell of cordite and the evidence that something very bad had just happened. I crouched down, picked up a single bullet and walked out of the room's only exit and into the sunlight.

On the other side two dead bodies lay on gurneys, with ambulances parked nearby. Judging by the size of the body bags they looked like adults, but I couldn't be sure. 'They are going home,' said a dark-skinned porter in a baseball cap as he tried and failed to load my bags onto his trolley. As if there wasn't enough death in Gaza, it had to be imported too. It was a one-kilometre walk through no-man's land before you reached the Gaza checkpoint. Men with beards and black uniforms stood outside a Portakabin to check everyone's credentials.

Behind them hung a sign. Alcohol would not be tolerated. Instead it gleefully informed visitors that any bottles would be opened and 'Poured down in the drain in front of the owner'.

Gaza was now firmly in the control of Hamas. The civil war between the secular nationalist Fatah of Yasser Arafat and the Islamic fundamentalist Hamas in 2007 had created a violent vacuum of kidnappings and tit-for-tat killings. The conflict had broken out when I was with the Palestinian national team at a tournament in Jordan. As the team travelled to Amman to take part in the West Asian Championship, Hamas forces had seized control of the Gaza Strip, trapping the entire squad in Jordan as the Israelis denied the team entry back into the West Bank. It was worrying enough for the players based in the West Bank. But for the 13 players that lived and worked in Gaza, it was a disaster.

I had come to Gaza for the cup final but also to see the spiritual home of Palestinian football. Every fan and official conceded that Palestine's best players came from Gaza. But for the past few years, football had slowly been dying there. The blockade and the internal fights had brought Gazan society to the brink of collapse. Gaza City was a hopeless place. Bullet holes, piles of rubble – once former housing blocks – and broken buildings sat untouched following the bombing that destroyed them months previously. The import of cement was banned by the Israelis in case it was used for military purposes. The black uniforms of Hamas now kept order on the streets, pacing in front of large, colourful murals of Palestinian martyrs. Huge piles of rubbish burned permanently, throwing up acrid plumes of thick black smoke. Manic children danced around them, throwing glass bottles at passers-by. One whistled inches past my head.

Gaza's football league had managed to survive even the darkest of days of the conflict, but it couldn't survive Hamas. When they took over Gaza, they cancelled it. It wasn't just the political and economic apparatus they seized: they had also forcibly taken over Gaza's top football clubs, angering the Fatah-dominated Palestinian Football Association based in the West Bank, leaving the fans, players and senior politicians angry. Now all that was left was a hastily arranged cup, branded as a so-called 'Dialogue and Tolerance' cup, organised by the clubs themselves, and resentment at the politicians that had tried to control the sport for their own ends. Ibrahim Abu Saleem, vice president of the PFA and the man in charge of football in Gaza, made some last-minute phone calls from the PFA's office on the morning of the cup final. These days they shared space with the Palestinian Olympic Committee, not out of choice, but because the headquarters of both organisations were levelled when Israel bombarded Gaza the previous winter. Now, though, the biggest threat to the game didn't come from Israel. 'We, as sportspeople, want to remove sport from politics but politicians on both sides – Hamas and Fatah – play on this, they try to make politics come into sport,' explained Ibrahim. 'The main problem lies with Hamas. When Hamas hands back the clubs to their legal board of directors, sport will be running again in Gaza as in the West Bank.'

More precisely, it was the military wing of Hamas that had refused to hand back the clubs to their rightful owners. 'The political wing wants to return the clubs to their legal owners,' Ibrahim explained. 'But they [Hamas's military wing] want to be within the Fatah clubs, to have control and channel the minds, the thinking, of the youth.' The chaos reminded me of my visit to the West Bank a few years earlier. Back then movement restrictions, checkpoints and a lack of political goodwill meant that no league could take place. But that had all changed when a new Palestinian Football Association president was elected. Jibril Rajoub was not a man to be messed with. He was a former national security advisor to Yasser Arafat, and once head of the Preventive Security Force. He had spent 17 years in and out of Israeli jails for throwing a grenade at an army checkpoint before being exiled to Lebanon. He spoke fluent Hebrew and English and had also just been elected to the Fatah Central Committee, making him one of the most powerful political figures in the West Bank. He was known for his fearsome ability to bash heads together to reach agreement and had achieved some stunning results. He had managed to persuade the Israelis to allow the building of a new national stadium in Al Ram on the outskirts of Ramallah – the Faisal al Husseini Stadium – right next to the Israeli separation barrier. The easing of Israeli checkpoints had allowed a new professional league to be started. A women's league was started too, giving Honey, the captain of the women's national team I had met in Bethlehem, the chance to finally play on a full-sized pitch against other international players.

Football was thriving in the West Bank. So much so that, the previous year, Palestine played its first-ever home match, a friendly against Jordan, just before the Palestinian civil war had broken out. As many as 15,000 fans turned up to watch their team draw 1–1 with Jordan in a hugely symbolic match. But in Gaza the civil conflict between Hamas and Fatah, and the subsequent Israeli war, had seen any gains in the West Bank go backwards in Gaza. 'The women footballers,' said Abu Saleem as he signed a pile of documents, 'they now can only play football in their bedrooms.' The crisis had hit the players hardest. Sitting in Ibrahim Abu Saleem's office was Hamada Eshbair, Al Shati's captain. Tanned with his hair cropped close to his skull, Hamada had played in the 2007 West Asian Championship, which marked the beginning of the end – at least for now – of a united national team. For months now no players based in the Strip had been allowed to leave. A lucky few, around 50, had been poached by the newly professional West Bank Premier League. But Hamada had remained, angry that his career had been put on hold due to internal and external conflict. 'As a national team player I've had big difficulties in playing because of the siege,' he explained. The last time he was allowed to leave was for a tournament more than a year ago. 'I can't play outside, to be the member of another team. I was offered chances in Jordan and Egypt, but I'm still here.'

Some were even unluckier. Three months before I arrived in Gaza, Mahmoud Sarsak packed his bags and travelled to the Erez Crossing. He believed that he was leaving to fulfil his potential and play for one of the West Bank Premier League's newly minted teams. Instead he was arrested by the Israelis, who believed he had taken part in a recent bombing. He was never charged with a crime, but was put into administrative detention – essentially being held without charge for an indefinite period. For three years he maintained his innocence whilst the PFA suggested that his arrest might come from the fact that Sarsak's brother had allegedly been a member of Islamic Jihad. When I asked a senior Israeli security source why Sarsak had been jailed they wouldn't go into specifics, only that he was 'in administrative detention due to security-related matters, including involvement in attacks on Israeli forces, and planned to perpetrate suicide bombings'. He wasn't freed until 2012 when he decided to go on hunger strike. His act of self-destruction brought his cause to global attention. FIFA president Sepp Blatter – the man behind granting Palestine FIFA membership – personally called for his release. The pressure worked. Sarsak returned home to Gaza having lost half his body weight, before managing to get out and find refuge in Ireland. I met him in London, where he was protesting against UEFA awarding Israel the right to host the European Under-21 Championship. 'I was harassed, brutalised, hit on the head with the guns they were using. They took me off into an army centre where they called my brother and told him I was in prison. I spent 45 days there. I saw death many times throughout that period,' he told me when we went to a nearby café to talk. The conditions he was held in, he said, weren't fit for an animal. 'It is a two-metre-by-two-metre bunker. Damp. No sun. No air. It is not a place where even animals should be. At first I had 18 days of investigation. I was chained to a chair. My eyes were closed. I was not allowed to sleep for 18 days. I was beaten up, humiliated. I was put in a fridge for a time where I was frozen almost to death and then straight from there to the hospital. Every time you go through these cycles you feel like you are going to die. And you could die at any moment under those conditions.' A hunger strike was, he felt, the only option left. 'This was the only way left to achieve my liberation. The Israelis killed my hope, killed my dreams, killed everything. It was either to live in dignity or be buried underground.' He was free now, but he would never play professional football again.

Back in Gaza, the federation was struggling to arrange any matches at all. 'There's a lack of funding for the PFA to launch competitions and so we can support ourselves,' Eshbair said, articulating the players' concerns that funding had been cut because of fears that any cash would end up in Hamas's hands. 'Jibril Rajoub is the [PFA] president, we appeal to him to support soccer in Gaza like he does in the West Bank. Political conflicts are the reason for this. I blame both sides [Fatah and Hamas]. They both have demands that harm the players.'

Ribhi Sammour scrawled his instructions in exaggerated flourishes on the faded green chalkboard that hung from the wall of the Palestine

Stadium's decrepit dressing room. The coach of Al Shati Sporting Club had gathered his players, all sitting in nervous silence, for one last briefing before the biggest match of the season would decide who would be Gaza's undisputed champion. They had good reason to be nervous and for Sammour to be especially exacting about his tactics for the big match. For one, their opponents, Al Salah Islamic Organisation, a new team aligned with Hamas, were an almost unknown quantity and the match was to be watched, if rumours were to be believed, by Hamas prime minister, and one of Israel's most hated men, Ismail Haniyeh. Equally as important was the weight of expectation. Al Shati, a mixed team of Fatah and Hamas members from the eponymous refugee camp, was one of Gaza's oldest and most popular teams. They had not won any silverware in almost a quarter of a century. But the most recent impediment to breaking their poor run wasn't the lack of talent or even motivation. There simply hadn't been any other teams to play against.

'We have no championship and we haven't won any trophies since 1983,' Sammour explained after he had directed his players onto the pitch. 'Hamas and the Fatah government in Ramallah do not give us the chance to play, so the 16 teams got together and we were given some money by the UNDP [United Nations Development Programme] instead.' Sammour strode out into the warm autumn Friday afternoon sun to a crescendo of cheers and drums. With little to do and even less to get excited about in Gaza, 5,000 hyperactive fans had made the journey to the stadium in Gaza City, the blue and yellow of Al Shati dominating the terraces. In front of them stood camouflaged members of Hamas's security forces armed with machine guns, ready for any crowd disturbance. In the spaces under the concrete stands, dozens of fans laid out their football jerseys and prayed as the referee blew his whistle.

The final was anything but an exhibition in dialogue and tolerance. As Hamas's forces prowled the touchline, fierce challenges flew as both sides desperately sought a breakthrough. The only time any unity was displayed was during half-time, when the press, Hamas security forces, players and officials lined up, 50-strong, to pray together on the pitch. They prayed in front of whatever they had in their hands at the time: a camera, a pair of boots, goalkeeper gloves, a club, a machine gun. By the time Al Shati scored in the 90th minute, the entire bench was on the pitch celebrating their unassailable lead. The referee had a brief stab at enforcing injury time before giving up, awarding a 2–0 victory to Al Shati and trudging back to his changing room, his authority neutered.

Now all eyes were on the small selection of dignitaries in the stand. The increasingly fraught armed guards gave a hint that someone important had arrived. Ismail Haniyeh took to the pitch in a camel-coloured jacket, flashing a wide smile before he climbed the hastily constructed dais that had, moments earlier, been dragged onto the pitch. Haniyeh himself had been a tough-tackling defender for Al Shati, where he grew up a few metres from the football club. He had been surrounded by machine-gun-wielding special forces in black flak jackets, eyeing the crowd with suspicion. Hamada Eshbair took the trophy offered by Haniyeh. The two spoke, Eshbair animated, as if pressing home an important point.

Haniyeh's appearance was fleeting. Al Shati's fans, still in the stadium to witness their rare piece of silverware, had begun to let off fireworks. The prime minister's stern-faced personal security men sensed danger. The Hamas politician had been targeted for assassination by Israel and, he claimed, Fatah in the past. Taking no risks, his security detail closed around him, forming a human battering ram that charged through the crowd. Haniyeh was bundled, still waving, into the back of a waiting parked limousine, past the lines of celebrating fans, seconds after he had handed out the last medal. The car screeched off into the distance.

It was the last time Hamada saw the cup he had just won. It would later emerge, outside the ground, in the hands of a yellow and blue mob, who proudly chanted as the cup was held at the apex of a tenuous human pyramid. Thousands of fans rolled down the dusty path towards the Mediterranean in the glow of the setting sun, before they, and their cup, disappeared into Al Shati camp. Hamada didn't mind too much. 'There is not a lot to be happy about here,' he said. 'The Beach Camp is very crowded, maybe 80,000 refugees. The Al Shati team wanted to make the people happy after the war and the martyrs and the siege, and we managed that.'

Later that night, Eshbair would sit in his home in the Beach Camp receiving well-wishers before a party was held in Martyrs' Square. But there was one thing that puzzled me. What did he say to Ismail Haniyeh as he was handed the cup? 'I told him: "You used to be a player, please solve this problem of the players quickly,"' Hamada retold with a wry smile.

'And what did he say?' I asked.

'He replied: "I hope so, I hope so, *inshallah*."'

RAMALLAH, MARCH 2011

The Palestinian national team trained in the cold, freezing light as a gaggle of young boys were being admonished on the touchline. 'Everyone is watching you, your mother, your father, everyone,' shouted a middle aged Singaporean match official to a dozen or so teenagers.

'Don't play with the ball!' he shouted in English. 'Don't slouch! Don't look unhappy!'

An interpreter rattled the rules back in Arabic to the ball boys, unhappy and slouching, their hoods pulled tight against the chill. The Palestinians were preparing for their first-ever competitive match on home soil, an opening qualification match for the 2012 London Olympic games against Thailand. The basics needed to be prepared. For one, the ball boys were being instructed how best to discharge their duties. It was unsportsmanlike, the Singaporean official explained, to not throw the ball back to opposition players during the match. Next to them another official taught a group of schoolchildren how to unfold and carry the flags of Palestine, Thailand and the Asian Football Confederation the right way up.

It had been just over a year since I left Gaza. The situation there was still dire, but in the West Bank Jibril Rajoub's football revolution continued. The president of the PFA's private office was a large villa in a quiet suburb of Ramallah, the colour of Jerusalem's famous sandstone. He sat behind his desk stymied by an ugly cold, occasionally coughing roughly into a well-used handkerchief. 'Getting the league started here was not easy but we have 15 to 20,000 coming now to games from the north, the south, from areas that are difficult to travel from,' he explained proudly. Rajoub looked fearsome, a huge man with a bald head and the gruff gait of a prizefighter. The blame for the failure of Gazan football to progress, Rajoub insisted, lay with Hamas. 'In the West Bank we have two members of Hamas on the board. We have teams for Hamas, the PFLP [Popular Front for the Liberation of Palestine],' he explained. 'There is a wall here between politics and factionalism in sport [in the West Bank]. I think the same should happen in Gaza.' The comparison between Ramallah and Gaza City was stark. Everything that lined a Gazan shopkeeper's sparse shelves, along with the cars and motorbikes that bumped along its unpaved and pockmarked streets, had to be smuggled in through the Hamas-controlled tunnels that stretched into Egypt. By comparison, Ramallah looked like Las Vegas. Brand-new, alien-looking shopping malls announced their arrival like visitors from the future. Basic foodstuffs in Gaza were scarce; in Ramallah a sign stretched across one road proclaiming that the new Nintendo Wii was back in stock after selling out, yours for just 1,690 shekels.

But this was Palestinian football's biggest moment so far, a chance to show the world that it could organise itself to an international standard. Yet some problems endured. Four Gazan players were granted permission to play in the Thailand game, but eight were refused, half of the starting line-up according to Palestine's Tunisian coach Mokhtar Tlili who was denied entry to the West Bank until the night before the match. Even the Asian Football Confederation's Qatari president Mohammed bin Hammam was held at the Jordanian border.

Rajoub's success had brought him some popularity. He was an enigma, a member of Fatah's inner circle and seen by some as a future Palestinian president. And yet his brother Sheikh Nayef was one of the top ministers in Hamas, dealing with religious affairs no less. He was Yasser Arafat's national security advisor in the West Bank, known as an enforcer and loathed by Islamist groups for targeting its members, including on one occasion his own brother. But he was also known as a moderate, backing a two-state solution, who had also learned Hebrew to translate some of the works of key Israeli Zionist thinkers into Arabic so that the Palestinians would 'know their enemy' better, as one PFA official put it. During the second intifada he was injured when his home was attacked by the Israeli Defence Force. Yet he now espoused the virtues of non-violent action. 'I think this is a rational decision by the Palestinian political leadership to focus on football,' he said. 'We need to expose the Palestinian cause through football and the values and ethics of the game. I do believe this is the right way to make business and pave the way for statehood for the people. The non-violent struggle is more productive and fruitful to the Palestinian cause. In the current situation in the twenty-first century, this is the best means . . . to achieve our national aspirations.'

Football was the medium Jibril now fought through. In fact, such had been his success in furthering the Palestinian cause through sport – he was also the head of the Palestinian Olympic Committee – that, as one unnamed PFA insider put it, 'he is popular and, more importantly, he is not corrupt. He will be the next President [of Palestine]'. Whilst Rajoub himself claimed to have no political ambitions, he left the door open, as any good politician would. 'My ambition is that sport has a national Palestinian identity. I have no personal ambition,' he replied when asked about any future political role. 'For me the [political] position is an option, rather than an obsession. I was popular, I am popular, and I will remain popular as long as I contribute to my people's cause. I was part of the freedom fighters, I spent 17 years in Israeli jails, I suffered a lot. I contributed to my people's cause, I want my cause to achieve something. This is the ambition of a person like me.'

Many within the Palestinian government believed that football not only provided a nationalist symbol, but was also part of Prime Minister Salam Fayyad's attempts to normalise the economic and civil institutions of the state so that, if the need arose, Palestine could announce unilateral independence. 'People know Palestine throughout the world because of the national football team,' said Palestinian defender Nadim Barghouthi. 'It is a perfect way to prove to the rest of the world that we are human beings. We are not terrorists. In the past, all the world thought that Palestinians threw stones. I consider the players to be soldiers without weapons. We are playing for freedom in Palestine.'

The big day arrived. The bus from Ramallah hugged the silver, graffiti-scarred separation barrier as it approached the Faisal al Husseini stadium. The wall was a mere 100 metres from the pitch, the stadium barely 4km from Jerusalem's old city. Thousands crushed inside three hours before kick-off, the sky dark and ominous from the earlier rains, coating the fans, the seats and the stands in lightly coloured mud. The police wore modern riot gear, pedantically removing poles from the supporter's Palestinian flags, confiscating fizzy drinks and checking for weapons, to prove that the Palestinians could organise a match to the newly required standard expected of competitive international football. But the numbers were too great; hundreds surged through the single metal door and into the stands, causing a crush. Fans scrambled up the sheer concrete walls, pulled up by other fans, to escape the dangerous ebb and flow of bodies until the police regained control.

Around the stadium, posters illustrated the importance that the Palestinian Authorities placed on football; huge portraits of Yasser Arafat, the Dome of the Rock, President Mahmoud Abbas, Jibril Rajoub and FIFA President Sepp Blatter all hung side by side. A hastily erected poster of AFC chief Mohammed bin Hammam, also here to witness history, hung from a nearby building. 'When this team plays, the people of Palestine are free, and these people [in the stands] are too,' shouted Motaz Abu Tayoon, a 21-year-old engineering student from the Askar refugee camp near Nablus. Around him fans chanted: 'Jerusalem, for the Arabs!' 'The Israelis are not here. I am very, very happy,' he added.

The ball boys successfully carried their flags onto the field, the national anthems passed without incident, and the politicians basked in the glow of international media attention. But it took 45 minutes for the stadium to come to life when Abdul Hamid Abu Habib, a player from Gaza, volleyed in Palestine's first goal. The stands erupted in song, chants, tabla drums and whistles. The captain took off his armband, kissed it and pointed towards Prime Minister Salam Fayyad, sitting in the crowd. 'The national team is very important. It is an important symbol. The national football team is a symbol of this country. It has that kind of significance, for sure. That [a player from Gaza scored] makes it all the more sweet,' Fayyad said whilst sheltering from the driving rain at half-time. But he urged a word of warning. 'We have the second half now. If the score stays as it is, we have an extra half hour of football.' Chances came and went until the final whistle blew at 1–0; 1–1 on aggregate over two legs. Salam Fayyad, with his white and black keffiyeh wrapped around his neck, paced through the stand, watching every minute of extra time unfold. 'I hate penalties,' he offered, rocking back on his heels with hands in pockets for protection against the freezing-cold early evening. 'I won't watch penalties. I'll look this way!' He pointed to the sky.

At the end, the collective weight of expectation rested on the lonely shoulders of a man called Zidan. A storm had now enveloped the stadium as freezing sheets of hail hammered down onto the pitch, and into the face of the white-shirted midfielder. A whole people, if not yet a whole nation, held its breath. Amjad Zidan stood 12 yards from goal facing the crucial penalty that would either continue Palestine's Olympic dream, or likely condemn them to familiar disappointment. As Salam Fayyad had feared, the match had gone to penalties. Everyone had scored. It was 5–5. Now it was sudden death.

The crowd of young men behind the goal, the players in the centre circle, even Salam Fayyad froze as they prepared for the ball to bulge in the back of the net. Zidan stood nervously in front of the Thai goalkeeper, awaiting his cue, the hail seemingly falling harder as the referee blew his whistle. But Salam Fayyad did watch; as we all did. The spot kick was saved. Half the crowd was gone before Thailand's Seeket Madputeh sealed Palestine's fate. The players, shattered from bombarding the Thailand goal, missing chance after chance even after the away team was reduced to ten men, left the field with heads bowed. It was too much for Nadim Barghouthi, the 'soldier without a weapon', who ran down the tunnel with tears streaming down his face, inconsolable.

It was still a remarkable turnaround. Five years earlier Israeli movement restrictions were so severe that it was impossible to organise a league in the West Bank. Now there was a professional league that was paying salaries comparable to lower division Israeli sides, which had begun to attract Israeli Arab players. Gaza remained isolated and impoverished, but there was a national stadium in the West Bank, and home games for the men's and women's national teams. Still, Mokhtar Tlili didn't find comfort in the moral victory. 'This leaves a bitter taste in the mouth,' he said in the tunnel as the press and fans melted away, back to the buses ferrying people to Nablus, Jericho and Jenin. 'We played well. But my heart aches tonight. It was a political victory, but I wanted it to be a sporting victory as well.'

14

The Death Match Replay

The Cairo International Stadium was already shaking to the sound of 100,000 songs six hours before kick-off, but by the time the Pharaohs were ready to take to the pitch the deafening screams had created a seemingly impenetrable wall of sound. No one knew for sure how many people were there. The official capacity stated 70,000 but anywhere up to 100,000 had squeezed in, evading the draconian riot police who were beating the ticketless and the poor outside the gates. It had been two years since I stood with Amr and his Al Ahly ultras in the same stadium – the same stand in the same stadium – to watch the Cairo derby against Zamalek in the Egyptian league. But this, a 2010 World Cup qualifier against Egypt's North African rivals Algeria, was different. Under the president Hosni Mubarak the security forces had tried to crack down on the unruly opposition they faced from the terraces during the Cairo derby. This time, for this match, there would be no such restrictions. The crowd had been encouraged to express its rage. Now it had gotten out of hand; frenzied, cathartic and ugly.

Such was the noise that every single note of the Algerian national anthem was obscured. The big screens focused on the worried faces of the Algerian players as they tried to sing against the tide. Several of them wore white bandages on their heads and across their faces, signs of recent, violent injury. If I'd been in any doubt about the ferocity of the rivalry between Egypt and Algeria up to that point, the boy standing on the seat next to me, head tilted back, screaming into the night, provided further evidence: the words 'Fuck Algeria' had been written on his and his friends' faces in crayon. A huge Egyptian flag with the words 'Welcome to Hell' written on it faced the pocket of Algerian fans, high up in the main stand. More than 2,000 seats had been left fallow around them, a protective barrier that gave sanctuary to the tiny rectangle of green and white flags.

After months of anticipation, mob violence, lies and political interventions, Egypt was about to play the Desert Foxes in one of the most politically charged football matches since a World Cup qualifier in 1969 sparked the so-called Soccer War between Honduras and El Salvador. At stake was a place at the 2010 World Cup finals, Africa's first. But like the Honduras–El Salvador conflict, it wasn't what was at stake so much as what lay beneath. History was repeating itself. The match took place nearly two decades since Egypt and Algeria had played in eerily similar circumstances in Cairo in 1989 for a place at Italia '90. That match, consequently known as the 'Death Match', became notorious. The game was marred by violence between players and fans of such ferocity that it has soured relations between the two countries. Egypt won that game 1–0 but, incensed by defeat, a dodgy offside decision and accusations of bias by the Tunisian referee, the fighting continued at the teams' hotel after the game, culminating in a supporter, an Egyptian doctor, being bottled and losing an eye. Algerian legend, and former African Player of the Year, Lakhdar Belloumi was blamed and convicted in his absence and an international warrant was issued for his arrest. Belloumi claimed innocence, pointing the finger at a former teammate. For two decades the shadow of the game hung over Belloumi until the reverse fixture between the two teams earlier in 2009. Then it took the personal intervention of Algeria's veteran president Abdelaziz Bouteflika to have the warrant quashed.

Algeria won that game 3–1, meaning that Egypt had to win in Cairo by three clear goals to qualify for South Africa 2010. Algeria merely needed a point. A 2–0 victory meant that the two teams would finish on the same points, goal difference, goals for and against. A play-off in Sudan had been scheduled for a few days later, just in case. The players carried not just the pressure of World Cup qualification, but also the joy and heartbreak of 1989 on their backs. Every little bit of help was required. Seconds before kick-off Egyptian striker Amr Zaki stood alone in the centre circle facing the Algerian players, his eyes closed, hands on his face. As two tribes swirled around him, and the referee prepared to blow his whistle to start the game, he was offering a solitary prayer.

Saleh Zakareya had got up before dawn for a chance to get a ticket for the game, but his efforts turned out to be fruitless. He had travelled down by train from the northern port city of Alexandria, where he was studying engineering, and queued for five hours in the hope of getting one of the official 70,000 tickets, but like the tens of thousands standing outside Zamalek stadium, his efforts were in vain. The police announced that they had come on the wrong day. They should come back tomorrow. The crowd was livid. 'This is because of the big people in the government who will get all the tickets and then sell them on the black market,' shouted Saleh, a short, bookish young man wearing glasses, as the angry crowd jostled with the policemen. The commanding officer, dressed in a black uniform, large Aviator sunglasses and adorned with numerous impotent honours, approached me and tried to grab my camera, before getting distracted by the rapidly worsening situation. 'There is so much corruption here,' Saleh shouted over the noise. 'They are supposed to be on sale for 15 [Egyptian pounds, about £1.50] but they will sell them for 150 [£ 11.50].'

In the two years since I was last here, life had got visibly worse for the Egyptians I spoke to. Poverty, unhappiness with President Mubarak's authoritarian rule and endemic corruption in all walks of life had proliferated. Wheat prices had rocketed and inflation had sparked bread riots the year before, reminiscent of similar protests over the price of bread in 1977 that led to nearly 80 deaths. The national team, though, had thrived. The Pharaohs were champions of Africa, winning the 2008 African Cup of Nations by beating Cameroon 1–0 in the Ghanaian capital, Accra. Mohamed Aboutrika had scored the winning goal.

Aboutrika was one of the greatest players Africa had ever produced. He was adored by all Egyptians, even Zamalek fans, thanks to his pious nature and devout faith. In an earlier round of the 2008 Africa Cup of Nations he had scored and revealed a T-shirt with the words 'Sympathize with Gaza' written on it, a reference to Israel's Operation Cast Lead that would cost the lives of over 1,000 people, mostly civilians. 'It was a personal statement from myself,' he explained afterwards.

'I feel great sympathy from the children of Gaza, who are under siege. I wore the shirt for Gaza's children who are suffering, who are starving, who are vulnerable and fear for their safety.' He was booked by the referee and warned not to do it again by CAF, African football's governing body. But Aboutrika had only further enhanced his heroic reputation in Africa and the Arab world.

The victory in Ghana meant Egypt had won back to back Africa Cup of Nations titles, making them one of the country's few current sources of pride. 'There is no Ahly or Zamalek today,' Saleh explained, in hope that the national team could unite Cairo's deep footballing divisions. As he spoke the police began to clear the crowd with their batons. The crowd replied by chanting what they felt about the Egyptian FA's president: 'Samir Zaher you are an asshole!'

'Unfortunately the media has made this match so huge. Some people will have heart attacks,' Saleh said, exasperated, now realising he would be taking the long train back to Alexandria empty handed. 'They have even asked that the female fans, the "ice-cream fans", don't come so that the true fans can come and make the stadium rock. They are making it like a fight between two armies.'

Saleh was right about that. After landing in Cairo it had become clear that the match had taken on a huge political importance. A media war between the Algerian and Egyptian press had slowly escalated since Egypt beat Zambia in an earlier round and the permutations needed for both countries were known. Suspicion was everywhere. There had been no press conferences and training was closed to the media, just in case any tactical secrets were leaked. Before Algeria's home match against Egypt earlier in the year, Algeria's veteran coach Rabah Saâdane, who had led his country into their last World Cup campaign at Mexico '86, broke down in tears, such was the pressure from the home press for victory. Every player and official was sworn to silence. The Egyptian league had been suspended for the previous month so that the team could prepare properly for the game, but the move had one unforeseen effect: the Egyptian press filled the vacuum with incessant coverage of the build-up, which had further stoked tensions between the two countries.

Many countries have been guilty of whipping up xenophobic feeling before an important match. But Egypt's press was tightly controlled.

Mubarak was a canny politician, and a huge football fan. He understood the power of a successful national team. When Egypt hosted the Africa Cup of Nations in 2006, Mubarak was there at the opening, waving to the crowd with his wife Suzanne. When Egypt won it, it was Mubarak who handed coach Hassan Shehata his medal. Before the Algeria game he would grace the team with his presence to offer words of encouragement, but behind closed doors. Aside from state television, the press was not invited.

It had been Mubarak's appropriation of the national team for reflected glory that had angered Amr, the leader of the Al Ahly ultras I had met at the Cairo derby. His group, he told me, had boycotted national team games even though much of the team played for Al Ahly, including Aboutrika, whom Amr adored. 'This is Mubarak's team,' Amr had told me as an explanation as to why he wasn't going to the game. But there were other reasons too. In the two years since they formed, Amr and his ultras had become virtual enemies of the state. As they grew from a few hundred into a few thousand, with their choreographed banners and increasingly poetic and political songs, the group had been harassed by the police. Arrests had been made to intimidate them. They were painted as violence-addicted hooligans in the state-run press. They had rebranded themselves the Ahlawy, and were regularly involved with violent confrontations with the state more than with their opposite numbers at Zamalek. It was best for everyone involved, Amr thought, that the Ahlawy stay away.

The media, both in Algeria and Egypt, had been trading insults, invoking the 'Spirit of '89' and using war-like imagery in their coverage. One of Egypt's popular weekly football newspapers ran with the game on all 20 pages. On the front page was a scene from the film 300, the Egyptian players' faces superimposed on the ripped bodies of the soldiers. At the front, leading the charge with the Egyptian flag in hand, was the coach Shehata. The headline read: 'Attack', smeared in blood. Even Coca-Cola handed out T-shirts that read 'I was there in 1989'.

In those circumstances it was surprising to discover that anyone from Algeria would risk travelling to the match, but some were still determined. A short drive from Zamalek's stadium journalists were ducking in and out of the guarded, high-walled offices of the Egyptian

FA. 'It is a war in the media only,' said Lyes Fodil, a correspondent for the Algerian newspaper *Echorouk*, who was there to pick up his press pass. 'The game in 1989, Egypt deserved to win, even if the goal was offside. I have been here a week and I haven't had any problems. The people have a good relationship.' He looked down at his press pass, with the word 'ALGERIA' splashed over the front and quickly stuffed it into his pocket. 'But Saturday is another day.'

The situation was different for the travelling supporters. Outside the Algerian embassy on Zamalek island, the 2,000 protesters knew they were on neutral, if not exactly safe, ground. The long, white-walled, tree-lined street was coloured green and white. They had gathered to show their displeasure at the way they and their country had been demonised. And they were not happy that so few tickets had been allocated to them. 'The Egyptians are so scared they will try any means to make sure there are only Egyptians in the stadium,' explained Elias Filali, a well-dressed British-Algerian businessman who had flown from London to get a ticket. 'It has become a dirty game in the press. The image of Egypt is at stake.' Others had driven from Algeria, through Libya, to get to Cairo. Some had travelled even further. Mohammed Touiza stood with a stiff military back and small moustache, dressed in a grey suit, shirt and tie with an Algerian scarf tied around his head. He was 73 years old and had followed the team for decades, back when Algeria was under French rule. On his lapel he wore the flag of the Front de Libération Nationale, the guerrilla movement that fought and won Algeria's independence in 1962. The FLN had famously launched a rogue 'national' team to promote its cause, attracting some of France's best French-Algerian players, several of whom had already represented the French national team. They had to leave the country under the cover of darkness to join the squad. But Mohammed had been much more directly involved. 'I used to be an FLN fighter and I got life in prison, life in arm and leg shackles, in a prison called the "Corridor of Death",' he bellowed, half to me, half to the crowd that had gathered to listen to what the old man had to say.

'What were you in prison for?' I asked.

'I killed someone, a French policeman and a *harki* [Algerians who served for the French army],' he replied, without a hint of remorse. 'I killed them with grenades, then I shot them. I killed him [the *harki*] because he informed on me. I was tortured in prison, they electrocuted my balls before they let me free after independence three years later. Football makes people popular and united. This match will make us forget the [Algerian] civil war.'

Although the 1989 match had been a pivotal moment for recent relations between the two countries, other issues ran deeper, touching on the colonialism that Mohammed fought against. As regional rivals, both had vied for supremacy: Egypt positioning itself as the leading force for Arab nationalism, Algeria assuming the position of tormentor-in-chief of colonial expansionism in Arab lands. Yet the Egyptians question Algeria's view of themselves, joking that they send language teachers to Algeria so that the Francophone nation can learn to speak Arabic properly. The Algerians, in return, accuse the Egyptians of cowardice, of selling out their Palestinian brothers by signing a peace treaty with Israel. The fact Egypt refused to play the FLN side hadn't been forgotten either. One disgruntled Algerian hacker defaced President Mubarak's personal website to air exactly those views. But for most ordinary people, there was still an Arab, Muslim fraternity that trumped all other grievances. As the crowd protested, a large group of Egyptian youths holding flags of both nations aloft approached. Rather than attack they applauded the Algerian crowd, who returned the favour. 'We wanted to let them know,' said one teenager who had painted his face both the colour of the Egyptian and Algerian flag for the occasion, 'that not everyone felt the same.' They were quickly bundled away by the police.

The limited fraternity didn't last long. 'Have you heard, the game is going to be cancelled, they have attacked the Algerians?' an Egyptian friend told me by phone that evening. Sure enough, within an hour the footage of the attack had been edited and uploaded onto the internet. The first video was dark and shaky, occasionally zooming into a huge hole that had been smashed through a coach window. The second showed the aftermath: several Algerian national team players exhibiting their injuries, blood pouring from head wounds. A hundred or so Egyptian fans had gathered to 'welcome' the Algerians as they arrived in Cairo, and had pelted the team bus with paving slabs, injuring three players. 'They let them do it,' defender Antar Yahia told Algerian state radio, accusing Egyptian security guards of standing back and allowing the attack to happen. 'You can't launch five-kilo rocks from 50 metres. They let them do it and watched. It's shameful. In our home game we welcomed them with flowers.'

The Algerian sports minister condemned the attack. The president of the Algerian Football Association asked for the game to be called off, citing safety fears. FIFA demanded the Egyptian FA guarantee security. 'I saw it with my own eyes, I videoed it,' Lyes, the Algerian journalist I had met picking up his press pass, told me later that night. 'I was standing in my hotel room, at the window, looking down at the bus. I saw them [the Egyptian fans] attack the bus.' But not everyone would be sure that he, or the Algerian team, was telling the truth.

The next day the streets of Cairo felt silent, the calm only punctuated by the rising, distorted cacophony of a thousand muezzins singing a thousand calls to prayer. Friday morning is usually a time for quiet reflection but the Egyptian press had gone on the attack. The initial reaction from the Egyptian authorities was to deny that the attack ever took place, feeding into a popular, conspiratorial belief that the Algerians were using the incident to call off the game out of cowardice. The government-run daily newspaper *Al Ahram* directly accused the Algerians of fabrication. 'The bus carrying the team from the airport to the hotel was at the centre of a strange incident in which some of the players started to smash the vehicle's windows claiming that they were the target of stone throwing,' it stated.

Every Egyptian I spoke to was utterly convinced the attack had been staged by Algeria to try and get the game annulled, so scared were they of playing in Cairo. For Saleh, the engineering student I met outside Zamalek's ground who, as feared, had to resort to the black market for his tickets, the truth was obvious. 'They destroyed their own bus, of course. Why? So after, when they lose, they can blame it on the Egyptian fans.' Even Ayman Younis – the former Egyptian international whom I'd met in Cairo before the Ahly–Zamalek match two years before – was suspicious. Ayman had actually played in the Death Match in 1989 and vividly remembered its viciousness. 'It was an incredible atmosphere, the Algeria team was full of stars,' he recalled, pointing out that it was Algeria that were the favourites back then. They had qualified for consecutive World Cups in 1982 and 1986. At Spain '82 they beat West Germany in their opening match.

They were only denied a place in the next round thanks to the 'Disgrace of Gijón', when West Germany and Austria manufactured a 1–0 victory for the Germans that would guarantee progress for both teams at the expense of Algeria. At Mexico '86 they narrowly lost to Brazil but went out in the group stages. In 1989 they were still considered the best African, and Arab, team around. 'On the pitch it was very crazy; 11 fights between every player,' Ayman said of that match in Cairo twenty years before. 'Everybody forgot what the coaches had to say and just fought instead. It was a battle, not a football match. It was like our war against Israel in 1973.' Ayman had driven to meet me outside Al Ahly's training ground. He had managed to find me a rare ticket. Ayman claimed he had incontrovertible proof of Algeria's duplicity. Security sources had told him that there was glass on the outside of the coach. Clearly, this proved they had broken the window themselves, *from the inside*. The bus driver, who he said had no axe to grind, had been assaulted by the players and had seen what was going on. 'What they did was make a movie,' Ayman said of the bloody video evidence that emerged afterwards. 'A very, very bad movie. The Algerian team are very bad people.' He warned me to be careful at the match and to leave early if I wanted to get in for the evening kick-off. 'Don't worry, I'll get there a few hours before,' I assured him. 'No, no,' he replied, leaning in as if I had quite grasped what he said. 'You have to get there at midday. A ticket doesn't mean you'll get in.'

Kick-off was at 7.30pm.

A burning sun greeted Egypt's big day. It was midday, seven-and-a-half hours before kick-off, but the side streets and concourses around the stadium were packed full of supporters and an almost equal number of security officers. The sea of people parted when a coach, led by a police escort, arrived full of Algeria fans. The Egyptian crowd closed around it as soon as it stopped, hurling vitriol at the scared passengers inside. One of the windows was missing. The Algerian fans filed out under a line of riot shields raised up high to protect them. 'They threw stones at us and gave us the finger,' explained Attef, an Algeria fan based in Cairo who had travelled with the convoy and had now been taken behind the relative safety of a police checkpoint. His friends eagerly showed videos on their mobile phones of their vehicle being

attacked minutes earlier. Others displayed cuts and bruises from flying glass. 'Not all Egyptian fans are like this,' he added. 'It's the kids.'
For the home fans the police set up three checkpoints on each route,
harassing and beating those that didn't have a ticket. I was carried
through in the crush. The line thinned out as more and more fans
were snatched away. As Ayman had told me, even having a ticket
wasn't a guarantee. At the last gate I had begun to take pictures of a
man in civilian clothes beating supporters who had tickets but weren't
allowed in. They waved them at me as they limped away. I was
grabbed from behind.

'Delete!' the balding man in the camel jacket demanded as he held
tightly onto my wrist. I flicked on the camera. The screen beamed back
an image of the same man, launching himself into a crowd of teenagers, his hand and stick a blur of rage. 'Delete.' The next was a close
up of his face, contorted and puce as he swung wildly. 'Delete.' We
went through deleting all the photos on the card, even the picture of
my pet dog, back home in England, licking the patch where his balls
used to be. Satisfied, he let go of my wrist and pointed me towards the
stadium gate.

Hours passed as the stadium filled and the blazing sun set. Hosni
Mubarak was nowhere to be seen. Instead it was an opportunity for his
sons Alaa and, more importantly, Gamal to step into the spotlight.
Gamal was an unpopular figure in Egypt, yet he was handed a leading
position in his father's political party and was obviously being groomed
as his successor. The match offered him a platform for statesmanship.

The noise from the crowd, as the teams walked onto the pitch, was
unlike anything I had heard before. Amr Zaki prayed and the referee
blew his whistle. Two minutes after the kick-off, and with Algeria
unable to get a touch of the ball, Egypt surged forward. Mohamed
Aboutrika hit a post and Zaki was there to poke in at close range. The
outpouring was almost viscous, a sound wave able to knock a grown
man off their feet. Everything – 1989, the World Cup, the accusations,
attacks, fabrications, the confected outrage – they had all led to that
moment.

Oddly, the goal had an almost anaesthetic effect on the crowd. The
goal had suddenly brought hope, but with it the reality of expectation. After the initial burst of euphoria the anti-Algerian chants died

down, the crowd subdued. Whereas before obscenities were screamed at the small patch of green and white high up in the stands, now the Egyptian fans stared blankly at the pitch, transferring their nervousness to the players. Egypt's initial fearlessness meant they had overawed Algeria in the first few moments. Afterwards, they could barely string two passes together.

Chances came, half-time went, but it was Algeria, their team punctuated by the white head bandages that marked those injured in the team bus attack, who edged towards the finals. After hours of queuing and singing, weeks of tit-for-tat media exchanges and a month of frenzied anticipation, and with 90 minutes on the clock, it looked like Egypt had fallen short of the World Cup finals by a solitary goal. Objects started to be thrown on the pitch. Grown men began to cry. The riot police lined up, fixing their gaze on the crowd and raising their shields. Unless a miracle happened the tension would inevitably explode onto Cairo's streets. But just as all hope was lost, in the sixth minute of injury time, substitute Emad Moteab rose and nodded in a looping header. The Algerians were silent, halted just 30 seconds from the finishing line. The Egyptian bench ran on to the pitch, the crowd erupting in disbelief. Egypt and Algeria had finished the group level on points, with the same goal difference and the same goals scored. They would have to do it all again four days later in Sudan.

Hundreds of thousands poured into the streets, firing rockets and plumes of fire from makeshift flamethrowers fashioned from hairspray canisters into the air. 'That we scored at the beginning and the end shows that we played until the last minute with the same soul,' shouted Essam Bilal, a fan I spoke to over the din of car horns from the gridlocked streets outside the stadium. 'Algeria are so disappointed now. It was bullshit that they were attacked because I know the bus driver and he said they invented everything so they deserved to lose,' he continued. 'Now we will beat them in Sudan, *inshallah*.' On the other side of the stadium, just as Essam and virtually every other Egyptian fan still insisted that the attack on Algeria's team bus had been a hoax, rocks once again rained down as Algeria's crushed fans left the stadium. Thirty-two people were injured in the clashes around the stadium that night, 20 of them Algerian. But the reverberations from Emad Moteab's late, late goal were felt around the world. In

France, hundreds of youths, mostly of Algerian descent, rioted in Marseilles, smashing shop windows and setting fire to cars and boats. In the Saudi city of Mecca, 50 Egyptians were arrested after celebrating too exuberantly on the Kingdom's conservative streets. The next day, in Algiers, fans who had gathered to try and buy tickets for the match in Sudan rioted, smashing up Egyptian businesses and ransacking the offices of Egypt Air.

Somehow the two teams, and the two nations, had to get themselves ready to do it all over again, a few days later, in Omdurman, Sudan. Sudan was a step too far from me. Without a visa, which was impossible to get in Cairo, there was no chance of making it. It seemed a strange place to have a neutral match. On the one hand, Sudan neighbours Egypt, and a huge number of Sudanese live and work there. On the other hand, they usually fill the most menial, lowest paid jobs and have to deal with endemic racism. It would not be the fraternal home match many in Egypt were expecting. Waiting at the airport, my phone rang. It was Ayman Younis. He could get me a seat on a plane for Sudan if I still wanted for just a few hundred dollars. But without a visa it would be pointless. Instead I would watch the match in the next best place I could find.

EDGWARE ROAD, LONDON

The green and white scarves had arrived early to find sanctuary in the Babylon Café in west London. A faded Truman Brewery sign hung on the wall, testament to its previous life as a pub. Now it was dry, taken over by an Algerian who had turned it into a halal café. Gone were the cigarette-and-booze soaked carpets of the English working class, replaced instead by oriental lamps, grilled lamb and beautiful women in green hijabs shouting: 'One, two, three, viva Algerie!' Directly opposite, through the former pub's dirty windows, I watched the Rose Café fill with Egyptian fans. Nasim, a young university student, stood and watched with me. 'At the end of the last game, you had the Algerians on one side of the road, the Egyptians on the other and the police lined up in the middle to make sure there was no trouble,' he said, not moving his gaze from the nervous men opposite. 'I didn't realise the Arabs hated each other so much. You could see it in the Egyptians' eyes, the Algerians' too.' As kick-off for the World Cup play-off between Egypt and Algeria approached cities across the world prepared for war. London's Edgware Road, famous for its Arab cafés like Babylon and Rose, had divided itself for the night. Almost every café within a half-mile radius was full of Egyptian fans. Babylon was Algeria's only ally. They didn't need many more than that. When Antar Yahia's first-half thunderbolt gave Algeria the lead, and eventually a place in the World Cup finals, the café emptied into the street where a long line of British police stood, separating the grim-faced Egyptian fans from the hundreds of celebrating, horn-blowing Algerians. Down Edgware Road they ran, the Egyptians on one side, the Algerians on the other, hurling insults at each other. I ran with them, towards Marble Arch and Oxford Street. The noisy mob snaked loudly through British shoppers, confused by the rattling drums and the occasional stops to pray. 'This is a big victory for the Algerian people,' shouted Qassi Ait Touati, a young chef who spoke with a deep French accent and marched with us. 'After what happened, Egypt deserved to lose.'

In Egypt, the accusations, rumours and conspiracy theories came thick and fast: Sudan had allowed its fans to be attacked; the Algerian government had sent thousands of violent criminals from its jails to teach the Egyptians a lesson; scores of people had died; Mubarak was about to send special forces into the country to protect his citizens. All weren't true. In fact, the Sudanese government summoned the Egyptian ambassador to explain the media coverage back in Egypt. Only five fans were lightly injured, they told the ambassador. Thanks were in order, not accusations. Such was the schism the Arab League even approached Colonel Gaddafi to see whether he would mediate between the countries. The whole sorry, ugly incident had left its mark and humiliated Egypt further. The biggest loser, though, seemed to be the Mubarak clan. The ailing dictator had placed the stewardship of events in the hands of his two sons, but it had gone badly wrong. Dictators can never resist the nationalistic catnip of international football for reflected glory, but the danger is in reflected defeat. Both sons were prominent at both matches with Alaa phoning an Egyptian TV show from Sudan to hysterically attack Algeria's 'terrorism' and vowing to avenge the attacks on Egyptian fans in Sudan next time the two teams played. 'These are not fans, these are terrorists,' Alaa Mubarak had whined. 'Thank God we've lost the game. Otherwise, it would have been a massacre.'

The two matches had stirred something in Egypt. It was the first time I had seen a whole propaganda machine lie in the face of irrefutable facts. Egypt would later be punished for the attack on the Algerian bus. For all the conspiracy theories, a TV crew from French network Canal+ had filmed the whole thing. A representative from FIFA was on board too and had watched the incident in horror. Egypt had been humiliated completely. If the Mubaraks had hoped that football could boost their support, defeat diminished their standing further. The Mubarak sons didn't look statesmanlike. They looked petty, jingoistic and weak. The match would prove to be the dark before the dawn.

The Pharaohs did exact some revenge. Before the World Cup, Egypt beat Algeria 4–0 in a heated Africa Cup of Nations semi-final. It would lead to Egypt's third African title in a row, a record. But when the World Cup came about, it was Algeria in the spotlight, even if they didn't make it past the group stage. But, back in London in the afterglow of the Sudan play-off, retribution and revolution were far from the Algerians' thoughts. One group of fans surrounded a thin, besuited middle-aged black man, out shopping on his own. The Algerian fans, seeing him as an avatar for their victory, joyously started chanting 'Sudan! Sudan! Sudan!' before hoisting him high. They ran down Oxford Street, with him teetering on their shoulders, with a huge smile on his face, towards Trafalgar Square where every Algerian had agreed to meet in case of victory.

His name was Dave.

He was from Brixton.

15

Return to Qatar

It had only been a month, but the posters had already warped, whitened and peeled from the walls and shop windows they had been fixed to in the afterglow of celebration. They could be found all across Doha, showing the same image: the country's leader, Emir Hamad bin Khalifa al Thani, wearing a Western suit and tie, lifting the World Cup with two hands over his left shoulder. A gap-toothed grin shone under an unfashionably bushy moustache. There were no words on the posters. There didn't need to be. The image said enough, the moment captured when Qatar had been chosen by FIFA to host the 2022 World Cup finals. The news had come as a shock, but not to Qataris who had gathered in numbers to watch a live feed from FIFA's headquarters in Zurich on large outdoor screens. They celebrated when Sepp Blatter fumbled with perhaps the most expensive envelope in history, and pulled out a piece of card with the word Qatar embossed on it. The image was quickly printed, distributed and pasted across the city. But unseasonably unsettled weather had seen the sun shine brightly between a *shamal*, the strong desert winds that blow from the planes of Mesopotamia down through the Persian Gulf, and bouts of cold rain. The posters extolling arguably the greatest moment in Qatar's short history were now fraying at the edges and warped, but that grin and that moustache and the gold World Cup remained untouched in the centre. No one dared take them down, as if removing them would loosen the emir's grip from the statue itself.

It had been seven years since I had first visited Qatar. I'd returned because the country was hosting the 2011 Asian Cup, just a few weeks after shocking the world and winning the 2022 World Cup bid. Qatar always had ambition, that was clear. I had seen how they poured money into their domestic league, the Qatari Stars League, later rebranded the Q League, to attract the biggest stars they could; the likes of Ronald and Frank de Boer, Marcel Desailly and Gabriel Batistuta. I had seen how they tried to pay Brazilian footballers huge sums of money in an attempt to naturalise them for the Qatari national team, only for FIFA to change the rules to prevent their efforts. I had marvelled as Diego Maradona and Pelé walked on to a stage together and embraced to mark the opening of the Aspire sports academy (and earn a phenomenal appearance fee in the process). All their efforts had been focused on raising the profile of Qatar internationally, and the standard of football at home so that the tiny nation with a population of citizens that could be counted in the hundreds of thousands could qualify for a World Cup finals. Back then it seemed like a distant, almost naive plan. It failed, of course, but there was a charm to the failure. It seemed so hopeless, so destined to failure. How could anyone buy their way to the World Cup finals? But no one could have predicted what happened next.

There had long been talk about one of the Gulf states hosting the world's greatest sporting prize. Dubai had once bragged that it would bid for the 2018 World Cup. Abu Dhabi followed with its own project bankrolling Manchester City. Qatar had tried and failed with its own quixotic bid to host the 2016 Olympic Games. It was rejected by the IOC as they wanted to move the date to a time in October when the temperature wasn't above 45°C. But this time was different. Qatar had become a serious contender to win the bid to host the 2022 finals. Qatar had invested heavily in the endeavour: sponsoring obscure conferences in Africa, paying for development projects in Asia and Central America, inviting the world to marquee friendlies involving Brazil or Argentina or Egypt in their magnificent Khalifa International Stadium in Doha, at the centre of their Aspire project, named after the father of Emir Hamad, who he deposed in 1995. A slew of famous stars backed the bid as Qatar World Cup 'ambassadors': those who played there in the past like Pep Guardiola, Ronald de Boer and Gabriel Batistuta. As well as Zinedine Zidane.

And then there was the vision thing. Yes, Qatar was a small country.

But this will be a World Cup for the Middle East, a World Cup that could unite a fractured land. Sure, no infrastructure existed yet. But we had unlimited pockets to build a new city, a new country. Yes it could hit 50°C in the summer. But we would build air-conditioned stadiums that would cheat nature. The technology would be solar, carbon neutral and, like the stadiums, packed up and sent to the developing world. It wouldn't just change Qatar. It wouldn't just change the Middle East. It would change the world.

Vision wasn't enough. The bid was plagued by accusations of corruption and vote buying. Members of FIFA's Executive Committee, the 24-person body that would ultimately decide the winner, had been caught taking cash and suspended. Two members, Nigeria's Amos Adamu and Tahiti's Reynald Temarii, were suspended before the vote after a *Sunday Times* sting filmed them asking for cash for votes. There was also the figure of Mohammed bin Hammam, the Qatari president of the Asian Football Confederation, one of football's most powerful men. He was rumoured to have played a vitally important behind-the-scenes role in lining up support for the bid. He was now being talked up as a possible challenger to FIFA president Sepp Blatter. When I met Bin Hammam in Ramallah's only five-star hotel a few months after the Zurich vote he told me he indeed intended to run for FIFA's top job, but wasn't quite ready to announce yet. There were whispers and accusations that Qatar had unfairly used its immense wealth to try and win the bid. But there was no smoking gun, at least not yet. They had played the game and, for now, they had a shot. Sepp Blatter even seemed surprised when he opened the envelope. In the end, it wasn't even close. Qatar had won every round of voting handsomely. The Qatari royal family delegation celebrated and embraced. The emir took to the stage and Sepp Blatter handed him the World Cup. Mohammed bin Hamad al Thani, his young son and the face of the bid, looked close to breaking down as he approached the podium and thanked everyone. 'We will not let you down,' Sheikh Mohammed promised, swallowing his tears.

How could this have happened? The press in England, but also the US and Australia, who both lost out to Qatar, was predictably negative. The legendary football writer Brian Glanville, giving his own viciously poetic spin on the issue, called Qatar a 'wretched little anonymity of a football country' and 'Bin Hammam's dismal desert state'. Almost immediately the calls had begun to re-examine the process. At the very least move the event to the winter, which would in turn cause havoc with the schedules of the powerful European leagues. Qatar must have bought it, the media alleged, without giving any concrete evidence. At one point a smoking gun appeared to have been found when Phaedra al Majid, a female media manager on the Qatar bid, went rogue, alleging to the *Sunday Times* that Qatar had paid two FIFA Ex Co members $1.5 million. The revelations were aired during a parliamentary select committee hearing on England's failed 2018 bid thanks to parliamentary privilege. Later Al Majid would retract her allegations. FIFA's general secretary Jérôme Valcke had claimed in a leaked email that Qatar had 'bought' it. He later said he meant they had used their immense wealth to inundate the process, which was all within the rules, of course.

The suspicions remained. But less well reported were perhaps more compelling and more strategic reasons for the bid's success. Not bribes or illegal inducements, but the glorified sports centre I had seen Pelé and Maradona inaugurate in 2005: Aspire. When Aspire had first opened its doors in 2004 it had grandiose aims that seemed at odds with reality. The Qataris would spot and nurture talent from across the world in the hope of finding the next Messi or Ronaldo. They had world-class training facilities for all sports at its sprawling Aspire complex, with Qatar's Wembley-esque national stadium as its centre point. But Aspire had also become a Forward Operating Base for the 2022 campaign. The Qataris had opened numerous academies around the globe looking to identify and recruit talent in previously overlooked or underdeveloped footballing nations. They had set up a programme called Football Dreams designed to mine for talent in Africa, opening a facility in Senegal. Whilst the rest of the world's media had looked for subterfuge in the bidding process, Brent Latham, an American sports writer for ESPN, had found a much more believable and accurate reason for Qatar's 2022 success. 'Football Dreams stands out not just because it throws money around to pluck prospects from the developing world,' he wrote. 'Six of the 15 programs are in countries represented on FIFA's all-power 24-man executive committee.'

Guatemala, Thailand and Paraguay had all seen Aspire arrive to build academies. Each had a member on the FIFA Ex Co. Players would be identified and whittled down to a handful who would then be awarded scholarships. It was a fast-track to success and a better life, in a much more controlled and ethical process than the agents' free for all that usually followed a talented player. Whilst the US and England were bragging to the world about their stadiums and their technically sound bids, Qatar was working under the radar funding what it viewed as a humanitarian project in the back yards of the men who would actually vote on the World Cup bids. But, along with currying favour with FIFA's Ex Co, the project may not be as altruistic as claimed for another reason. There was one main fringe benefit for Qatar. The hope of finding players for its own national team.

Before the start of the Asian Cup, I went back to the Aspire complex. Inside its main hall small groups of children trained in front of five-a-side goals. The young boys were a mix of ethnicities and nationalities: Arab and African; Qatari and Senegalese. On the touchline Aspire's sporting director Wayde Clews watched as the kids were run through their paces by European coaches. 'Two thousand and ten was a watershed year for Aspire because some of the boys that came through the academy are now starting to find their way into the Qatar Olympic squad,' he said. In fact eight Aspire students had just made it to the Qatar squad for the 2010 Asian Games in China. 'We are also now seeing three or four making their way into the [full] national squad,' he added. He denied that Aspire was an exercise in looting talent from the developing world to build a new Qatari team. 'I think there's no evidence to support those sorts of notions. What we have done is brought boys from Third World nations. There is absolutely no obstacle to those boys playing for their home countries. It can be seen as an altruistic move by Qatar.'

This was true too. Various Ghanaian and Nigerian national youth squads had benefited from returning Aspire graduates. But Qatar had form in this area, naturalising athletes from Africa, Asia and South America so that they could compete in the Olympics. The national football team had also seen several Brazilians and Uruguayans play for it, naturalised before the Qataris went too far and tried to 'sign' the then Werder Bremen striker Ailton, forcing FIFA to change its rules on eligibility. One Uruguayan, Sebastián Soria, remained Qatar's first-choice striker. Clews was adamant that naturalisation wasn't a goal, but it didn't mean a young African player *couldn't* choose to be Qatari if they so wished. As Aspire's director general Andreas Bleicher explained: 'When making agreements, we are not requiring them to play for Qatar. We leave it up to them. A player might be here for five years, and if he wants to play for Qatar, it is upon the player concerned.'

That raised a much more fundamental question. A young kid in Senegal or Kenya or Benin might have a life of poverty and insecurity at home, ruled by governments that had invariably failed to offer much in the way of opportunity or a future. At best they could take a long shot in Europe's talent-trafficking grinder where they could find themselves signing for Manchester United, or playing in the Ukrainian second division or begging on the streets of Marseilles. Or they and their families could be taken to Qatar, educated and fed. If they failed, they at least now had options, an education. The question wasn't: why would an African kid choose to represent Qatar? The question was: why *wouldn't* an African kid choose to represent Qatar? That was what terrified African and European football. One African football journalist captured those fears when he told me Aspire was 'stealing' the continent's talent. The next generation of Weahs and Drogbas would be lost to them. This, at least in theory, was partially true. But for European football they had met an entity that threatened its pre-eminence in identifying and exploiting talent. If Aspire was engaged in theft, as some in Africa saw it, they were simply better at the game than the Europeans, who had engaged in talent plunder in a manner that had no rules and few concerns on what would come of those who didn't make it. At least Aspire offered more than an agent's meal ticket. The young boys walking off the state-of-the-art pitch and into the changing rooms were all between 12 and 14 years old. By the time the 2022 World Cup came along they would be in their mid-20s, in their prime, and possibly wearing the maroon shirt of Qatar.

The Asian Cup wasn't just about judging Qatar's suitability as a host. It was a chance for many to see Qatar play football for the first time. On the pitch, things hadn't started well. In front of a packed 40,000 near all-Qatari crowd, after a lavish opening ceremony, the team had conspired to lose 2–0 to Uzbekistan. The holders, Iraq, also had great expectations to fulfil. The Iraq team trained next to the Gharafa Stadium, where I had met Marcel Desailly. That felt like a lifetime ago. Iraq's previous coach Jorvan Vieira, the Brazilian Muslim who had masterminded Iraq's stunning Asian Cup triumph in 2007, was long gone. Now Wolfgang Sidka, a German who eyed me with suspicion, was in charge of defending the title. He was preparing his team for a group match against their perennial rivals Iran. Younis Mahmoud, the captain that had dragged his team to victory through sheer force of will in 2007, scoring the only goal in the final and being nominated for the FIFA Player of the Year in the process, greeted me warmly on the touchline. He had remembered how his teammates had humiliated me on the Iraqi team bus in Jordan four years ago by filming me dancing topless. 'It's considered a derby game, just as Saudi Arabia is considered a derby,' Younis explained of the up-and-coming match against Iran. This was an understatement. I had watched him play in the final of the West Asian Championship against Iran in Amman, and seen the outpouring of vitriol from the Iraqi crowd towards the Iranian team. 'There were also problems between us and Iran and years of war. So I think it is considered a derby and also a challenge.'

The team had experienced mixed fortunes since that day in July 2007. It was hard living up to an achievement like that. Younis still remembered those last few matches as if they were yesterday. He remembered being in the dressing room after the semi-final with South Korea. Iraq won on penalties but, moments later, a suicide bomber detonated his explosive vest in two crowds of celebrating fans in Baghdad. Some of the team had wanted to pull out of the final, partly out of grief, partly out of guilt. But something stopped them. 'All our players wanted to take this cup because we saw on television one woman whose baby was dead,' he recalled of that moment in the dressing room when they heard the news. They switched on a TV to see the carnage, and saw the woman who had lost her child, overcome with grief. 'She said, "I need the players to take this cup . . . because my son is dead,"' Younis recalled. She became known as Umm Haider, Mother of Haider, the name of her murdered 12-year-old son. Her testimony, Younis told me, made the difference between going home and fighting for the title. 'I was fired for this game, I killed myself in that stadium to take this cup,' he said. 'Before we started the game we had won. Because our heart was in this game. We killed ourselves to win this game.' Younis didn't return to Iraq for the planned reception with the prime minister Nuri al Maliki. It was just too dangerous. Some of the squad did go back and they were welcomed by Maliki, who had invited Umm Haider too. 'This courageous woman's attitude is what we expect to see from Iraqis. She showed true love for her country and her people. She was very courageous and we cannot do enough to thank her,' Maliki said. The prime minister placed garlands of white carnations around the players' necks, and promised them all diplomatic passports. Umm Haider was promised land and money, so she could start her life again.

After the adulation, the comedown followed. Mahmoud had been close to securing a dream move to France, but the issue of whether his extended family could come with him prevented him from going. He stayed in Qatar. Then the team failed to qualify for the 2010 World Cup after losing, ironically, to Qatar. Later it would emerge that one of Qatar's naturalised Brazilian players was ineligible to play in that game. It was an open and shut case. Iraq should have been awarded the tie and a place in the final round of qualification. But FIFA rejected it on the grounds that they received Iraq's appeal past the deadline. And then there was the battle within the Iraqi Football Association itself. Hussein Saeed Mohammed, Iraq's all-time top scorer and, some alleged, Saddam Hussein's favourite player, had only just managed to keep his job as president of Iraqi football. The Iraqi sports ministry was now run by a Shia politician, who tried to oust Hussein for his perceived silence during the Saddam years. FIFA suspended the federation, threatening their defence of the Asian Cup. He was reinstated but was on borrowed time. Unity and a common purpose were harder to come by in the new Iraq. Results had suffered and the sectarian bickering – within the IFA, if not the team – had begun to rise.

Yet back then, in 2007, with the country tearing itself apart the squad had found that unity in the face of adversity. Something approaching normality had since begun to return to Iraq. In fact, July 2007 marked a watershed for Iraq. According to US military statistics it was the worst month for civilian deaths since the start of the war.

But after July the deaths started falling, and they kept dropping. A US troop surge had been an important factor on the ground, but the players believed that the Asian Cup final had had a marked psychological effect too. 'The situation in 2007 was very bad. There was fighting on the streets. We won the Asian Cup and now that situation is gone,' explained Nashat Akram, the midfielder who was a key player in that team and who came close to joining Manchester City only for the British government to refuse him a work visa. 'We don't have kidnapping in our country any more,' he said. 'We have a very safe country.'

On the next pitch the Iranian-American coach Afshin Ghotbi was training the Iran team. When we had spoken in 2009 he was trying to deflect accusations of treason away from his players. Several had worn green armbands during a 2010 World Cup qualifier against South Korea. The armbands, it was alleged, were worn in sympathy with the Green Movement that was taking place back home. It was crushed and the players had to face the music. Ghotbi kept his job, and even recalled some of those players despite claims they would be banned and imprisoned, including the country's best player Ali Karimi. But Ghotbi had been given a hard time by the press, especially those that couldn't see past his American upbringing. Dozens of Iranian sports journalists crowded around him as he left the pitch, shouting vociferously at him.

'You always have big rivalries like this with neighbours, take USA–Mexico, or Holland–Germany, Korea–Japan,' he said as the team filed onto the team bus painted the colours of the Iranian flag. 'There are a lot of beautiful rivalries in football that excite the fans. It is a rivalry. There's a long history of sports and politics. So my feeling is that it will be an exciting game. And I hope that energy from outside the game will be transferred to the pitch. It will be a spectacle.' He wouldn't talk about the Green Movement any more, not now anyway. This was his last tournament for Iran. He would soon leave to take charge of a team in the Japanese J.League. But he hinted at more. 'I will tell you the truth when I leave here,' he would later whisper to me conspiratorially. 'Perhaps I will write a book about it.'

As dusk fell on the Al Rayyan stadium, migrant workers sold Iraqi and Iranian flags side by side. The atmosphere was good natured, conciliatory even, a far cry from the febrile booing of the national anthem I had seen during the final of the West Asian Championship in Amman a few years back. Of course, it was Younis Mahmoud who scored first for Iraq but Iran stormed back, winning 2–1. After the game the Iranians, almost all wealthy expats living in Doha, danced and sang in the streets outside. Both teams, in the end, qualified for the quarter-finals but that was as far as Iraq and Iran would reach, losing to a single extra-time goal against Australia and South Korea respectively. Qatar, too, had reached the quarter-finals. I sat in the Khalifa International Stadium along with 30,000 white-robed Qataris as they prayed for a miracle. They beat China 2–0 but succumbed to Japan in the next round 3–2, despite being 2–1 up with 19 minutes to go and putting in their best performance of the tournament. The two goal scorers were Sebastián Soria and Fábio César Montezine, the former born in Uruguay, the latter Brazil.

The tournament didn't go without its problems either. Empty seats were an issue, usually dealt with by bussing in hundreds of Indian migrant workers from their day jobs building Qatar's gleaming future, as if they were little more than human seat warmers. It only went to highlight the plight of the migrant workers in the Gulf, usually on contracts tied to the employers, known across the Middle East as the *kafala* system, with no freedom of movement and extremely low wages. Their plight had been taken up by the international trade union movement who launched a 'No World Cup in Qatar without labour rights' campaign. 'It is not too late to change the venue of the World Cup. This is not an industrial skirmish about wages; this is a serious breach in regard to human and labour rights,' said Sharan Burrow, general secretary of the International Trade Union Confederation. 'The country is incredibly wealthy and is portraying itself as a model country. That is simply not true. Our members are football fans and they don't want to see the game played in a country that practices slavery.'

But there was still context to be found here too. During India's match against Australia, a few thousand workers had been given the day off – and free tickets – to watch their countrymen play. None of them liked football, but willingly attended for a glimpse of home. They were mostly from the south, where cricket was supreme. But it was still India, and the tickets were free. Almost every worker was cautious about Qatar. There were still problems but, as one engineer told me: 'Thank God I'm not in Saudi Arabia or Abu Dhabi.' The difference between their list of gripes – some still very serious – and their countrymen's utter despair when I had visited a sewage-filled labour camp in Dubai was telling.

The final between Japan and Australia was chaotic. Thousands of fans with tickets (although the organisers claim only 700) had been locked out, supporters who had travelled from Tokyo and Sydney to be there. The gates had been closed half an hour before kick-off, the organisers explained, as part of the emir's security detail, the kind of move that would have caused a riot at a World Cup final. In the months that followed more allegations about the World Cup bid came to light. According to one investigation into Russia and Qatar's winning bids in the *Blizzard* by journalist James Corbett, Qatar's state-owned airline, Qatar Airways, unveiled massively subsidised routes to Argentina and Brazil around the time of the vote. In August, the emir of Qatar visited Paraguay on an official state visit to finalise one of the biggest trade deals in the country's history. Ex Co members from all three countries – Argentina, Brazil and Paraguay – apparently voted for Qatar. Of course, it all could be a coincidence.

Most intriguing of all was the mess that the French found themselves in. It was alleged that UEFA president Michel Platini was asked to vote for Qatar by then president Nicolas Sarkozy. Several commercial and military airline deals with Qatar hung in the balance at the time. The allegations, made in a 15-page *France Football* investigation under the headline 'Qatargate', laid out how the president had hosted a secret lunch at the Élysée Palace for the crown prince of Qatar, Sheikh Tamin bin Haman al Thani, Michel Platini and representatives of Colony Capital who owned PSG, Sarkozy's team. At the lunch it was alleged that Sheikh Tamin had offered to buy PSG, clear its debt, and spin off a new sports TV network from Al Jazeera, what would become known as beIN Sports, to buy French televised football rights for £70 million a year. Platini responded forcefully. 'To say that my choice ... was part of a deal between the French state and Qatar is pure speculation ... and lies,' he said. 'I do not rule out legal action against anyone who casts doubt on the honesty of my vote.' The

Qatar Investment Authority went on to buy PSG, transforming it in the same way the royal family of Abu Dhabi transformed Manchester City. Six months after the 2022 World Cup vote, Al Jazeera agreed a TV rights deal worth 450 million euros over five seasons. The money and the influence and the power of the Gulf were in the ascendancy. Qatar now had over a decade to deliver. But it also provided for a decade of scrutiny and criticism that would turn it into a global pariah, become central to a regional cold war and threaten the World Cup itself.

But as Japan lifted the Asian Cup on 29 January 2011, another powerful force destined to shape the region, and the world, over the next decade was breaking cover. The capitals of the Middle East were burning with the fires of the Arab Spring. And in Cairo, on that very same day that Japanese captain Makoto Hasebe lifted the trophy after they beat Australia with a single goal late in extra time, 50,000 protesters had filled Tahrir Square calling for the resignation of President Hosni Mubarak. Nineteen protesters were shot dead in Cairo. Riots broke out in the nation's prisons. Arms dumps in Port Said were raided. And on the front lines of the battles for control of Tahrir Square stood a force – nurtured on the terraces of Egypt's football stadiums – that was in the process of helping to bring down a dictator.

16

Egypt and the Revolution

CAIRO, ARAB REPUBLIC OF EGYPT, APRIL 2011

It was 61 days since the fall of Hosni Mubarak and the 7,000 supporters of Al Ahly crowded into one end of Cairo's Military Stadium for the restart of the Egyptian football league were finally able to gloat in front of the people that had made their lives hell for the past four years. Hundreds of police officers stood looking at the crowd as the fans, led by the Ahlawy, gleefully reminded them and their former paymasters of their position in the new post-revolutionary Egypt. Around the group revolutionary flags had been hung: from Tunisia, Libya and Palestine.

'Fuck the mother of Hosni Mubarak!' the crowd chanted.

'Go fuck your minister, Habib al Adly!'

This show of dissent would have been ruthlessly cut down a few months previously. But now Mubarak was under arrest in a hospital bed near the Red Sea, and Al Adly – the former minister of the interior and the man formerly in charge of Egypt's hated police force – languished, along with Mubarak's sons, the ex-prime minister and other members of the country's elite, in the same jail he would send the former regime's political prisoners. 'Can you imagine? What must they all be saying to each other? You could write a film about it!' shouted Amr, standing in the middle of the throng, over the deafening sound of abuse. 'The police would abuse us every day. Now it's our time.' It had been a while since I had last seen Amr but the circumstances couldn't have been any more different. When we first met, at the birth of his Ahlawy ultras group during the Cairo derby four years previously, the group numbered a few hundred. But their numbers exploded thanks to their persecution by the police under Mubarak. It was a move Mubarak would live to regret.

The world watched transfixed as the Egyptians deposed its hated president after 30 years of stifling repression. Every day, tens of thousands would turn up to Tahrir Square and fight pitched battles. But what could explain how a country, where civil society had been so sanitised, and any opposition so ruthlessly crushed, could rise up against one of the world's largest police states? This was called the 'Facebook Revolution' but, improbably, it was also – at least in part – a football revolution too, where organised fan groups, the ultras of Cairo's two biggest teams – Ahly and Zamalek – united, if only for a little while, to play a crucial role in bringing down a government.

Amr picked me up outside the same KFC on Tahrir Square where we had first met in 2007. He looked different now: his glasses were gone and his hair was cut short like a soldier. 'Living under Mubarak was like living under communism in Eastern Europe: nobody could talk to each other who might have the potential to organise,' he explained as we drove out of Cairo's clogged centre to the Military Stadium on the outskirts of town. 'The whole concept of any independent organisation didn't exist, not unions, not political parties. Nothing was organised, and then we started to organise football ultras. It was just sport then. But to them it was the youth, in big numbers – very smart people – who could mobilise themselves quickly. They feared us.'

The Ahlawy grew into something more violent and anti-authoritarian. Members were arbitrarily beaten and arrested, fans harassed by being strip searched or humiliated. Amr himself had been arrested and thrown in jail. Ahly's football matches provided a micro-cosm of the heavy-handedness that the rest of the country felt on a daily basis in Mubarak's Egypt. But unlike the activists and the other opposition groups that had been neutered, the ultras found that the country's football stadiums provided a space to organise and fight back. 'The more they tried to put pressure on us, the more we grew in cult status. The ministry and the media, they would call us a gang, as violent,' said Amr. The police were now in small numbers, lurking on the periphery in the shadows of the stadium. 'It wasn't just supporting a team, you were fighting a system and the country as a whole. We were fighting the police, fighting the government, fighting for our rights . . . The police did what they wanted. The government did what they wanted. And the ultras taught us to speak our mind. This was something new, a little bit of a seed that was planted four years later.'

Now the Ahlawy were in charge. As much as the match against Itti-had el Shorta – ironically the police's own football club – was a celebration for the Ahlawy, it was also one of the first large-scale pub-lic outing for the police force. After viciously trying to put down the revolution with tear gas, rubber bullets and then, finally, live ammuni-tion, the police fled their positions and melted into the population. Now they had returned, chastened; politely asking for tickets and meekly asking the supporters to go through the turnstiles. Before, Amr explained, a swing of the club would have sufficed. The skills that Amr and the Ahlawy had honed during four years of fighting the police came in handy when the January 25 Revolution, and the 'Day of Rage' that took place three days later, saw the confrontation between the authorities – who had decades of experience quashing dissent – and a wholly unprepared public turn increasingly violent. 'I don't want to say we were solely responsible for bringing down Mubarak!' Amr laughed. 'But our role was . . . letting them [protesters] know if a cop hits you, you can hit them back, not just run away. This was a police state. Our role started earlier than the revolution. During the revolu-tion, there was the Muslim Brotherhood, the activists and the ultras. That's it.' Fittingly, the final score was Al Ahly 2, the Police 1.

Later we met in the Horriya bar, an old, yellowing relic of Egypt's 1950s heyday, on a road near Tahrir Square. The leaders of the Ahlawy sat around, discussing the day the revolution began. 'After three or four days, you can't really feel the tear gas as much,' said Mohammed, one of Ahlawy's lieutenants. 'But we had been in contact with other ultra groups from Tunisia who had been involved in the protest there. They told us to dab Pepsi under our eyes. It worked!' And what of their hated rivals Zamalek and their group the Ultras White Knights, who the Ahlawy would fight when they weren't fighting the police? Did you join forces on the front line? 'For a few hours,' Amr said, as if he had made a pact with the devil. 'But I couldn't do it for long.'

Tahrir Square felt anarchic. Compared to the suffocating security of the past, there were no police on the street. A camp of activists still occu-pied the centre. People argued about politics on the street. Sometimes they would end in a fist fight. On one occasion a man wearing a women's abaya was lynched by a crowd when he was denounced as an Israeli spy. On another occasion an angry crowd surrounded a different man after he was denounced as a police informer. Both had to be rescued by the army. It was flawed and chaotic. But it was free. There was hope. The police had been bested. Tomorrow could be a better day.

Things had been tougher for the white half of Cairo, for the supporters of Zamalek. The Ultras White Knights (UWK) had been in hiding, but agreed to meet me in Nasr City, a district of Cairo, in secret. The day before, 4 of its 15 leaders had been arrested, along with 18 of its members. Two days had passed since Ahly had beaten the Police team but the UWK had bigger problems to deal with than the fact that Ahly had cut Zamalek's lead at the top of the table to three points. Earlier in the month Zamalek fans had stormed the pitch during an African Champions League match against a Tunisian club, destroying the goals and attacking the players. The interim military government considered cancelling the league, until the clubs pointed out that most would end up going bankrupt. The UWK had been blamed for the violence, and now the authorities were purging its ranks.

The three men sitting in Costa Coffee couldn't have looked less like violent football revolutionaries. Amir, a gentle-natured, heavy-set man in his early 20s, was a production manager. Mohammed was a lawyer; Massoud a student. But they, along with the rest of the UWK leadership, were being hunted down by the authorities. 'We have suspended our activities,' explained Amir, who suggested, like many White Knights, that the pitch invasion was a false-flag attack, led not by them, but by those seeking to discredit them. 'It is only temporary, we will return . . . They [the police] want to be in control again. It is some kind of propaganda for them. They want to control us.'

Zamalek had also played their first league match in post-revolutionary Egypt, against Haras el Hodood and also at the Cairo Military Stadium, which Zamalek won 2–1. But compared to the Ahlawy's show of unity and force against the police team, the UWK were not officially there. The arrests had forced many underground, and without them, the fans had begun fighting among themselves. One group had crossed their wrists in unison as the teams entered the pitch, in solidarity with the arrested. Another group stood in silence, angry that some Zamalek players were complaining about non-payment of wages. A third sang revolutionary songs, ignoring the other two. The crowd was watched by close to 2,000 armed police, some with machine guns, others with dogs. It was a long way from the unity that had seen the UWK come to prominence on the front line of the protests. The *New York Times* noted that the ultras had been part of the group that stormed, and then torched, the headquarters of Mubarak's despised National Democratic Party. At the so-called 'Battle of the Camels' – when Mubarak supporters, mounted on camels and armed with machetes, stormed Tahrir Square – the UWK had used their experience of dealing with the police to stop and then detain the riders. 'There is a war between us and the police,' said Amir. 'We are fighting them in every match. We know them. We know when they run, when we should make them run. We were teaching them [the protesters] how to throw bricks . . . hit-and-run tactics . . . At the beginning of the Battle of the Camels people were afraid but we got up and attacked the riders.'

'On the Day of Rage [28 January] we made a plan,' Mohammed continued. 'Every group, 20 each, travelled separately . . . On our own, it was nothing. But together as a group in the square we were a big power . . . 10,000, 15,000 people fighting without any fear. The ultras were the leaders of the battle.' The victory didn't come without its cost. Three were killed, according to Amir, 'one in Suez, one in Alexandria, one in Cairo. And a lot of injuries. One was shot in the stomach.' Just then Mohammed's phone rang. It was one of the UWK's leaders. The army had just raided his home. He had narrowly avoided arrest and was now on the run.

Would your old rivalry with Ahly return? I asked finally.

'During the march we celebrated with each other. We were fighting with the Ahlawy on the front line,' Amir recalled. 'We are trying to make a peace treaty with the Ahlawy, because we are fighting in the same direction. But you've just heard. The police are chasing our leaders.'

On 1 February 2012, almost a year later, the Ahlawy was preparing for a long away trip to Port Said for what was usually a bad-tempered clash in the Egyptian league against Al Masry. There was no deep historical rivalry between the two clubs, just provincial jealousies provoked by the big city. The Ahlawy was expecting a hostile reception. The last time they travelled to Port Said they had been attacked by Al Masry's ultras, the Green Eagles. This time it should have been a routine win for Al Ahly. But Al Masry pulled off a shock and won 3–1.

As soon as the final whistle was blown, hundreds of Al Masry supporters stormed onto the pitch. The security for the match had been lighter than under Mubarak but the Al Masry fans got on to the pitch far too easily. Something didn't fit. The Al Ahly players fled for their lives. 'The fans were coming, sprinting after the match,' recalled Egyptian international defender Ahmed Fathi, when I later asked him about his recollections of that night. He was on the pitch at the time and scrambled for the sanctuary of the dressing room. 'I knew they hated me and all the players. All the players ran,' recalled Ahmed. 'I didn't know what was happening outside. But something was happening outside. After this they killed the boys. Not the men, the boys.'

That 'something' was the deaths of 72 young men. Most were crushed to death in a stampede, others – the ultras claimed – stabbed. Some were thrown to their deaths from the top of the stand, four storeys up, onto the concrete below. It was one of the worst football disasters of all time. The true horror had only become apparent in the cold light of the next morning. Dozens of odd shoes, discarded by those that had fled and those that had died, piled up as if left for collection by those that could never return. Pools of blood had collected in the depressions of the plastic seats. A huge metal gate had been carefully moved and left against a wall after it had been sheared from its concrete pillar by the sheer weight of the crush. In the aftermath the authorities blamed the violence on football hooliganism. But as eyewitness accounts began to emerge, a very different story formed, one of official complicity in the deaths; of a police force who had stood back and watched on as young men were stabbed, beaten, crushed and thrown to their deaths; of an army that, either through foresight or ineptitude, was complicit.

I arrived back in Tahrir Square a few days after the tragedy, just as Cairo's blood-red sun was dying. A protest seemed to be coming to an end. Hundreds of young men and women – most of the women covering their hair with the hijab – stood in front of a steel, stone and razor wire barricade. They chanted at the police, who had formed a line to protect the country's parliament. Every side road was blocked by newly constructed concrete walls. Every reflective surface smashed; windows, ATM screens, mirrors. Every wall was daubed with revolutionary graffiti.

'Fuck the Police'

'Fuck the Military'

'Fuck Mubarak'

One protester lay down on a piece of cardboard and prayed next to a wall under a freshly sprayed anarchist symbol. It had been over a year since the toppling of the Pharaoh. The January 25 Revolution that swept Hosni Mubarak and his cabal of criminals, perverts and cronies from power – his sons Alaa and crown prince Gamal included – was the high tide of the Arab Spring. But for the young people who had congregated here a new threat needed to be combated. Egypt had become what they saw as a military dictatorship. The iron grip hadn't loosened since the fall of Mubarak, they argued, but merely changed position from Egypt's neck to its wrist. Protests continued but not in the same numbers or ferocity. Perhaps it was protest fatigue. Perhaps it was the fact that the directions sent out by the organisers via Twitter were vague. The crowd had slowly drifted away; each revolutionary slogan met with diminishing vigour. The police line took a step forward, sensing the changing tide.

The darkness was suddenly illuminated by fire. A flare had been cracked open by a young man wearing an Ahly shirt, held aloft triumphantly. Next to him another unfurled Ahly's flag, with a soaring eagle embossed on a shield. Suddenly the protest was reborn, as if spirit had been thrown on embers. The young men stormed the barricades, urging others to climb with them. Even the man praying by the anarchist symbol had re-joined the fray. They flew their flag and urged the rest to sing.

'*Horriya! Horriya!*'

Freedom! Freedom!

The police line took one step back.

The next day Amr met me under the hanging needle in the lobby of the Ramses train station in central Cairo. It had only recently been renovated, but already it looked old and worn, as if the chaos and pollution of the city had quickly reclaimed it like an advancing desert.

It had been almost exactly a year since I had said goodbye to Amr and the Ahlawy at the Horriya bar. Then he was blazing with hope. Now he looked smaller and older. He stooped slightly as we met, hair now shaved close to his skull (the product, I later learned, of having to be treated for a gash delivered by a policeman's club). 'The military were clever,' Amr said after we embraced, looking at the floor as he spoke. 'They played their cards well so that it looked like the police.'

Several dozen of the Ahlawy had gathered to take a train north to the famous northern coastal city of Alexandria, founded by Alexander the Great and once considered a centre of the Hellenic world. Everyone present had lost someone at Port Said but the trip has been organised to commemorate the death of one man in particular: Mahmoud Ghandour, the leader of the Ahlawy group in Alexandria. He was 24 years old. A march was to be held in his memory. Thousands were planning to attend, marching towards the northern headquarters of the Egyptian army to demand justice for the dead. Seventy-six people had been arrested in connection with the massacre at Port Said, mostly Al Masry fans who had asserted their innocence. But some high-profile figures had been blamed too. The head of security in Port Said was arrested. It was rumoured he would face the death penalty, but it wasn't enough for the Ahlawy.

'We don't want resignations,' Amr said as we boarded the express train north. 'We want arrests. Not the people who were holding the knives but the people who put the knives in their hands.' The group gathered in a café close to the Alexandria seafront. At the beginning of the twentieth century Alexandria was once famed for its cosmopolitanism, Francophile architecture and its parties, where Muslims, Jews and Europeans would mix freely. Now the city seemed like it was crumbling into the sea, the incongruous metal and glass of the famous Alexandria Library on the shore of the Mediterranean the only splash of modernity in the city. Graffiti honouring the Port Said dead was everywhere. The stencilled face of Ghandour had been sprayed on what seemed to be every wall along the seafront.

Amr sat with his lieutenants, drinking Turkish coffee. The weeks after the tragedy had been spent on the streets in clashes with the police and army, and visiting the families of the dead. Amr felt responsible in some way. After all, this was his gang. What had begun five years ago as an expression of support for a football team – catharsis in the face of oppression, even – had ended in the homes of mothers distraught with grief after losing their only son. It had left its mark. So far he had visited 38 families, all the time prepared for a backlash. But it never came. 'They weren't angry,' Amr said as the group discussed how to get to the march and where to find Ghandour's grave. 'They told us that they were proud their sons were loved by so many people. They all told us one thing: get justice.' Football had long melted into the background. After the tragedy the league was suspended and later cancelled altogether. The Egyptian FA board, including the hated president Samir Zaher, resigned and Al Masry were provisionally banned from all competitions. Egypt's home 2014 World Cup qualifiers were to be played behind closed doors. The only football left for Ahly was the African Champions League. 'We will play in the Champions League and we will win it to honour the dead,' Amr predicted forcefully. The delegation left for the graveyard.

The taxi bus pulled to a stop outside a high-walled compound in a quiet suburb of Alexandria. Inside the graveyard, old women covered head to toe in black sat crying on the tombs of the deceased, as if clinging to a fading memory. Dozens of cats stretched and bathed in the warm sun, blissfully ignorant of the grief around them. The Ahlawy weaved silently through the graves until they reached the final resting place of Mahmoud Ghandour. They were joined by one of Ahly's greatest players. Shady Mohamed was Ahly's most successful captain and in the decade between his first game in 1999 and his departure a decade later he had won six league titles, nine domestic cups and clinched the African Champions League on four occasions. He also won the Africa Cup of Nations with the Egyptian national team in 2008. He didn't play for Ahly any longer but that didn't matter.

Shady, Amr and the Ahlawy stood by the grave, heads bowed, each mouthing a prayer in silence. A few minutes passed before Amr moved. The rest followed. Outside the high walls Ibrahim, one of the group that had travelled north from Cairo, pulled on a cigarette. Ibrahim was one of the founding members of Ahlawy, a working-class hotel worker who tried his hand at working in Eastern Europe a couple of times. He'd even married a Polish girl at one point, but that didn't work out. And the cold was excruciating, so he returned home. Like the rest of the delegation he knew Ghandour. Ibrahim had been there on that day in Port Said. It was his devastating testimony of what happened in Port Said that turned the tide of public opinion. At first people assumed it was just football thugs settling scores, but Ibrahim's appearance on a talk show on Egyptian TV changed all that. He seemed to sink when he recounted what happened, how Al Masry had beaten Al Ahly on the pitch before the police and army turned a blind eye to thousands of charging home fans:

We saw they were not celebrating, but heading towards us. We could see the cops in front of us but we thought they would stop them from attacking us. But suddenly we saw the cops moving and the gates are opened. And the fans are coming like a storm of people. Hundreds of people.

We were so surprised the gates [behind them] were locked. Eight hundred people were stuck in this tunnel. Sixty square metres. We started to fall down on each other. There were like five levels of people on top of each other. We couldn't see a complete human, only half a human. Just an upper part, a head, the body is buried by the other bodies. Just one hand sticking out trying to say help. The cops were just watching. The army were guarding this gate and just watching. I was inside the tunnel. The gate, which was locked, it collapsed under the weight of all the people. The first person who died, his name was Yousef. He was a great hero. He was outside the gate because he went to the bathroom 15 minutes before the end of the game and when he came back the gates were locked. So he got a stone and tried to break the lock off the gate. He couldn't do it. He was pulling it with his own hands and then it collapsed on him.

We were just waiting for the moment to die. I couldn't step because there were a lot of guys falling on each other. I was down and someone was on top of me. I had two choices. If I stand up someone will stab me or burn me. The other choice is to step on these boys. I could hear they were killing people. I could hear people screaming for help. When they took the guy on top of me I heard him screaming so bad so I guess they stabbed him or something. In this moment I took the hard decision to move.

Ibrahim got out and managed to find refuge in the dressing room, where the Al Ahly players held some of the bodies, distraught. The Egypt national team's American coach Bob Bradley would later tell me how Mohamed Aboutrika held one of the protesters in his arms as he died. 'You know the story?' Bradley asked. I didn't. 'The fan says to Aboutrika: "Captain, I always wanted to meet you . . ."'

Tens of thousands of crying mothers, fathers, brothers and friends awaited Ibrahim and the other survivors when he returned to Ramses train station that night, all desperate for news. The carriages had left packed four to a bench. The survivors were spread out, silent. Ibrahim was under no illusion who to blame:

> We blame everyone. We blame the army who were guarding the locked gate. We blame the police. We think it was a mix. It happened because of the rivalry between the two teams. And also as punishment for the ultras standing with the revolution, for protecting the revolution. We are a big pain for the regime because the people of the revolution believe that the old regime is still controlling the country. It was because of the Masry fans, it was because of football and it was because of politics too.

The march began on Port Said Street, behind Alexandria's famous library. Tens of thousands of men and women filled the streets as far as the eye could see. Those with the loudest voices sat on their friends' shoulders to face the crowd and lead them in revolutionary song.

> They say violence is in our blood
> How dare we fight for our rights
> Stupid regime
> Hear what we say
> Freedom!
> Freedom!
> Freedom!

The smiling face of Mahmoud Ghandour stared back from T-shirts and banners. Before the revolution a protest like this would never be allowed. Now what little police were there, perhaps half a dozen, looked the other way as two ultras with spray cans rechristened the street sign 'Ghandour Street'. It took three hours for the march to snake through the streets. All the while they were cheered by the watching crowds on the balconies. An old lady held up a handmade placard denouncing the army. The march eventually stopped at the gates of the headquarters for Egypt's army in the north of the country. Troops stared back atop armed APCs, a tank and a dozen foot soldiers. All their guns were trained on the crowd. 'The people demand the trial of Port Said,' they chanted. The troops didn't move. The gate stayed locked. Instead the ultras knelt down and prayed in front of the troops before peacefully dispersing.

Even old enemies were welcomed on the march. White flags of Ahly's main rival Zamalek could also be seen. And in a gesture of revolutionary fraternity, the ultras of Alexandria's own Premier League side Ittihad – the Green Magic – arrived too. They requested a meeting with the Ahlawy, and offered an invite back to one of their houses. 'They said to me: "We've wasted 20 years hating each other, let's make peace,"' Amr explained as we climbed into a taxi. The Green Magic were poor men, too poor to rent an apartment and therefore too poor to marry. Instead the group of middle-aged men lived together in a derelict building. Both groups squeezed into the front room, overlooking the city's courthouse. One pulled out a large hunting knife. He plunged it into an empty bottle of Sprite, carefully sawing it in half. In the centre of the room, under a bare bulb hanging precariously to its wire, one member of the Green Magic crumbled hash into a big brown pile. The plastic bottles were filled with water and hastily constructed into makeshift water pipes as the room broke out into song and dance. The leader of the Green Magic – a fisherman blessed with a beautiful singing voice – led the two groups singing sad old songs of regret and longing, as he glided gently across the room. The rudimentary pipe was passed to each and every person. Outside, in the middle of the street, long tables were being set. Whatever few Egyptian pounds the Green Magic had left, they had spent on plates of Alexandrian *hawawshi*, bread stuffed with beef mince and peppers. The future and the past were forgotten. Everyone breathed deeply.

The next evening there was a gathering outside the Cairo International Stadium. The meeting had been arranged on the Ahlawy's

Facebook page. Amr never looked forward to the meetings before, but that had changed. 'We used to take these meetings a little for granted, but not after Port Said,' he said as he swung his BMW into the car park. On the radio was a CD of chants and anti-regime songs the Ahlawy had recorded long before Port Said. 'After speaking to the families and what it meant for them to come here and get the shirt, well . . .'

The crowd were here to buy a new shirt made by the Ahlawy. They were selling them to raise money for a children's cancer hospital. If they sold enough they could have a ward dedicated to the victims of Port Said. 'We will call it "Shahid Ahlawy Port Said",' Amr said as he took the orders. The Ahlawy martyrs of Port Said. They took 600 orders in half an hour. The popularity of the Ahlawy could not have been higher. Nor could their standing in Egyptian society, as the so-called 'protectors of the revolution'. But Port Said changed everything for Amr. 'Because of the political situation in the country, we [the ultras] developed so quickly that I can't really still believe it. We had no political ambitions at first but when the regime started oppressing us they turned us into what they feared,' he said. 'Everybody knows Port Said was a set up, everyone knows that.'

Amr regretted the loss of what made the Ahlawy in the first place: the football team. But now there were bigger things to fight for. 'We are victims for our values and victims for our ideology and we are victims of what we stand for. It is destiny that we were made to suffer that. We are one of the purest entities in the country and they are try-ing to destroy us. Seventy-four [72 who died in Port Said and another 2 who died during the revolution] people is not enough. If you want to terminate our ideas then you have to finish us all. It makes you more focused to get what these people died for. They died for certain values . . . I don't know if we will achieve it but what is certain is that we'll all die for them. We'll die for it if that is what it takes.'

The Al Ahly flag took pride of place on the barricades. The club's crest, the eagle on the shield, was now flown with revolutionary pride. But there had been no football. With the league cancelled the only competition left was the African Champions League, which Amr and the Ahlawy believed Ahly was destined to win. In the second round the team travelled to Mali for a two-legged tie. No sooner had the team landed than a coup started. The players were stuck in their hotel for a week after their 1–0 loss as street-to-street fighting broke out around them. They quickly went 1–0 down in the first half of the second leg too, in the empty Military Stadium in Cairo. That was until Mohamed Aboutrika – the 'captain', the man who held a dying fan in his arms in the dressing room on that night in Port Said – scored a second-half hat-trick after coming on at half-time.

There was a rash of arrests in the aftermath of Port Said. The Supreme Council of the Armed Forces blamed hooligan elements for the violence and strongly denied it was a conspiracy, insisting it was a mixture of thuggery, bad luck and incompetence. When the accused were taken before the judge, in a large cage, they protested their innocence – claiming they were scapegoats for a wider conspiracy – and prayed together in an act of defiance. The trial's continued postponement meant the Ahlawy would keep protesting to prevent the league from restarting until they had secured justice for the Port Said dead.

After the T-shirt orders had been taken Amr and Ibrahim led the group to their café, their local, in a district near Tahrir Square. It was already full, the Ahlawy spilling out onto the pavement in front; rich and poor, Muslim and Christian. 'My mother thinks Egyptian society should follow us,' said Ibrahim, fanning his arm around in a semi-circle. 'Look. We have low class and high class. Amr is high class. But we have another guy who works as a baker making a couple of [Egyptian] pounds a day. There is no religion here. Christian, Muslim, it's all the same. Everyone is equal.' Amr agreed as a joint was passed around the group. 'Even before the revolution, this place, the café, it was a free place.'

But the ghosts of Port Said still walked here. The talk was of sacrifice and martyrdom. If the authorities had hoped to silence the Ahlawy they had instead, as Amr said, created what they feared. They had thrown spirit on the embers of a fire. 'We now have a big battle against all the officials. Nothing will make us calm until we see them all hanged,' Ibrahim said, betraying his anger for only a few moments. 'Everyone who was responsible for this. The Al Masry fans who did this. The police. The cop leaders in Port Said, the minister of the interior. Everyone.' Ibrahim lit a cigarette before he and Amr melted back into the night.

CAIRO, JANUARY 2013

Red smoke billowed all around, heaving upwards from canisters held aloft. The thickness enveloped everyone who had stood for hours waiting for the news, forcing its way through the crowd like a flood, but rising like a fire, leaving a permanent crimson haze. It was a sign that word had arrived. It still wasn't clear what that word was. Or whether a word had even been spoken. Had justice been served? Or had, as the 15,000-strong crowd that gathered outside Al Ahly's walled training complex in Cairo always suspected, justice been denied, compromised, denigrated, postponed?

The thousands of Ahlawy stood in front of a huge black billboard, 50-foot wide and 10-foot tall. This was still a good part of town, on Zamalek island in the Nile, one of the few upmarket districts that the rich of Cairo still bothered to populate. Most had left for the gated communities of the new suburbs that had been growing steadily over the past decades. Cairo proper had become too poor, too chaotic and too polluted for those with choice. Most people in Egypt didn't have a choice. The rest remained, struggling with the realities of a city that had become too big for its clothes. But Ahly remained, an anchor to the old world, to the hope that burned and then crashed between Nasser and the assassination of Sadat.

A few dozen of the Ahlawy had climbed onto the shelf in front of the billboard via a pale, sick-looking, leafless tree nearby, to see the expectant but pessimistic crowd below. Aside from the crazy few who had clambered to higher ground, the crowd faced the pictures of the young men who had died. It was a few seconds after 10am and the verdict of those accused of their role – or complicity or acquiescence – in the deaths of 72 Al Ahly fans killed during a match against Al Masry in Port Said nearly one year previously was about to be known. The billboard, a collage of 72 portraits shorn from Facebook, passport photos and family gatherings, looked down on the crowd as if they too were expecting justice. Except there weren't 72 faces. There were only 68 pictures. Three of the dead had no picture. One of the dead had never been identified. As the grieving families claimed their departed one by one, he was left orphaned at the morgue. All that was

known was depressingly medical: he was male, Egyptian, in his forties. He could have been an Ahly fan, he could have just been passing
by that night and caught up in the tragedy. He was buried in an
unmarked grave. Everyone on that billboard had a name, if not a
picture, but under his generic black space he was known simply as
'The Martyr'.

Information crackled through the crowd like a loose electrical wire.
Gunfire boomed, ear-shattering blasts that scorched the face. The Ahlawy, at least some of them, had come armed for the verdict. A few
that I saw carried homemade, sawn-off shotguns, fashioned into pistols. They fired them in the air, birdshot spraying those nearby. One
young man fired an automatic pistol in the air repeatedly before it
jammed. His friends gathered around to try and make it work again,
but they didn't have the technical ability, as if the gun had been stolen
out of a father's closet. Fireworks exploded too, adding to the chaos.
Gunfire and gunpowder mingled effortlessly.

Many of the Ahlawy I had known for all these years, from the
Zamalek derby in 2007, to the hope and anarchy that immediately
followed the revolution to the aftermath of Port Said and to now,
were here too. Mohamed, one of the founding members, crouched
down, the hot morning sun burning our faces, as he tried to decipher
the code. The gunfire and the fireworks suddenly intensified. 'Fifteen
death sentences, a lot, a lot, a lot for the Port Said people I don't know
what's for the police,' he relayed, calmly, mobile phone pressed to one
ear, his other hand trying to muffle the outside world. Next to us a
teenager with a homemade shotgun, his head covered by a hood, his
face smothered by a red scarf, blasted another couple of rounds in the
air. Mohamed looked up at me. 'It's over.'

The court had delivered an unexpected verdict. As the fog cleared
the decision was better than almost any of the Ahlawy had expected.
Twenty-one of Al Masry's fans had been sentenced to death. The year
previously, in the macabre glow of Port Said when I had marched
with the Ahlawy in Alexandria and spoken to Amr and Ibrahim –
Amr the founding force of the Ahlawy and Ibrahim an original
member who was at Port Said and had been forced to step on the
bodies of his friends as they died underneath him – the ultras had
demanded blood. Executions. Not the people who are holding the

knives but the people who put the knives in their hands. Since then they had embarked on a campaign to ensure that justice was served. They had successfully boycotted the league until a verdict had been delivered. In some cases the Ahlawy would picket stadiums where matches were about to take place. The Egyptian FA, so tainted by their close association to, and sycophancy of, the Mubarak regime, crumbled in front of the Ahlawy's opposition. August, September, October passed and still no league could restart without the Ahlawy's say so. The only football, other than a handful of Egyptian national team World Cup and Africa Cup of Nations qualifiers, was the African Champions League. Port Said had scarred Ahly's players. Many said they would never play again. It took months for some of them to emerge for training. It was understandable.

When I had said goodbye to Ibrahim and Amr they had vowed justice and victory. Victory in the Champions League, they said, would honour the martyrs. Somehow, despite not playing any league games, Al Ahly progressed. First there was the tie in Mali when the team was caught up in the coup. And then there was the semi-final against Nigeria's Sunshine Stars. The match in Cairo was again played behind closed doors but the hotel where the away team was staying was inundated by Egyptian protesters. They weren't the usual protesters you would see at Tahrir Square, but a gathering of professional footballers, angry that their livelihood had been taken away from them. They were equally angry that Al Ahly had still been allowed to play, tapping into a resentment that had existed long before the revolution that the club received special treatment. The players hoped that if they barricaded the Nigerian team in the hotel, the match would be cancelled, Ahly would be kicked out of the competition and their cause would finally be understood. But Mohamed, now crouching in the street outside Ahly's training complex trying to relay news of the Port Said verdict to his friends, had other ideas.

'We only found out during rush hour that the players were having a march,' he told me at the time. 'We embarked on a mission to "free" the Sunshine Stars players. We contacted each other by BBM and SMS and congregated. There were fights with the players. I think one of the players had a gun. They prevented the Sunshine players from going to the game. We had to let the game go on. We cleared the way for the bus.' The Ahlawy led the players to the bus and arranged an escort to the stadium. Nigerian journalist Colin Udoh, who was embedded with the Sunshine Stars, saw the whole thing. 'When the players were coming down the fans were applauding them,' he said. 'On the drive to the stadium 2,000 fans were lining the road applauding us. Inside the bus they didn't understand it. They thought they were angry with them . . . It is a unique position to see fans with that much power.' Al Ahly won that game and won the final too. Despite having no league, no fans and experiencing unimaginable horror, they had become champions of Africa, and with it a place with the other confederation champions – Chelsea from Europe, Corinthians from South America, Monterrey from Central and North America – at FIFA's Club World Cup in Japan.

A dozen Ahlawy had made the insane trip to the city of Nagoya, west of Tokyo, for the first match against the Japanese champions Sanfrecce Hiroshima. It was December 2012 and the snow fell thick on the freezing stands. Amr, Issa, a Christian member of the Ahlawy, Hassan and I watched Ahly play in the snow for the first time in their history. It was also the first time the Ahlawy had attended a match since Port Said. It had been an incredible journey for the team, as much as it had been for the Ahlawy. Amr was optimistic. He wanted to get back to the football. Politics was a dirty business. He despised the government and the police, but now they at least had a mechanism for change. Egypt wasn't just a post-revolutionary society any more, ready to be moulded into whichever street force emerged strongest. It was now a presidential democracy. Mohamed Morsi and the Muslim Brotherhood had won, just as Mubarak and his allies, especially in the UAE and Saudi Arabia, had feared.

It wasn't who he would have chosen as president, Amr reasoned, but it was better than what they had before and now they had the prospect of justice too. 'Already a date has been set to announce the verdict which should be 26 January [2013],' he said as Al Ahly took the lead. Around him the Ahlawy sang the familiar revolutionary songs that had not been heard in a football stadium since Port Said. 'We are very optimistic and hopefully the court will bring the justice the victims deserve. It will be unimaginable to think of how emotional and special it will be to return to football after 13 months.' Next to the Ahlawy, a bigger group of Ahly fans, mostly students studying in Tokyo, watched the game too. They wore heavy beards and carried banners proclaiming their support for President Morsi. They began to chant pro-Morsi slogans. The ultras chanted back, louder, about freedom and control. Scuffles broke out between the two. They only ended when Mohamed Aboutrika intervened. With the match drawn at 1–1 Aboutrika took the ball down on the right and blasted the ball past the goalkeeper. It was later voted the goal of the tournament. The banners were put away and the chants stopped.

As the day of the Port Said verdict neared, the new regime of Mohamed Morsi breathed in, fearing the court verdict would spark an already combustible situation on the ground. The sulphuric burn of tear gas now permanently hung around Tahrir Square. Next to the Nile, outside one of the big five-star hotels, young protesters, many wearing Ahly flags and scarves, and the police force traded blows. The police would fire tear-gas canister after tear-gas canister high into the air, smoke marking its trajectory as it looped and then landed at the feet of the crowd 100 metres away. The protesters would pick up the canisters and hurl them in the Nile before aiming the only weapons they had, fireworks, in the direction of the police.

None of the Ahlawy I knew was here, still fighting these battles. They had become more than a revolutionary force. They were now a revolutionary aesthetic. Street hawkers who would sell religious flags during marches by supporters of the Muslim Brotherhood now sold Ahly flags too. Their biggest seller was the Ahly-branded black balaclavas. Being an ultra was now a synonym for resistance. Many young people with a grievance on the street now said they were an ultra and sung the revolutionary songs that had emerged from the terraces. For them being an ultra wasn't first an expression of love for your team, it was an expression of discontent. But that was because the core of what had brought them together in the first place had skipped a generation. There was no terrace to stand on any more, no team to discuss, no matches to watch, no schedule to keep by. The metronome of a football season was gone.

The Ahlawy lamented the loss of their club and the game they loved. Others had taken the mantle and ran with it. But it had little connection to them nor to the roots of what had made them strong in the first place. Justice for the dead at Port Said had already held them together longer than anyone had expected. Many of them were now approaching 30. They had jobs and lives to live. Amr couldn't be here for the verdict. His day job at the Confederation of African Football, ironically, meant that he was out of the country. Real life had intervened.

Outside the ground, as the extent of the court's verdict became known, the mood changed from menace to celebration to confusion. Twenty-one were sentenced to death, yes, but the verdict of the other 52 accused, including several security officials, had been postponed. Some believed the verdict was political, a way of taking the sting out of a potentially explosive situation. 'It's a very good decision by the court,' said Issa, the Christian member of the Ahlawy who had travelled to Japan to see Ahly for the first time in a year. 'We hope it will be a perfect ending for this story. We have been waiting for this for so long. For 21 to get executed is a very good decision. So now we wait for the police decision. For sure, it wasn't just them [the Al Masry fans] that made this.'

Ahmed, another founding member of the Ahlawy I had met in Alexandria, was equally as unequivocal. 'I feel satisfied that some of those who committed what we suffered a year ago are going to face what they deserve,' he said, as the crowd began to move inside the training complex and gathered together on the pitch. 'It's a strong verdict but they don't deserve less than a strong verdict. Nobody ever wants to see someone dying but when someone kills he deserves a death sentence. He deserves that his life is taken. I don't see a way the police can get away with this.'

It was conflicting, watching thousands celebrate executions on the pitch inside the training complex. But if the courts had hoped to take the sting out of the situation, it had worked in Cairo. The crowd melted away, satisfied at least until the next verdict a month later. The Ahlawy I had known for the past six years were always accidental revolutionaries. Now the battles were to be fought by other people carrying their flags, the next generation. The Ahlawy left for Mohamed's flat nearby, to spend the rest of the day getting stoned and watching the protests in Tahrir Square on TV.

But what had averted disaster in Cairo had ignited the city of Port

Said. The verdicts were greeted with astonishment, disbelief, and anger by Al Masry's fans and the families of the 73 accused who had gathered outside the prison in Port Said where the suspects were held. Like the Ahlawy supporters in Cairo, they too had come prepared. Two policemen were shot dead as the relatives tried to storm the prison. The police fired back. At least 30 people were killed in clashes. Among them was a former Al Masry player. President Morsi addressed the nation and announced a 30-day curfew, from 9pm until 6am in the cities worst affected by the violence.

A few hours before the first curfew was due to fall, a storm rolled into Port Said. I had taken the last bus from Cairo and entered the city just before it was to be sealed. The streets were empty, the skies dark and pregnant with rain. The only sound was the faint, periodic burst of gunfire. It emanated from near the Al Arab police station by the sea. I walked through Port Said's deserted streets, using the rising smoke and gunfire, getting louder as I approached, as a compass. Ominously, down one deserted street, an orphaned tire barricade burned in its centre. Suddenly, the dead streets came alive, as if the entire energy of the city had been focused on one point. Young men exchanged rocks for gunfire over the burning tyres. The clashes had followed the funeral of more protesters, killed the day after the violence outside the prison. Down side streets members of the Red Crescent peered nervously around street corners to check for the injured, before ducking back when the police fired off a few rounds. 'There are some injuries here,' one paramedic said as he sheltered from the latest volley. Ambulances flew by, their sirens blaring. 'We've seen gun bullets from the government. In four days we have seen more than 450 injured.'

Yet, despite the gunfire and the curfew, a march had been arranged. At 8.30pm a crowd of thousands gathered near the same spot the Red Crescent had been waiting to ferry the injured to hospital. They marched through the smouldering barricades towards where the gunfire had previously come from. Now the army, not the police, was in charge. APCs and armed troops were stationed on street corners and outside important military and civilian buildings. At the march's core were Al Masry's ultras group the Green Eagles. But they were by no means alone. The marchers had come from all sections of Port Said.

Several hundred women marched together, denouncing Morsi and Cairo. The curfew came and went, the crowd mocking its passing. 'It's nine o'clock!' they chanted as they passed the stationed troops. There was no animosity towards the army. The police were the enemy. Protesters took it in turns to hug and kiss the young soldiers that had lined their path.

No one wanted to admit to being an Al Masry fan, nor say whether they were there on that fateful night almost a year ago that set in motion the chain of deadly events. What they would say was that they believed a miscarriage of justice had taken place, that Morsi had sacrificed Port Said to prevent chaos in Cairo, that traditional antipathy towards Port Said, a poor and neglected city, was at play. 'People are truly sure that these people [the 21 sentenced to death] didn't kill anyone. We didn't do it and they [the Ahlawy] don't believe we didn't do this,' said Tariq, an accountant who was on the march with a friend. 'Al Masry will not be back for five years. I'm a big Masry fan. But I can't go anywhere. All the supporters of the big teams in Cairo or anywhere believe that Al Masry supporters did this.' For Tariq, admitting to being an Al Masry supporter outside of Port Said was impossible. 'They say, "You killed them, the Ahly supporters. You are like a terrorist." Nobody believes us, we didn't do anything here.'

As the march moved back towards the place it had started, machine-gun fire rang out once again. This time it was all around the march, front and back. The crowd scattered. A protester was shot dead at the back of the march, next to the Al Arab police station. 'In three days we have lost 21 people, judged to be executed, and also about 39 murdered and many injured so there is no family which have not lost a friend, a colleague, a neighbour. You can consider this a sort of vendetta between the people and the police,' said Muhammad, an English tutor. 'People are going to stay out all night, every day for a month. They reject and refuse the curfew imposed by Morsi.' But they didn't stay out all night. Their message had been heard and, with one protester already dead, it was time to leave. As gunfire crackled in the night sky, I moved through Port Said's deserted streets, hiding behind cars every time a new volley broke out until I finally reached safety.

The next morning I decided to visit the Port Said stadium. I circled its grey walls looking for a way in, past graffiti from the Green Eagles, denouncing the verdict. Another said: 'NO TV. GO TO THE STA-DIUM.' Each door to the stadium was firmly shut with brand-new padlocks. But one gate had been carelessly left open. I pushed it open. It was next to the gate where the 72 Ahly supporters died. The stairwell where they were crushed looked horrifically tiny. The gates that had eventually sheared away from their concrete pillars still lay discarded on the floor 12 months on. Someone was still watering and cutting the grass. I took some pictures before I was chased out of the stadium by a security guard shouting that I was an Israeli spy. I ran back to the main street, which was full of burned-out cars. Hundreds of people were here now, gathered outside a mosque. As in the preceding days, it was the funeral of a young man killed in clashes with the police the night before. His body was carried through the crowd on a stretcher, wrapped tightly in linen, back towards the barricades, where the cycle of protest and murder would continue.

I FEBRUARY, 2013

The streets outside Ahly's training ground were deserted now. On the same spot where 15,000 Ahlawy had gathered to hear the first verdict in the Port Said trial a week before, a crew of eight graffiti artists were busy covering the walls of the training ground with the faces of the dead. It was exactly one year since that night in Port Said and the club had arranged for an evening memorial service for the victims of the tragedy. As the sun set, the Ahlawy slowly arrived, chaste and introverted. Mohamed and Issa had met with others I had come to know well. They embraced and led each other up into the stands where thousands more were waiting for them. On the pitch four of the Ahlawy were arranging a pyrotechnic display to mark the exact minute when tragedy took place: 74 flares were to be lit, each held by a different ultra, standing in the shape of a '7' and a '4'. The organisers ran around flustered, trying to move the men into the correct position as if herding cats, phoning friends stationed high up in the stands so that they could guide the design below.

The families of the martyrs walked on two by two. Mothers who had lost sons, sisters that had lost brothers, wives who had lost husbands, daughters that had lost fathers. They wept as they saw the crowds that had gathered, the name of each read out on the crackly speaker system and chanted by the crowd. When the moment came, and the sun had almost vanished from the horizon, the flares were lit. The number '74' burned brightly. Tomorrow another chapter in the tragedy was to close. The football league would return. The fans would still be banned from attending but that was the next battle, to fight for the Ahlawy's rightful return.

When the second verdict was read out a month later, two of the main security officials on trial were jailed for 15 years. But 28 were acquitted. Riots near Ahly's training complex followed as the nearby Police Club was burned down. Some of the Ahlawy claimed responsibility. But no one could be sure who it was. The Ahlawy had become so big, so stretched, so removed from the original core of fans who had fought the regime in Egypt's darkest days that the claim was virtually meaningless. Perhaps it was a supernova, the blinding flash of brilliant white that marked the death of a star. Perhaps it marked a new phase under a new leadership. But, at the one-year anniversary memorial, it felt like an end, a chapter that had closed on all of their lives. The flares burned and the victims wept as we stood and paid our respects. Tears streamed down Issa's face as the flares began to fade and the Ahlawy began to sing – a song that had never been sung at an Al Ahly match before – into the darkening Cairo night.

Wearing a red T-shirt
Going to Port Said
Came back in a white coffin
I became a martyr in my own country
In heaven a martyr
Revolution all over again.

17

The Rebel Players

The Arab Spring came to Bahrain on Valentine's Day. Although progress in uniting the country's Sunni elite and Shia majority had been made in some areas, it wasn't fast enough. The reform process had stalled. The king still reserved the right to pick Bahrain's prime minister, a key demand of the opposition. Although King Hamad had never needed to pick a new prime minister: Bahrain had only ever had one. Khalifa bin Salman al Khalifa had been in place since the country's independence in 1971. He was the longest serving prime minister in the world. But with Tunisia and Egypt leading the way with huge street protests, Bahrain followed. Memories were still fresh of the last uprising that had ended just over a decade previously. Yet the discontent had burst forth this time in a different world. Social media meant that protests could be organised much easier. And there was also the increasing power of Iran, which had frightened the Gulf states. Bahrain's Sunni elite had always believed that Bahrain's Shia political leadership were mere puppets controlled by Tehran. It was a familiar refrain for the Shia everywhere in the Middle East, be they in Lebanon, Iraq, Saudi Arabia or Bahrain; that their allegiance was to their spiritual leader in Iran and not the country they called home. For those on the street on Valentine's Day at the Pearl Roundabout in Manama, the issue of Iran was a smoke screen. They wanted greater democracy, not an Iranian-style theocracy. They wanted more accountability, not an infallible ayatollah. They wanted jobs and a future that was based on meritocracy, not patronage based on religion or family.

The crowds that gathered were from all areas of Bahrain too, Shia and Sunni. And among the crowd were dozens of sporting heroes; wrestlers, handball players and, most significantly of all, several national football team players. It had been just over a year since Sayed Mohamed Adnan, A'ala and Mohamed Hubail had seen their World Cup dream end in Wellington. A'ala and Mohamed now played on the same team, Al Ahli Manama, whilst Adnan had stayed in Qatar playing for Al Khor. But when the protests came they decided it was their duty to take to the streets too. According to an interview A'ala gave to the Associated Press, he'd only agreed to go on the march after hearing that the royal family had sanctioned, even encouraged, peaceful protest. It was the biggest mistake of his and his teammates' lives.

The Pearl Roundabout protest was crushed. Activists claimed four people were killed when the military rolled their tanks in to clear the makeshift camp that had been erected. Eventually they destroyed the monument at its centre too, in case it became a symbol, a rallying point, for future protests. A Pakistani migrant worker in his forties was killed when one of the arches collapsed onto the cab of his crane as he demolished it. The King Fahd Causeway, once the conduit for a thousand young Saudi men to travel to Manama every weekend to raise a little hell, now rumbled with a new convoy: a Gulf Cooperation Council (GCC) force from Saudi, Qatar, the UAE and beyond to help the Bahrainis mop up whatever opposition was left. At least another 30 people died.

The players survived but they were now marked men. The three, as well as Bahrain's goalkeeper, had been spotted at the protests. A video of A'ala surfaced on social media addressing a large crowd, calling for peaceful change. The video was analysed on a popular Bahrain sports show, with the players' faces ringed in red to highlight their role. A'ala was shamed on national TV, the host of one talk show labelling the protesters 'stray hyenas' and subjecting him to a 15-minute grilling about his 'treachery' on state TV. According to the Bahrain Institute for Rights and Democracy, the son of the king, Prince Nasser bin Hamad – who was also the president of the Bahrain's National Olympic Committee – went on state TV and threatened the protesting athletes, vowing that 'judgement day' had come. The next day the police came and arrested both A'ala and his brother. 'We saw some masked men get out of the car. They said: "Captain A'ala, get your brother" and we went with them,' A'ala later explained in an ESPN documentary, *E60: The Persecuted Athletes of Bahrain.* 'They put me in the room for the beatings. One of the people who hit me said I'm going to break your legs. They knew who we were . . . We were forced to endure it. I had to endure it. If I didn't, something worse would have happened to me.' Eight days after the brothers were arrested, the country's state news agency – the Bahrain News Agency – announced that a committee would be set up to identify and punish sportsmen and women who had been involved in the protests. It was chaired, they announced, by the president of the Bahrain Football Association, Sheikh Salman bin Ibrahim al Khalifa. Its first meeting, it claimed, had already taken place.

Those that played in Bahrain – like the Hubail brothers – were later fired from their clubs and effectively banned from the national team. Two clubs, including Al Shabab, were dissolved for being an apparent hotbed of Shia agitation. They would later be reinstated but demoted to Bahrain's second tier. Yet no one spoke up for the footballers initially; not FIFA, not the AFC and not the US or British governments that had supported other such uprisings in Libya or Syria but who considered the Bahrain royal family a vital ally against the rise of Iran. It was British and American-made tear gas and rubber bullets that silenced the uprising. 'The violence and abuse is so huge. We have too much work. We can't cope here. A lot of doctors, a lot of people have been targeted, soccer players, basketball players, teachers, unionists,' explained Nabeel Rajab, head of the Bahrain Center for Human Rights. Rajab was the most prominent human rights activist in Bahrain and had spoken out against the targeting of high-profile sportsmen and women as well as criticising the continued hosting of the F1 grand prix in Bahrain. He had agreed to speak to me a few months after the Pearl Roundabout uprising, over Skype. He wouldn't speak on mobile phone nor write by email. He was worried that, as the most visible opponent in the foreign media, his communications were being monitored. Rajab was himself arrested in the middle of the night on charges that he had fabricated a picture showing a dead protester, allegedly killed by the army. He claimed he was tortured, threatened with rape and then released. 'The people who are in charge, they don't care about international image,' he said. 'They are military people. All of the sport associations are headed by the royal family. We have 100 associations headed by the royal family.' But Rajab reserved his harshest criticism for FIFA. 'Footballers have rights like any other human to be a citizen. It's time for FIFA to raise their voice. The people of Bahrain are looking at them and asking: "Where are you?"'

The three players were imprisoned for up to three months. After media pressure made ignorance impossible, FIFA belatedly enquired whether their detention broke their own rules on political involvement in the game. 'The players have obviously been in custody after their involvement in the demonstrations and acts of violence against governmental officials was proven,' said Sheikh Ali bin Khalifa al Khalifa, the genial vice president of the BFA who had been achingly friendly when I met him in 2009, in a statement when I contacted him. 'The players have been arrested, investigated and detained for having opposed the general laws and by-laws of the country. The fact that they happen to be footballers and national team players is highly irrelevant . . . If tolerance was shown to those who happen to be athletes, it will result in the disintegrating of the equality under the law spirit, a matter that goes beyond everything our revered government stands for.'

When the players were released their national careers appeared to be over. Mohamed Hubail was sentenced to two years in jail (although it was later thrown out on appeal). A'ala fled to Oman where he played in the local league, his family still in Bahrain. Sayed Mohamed Adnan left for Australia and starred for the Brisbane Roar as he powered them on to win the A-League championship. But what had once united a nation had been broken for a generation at least. The national football team had been shorn of its best players, its legends tainted and abused. Former Leicester City coach Peter Taylor took charge of Bahrain's attempts to qualify for the 2014 World Cup finals. Taylor's campaign was not a success. Bahrain was eliminated in the first group stage. They lost 6–0 to Iran and won just two games, both against the lowest ranked team in the group, Indonesia. The second was an incredible 10–0 victory in the final game of the group. But as Bahrain needed to beat Indonesia 9–0 and hope Qatar lost to Iran, FIFA launched a 'routine' investigation. Taylor gave a disastrous interview claiming to have never heard of the three detained players. 'I knew nothing of the politics of the situation,' a contrite Taylor told me when I spoke to him on the phone a few months later. 'I was just a coach, in charge of a team. That was it.'

The golden era of Bahraini football, an era that saw one of the smallest nations on the planet humble Asia's giants, an era that saw a team which, in Milan Máčala's words, 'represented the whole country', an era that produced two of the finest Asian players of the last ten years, was over. A'ala Hubail's words in 2009, after a serious injury ruled him out of that second-leg play-off against New Zealand, also returned to haunt him. 'We don't know what will happen in the next four or five years, and it is difficult to know who will still be playing with the national team,' he said. Instead he was left to reflect on his evisceration. As he said whilst living in exile in Oman: 'I didn't do anything wrong to deserve this humiliation.'

Yet A'ala and his brother's experience had at least become public knowledge. Their stories had been told. Below them, dozens if not hundreds of other players and athletes had been arrested, persecuted and tortured in secret. One young player who was just breaking in to the national team was about to find out the lengths the Bahraini regime would go to seek out and punish players who rebelled.

TUNIS, TUNISIAN REPUBLIC, OCTOBER 2011

Under an immaculate blue Mediterranean sky, Marcos César Dias de Castro 'Paquetá' stood alone on the sidelines in ankle-deep grass at the Stade Abdelaziz Chtioui, Tunis, watching his goalkeeper Guma Mousa writhe on the floor in agony. The coach of the Libyan national team rubbed his temples with his right hand, exasperated. Many things should have gone wrong over the past year for the Brazilian, but Paquetá and his team had somehow stumbled their way around fate. Until now. In a few days his team was due to play a final 2012 Africa Cup of Nations qualifier against Zambia. The sporting facts were daunting enough as it was. Unlike their North African neighbours – Egypt, Tunisia, Algeria and Morocco – Libya had never had its own golden era. They had never qualified for a World Cup finals, instead being forced into long periods of petty self-exile and failure thanks largely to the unpredictable manoeuvrings of the country's dictator Colonel Muammar Gaddafi. They had qualified for the Africa Cup of Nations in the past, once as hosts, but this was different. Paquetá had begun his campaign with Gaddafi's iron grip still in place. He was about to end it with the country mired in a civil war.

The team had met for a training camp in the birthplace of the Arab Spring for a series of friendlies against local Tunisian club sides. So far Libya had lost once, eked out a 0–0 draw against another and were now, in their final game against Avenir Sportif de La Marsa, losing 2–0. One of Paquetá's best players had been injured thanks to the insane over-exuberance of La Marsa's players. He lay on the stretcher weeping, his knee held together in a leg brace. The coach turned and shrugged sarcastically at the concerned bench as Guma Mousa hopped off the pitch, arm around his physio. That Mousa should have succumbed here, of all places, would have been comedic were it not so tragic. He was one of the team's three rebel players. For the past few months, like fellow national team players Walid el Kahtroushi and Ahmed Al Saghir, Mousa had been fighting for the Libyan rebels against Colonel Gaddafi, an uprising long in the making that had found traction in the Arab Spring. He had survived Libya's haphazard frontline. He had survived the privations and exposures of a modern insurgency. But he could not survive 90 minutes and the swing of a Tunisian boot. 'Why are they playing like this?' Paquetá asked no one in particular, tapping his forefinger against his temple. Mousa lay behind him, grimacing as an ice pack was laid on his injured knee. 'It's crazy,' he added.

Paquetá was right: it was crazy. Everything had changed since he had taken the job in June 2010. Back then Gaddafi and his regime looked impregnable. Gaddafi's football-crazy sons had offered a fine package for the coach. The team was to be a symbol of Libya's growing might. Its oil wealth would build state-of-the-art facilities, some of the best in Africa. In return he was to deliver qualification for the 2012 Africa Cup of Nations and the 2014 World Cup in Brazil. Libya was also due to host the next Africa Cup of Nations. Victory in that was expected. No expense was to be spared.

And then a street seller in Tunisia set fire to himself, about 25km from where I was standing.

When the first protests against Gaddafi began in the eastern city of Benghazi at the start of Paquetá's Africa Cup of Nations campaign, his key players spoke out in favour of Gaddafi and denounced the rebels. The national team was for the nation, they would tell the press. It was united behind Gaddafi against the terrorists. But the illusion of unity melted away as quickly as spring snow. As the civil war went on, players started disappearing from the national team's training camps to go and fight with the rebels, unable to stomach the pro-Gaddafi sentiment as they nervously waited on news from family and friends, pinned down in districts being shelled by the army. As the facts on the ground changed, the pro-Gaddafi players disappeared too, more out of self-preservation than anything else. Now Gaddafi's whereabouts were unknown. He was on the run after his forces had lost the capital, Tripoli. Three weeks before this game the UN recognised the National Transitional Council as the legitimate government of Libya, and the national team had taken a very different role. It was to be a symbol of the new Libya. Before they took to the pitch against Avenir Sportif de La Marsa, the team's new kit arrived, expunged of all traces of the old regime. The rebel flag was now stitched on each player's breast. It sat atop black and white stripes, an almost exact copy of the shirt worn by Juventus. A club, ironically, that was 7.5 per cent owned by Libya's sovereign wealth fund.

The new kit had so far brought nothing but defeat and injury. It had been an inauspicious start for the new Libya. But the second half brought better news. Paquetá threw on his wild card. Ahmed Zuway was a young battering ram of a striker from the rebel stronghold of Benghazi. Zuway was built like an ox, his powerful demeanour belied his childlike face. Three goals were scored, two from Zuway, securing Libya's only victory during their brief tour of Tunisia. In the tunnel players from both teams forgot the brutal challenges and embraced, exchanging best wishes before the Zambia game. The players made sure not to exchange their new shirts. There was only enough for one each. Paquetá did not hang around. He walked straight to the coach.

As they left the stadium, the players were stopped in their tracks. A group of young men wearing rebel flags waited to meet their heroes on crutches, wrapped in bandages or sitting in wheelchairs. Amputees with fresh faces, clear and unlined under thick, dark beards. The rebel fighters who weren't so lucky had carried their permanent scars to Tunisia for treatment. The players fell quiet as they passed the young amputees, shaking their hands – or wrists if need be – whispering thanks for their sacrifice into each of their ears.

*

The team was due to take a ten-hour chartered flight from Tunis via Cameroon to Chingola, a small town next to the Zambia–Democratic Republic of Congo border that had grown rich on copper. The problem was getting myself on the flight too. Libya's team manager had viewed my letters of invitation with suspicion. Ali wore a red team tracksuit and a bushy moustache that was rarely seen without a cigarette poking through it. He had been with the team for years, essentially a fixer getting the team from A to B whilst trying to navigate, and sometimes negate, the suspicious, bureaucratic demands of a dictatorship. Even though a civil war was now being openly fought, and Gaddafi's days looked like being numbered, old habits seemed to die hard for Ali.

Ali, like most Libyans who had worked under the regime, was hedging his bets. His innate suspicion of outsiders was clear. He took a long drag on his cigarette before passing the letters back to me. 'Without a stamp I can do nothing,' he said. He attempted to look sorry that my trip was to end here. But a last-minute fax from Libya's National Transitional Council arrived a few minutes before the team bus was due to leave for the airport. Ali looked at the new fax, realising that even with years of experience in obstruction there was nothing he could do. He smiled and put out his cigarette as the team threw their bags into the coach. 'I guess you are coming.'

It was a moral quandary that almost everyone connected with the national team had to address. How could they explain the years of working for the regime now that the team was essentially against it? As the coach crept through the gridlocked streets of Tunis towards the airport, Marcos Paquetá cautiously explained how it was he got here in the first place. 'When I was there [in Libya] the first time I contacted only the federation people, but then one time I have one meeting with Dr Muhammad,' he recalled. Back then Colonel Gaddafi's regime was being rehabilitated as Western governments were eager to tap into Libya's vast oil reserves. His eldest son Dr Muhammad Gaddafi was head of the Libyan National Olympic Committee and the Libyan Football Federation. He shook hands with Paquetá and agreed to hire him with one eye on the 2012 Africa Cup of Nations, the other on the World Cup in Brazil two years later. 'We talked about my project. He was happy because I had made a project for the national team and Libyan football.'

Paquetá was a good choice by Dr Gaddafi. The Brazilian had taken

Saudi Arabia to the 2006 World Cup finals in Germany and held the distinction of winning two World Cups in one year: both the Under-17 and Under-20 titles for Brazil in 2003. He proudly opened his laptop to show me his team photos. He knew where each of his former players were now. 'Do you recognise him?!' he laughed, pointing at one. It was Barcelona's full-back Daniel Alves. But he also had experience operating in closed societies, and Libya was one of the most repressive regimes on earth. Like almost everyone that worked in Libya before the fall of Gaddafi, Paquetá was reluctant to talk about life under the previous regime. He had a good life, a beach-side house and a large salary. 'I focused only on sports,' he said. 'At that time you don't know about the country.' Under Paquetá Libya's Africa Cup of Nations campaign got off to a slow start. But a 0–0 draw was followed by a shock 1–0 victory against favourites Zambia in Tripoli, putting them top of the group. It was to be the final game that Libya would play at home as civil war broke out and the Gaddafi regime crumbled.

The Gaddafis had developed a love/hate relationship with football. The colonel's son Saadi had grandiose delusions of international stardom. He played for Al Ahly Tripoli and installed himself as captain of the national football team. That wasn't enough. Saadi wanted to test himself on the biggest stage. So he signed for Italian Serie A side Perugia in 2003, just one of a series of outlandish moves by then president Luciano Gaucci. Gaucci's eccentricities included trying to sack South Korean striker Ahn Jung-hwan for scoring against Italy at the 2002 World Cup finals and trying to use a loophole in the Italian FA's regulations to sign a female player for the men's senior team.

The inspiration for Saadi's signing, though, seemed to come from a higher power: then AC Milan owner and Italian prime minister Silvio Berlusconi. Gaucci, who would later be declared bankrupt and flee to the Dominican Republic (where he died in 2020), released a statement at the time that claimed: 'Berlusconi called me up and encouraged me. He told me that having Gaddafi in the team is helping us build a relationship with Libya. If he plays badly, he plays badly. So be it.' And play badly he did. Gaddafi hired disgraced Olympic sprinter Ben Johnson as his personal trainer to get him in shape, and stayed for two years. He made three appearances in that time and was banned for failing a drugs test. He is still to this day referred to as the worst player in Serie A history.

But it was the Gaddafis' tenure as head of the Libyan Football Federation – first under Saadi and then later under the more circumspect rule of his brother Muhammad – that saw their father's brutal streak emerge. Under Saadi's control the LFF was used as a tool of political persecution, punishing fans and teams for daring to show any dissent on the football terraces, which remained, along with the mosque, one of the few available forums for mass opposition. In 2000, Saadi's Al Ahly Tripoli travelled to Al Ahly Benghazi for a league match. Benghazi had long been associated with Libya's opposition movement and fans would complain that referees and players were bribed to ensure that Al Ahly Tripoli, the regime's team, would always win. But this time the Benghazi fans had a surprise for Saadi: they paraded a donkey wearing his numbered shirt. 'It is a bad story, not a funny story,' 29-year-old defensive midfielder Moataz Ben Amer, the current captain of Al Ahly Benghazi, would later recall. 'The first half, Ahly Tripoli are winning. But the referee is no good. So Ahly Benghazi leaves the ground and goes to the airport [in protest]. Saadi Gaddafi turned up with his dogs and the police and said: "If you don't play the second half, we will kick you." Al Ahly Benghazi was afraid. We ended up losing 3–0.' The incident revealed the Gaddafis' dark psychology. When his father heard of the intemperance, he ordered Al Ahly Benghazi's headquarters be razed to the ground. The club was banned from playing any football for six years. 'It wasn't Saadi,' Ben Amer added. 'Muammar Gaddafi said Al Ahly [Benghazi] is finished, and closed it. People in Benghazi who were with Gaddafi came and destroyed their building.'

Unlike other dictators that saw the political and nationalistic benefits of a strong, successful football team, the colonel himself had a far harder time coming to terms with the passion and the popularity of the game that his sons adored. In the final chapter of his 1975 *Green Book* manifesto, Gaddafi outlined his disdain for spectator sports:

The thousands who crowd stadiums to view, applaud and laugh are foolish people who have failed to carry out the activity themselves. They line up lethargically in the stands of the sports grounds, and applaud those heroes who wrest from them the initiative, dominate the

*field and control the sport and, in so doing, exploit the facilities that the
masses provide ... sport is a public activity which must be practised
rather than watched.*

Still, Ali al Aswad was remarkably stoic about the end of his playing days at the age of 29. The 60-year-old was the team manager of
Libya's youth and senior national teams and was a legend in his day,
playing for the national team and scoring over 150 goals for Al Ahly
Tripoli. Whilst the likes of Saddam Hussein and even Mahmoud
Ahmadinejad held their national football teams close in the hope of
basking in reflected glory, Gaddafi was deeply jealous of the game, a
jealousy that effectively ended Ali's career. 'I played until 1979 and do
you know why I stopped?' Ali asked as the coach approached the airport. Outside hundreds of Libyan supporters had gathered to send the
team off with flowers and kisses. 'Gaddafi stopped the clubs and the
leagues. He only wanted us to play in the streets and for the national
team abroad.'

I asked him why Gaddafi Senior disliked football so much.

'Gaddafi would pass people playing football and see names written
on the wall,' he replied. 'He'd ask: "Who are these people's names?"
He was told they were footballers so he went out to stop it. Yes, he
was jealous.' The jealousy was such that Gaddafi banned all names
and numbers from shirts of all Libyan football teams, to prevent anyone from challenging his cult of personality. The only player allowed
to carry a name and number on his shirt was his son Saadi. 'We used
to call him "Big Lips" before the revolution,' whispered Esam, the
team's masseur, as if careless talk could still, one day, come back to
haunt him.

Did you ever say that in front of Saadi?

'No!' he laughed, folding his fingers in the shape of a gun and pressing it to his forehead. The most telling example, though, came from
Libya's most successful AFCoN campaign. They reached the final as
hosts in 1982. Ali shook his head whilst grinning sarcastically at the
memory of it. 'At the opening ceremony, [the colonel] gave a speech.'
It was, by all accounts, two hours long. 'You know what he said? "All
you stupid spectators, have your stupid game."' Gaddafi, he said,
stormed off the stage in a rage.

CHINGOLA, REPUBLIC OF ZAMBIA

The plane landed at night on the tarmac of Ndola airport. Nearby the lights of Lubumbashi, one of the Democratic Republic of Congo's most important, mineral-rich cities, twinkled benignly. Ndola's small airport serviced the workers who came from across Africa to work in the region's copper mines. But it also had a footnote in history. It was here that the former UN secretary general Dag Hammarskjöld was killed in a plane crash. The official report claimed the crash was due to pilot error. He was due to mediate talks over violence in nearby Katanga province in what is now the Democratic Republic of Congo but there have long been suspicions that the plane was shot down.

The match was due to be played in Chingola as Zambia's national stadium in Lusaka was being renovated. The benefits inherent in the awkwardness of the journey would not have been lost on the Zambian FA. The flight itself had taken a bizarre turn. Half the Libyan players danced and sang in the aisles to Arabic pop songs whilst the other half lay in their seats reading copies of the Quran. At the back the physio and team doctor puffed away on cigarettes – still the only time I have ever smoked on a flight – as Marcos Paquetá shot them disapproving glances over his shoulder. The plane had to refuel in Cameroon, but an election was about to take place and Cameroon's air space was to be shut for 24 hours. There was only a window of a few hours before the plane would be grounded. Libya's crucial game would be over before it had started. According to the Libyan delegation, the ground staff raised the price of fuel. A stand-off followed for the next three hours and the pilots refused to give in to their alleged extortion. But they blinked first. A member of the air crew was dispatched down to hand over several large bricks of $100 bills so that the flight could carry on to Ndola.

Even at night you could see the shifting political and economic landscape of Zambia. The north of the country had seen a huge influx of Chinese money in recent years, part of a wider policy of African investment by China to secure the natural resources needed to feed its rapidly growing economy. And the Chinese had left their imprint. As the coach bumped along the single, unlit road towards Chingola we passed a huge new stadium built by the Chinese government. The 44,000-capacity Levy Mwanawasa Stadium was a state-of-the-art construction with a running track around it. It wasn't ready in time for this match, but would soon be one of the finest stadiums in Africa. The front gate was adorned with two Chinese dragons atop a sign. 'The Ndola National Stadium,' it said. 'In Zambia, Aided by China.'

Walid el Kahtroushi sat quietly in his hotel room with his baseball cap pulled down tightly over his eyes, head bowed, as if carrying the weight of the world on his shoulders. The team had arrived in the early hours of the morning the day before the match. There hadn't been enough beds for the team and some had to sleep on the floor. It wasn't the late night or the pressure of expectation that now weighed heavily on the 27-year-old midfielder. It was the guilt that wouldn't leave him. 'If it was about me I would never come back, you would never find me here playing football,' he said firmly. 'But my friends on the front line, they told me: "This is your future, you must go there [to Zambia]. This is also like a war for you. This is your duty. You must go there and play and then you can come back." And that's why I'm here.'

The Libyan civil war had broken out eight months previously, midway through Libya's qualification campaign, forcing the players to choose sides. Some, like the 34-year-old captain Tariq al Taib, were virulently pro-Gaddafi. When Libya beat the Comoros 3–0 in a qualifier in neutral Mali a few weeks after the civil war started, it was Al Taib who had declared that the team was 100 per cent behind the regime, even declaring the rebels 'dogs' and 'rats'. 'The whole team is for Gaddafi,' he declared to AP after the game. 'We dedicate this victory to the Libyan people who are suffering.'

But under the surface nothing could have been further from the truth. Kahtroushi had scored the first goal of that game, but when the return match was due to take place he couldn't bear to pull on the jersey that bore the Gaddafi-era flag.

'I was in the camp for the second match against Comoros [in June 2011]. Some people came to me and told me one of my dear friends was in the hospital and lost his arm,' he said. Straight away he decided to leave and return to fight for the rebels. The coaching staff only realised what he was planning when they saw him waving from beyond the gate. 'I went there [to Tripoli] to see him in the hospital. I saw him and saw many Libyans injured in a very hard situation.' Kahtroushi decided to join the rebellion at Jebel Nafusa, then a small pocket of resistance against Gaddafi's forces near the Tunisian border. 'The first time I went there they didn't let me pick up a gun and try to fight,' he said. 'They gave me some missions, gave me some money to go bring them some food and some help. Living there was so hard. As a football player they wouldn't let me on the front line. They were always trying to give me other missions to keep me alive. At the time even one of my friends said: "Just go behind me, I'll go in front of you so if there's a bullet I can have it."'

The fighting got so fierce that his status as a footballer in need of protection melted away. 'In the end it was so hard and there's no way [I couldn't fight] so I just took the gun and I went out fighting. It was so hard, you can imagine, you could lose your life at any time.' Kahtroushi survived, as did the goalkeeper Guma Mousa, but not all were so lucky. Ahmed Al Saghir was shot in the shoulder and spent a month in hospital. The squad went and visited him before Al Saghir decided to re-join the rebels rather than play against Zambia. By the end of August, Gaddafi had been toppled. A week later the team had to play their penultimate qualifier against Mozambique behind closed doors in Egypt. Aside from the trouble of getting the players out of the country, there were some more practical concerns to deal with. Nobody wanted to wear the old Gaddafi-era kit and it would be months before a new official kit would arrive. So the team stitched rebel badges onto their shirts instead. The Libyans fought out a 0–0 draw and celebrated, dedicating their victory to freedom and to the Libyans who had lost their lives.

'In football we don't have to represent politics. We played with the first government, yes, but we represented the people of Libya and the country of Libya,' explained 26-year-old midfielder Abdallah al Sherif, now sitting on the bed next to Kahtroushi. 'We are one of the people and we are still representing and playing for Libya and the Libyan people.' Sherif lost family during the NATO bombing of Tripoli. 'The whole family is from Tripoli. I lived a lot of moments during the troubles in Tripoli. We were sitting at home it was so hard to get out. You'd only get out for necessities. To get some food or something like this. To go back home quickly. I had a cousin that died because of a NATO bombing. This situation, this very bad situation we have been through, in the soul of Libya, was caused by the regime because it started the hard way, the way of killing people.'

The issue of what to do with those who had supported the regime was swiftly dealt with by coach Paquetá. Tariq al Taib was nowhere to be seen in Zambia, replaced as captain by 39-year-old veteran goalkeeper Samir Aboud. 'The first time after the war I made a meeting with the players before we started training,' Paquetá had explained back in Tunis. 'I said: "Forget the war, forget Gaddafi and focus on the people. Because Libya is Libya. It is not Gaddafi, it's not the revolution. It's Libyan."'

Like in Iraq or Poland or Spain – countries that had lived under divisive brutal regimes where compromises were required just to survive – Libya's footballers were trying to move on. In the month since Gaddafi fell, over 20 players had signed for foreign clubs, something that had been banned thanks to the paranoia of the previous regime. 'As a Libyan player you didn't have the right to decide for yourself. You just had to come back to the president's son who was controlling everything,' said Kahtroushi. He recalled the Mozambique match and how that result, even a goalless draw, was met with jubilation back in Libya. The match against Zambia, and qualification for the Africa Cup of Nations, would have a greater effect. 'Things are changing, the future will be more beautiful,' he said. Now Kahtroushi didn't look like he had the world on his shoulders. His baseball cap was tipped to the sky, his chin – covered in a large, well-kept beard – thrust forward. Now victory was a matter of duty. 'We will do everything to qualify, *inshallah*, because this will help our country too much. At least to bring them some happiness after all the sadness they have been through.'

The vuvuzelas and the horns began blowing early in Chingola. It was the day of the match and Zambia's fans had descended on the usually quiet mining town dressed in green, creating a low, menacing drone. The Chipolopolo Boys only needed a draw, even if the majority of the fans expected Zambia to hammer Libya. The Libyans needed to win. A draw would see them at the mercy of other results in Ghana and Nigeria. The skies above the Nchanga Stadium were a fresh, light blue, disturbed by a few white clouds that meandered by. The stadium was full well before the Libyan team arrived at there. When they did show up they sat nervously in the changing room as Paquetá gave them their last-minute instructions before praying together. They all wore the new kit with the new badge and carried the new flag. The new national anthem was a little more problematic. With the political and military situation still fluid on the ground, the Zambian government had yet to recognise the new Libyan administration. Officially they had to play the Gaddafi-era anthem. The Libyan officials ran between the changing room and the main stand, trying desperately to avoid a diplomatic incident. The players lined up next to a chain-link fence. Walid el Kahtroushi and his teammates bounced from foot to foot before they walked out onto the pitch. Thankfully, a diplomatic incident was avoided. Libya's new anthem was played, but at such low volume that no one could hear it. None of the players realised it had even begun.

The game was atrocious. The few Libyan journalists that had followed the team knelt by the side of the pitch and prayed as the match played out in front of them. The veteran goalkeeper Samir Aboud, the new captain, made three stunning saves. Zambia hit the post twice. The referee waved away two certain Zambian penalties. Somehow the game ended 0–0. The Zambian fans were livid at their team's inept performance. So angry, in fact, that shortly afterwards the Zambian FA sacked the team's Italian coach Dario Bonetti, despite the fact they had topped their qualification group. Libya's players collapsed on to the pitch. Some cried, others prayed. But they still did not know whether they had done enough to make it. Aboud wept openly on the shoulders of his teammates as they returned to the sanctuary of the dressing room. There we waited for news.

The players sat in their kit, sweating in silence. No one talked, no one speculated. The room grew heavier with humidity and fear. We could have waited an hour. It could have been 30 seconds. The thick fog of confusion was broken when the kit man sprinted into the room. Ghana had beaten Sudan, he shouted, and Nigeria conceded a late . . .

He didn't finish his sentence. A 90th-minute Ibrahima Traoré goal for Guinea in the Nigerian capital Abuja had changed the qualification calculus in Libya's favour. They had made it. The room ignited. The players and coaches held each other as they screamed the national anthem until, exhausted, they sat back on the wooden benches. Somehow, Libya had made it through, ending their campaign with three victories and three draws. They were undefeated.

Libya arrived at the Africa Cup of Nations in Equatorial Guinea as underdogs but were handed the honour of playing in the tournament's opening game against the hosts. They lost 1–0, but drew against Zambia 2–2 before beating Senegal. It wasn't enough to qualify for the next round, but the Libyan team had already shown the world that war wasn't going to hold them back. Zambia went on to appoint Frenchman Hervé Renard after sacking Bonetti, and promptly won the tournament for the first time in their history.

Yet a more significant moment happened three days after that match in Chingola. A convoy of cars near Gaddafi's home town of Sirte was attacked by NATO forces. Colonel Gaddafi and a handful of loyalists managed to escape and hide in a nearby tunnel. But they were caught by rebel fighters. Gaddafi, his face bloated and bloodied from the attack, was dragged through the sand and beaten. He was executed within the hour. Video footage suggested that, in his last, frenzied, brutal moments, Gaddafi was sodomised with a knife by one of his captors.

But, in Chingola in the aftermath of Libya's qualification, the memories of those who had sacrificed their lives to overthrow a dictator were still spoken of in the present tense. The coach returned to the hotel, the first leg of its long journey home. Ahmed Zuway and Walid el Kahtroushi led the team in song as they entered the hotel lobby. Confused white South Africans looked on before joining in with the celebrations. They clapped, not understanding what the Libyans were singing.

The blood of the dead,
It will not be spilled in vain.

AMMAN, HASHEMITE KINGDOM OF JORDAN, MARCH 2012

It took just one question – the first question – for the press conference to degenerate into a farce. In a half-empty room that still smelled of fresh paint at the offices of the Jordanian Football Association in Amman,

Haitham Jattal and Ahmad al Salih, coach and captain of Syria's under-23 team, sat in silence in front of a handful of Asian football journalists as an argument raged around them. It was the day before Syria played its final group qualifier for the London 2012 Olympics, against Malaysia. It was supposed to be a home game but football was now impossible in Syria. An uprising against the rule of Bashar al Assad had plunged the country into civil war, a war that began in the belligerent city of Homs before its shockwaves had covered the entire country. As many as 10,000 people had been slaughtered in the violence so far as Assad tried with diminishing success to reimpose his will on Syria's restive provinces. With the uprising intensifying, FIFA decided that international football was too dangerous to be held in Damascus. Amman was deemed a safer bet. Yet exile had not led to defeat. The Syria team had come within one game of qualifying for the first major football tournament in their history, beating Japan – Asian champions no less – 2–1 in the process. Syria needed to beat Malaysia heavily and hope that Bahrain beat Japan on the other side of the world in Tokyo. It was an incredible achievement in the face of such chaos, but the regime was not giving up its control easily.

'We can't answer about this,' a voice shot angrily across the room. A large, middle-aged man in a suit who had been watching the press from behind the door had entered the room at the first sign of trouble. 'No comment about that,' he said, wagging his finger. 'I am in charge of the media for the team and I say you cannot ask that!'

'No questions about politics!' shouted another from the other side of the room who claimed to be an interpreter. The question asked was a seemingly innocuous one: how had the Syrian team coped playing its games outside the country given the situation back home? The room bickered about the nature of the question with the two men who claimed to be interpreters for the team, although few were convinced by their aliases. The Syrian coach and captain watched on stony faced as the circus continued around them. 'We play in the name of Syria,' coach Jattal was eventually allowed to answer. 'It is well known everyone back home will be watching the match and they will be hoping for us to win. Of course, playing in your homeland in front of our own people would be much better than playing outside. But we have overcome this difficulty and turned it into an incentive to reach the Olympics.'

It was a universe away from what I had seen four years previously at Al Jaish. Back then there was stability, if not peace and happiness. Football had successfully challenged the army's monopoly and won. The league had gone professional. Young players were finally given the chance to reach their potential as Syria's various national youth sides had begun to qualify for international tournaments. There had been hope that Syria might even make it to the 2014 World Cup finals, but the team was kicked out early in qualification after it was discovered that they had fielded a player – George Mourad – who had previously played for Sweden. Still, there was always the Olympics. But then the people of Homs rose up against Assad and everything changed. Except the suspicion. Another question about how the coach had managed to forge unity in a squad that included players from across Syria's sectarian and geographical divides, including several from Homs, was met with the same howls of protest. 'It is easy and simple. Everybody came a few days before the match [for a meeting] in the capital Damascus,' insisted the interpreter eventually when pressed on the issue. 'We have no problems with the players.' When asked whether the coach would like to answer the question, the interpreter stopped, as if taken back by the question. 'He says the same as I said.' Except this was a lie. The Syrians did have a problem with one rebel player in particular, the team's goalkeeper, Abdul Basset al Saroot. He was nowhere to be seen. But that was to be expected since no one knew where he was. The only way to find him was on You-Tube, where he had become an early hero of the revolution.

The footage was grainy. A young man stood proudly, defiantly even, if a little nervously, in front of a Syrian national flag. The date on the screen stated that the video was shot in July 2011 in the city of Homs. He was wearing a dark T-shirt, his arms folded across his chest. 'In the name of Allah, the most merciful and compassionate. I am Abdul Basset al Saroot, a Syrian citizen,' the young man began. 'I am the national goalkeeper of the Syrian national youth team and of [local Syrian team] Karamah club,' he continued. 'I am now wanted by the security agencies, which are trying to arrest me. I declare with sound mind and of my own volition, that we, the free people of Syria, will not back down until our one and only demand is met: the toppling of the regime.' The video ended abruptly, but not before Abdul Basset al Saroot delivered his coup de grâce. 'I hold the Syrian regime responsible for anything that happens to me,' he said, calmer now. 'Long live free Syria, long live our proud people that reject humiliation.'

The 20-year-old goalkeeper had not turned up for training with the squad the previous summer. Instead, he was so sickened by the army's atrocities in his home city of Homs – the centre of the rebellion – that he left football and joined the rebels. At first he seemed like any other defector. But he soon became more than that, as another YouTube video a few months later proved. Shot by Al Jazeera it showed Abdul Basset al Saroot sitting low in the front seat as his car careered from stop to stop. He now had to take special precautions. The regime had already tried to assassinate him on several occasions, claiming the lives of his best friend and his brother. Now he travelled from safe house to safe house. It was too dangerous to stay in one place for long.

Eventually he arrived at his destination. Abdul Basset al Saroot was to sing revolutionary songs for a large crowd of a few thousand that had gathered especially for him, to see the now legendary 'singing goal-keeper' give thanks to those who had died so far in the uprising. His beautiful singing voice had been put to good use since he had gone AWOL from Syria's Olympic football squad. The crowds had got big-ger and bigger to see the new hero of Homs. Every time the regime tried to silence him, the crowds grew. In the previous YouTube video, filmed shortly after the first assassination attempt, Saroot had appeared – seriously injured and clearly shaken – to prove that he was still alive. Now he was talking to Al Jazeera, explaining his life of perpetual move-ment that had become a symbol of hope for the anti-Assad rebels. 'I am free. I have travelled all over the world to play football. But freedom isn't just about me or about travelling,' he told the reporter. 'What about everyone else? Freedom is a big word. Freedom is about freedom of speech and freedom of opinion . . . the Syrian regime has made it so scary that a son is too afraid to even talk to his own mother.'

Abdul Basset al Saroot's defection had been an embarrassment. Now the players were looked on every bit as suspiciously as the for-eign journalists sitting in the room. 'You didn't think that guy was an interpreter did you?' a Jordanian official said to me shortly after the press conference had finished. 'If the coach or any of the players talked about politics they would hang them.'

*

The Syrian squad trained in silence at the King Abdullah stadium on the outskirts of Amman. The team had been chosen from all of Syria's football clubs – including the country's biggest team Al Karamah and Al Wathba, both based in Homs. It was hoped that the team could become a symbol of normality and unity. But Abdul Basset al Saroot's absence loomed large over the squad, even if some would have liked that not to be the case. 'Everyone is looking for him, he's hiding in houses in Homs,' one Syrian official said dismissively, and anonymously, pitchside, shortly before the delegation decided to close the training session to the media. 'Every time they look for him they find women in all black [wearing religious clothing]. He's friends with number nine [striker Nassouh Nakkdahli] but they haven't spoken to him for seven months.'

His ghost – a free spirit cut loose from the shackles of the regime be they in Homs or here, in Amman – still haunted those all around. It had been a while since he had posted on YouTube. Some thought he had been killed. But his former teammates still held out hope that he was alive and might even one day play with them again. In the stands watching the team train, two injured players sat separately from the rest of Syria's delegation. 'We hope that he will return. He is a good goalkeeper and he was also our friend before,' said Thaer Krouma, a midfielder also from Homs who played for Al Wathba. For Syrian players like Krouma, qualification for the Olympics would be a gift to the people, separate from the politics and bloodshed that had dominated the previous 12 months. 'The players have a strong bond and love for each other and are committed. [Olympic qualification is] a big dream to accomplish but we represent Syria, the people of Syria and anyone who loves the Syrian country. We represent the 23 million people and their hopes,' he said. Krouma was worried about the worsening situation back home. He had spoken to his family in Homs, who were safe despite the army pounding several rebellious districts into dust. Saroot didn't believe that the Olympics would be a gift for the people, nor that you could separate victory for the Syrian national team from victory for the regime. The Olympics would give Assad more legitimacy than he deserved.

When kick-off arrived, the King Abdullah stadium was virtually empty. A few hundred Malaysian fans – almost all of them university students – filled one small section despite the fact they had nothing to play for. In the 'home' end just 20 Syrians noisily sang pro-regime chants. 'It's a conspiracy,' argued 18-year-old Jneid, a leather market trader originally from Aleppo, of what he viewed as the anti-Assad media coverage of the conflict in Syria. 'The Gulf countries, like Qatar who own Al Jazeera, and his friends, they make a conspiracy on Syria. [In Homs] After the last prayers they [the Gulf countries] take the money and go to the young people with no job, offer them money and tell them to go and shoot, go and bomb the hospitals.'

They watched as Syria easily overcame their inferior opponents, beating them 3–0. It wasn't enough for automatic qualification as Japan dispatched Bahrain. Instead Syria would have to travel to Vietnam two weeks later to play Oman and Uzbekistan in a round-robin tournament. The winner would go into a final play-off against Senegal in the English city of Coventry for the last place at London 2012. A downbeat coach Jattal tried to see the positives in the victory and the three potential extra matches, played thousands of miles apart in less than a month, that came with it.

'[We feel] happiness but not that much happiness as we would prefer to go to England without the play-off,' he said. The players barely celebrated as they left the pitch, the pro-Assad chants from the handful of Syrian fans almost, but not quite, drowned out by the drums of Malaysian students.

'God, Syria. Bashar [Al Assad] is all we need,' they chanted.

Syria never made it to London. They mysteriously arrived in Vietnam with a different coach. A draw against Oman meant that Syria had to beat Uzbekistan. They took an early lead too but the intense schedule of matches and travel took their toll. Uzbekistan scored two late goals and Syria's hopes of making it to the Olympics were over. By then others had opened their eyes to the horrors in Homs. Syria's army would crush the rebellion and regain control of the city. The world watched as the district of Baba Amr, the centre of the rebellion in Homs, was flattened and innocent lives lost. The thought that Syria might be represented at London 2012 appeared abhorrent. The British government even moved to ban any figures aligned to the regime from attending the Olympics. 'If the British government has decided to ban anyone connected to the regime and to President Bashar al

Assad, I am telling you in advance they should ban all Syrian citizens, because we all support President Assad and support Syria,' an angry General Mowaffak Joumaa, chair of the Syrian Olympic Committee, told the BBC. But the football team, who returned to Syria empty-handed, was no longer part of that game.

A few weeks later the British government confirmed the news: 'The General', the same general I had met in Damascus four years earlier shredding documents in front of a picture of him embracing the president, had been refused a visa to attend the games.

The General may not have travelled to London 2012, but the national football team had enjoyed something of a renaissance. The exile and war had, much like with the Iraqi national team and their 2007 victory in the Asian Cup, focused minds. Many of the same players that had gone so close to making it to the London Olympics had starred in the AFC U-19 Championship in the UAE a few months later. They were knocked out in the quarter-finals but not before they had smashed Saudi Arabia – a country that the Assad regime and his supporters had accused of funding and supporting Syria's rebels – 5–1. A few months later Syria won the 2012 West Asian Championship, beating Iraq in the final. In some respects it had been Syrian football's greatest year. But their success wasn't like the Iraq team in 2007. Back then Iraq didn't have a regime to follow or resist, just the morality of their own unity. The fingerprints of the Syrian state, on the other hand, remain on the country's recent football success.

It had been a while since the world heard from Abdul Basset al Saroot, the rebel goalkeeper. His last dispatch came on 4 April 2012, from the Syrian village of Bayada. A huge crowd had gathered in the city's main square. It was dangerous to gather in such numbers here given that the Syrian army was in the middle of razing the district of Baba Amr in nearby Homs to the ground. Thousands had died in the shelling and from the snipers. Countless more had been picked up and disappeared, presumed liquidated in one of Assad's many medieval torture cells. But thousands of people, maybe as many as 10,000 people, had taken the risk to see Abdul Basset al Saroot sing. He stood at the front, high above his audience, and addressed the crowd.

'*Allahu Akbar!*' he shouted to the crowd.

'God is great!' they repeated in unison.

Saroot's voice was strong, his singing clear.

'We won't back down from this revolution!' he sang.

'*Allahu Akbar!*' replied the crowd.

'We won't be quiet on the wound inflicted on Baba Amr. Either we are victorious or we die. Allah is witness to what we say. If we walk on this path we shall, inshallah, die as martyrs.'

The thousands of people hanging off Abdul Basset al Saroot's every word agreed.

MELBOURNE, AUSTRALIA, FEBRUARY 2016

Hakeem al Araibi can still remember the excitement of getting up at dawn in the hope of watching Bahrain qualify for the World Cup. Hakeem was 15 years old when Bahrain played New Zealand in Wellington. He was a promising youth player for his local club, Al Shabab, and the whole family had gathered around the television to watch the game at his home in the village of Jidhafs, a few kilometres west of Manama. 'We were screaming at the television, me and my family, at the house,' he recalled of the second game against New Zealand. 'We were wishing we could win and then go outside of the house in the village to celebrate and go to see my mates and celebrate with them.' He remembers praying seconds before Sayed Mohamed Adnan took *that* penalty. Adnan, and A'ala Hubail, were Hakeem's heroes. He hoped to emulate them by playing for the national team too. 'Mohamed Adnan missed that penalty,' he said, sounding as if he was still disappointed five years later. 'We couldn't do it. It happens in football. We were unlucky.'

Still, it was the start of an emotional 12 months for Hakeem. He was thriving at Al Shabab. A school teacher had seen him play and suggested to a local scout that he come and see him. Soon enough he had also appeared on the radar of the Bahrain Football Association. The national team's exploits over the previous ten years had inspired Hakeem. If a country as small as Bahrain can almost reach two World Cup finals, what did it matter if he was from a small village outside the capital? So, in 2010 he was called up to the under-17 squad. 'I was 16 years old when the national team called me up and I was so happy,' he said. 'I put so much effort into being a good representative of the national team.' Like the former national team coach Milan Máčala, Hakeem saw the national teams as symbols of unity. 'It didn't matter whether we were Sunni or Shia,' he said of that time. 'They [Sunni players] were attending the same prayers as us, religious rites with us. I remember they would sing our religious songs, no problems at all.'

But by the end of 2010 that had changed. Tensions between Shia political groups and the government had begun to boil over. Hakeem's brother, Emad, was a well-known activist who had become a person of interest to the police. When Hakeem returned to Bahrain after playing an under-17 national team match in Kuwait the police raided his home. 'I arrived in Bahrain at midnight and then the police attacked my house at 3am,' he recalled. The police, he said, were look- ing for his brother. Hakeem was the only male in the house. 'They took me instead,' he said. He was accused of burning tyres, something he denied, and was held for three months, until February 2011, when the Pearl Roundabout revolution was in full swing. 'I was so proud when I came out,' he said of his release. 'I couldn't imagine that so many people would be out on the street and asking for their rights and participating in parliament and other powerful positions in Bah- rain. I wasn't involved in politics but I thought it was something really strange to see.'

He remembers the aftermath, and watching the now infamous pro- gramme on Bahraini national television where prominent footballers and other athletes were highlighted in the crowd and then denounced. 'I'm an athlete and I was afraid I would be in jail again and they would target me again. Usually, when you have a history, they will target you again,' he said. 'I was really surprised when I saw two of my heroes [A'ala Hubail and Sayed Mohamed Adnan], the most famous in Bahrain, being mistreated and tortured and thrown in jail. I was really afraid the same would happen to me as in my village there was a big uprising and it took a big part in the Bahraini revolution. I was really afraid to go out of my house. I couldn't imagine that they would be mistreated. Everyone loved them in Bahrain.'

Hakeem kept his head down although it was tough to play football. His club, Al Shabab, had been targeted by the Bahrain Football Association. For almost a year after the revolution there was no football at Al Shabab. Eventually, the BFA decided to demote the club to the second division, punishment – Hakeem says – for it being a club from a Shia area heavily involved in the protests. 'They stopped the activities in the club because most of the players were Shia,' Hakeem believed. 'I couldn't do anything. No one was playing in my club. I was going to train at the club by myself to keep fit.' He was still being picked for the under-17 team but he didn't play any club football until the spring of 2012. When the club returned in the second division he established himself as first choice. It was on 3 November that year Hakeem was chosen in the starting XI against Busaiteen Club, at the Al Muharraq Stadium. 'I remember everything about that game I played against Busaiteen Club,' he said. 'I remember seeing the doctor from the club. I remember we were all together in the bus. I remember we were defeated 3–0. We took a shower and went back to the bus and after that we went back to the club. We were talking to a player from Morocco about his career and what he had done.'

I'd managed to get hold of a recording of the game. The video was of terrible quality, but the faces of the players can be seen and their names clearly heard as each was announced by the Arabic commentators. The sun had set and the floodlights were on. There weren't many fans in the stadium, a sand-coloured bowl with a shallow terrace of no more than half-a-dozen steps. Two red and white Bahraini flags made of cloth had been fastened to a wall either side of the halfway line, directly opposite the camera position. In the middle of the two flags was a banner bearing the face of Bahrain's king. The game was pretty unremarkable. A goalless first half was followed by Busaiteen Club scoring three goals without reply in the second. As the players walked off the pitch at the Muharraq Stadium, Hakeem al Araibi looked exhausted and dejected as he shook hands with his opponents and the referees. It had been a heavy defeat. The time was 19.20, which was important to note. Twenty kilometres south-west of the stadium, on the other side of Manama, a riot had broken out outside the Al Khamees police station. According to the official police report, a mob of 150 people attacked the building, throwing Molotov cocktails and smashing windows. Among the crowd, according to eyewitnesses and, later, a confession extracted by the police, was a young man by the name of Hakeem al Araibi.

According to the Bahrain police report, Hakeem left the stadium, got dressed, raced through the rush hour to the other side of the city so that he could attack the Al Khamees police station 40 minutes later. Such a journey would be virtually impossible without a helicopter. There was also another problem with the police report. The match was shown live on Bahraini television. Regardless, Hakeem and his brother were arrested a few days later. 'In the investigation room they were telling me that I had attacked a police station in Al Khamees on the night of 3 November. I told them: "I was playing live on TV! I have evidence!"' he said. 'The stadium I played in was not close to that police station. But they kept saying: "Don't say that because you are a liar. You shut up. You lie."'

It was at this point that Hakeem alleges that he was tortured by four men, three to hold him, one to beat him whilst he was blindfolded. 'In the interrogation room they asked me all the questions and said: "Do you need an introduction or shall we start?" I didn't know what they meant. They started beating me. They cared about putting no marks on me. But they were focused on my legs. They would say: "You are a football player and we will destroy your future." They were beating me on my legs every ten minutes. When it was red they would stop and let me shake the blood back into them and then I felt them beat again and again without leaving a mark.'

He was released three months later but the trial continued. Meanwhile, Hakeem had returned to play for Al Shabab and was eventually called up for the senior national team by another English coach who had just taken over, Anthony Hudson (later manager of New Zealand). 'I had no problem with the coach [Hudson] because he had no problem with Shia or Sunni, only how you played football and are you good enough?' he said, admitting to feeling strange about being around the Bahraini administrators of the national team. 'I felt really weird towards the administration of the Bahrain national football team though because most of them were Sunni and I was a little afraid. But it went OK, away from politics. I was playing regularly, not saying anything about the uprising . . .'

This, it turns out, wasn't enough. Hakeem travelled with the national team to Qatar at the end of 2013 for the West Asian Football Federation Championship. Shortly after Bahrain's 0–0 draw with Iraq, as they trained for the next game against Jordan on 4 January 2014, Hakeem was informed that he had been convicted of attacking the police station and had been sentenced to ten years in prison. Despite the evidence that he was playing football that time live on television, the court upheld a confession extracted from his brother Emad that also placed Hakeem at the scene of the crime. Emad claimed he had been tortured into giving the confession. But the judge, who was also a member of the Khalifa royal family, dismissed the allegation, as well as testimonies from Hakeem's teammates that he was still with the team well past 8pm when the attack on Al Khamees police station took place. He told Hudson of the news before federation officials, he said, frogmarched him to the airport to put him on a flight back to Bahrain. I sent Hudson a message on Facebook, which he initially responded to before going dark when I asked him specifically about Hakeem.

'No way, I am not going back. I've experienced really horrible days before, being tortured, mistreated. How can I be assured I won't be killed back in Bahrain?' Hakeem recalled thinking at that moment. 'When I got inside the gate I waited until the guys from Bahrain's football administration went outside the airport. And then I left the airport. I went to one of my friends in Qatar and asked them to help me and book me a ticket to anywhere else in the world so I can survive.' What followed was a nomadic four-month escape. He left for Iran, then Iraq, then Iran again, Malaysia, Thailand and, finally, Australia. 'I was just thinking of playing football and living a peaceful life.' Hakeem hadn't set out to rebel. The regime would turn him into a rebel player.

Hakeem and I had spoken for over an hour as he told me his story. He was in Melbourne now and was happy, playing state football, preparing to get married and waiting for his permanent refugee status to come through from the Australian authorities. But he was angry too. It was a few days before FIFA's 2016 presidential election was about to take place. Gianni Infantino was the slight favourite to win the vote but his main challenger was Sheikh Salman bin Ibrahim al

Khalifa, the former president of the Bahrain Football Association and member of Bahrain's ruling Khalifa royal family, the same Sheikh Salman who allegedly chaired a committee to identify protesting athletes. Two years later he had been elected president of the Asian Football Confederation and now he was up for football's top job. A spokesperson for Sheikh Salman told the *Guardian* in 2016 that 'the allegations are entirely false and categorically denied by Sheikh Salman bin Ibrahim al Khalifa. While it was proposed that Sheikh Salman lead a fact-finding committee in relation to the events of 2011, that committee was never formally established and never conducted any business whatsoever.' But for Hakeem those denials were not plausible. 'I can guarantee he [Sheikh Salman] knows what happened in Bahrain,' he said. 'He was the Bahrain Football Association president so there is no way he doesn't know what happens regardless of the committee. Players have been mistreated in a violent way. If you will deny that things happened to other players, what about me? I am one of the big examples in your history. I have been tortured. I have evidence I was playing live on TV. And you haven't defended me. At least say a word about me. He didn't say anything about me. Which means you have wronged me.'

The run up to the FIFA vote then took a surprising turn. Back in Bahrain Sheikh Salman gave an interview to the Associated Press where he called the accusations 'dirty tricks and dirty lies' before wheeling out a secret weapon to pledge support for his candidacy: A'ala Hubail, Bahrain's all-time top scorer who had been humiliated on national television, jailed and later claimed he was tortured after being involved in the protest. Now, incredibly, he was in favour of Sheikh Salman's candidacy, claiming that his protest was not political, but rather aimed at improving sports facilities. 'I have known Sheikh Salman for a while. I don't think that he was involved in this ... I would never lie. I don't think he did this and I am sure of it,' he said. 'We didn't want to harm anyone or offend anybody ... On Bahrain television, some people wanted to take advantage of the situation and use the players for their own good ... so I was arrested for about three months and then I was released.' It was an absurd turnaround, but one that Hakeem believed was made under pressure. 'If I was in Bahrain, you would not hear something bad from me about Sheikh

Salman,' Hakeem told me when I asked about Hubail's recent comments. Sayed Mohamed Adnan had also been somewhat rehabilitated by returning to Bahrain and playing again briefly for the national team. 'If I said anything opposite I would be mistreated and in jail,' added Hakeem. 'They changed their words because they are in fear.'

Sheikh Salman narrowly lost the FIFA presidential election. He won 85 votes in the first round of voting, just behind Infantino who led with 88. But, during the second round of voting, Infantino ran away with it. Of the 34 votes available in the second round, only 3 switched to Sheikh Salman. He returned to his presidency of the Asian Football Confederation. Meanwhile, at the end of November 2017, Hakeem al Araibi was finally granted permanent leave to remain in Australia as a refugee. He moved to Pascoe Vale FC, a semi-pro club in Australia's National Premier Leagues Victoria and got married. In November 2018 Hakeem and his new wife decided to go on honeymoon in Thailand. But when the couple arrived in Bangkok, Hakeem was arrested. Bahrain had issued a 'Red Notice' through Interpol, in effect an international arrest warrant, even though Interpol's own rules prevent refugees from being issued a Red Notice by the countries from which they have fled. He was in jail and on the verge of being sent back to Bahrain at any moment. 'This is nothing to do with my conviction, Bahrain wants me back to punish me, because I talked to the media in 2016 about the terrible human rights and about how Sheikh Salman is a very bad man who discriminates against Shia Muslims,' Hakeem said from jail. 'I am so scared of being sent back to Bahrain, so scared because 100 per cent they will arrest me, they will torture me again, possibly they will kill me.'

I thought of Milan Máčala back in 2009, sweating in Manama's humidity, telling me how the team was a symbol of unity that successfully harnessed a preposterous amount of talent for the tiny size of its population. I thought of the time when I turned up to a Brisbane Roar game in Sydney, not long after Sayed Mohamed Adnan had arrived, and how his club spokesperson told me he feared retribution and was too scared to talk about what had happened to him. And I thought of Hakeem, alone in his Thai cell, unsure whether he would live or he would die.

18

The Soccer War

Xavi Hernández arrived late and a bit flustered. 'I recorded this video, in English, and it was not easy!' he said, sitting down, a little out of breath, looking for his phone so he could show me what he was talking about. We were sitting at a café high up in the Aspire Tower, a 50-storey, near 1,000-foot-high skyscraper built to look like a flaming torch that watched over the Aspire Zone, the state-of-the-art training facility I had seen opened by Pelé and Maradona back in 2005. Xavi was one of the greatest players of his generation, Barcelona's metronome during arguably the defining golden era in the club's history. After joining La Masia, Barcelona's youth academy, at the age of 11, he went on to replace his mentor Pep Guardiola and win everything in the game, including eight La Liga and four Champions League titles. He was equally as devastating with the Spanish national team, where he won back-to-back European Championships and the 2010 World Cup.

Today he played in Qatar, for Al Sadd.

When I'd first arrived in Qatar, and Manfred Hoener was pulling the strings, the Q League was full of stars like Gabriel Batistuta and Marcel Desailly. It had become harder to match those big names but Xavi was different. He was a genuine superstar. This was to be the final, well-paying stop of his record-breaking playing career. The evening before I had watched him play at Al Sadd's Jassim bin Hamad Stadium. It was an oppressively humid evening but the stadium had deployed its much trumpeted outdoor air-conditioning system. It had been mentioned in Qatar's bid document for the 2022 World Cup finals; a fix to keep players and fans from collapsing in the 50°C summer heat the tournament had been due to be played in. The system worked. It was ten degrees cooler pitchside. But that was immaterial now. FIFA had agreed to move the World Cup to November and December 2022, in Qatar's winter. Al Sadd beat Al Gharafa 2–1 and Xavi had shown the same pin-sharp clarity of passing and awareness that had characterised his time at Camp Nou, even if he didn't quite have the legs any more.

This was to be his third and final season in Qatar as a player. Retirement and coaching beckoned. Yet, as he finally arrived at the Aspire Tower – flustered but apologetic and friendly – his thoughts weren't in Doha, but Catalonia. A long-gestated independence referendum had been held, and violence against voters and protesters at the hands of the Spanish police had followed, images that had shocked the world. Xavi too. He unlocked his phone and showed me the video he had recorded that morning, and the reason for his delay. It was a message of solidarity with the people of Catalonia, in English, a language he had only begun to seriously learn when he arrived in Qatar at the age of 35.

What is happening today in Catalonia is a crying shame.
In a democratic country, people should be able to vote.
My whole support goes out to Catalans trying to vote.
Visca [long live] Catalunya!

'Only Catalonia people want to vote. Just want to vote. Is there a democracy or not in Spain?' he asked rhetorically after he'd shown me it. 'Look at the videos in Barcelona now. Look.' He flipped through picture after picture. The first was of a group of young protesters being beaten. The next was an old lady with blood on her face. He got more and more agitated as he flipped through perhaps 20 more. The images of blood and violence blurred. 'This picture is the reality, look,' he said, stopping at the picture of an old man being manhandled by police near a polling station. 'One old man trying to vote and two police beat him. For me it is a crying shame. It is a reality in Spain now.' He took a moment to compose himself. We were, after all, here to talk about football, and how he ended up in Qatar, a country that unlike Spain really did have zero democracy. 'I am trying to be calm,' he said. 'But it is very tense.'

Xavi liked living in Qatar. He was 37 now and although he still thought about the game at the same speed he always did, his legs weren't following the brain's instructions quick enough. 'The main reason I came here is that I can continue to play, in a different rhythm and a different intensity than in Europe,' he said when I asked whether it was the money that brought him to Qatar. 'In Barcelona it was too hard to play every three days. I was going to the national team for many, many years. It was difficult to continue to play at 35 years old. So I can continue to play football here, I can start as a coach here in Aspire. I am learning a lot in the academy. And the country permits my whole family to come here.' It didn't sound that different to the reasons Ronald de Boer and Marcel Desailly told me they had moved to Qatar for. But that was 12 years before, and Qatar was a completely different country now.

Very few people would have been able to point to Qatar on the map before that fateful night in Zurich, in December 2010, when Sepp Blatter announced that Qatar would host the 2022 World Cup finals. But the world knew about Qatar now, and not all of it was good. The bid was embroiled in serious corruption allegations that had almost destroyed FIFA and brought an unforgiving microscope that had magnified Qatar's human rights abuses, especially the appalling treatment of migrant workers who built the Gulf's infrastructure. The full accounting of the scandals would be almost too long to list in a single book. In the immediate aftermath of the 2010 vote FIFA president Sepp Blatter was challenged for the top job by the Qatari AFC president Mohammed bin Hammam, who had played an important behind-the-scenes role in delivering Qatar's World Cup. He'd told me back in 2011, as we sat in a hotel café in Ramallah at the height of his power, that he was ready to run against Blatter. He was perhaps, back then, the most powerful man in world football. And he was close to dethroning Blatter too, but then he was destroyed by allegations he had approved bribes, bricks of cash handed out to federation chiefs in the Caribbean, in return for votes. He was later banned from football for life and was accused of facilitating huge bribes for members of FIFA's Executive Committee ahead of the 2022 vote, which he denied and appealed against. As various courts and committees weighed up his guilt, he quit and returned to Qatar to tend to his family's engineering business.

As accusations of corruption related to the Qatar and Russia bids continued to mount, FIFA was forced to commission an investigation. Former US attorney for the Southern District of New York Michael J. Garcia was put in charge and two years later he delivered what became known as the Garcia Report. FIFA at first refused to release the report except for a heavily truncated executive summary, and claimed it exonerated Qatar. But Garcia resigned saying that his work was being misinterpreted. It seemed like the shock 2010 vote had started a chain reaction, which led to the Bar au Lac Hotel in Zurich being raided at dawn in May 2015, with FIFA officials being dragged out of bed at 6am and arrested before their annual congress. Ever since the US lost the 2022 bid to Qatar the FBI had taken a closer look at corruption in world soccer. It didn't take them long to find dirt on Chuck Blazer, the garrulous, morbidly obese general secretary of CONCACAF who owned two apartments in Trump Tower and would often been seen driving his mobility scooter in New York with his pet parrot on his shoulder. Blazer hadn't paid tax for years and was easily flipped to become an informer when prison looked likely. He even wore a wire whilst at the 2012 Olympics to gather evidence of bribe-taking and corruption, which led directly to the Baur au Lac arrests. The Office of the Attorney General of Switzerland opened a criminal investigation into the Qatar and Russia vote the same day. Blazer died of cancer in July 2017.

The arrests took place just before FIFA's presidential elections. Sepp Blatter initially won against his rival Prince Ali of Jordan. But it didn't last long. The outcry over the arrests and the perception that corruption within FIFA was out of control under Blatter's reign saw Sepp resign a few days later. Both him, and his then likely successor Michel Platini, who had voted for Qatar's World Cup and had been implicated in *France Football*'s 'Qatargate' investigation, were later suspended and then banned for eight years over a 1.5 million-euro payment made to Platini, approved by Blatter, in 2011, around the time Platini was rumoured to be considering running against Blatter. When the election finally took place the previously unfancied secretary general of UEFA Gianni Infantino beat Bahrain's Sheikh Salman. Infantino likely won because of a last-minute shift of votes from federation chiefs uneasy about the allegations surrounding Sheikh

Salman's involvement in punishing Bahraini sportsmen and women after the failed Pearl Roundabout uprising. Sheikh Salman had continued to claim his innocence. Of the 24 FIFA Executive Committee members who voted on Qatar's World Cup in 2010, 21 were now either banned from football, indicted by the FBI or credibly accused of corruption. Several had died before justice could be served.

The worst scandal, though, was the appalling treatment of migrant workers under the system of *kafala*, which means 'guardianship' in Arabic. It is a system where your employer is responsible for all that you do and, effectively, gives bosses absolute control over a worker's life. It was something I had seen and was appalled by as soon as I had arrived in Dubai for the *Time Out* job. Yet it had been completely normalised in all Gulf states, not just Qatar. In fact, many workers would tell me that the situation was far worse in Saudi Arabia and the UAE. Western expats would go about their business as Indian, Pakistani and Bangladeshi workers lived in miserable ghetto camps, toiling on building sites in 50°C heat for a pittance. Everyone who worked in the Gulf, from the CEO to their driver, was employed under the *kafala* system. But the country you came from and the colour of your skin decided how restrictive it was. Most Westerners could freely move about, leave the country, and not give up their passports, earning tax-free salaries better than at home. As long as they didn't ask any questions, or make any trouble, they could still drink alcohol in their nice bars, play golf on championship courses that sucked down a country's worth of water to stay green and shop in their luxury malls (one of the few public spaces in the Gulf, which poor black and brown workers were effectively banned from). Female migrants had it even worse, trapped in domestic work often separated from anyone else and ripe for abuse and exploitation.

Westerners told themselves stories that the migrant workers they saw in blue overalls packed onto buses on their way to work at dawn, returning home exhausted and covered in dust at dusk, were like the Irish or Italians that arrived in the US at the end of the nineteenth century; arriving in a land of opportunity denied them back home, taking a few years of hardship on the chin so they could have a better life in a few years' time. They were like us, in effect, but just at a different stage of the immutable, ever-turning economic cycle of development.

The expats were mostly lying to themselves. These workers would never be recognised for their role in building their adopted countries. They had no rights, and were beaten, arrested and deported if they asked for them. They were often trapped in a form of indentured slavery and would be sent home once their employer had drained them of strength and life. We will never know how many men and women have died over the past few decades because of the heat and the abuse. Keeping records wasn't in the interests of the Gulf states that relied on them, nor the governments in the developing world that craved their remittances, and not the Western corporations who exploited their labour to build fabulous towers and islands. It was a vicious form of economic apartheid. Yet the British press didn't think that a system of slavery operating in the open was much of a story before 2010. I'd heard that one well-known editor who arrived in the UAE to take charge of a newspaper had told their staff to bin any job applications from journalists that included cuttings of workers' rights stories. People, they said, had 'moved on' from the story. But they hadn't moved on. The intense scrutiny that the World Cup victory brought, tinged with some additional anti-Arab racism, meant that suddenly people started noticing that millions of people's lives were being crushed by one of the great injustices of twenty-first-century global capitalism.

The dangers of 'making trouble' were clear in the case of Zahir Belounis. In 2013, the French-Algerian footballer was trapped in Qatar because of the *kafala* system. He played for El Jaish, Qatar's army team, but was loaned out against his wishes. His wages were stopped. Qatari law back then required employees to get permission from their employer to get an exit visa. Belounis claimed his club refused to give him one unless he agreed to not claim his wages. So for nearly two years he had been living on handouts, unpaid, unable to work, unable to play. He had just decided to go on hunger strike. 'It's going to start next week. They treat me like a dog but I will fight. I will die here in Qatar,' he told me when we spoke on the phone. Another player, former Moroccan international Abdeslam Ouaddou, had a similar experience. He'd signed for Lekhwiya but after falling out of favour his wages stopped. He made a complaint to FIFA and tried to leave the country. 'When I asked for my exit visa from my first club, my sponsor at Lekhwiya, he told me: "We will not give you an exit visa until you take out your complaint. Qatar has many interests in FIFA and it is not good."' He'd already not been paid for five months so he decided to tell his story, and his case was picked up by human rights groups. Both Zahir and Abdeslam were eventually allowed to leave after their cases became public and highly embarrassing for Qatar. 'When you work in Qatar you belong to someone. You are not free. You are a slave,' Abdeslam told me. 'Of course it is not the same situation as the [construction] workers in Qatar, but there is a parallel. It is the same methodology. They can throw you away like old socks.'

By 2016 Qatar had been dragged kicking and screaming into talking about reform, promising to end *kafala*, end exit visas, end non-payment of wages and passport confiscations, end the discrimination where workers were paid depending on their nationality, and ban agents from charging workers fees to find jobs in Qatar. This was one of the biggest issues as a huge agent business had mushroomed in Asia to exploit workers along every step of the pipeline that funnelled poor rural workers to building sites in the Gulf. But it also needed someone on the other side to give the visas in the first place. Every worker to whom I spoke had to take a loan to pay the agent, meaning that their wages, sometimes for decades, were being garnished back home.

Qatar had also promised to improve the miserable living conditions that saw workers living 8, 10, 12 to a room next to open sewers. A series of camps had been built for World Cup workers, which were clean and air-conditioned and only had four people living in the same room. I'd visited Qatar in 2016 to see the Workers' Cup, a football competition set up by the Supreme Committee for Delivery and Legacy, the body organising the 2022 World Cup. Teams of workers from Qatar's big employers played in front of packed crowds as their campmates cheered them on, a genuine moment of escape and joy.

Gianni Infantino turned up – it was one of his first trips since his election as FIFA president – to watch some of the games and to talk to the new emir about the workers' rights issue. Emir Hamad, who had held the World Cup aloft in Zurich next to Blatter in 2010, had abdicated and passed the throne on to his son Tamim. But the issue of workers' rights was seriously damaging Qatar's international reputation. A new report by Amnesty International into the promised reforms was damning. Infantino smiled as he walked on the pitch, his head glistening in the hot midday sun as he took selfies with the workers from Ghana, Kenya, Egypt and India. But as soon as the tournament was finished I went back to the workers' camps and little had changed. They were still trapped, treated like third-class residents, effectively banned from visiting malls and paid less than £200 a month in wages in the world's richest country. Getting access to the camps was hard as the Qatari authorities banned journalists from visiting them without permission. And even then, we would be taken to the equivalent of Potemkin villages: show camps where a fraction of workers lived. Most lived in the vast networks of camps in Al Shahaniya in the middle of the country. One evening, a Ukrainian photographer and I snuck into one of the camps at night, running behind a water truck to avoid being spotted by security. Inside was a very different story. The men I spoke to from Ghana and India lived in miserable conditions; open sewers, workers sleeping in bunks three beds high, cooking facilities blackened with soot and dirt. They had all been brought to Qatar on the promise of helping to build the World Cup. But now the reality was different. The wages were lower than promised and the conditions terrible but the debt to the agent back home still needed to be repaid. They were trapped.

An hour later, once we had snuck out of the camp without getting caught, we jumped into a taxi and headed to a five-star hotel in the centre of Doha where I met Hassan al Thawadi, the man in charge of delivering Qatar's World Cup (who famously claimed in 2022 that critics of Qatar were 'ill-informed'). The disconnection between the squalor I had just seen an hour ago and the luxury I now stood in wasn't just stark, it was immoral.

Is it ethical in such a rich country for someone to be paid £200 a month? I asked.

'I can't, I am not fully aware. I'm not the right person,' Al Thawadi responded. 'In the areas we are responsible . . . I look at worker welfare, where we can influence and have a say on that. Ethical recruitment. Getting rid of worker fees so any new worker doesn't have to pay. Accommodation, making sure it is healthy. How many to a room. We can address those. Safety in the workplace, transportation. Repatriation. These are the areas we are responsible for.' Two hundred thousand good-quality rooms were being built for workers too, he claimed. But why herd workers into faraway camps in the first place, as if they were Qatar's dirty secret? And where will the new 'quality rooms' be built? I asked. 'That is for the market to dictate,' he replied. It was true that *kafala* was popular among Qatar nationals. They were a minority in their own country. It's not hard to imagine a similar demographic imbalance in the UK or the US promoting an even more punitive system. And Al Thawadi had a tough job. He seemed to genuinely want to reform the system, but he wasn't a member of the royal family and so, ultimately, his influence was limited. So, the reforms never went far enough. The workers I had met were not official World Cup workers and so were outside of the Supreme Committee's scope. But Qatar was only 50 miles across. Everything was being built for the World Cup, whether it was official or unofficial. To say or think otherwise was to be deeply disingenuous.

Xavi thought that Qatar was dealing with the workers issue well. 'It is normal [the criticism] because everyone wants to be the host of the World Cup,' he said when I asked him about it, boiling the criticism down to jealousy, a common theme I would often hear Qataris return to. 'Everything is right here. For example, Gianni Infantino is coming here sometimes. Last week he came here to discuss football, about the stadiums, and everything is right.' Xavi was here for other reasons. An easier life, for one, but also, in his words, to help build Qatari football culture and a Qatari team that might be able to compete in 2022. It had been one of the biggest criticisms when Qatar won the bid for the World Cup; that it had little football history of its own. They'd never qualified for the World Cup and hadn't produced a star player of note on the world stage. It was hoped Xavi's example would rub off on his teammates and the rest of the league. 'They are new to football. They don't have a long culture of football,' he said. 'It is difficult for them, for us to come here and try to motivate them to play football. They are a rich country. The new generation now has passion and are motivated to play football. But it is difficult because Qataris is only maybe 10 years, 15 years since they started to play football. It is not easy but we are trying to put in their mind the motivation and culture of European football.' He thought that his teammates were good technically but that he could help them tactically. 'I'm trying to use my experience of Barcelona, of the national team of Spain,' he said. 'I'm trying to put inside them my philosophy.'

It had been hard to get used to Qatar at first, he said. The stadiums were rarely full ('It is really empty!'). And the heat was a problem for half the year. But he stayed and wanted to fulfil an ambition. 'I want to be a coach,' he said. 'I feel I can do it. At least I will try. Because I love football. I love staying on the pitch. I love helping players. I love football, the game. I can't imagine myself in an office. With a computer? No. I feel I can help improve the players on the pitch. It is really soon. I have to take my licence. I'm thinking now as a coach.' This had got everyone excited, that Xavi would be the next coach of the Qatari national team. 'Yeah, everybody asks me on the street. In the malls: "Xavi, will you be our coach for 2022?!"' he recalled. 'OK, it is a big honour that people are thinking of me as their coach. But, I'm still playing, still enjoying football as a player, but we will see.' Xavi (who in fact became manager of Al Sadd in 2019 before being lured back to Barcelona for the top job at Camp Nou) was getting a little ahead of himself. In the past few months Qatar's World Cup suddenly had bigger problems to deal with. Qatar's World Cup was in danger of not happening at all.

At midnight on 24 May 2017, Qatar's official news agency, the QNA, posted a story on its website purporting to be from Emir Tamim. The story seemed wildly florid and undiplomatic compared to the QNA's usual stories welcoming various political figures from around the world. The story quoted the emir lavishing praise on Iran, the Muslim Brotherhood and Hamas, whilst also criticising the recently elected US president Donald J. Trump. It was only up for a few minutes but the damage had been done. Qatar's neighbours, specifically the UAE and Saudi Arabia, were furious that the emir had praised the exact groups and countries they viewed as existential threats. Over the following days, they built a coalition of countries to isolate Qatar, both diplomatically and physically, blockading it by sea and air. According to some US officials, there was even a plan to invade Qatar via its one land border with Saudi Arabia. The coalition announced 13 demands that needed to be met for the blockade to be lifted, including shutting down Al Jazeera and distancing themselves from Iran. The demands equated to Qatar giving up its status as an independent nation. The problem was that the story was fake, uploaded by a suspected Russian hacker who, Western intelligence agencies believed, was most likely commissioned by the UAE itself. The Gulf now had its very own cold war, and Qatar was facing its greatest crisis since independence. The World Cup would become a target, and a weapon, in this new Gulf War.

Antagonism between the various Gulf royal families stretched back decades, sometimes centuries. But the root of the blockade could be found in the Arab Spring, which began in Tunisia and spread across the region. In Egypt the long-time dictator Hosni Mubarak was removed from power after hundreds of thousands of people, including the ultras I had met from Al Ahly, filled Tahrir Square. After Egypt's first free elections, Mohamed Morsi became president, a candidate aligned with the Muslim Brotherhood. The Muslim Brotherhood was a popular Islamist organisation banned in much of the Middle East as it posed the biggest threat to the Gulf's conservative, autocratic monarchies. The Arab Spring terrified the Gulf Arab states, who feared they would be next.

Meanwhile, two crown princes had risen to power who both viewed the Brotherhood (and Iran, a historic rival to Saudi Arabia) as a threat to their rule: Sheikh Mohamed bin Zayed in the UAE, the brother of Manchester City's owner Sheikh Mansour, and Mohammad bin Salman in Saudi Arabia. MbZ, as the former is known, was already de facto in charge of the UAE and its formidable security apparatus. The Arab Spring had seen the UAE change. It had become more aggressive with critics, both inside and outside the country, to prevent regime change there too.

Mohamed bin Salman, MbS, was much younger and had ruthlessly accumulated power after his father became the Saudi king in 2015. MbS was appointed deputy crown prince and defence minister. Despite several decades separating them, MbS and MbZ shared a vision for the region and an impatience with implementing it. It was a mentor–mentee relationship. MbS pushed for some social liberalisation, namely reducing the power of the Saudi religious police, and allowing women to drive and attend football matches. Cinemas would reopen. And a huge investment fund, Vision 2030, would diversify the economy away from oil. Western leaders and businessmen seemed to be seduced by the young deputy crown prince, who they viewed as a can-do reformer.

Yet MbS and MbZ had also embroiled themselves in the disastrous conflict in Yemen, ordering a bombing campaign and naval blockade that had killed tens of thousands of people. They also intervened by proxy in various conflicts – especially Syria and Libya – where they saw Islamist groups gaining a foothold. Billions were spent by both countries building cyber-security capabilities that had turned both UAE and Saudi Arabia into surveillance states that could also monitor, attack and drown out criticism from dissidents abroad. Qatar, meanwhile, maintained an independent foreign policy and broadly supported the Arab Spring uprising, as well as Islamist groups like the Muslim Brotherhood. Billions of dollars had been loaned by Qatar in a failed attempt to prop up the Morsi government in Egypt. There was also support for other Islamist groups in the Middle East. Qatar would host leading figures of Hamas and the Taliban in Doha. There were allegations of funding fundamentalist militias that were fighting Bashar al Assad's government in Syria's civil war, a complicated patchwork of armed groups that were being funded by various outside actors including the US and the Saudis, sometimes fighting on the same side, sometimes against each other. When Morsi was eventually removed from power in a military coup in 2013, the UAE and Saudi Arabia promised upwards of $12 billion of aid to support Abdel Fattah el Sisi's new anti-Muslim Brotherhood regime. Qatar was also responsible for paying government wages in Gaza, which meant Hamas. Pro-Israeli commentators and activists accused Qatar of funding 'terrorism'. It wasn't helped that, largely because they shared access to the world's largest gas field, Qatar also had closer relations with Iran, another country that both the Sunni Arab autocrats in the Gulf and Israel viewed as a threat to their existence. It also put Israel, the Saudis and the UAE on the same side. The UAE and Saudi Arabia on one side, and Qatar on the other, had already been at war via their various proxies in Syria and later Libya for years. But what really antagonised Qatar's neighbours was Al Jazeera, which gave airtime to dissidents who openly criticised the policies of Saudi and Emirati leaders whilst refraining to criticise the Qatari royal family who bankrolled it. They accused Qatar of using Al Jazeera to agitate opposition in their own backyards.

And then there was the scandal over a group of kidnapped Qatari royal family members who had been snatched by Shia militias whilst hunting in southern Iraq, looking for the houbara bustard. Qatar is thought to have paid up to a billion dollars in ransoms to free the captives, money that found its way into the hands of militias with ties to Iran and Hezbollah in Lebanon. According to Robert F. Worth, writing in the *New York Times Magazine*, the ransom enraged the Saudis. It 'began to figure, often in highly distorted form, in a Saudi-financed P.R. blitz that portrayed Qatar as a fountainhead of terrorism. The anti-Qatar campaign was a patchwork of true and false or questionable claims that only muddied the waters around the ransom and Qatar's broader culpability in bankrolling Islamist groups.'

There had been various crises before. The UAE had once supported a coup to remove Emir Hamad of Qatar when he took power from his father in 1995. There was a diplomatic break in 2014. But the 2016 election of Donald Trump presented an opportunity. The Saudis and the UAE had been supportive of a Trump presidency after becoming enraged with President Barack Obama's nuclear deal with Iran. A few days before the fake QNA story dropped, Trump had been invited to Riyadh for his first foreign trip as president. He was received like a king, and charmed by MbS. The Saudis convinced him that Qatar was the bad guy. So, when the blockade began, Trump took a side. He tweeted: 'During my recent trip to the Middle East I stated that there can no longer be funding of Radical Ideology. Leaders pointed to Qatar – look!' A week after the start of the blockade, MbS was officially elevated by his father to crown prince, replacing his cousin Mohammed bin Nayef. MbS would later have him arrested for treason.

With the land border with Saudi Arabia closed, supermarket shelves in Doha emptied. Flight plans had to be re-routed. New shipping supply chains had to be built via Oman to keep the raw materials that were needed to build the World Cup flowing. Qatar played a 2018 World Cup qualifier against South Korea at the Jassim bin Hamad Stadium a few days after the blockade began. The players wore T-shirts with a stylised black-and-white profile silhouette of the young Emir Tamim on the front. They won 3–2 thanks to two goals by their captain Hassan al Haydos but FIFA later fined the Qatari FA for 'displaying a political image' and 'political displays' by fans. Al Haydos was fined 5,000 Swiss francs for 'unsporting conduct' for taking one of the T-shirts off a fan and displaying it to the crowd after he scored. Xavi, following on from his message to the Catalan people, had also recorded a new video, this time calling for an end to the blockade.

During this month of Ramadan I will like to call for an end to the crisis in the Arab world.
And the end of the blockade against Qatar.
It is affecting many people.
Families and also football and sport.
I hope there will be a solution soon so people can live in peace and enjoy football together.

Turkey's president Recep Tayyip Erdoğan stepped in to supply Turkish food. Four thousand Holstein dairy cows were airlifted from Europe to Qatar so the country didn't run out of milk. Turkish troops were stationed in Qatar.

As Qatar struggled to survive in the new regional order, a succession of policies was announced by the blockading countries. Bahrain, the UAE and Saudi Arabia passed laws that imposed a 15-year prison sentence on anyone who showed 'sympathy' for Qatar. Saudi Arabia announced it would build a trench to separate Qatar from the mainland and fill it with nuclear waste. There was the case of beoutQ, a TV network that emerged overnight that began brazenly bootlegging beIN Premier League and World Cup football matches in Saudi Arabia. But the 2022 World Cup was the biggest prize of all, something in which Qatar had invested huge resources, perhaps as much as $200 billion, and political capital. When the emails of the UAE's ambassador to the US – Yousef al Otaiba, a well-connected scion of Washington's political elite – were leaked they laid bare a trail of plans aimed at destroying Qatar's economy and its ability to host the World Cup, including one that would force Qatar to share the World Cup with its neighbours. In a strategy document allegedly put together by Banque Havilland, a private bank that does business with Abu Dhabi's royal elite, a PR plan was outlined to try and force Qatar to share the tournament with its neighbours by appealing to FIFA that a GCC World Cup would 'display football as a tool to stabilise the region'. In the meantime, a PR campaign would help so that 'negative publicity can resurface around the original award of the tournament, bribery allegations, conditions of construction personnel and other issues.'

Allies of the UAE claimed the emails were stolen by Qatari hackers. In fact, a dirty information war had long been underway, with accusations of hacking and counter hacking; of astro-turfed human rights organisations popping up and disappearing overnight as well as mysteriously slick anti-Qatar 2022 Twitter campaigns. Millions of dollars were poured into DC's amoral think-tank laundromat to skew research and PR one way or the other. Qatar's World Cup was in danger, and the UAE and Saudi Arabia knew a man who shared their vision. Gianni Infantino happened to have had the same idea.

Qatar's skyline was changing fast, like dunes remodelled by the wind. Every time I returned I remembered the rough contours of the city, the same roads and sand-coloured mosques. But the buildings were growing up and out fast, scrambling my internal compass as I tried to orientate myself. Every time, I noticed something new. A building site was now a football stadium. Entrances to an underground station for a brand-new metro system had started to pop up. Whole new cities, like Lusail, to the north of Doha, where the World Cup final was to be played. The city had changed in other ways too. The blockade was now in its fourth month. The initial shortages had passed. The taxi drivers complained that there weren't enough fares now that the rest of the Gulf was barred from travelling there. I'd kept in touch with a network of migrant workers I'd met over the years and they seemed to still be in work. The shops were empty for the first few days, one Bangladeshi worker told me, but were soon filled up by Turkish goods. They still worried about what the future might hold. The face of the newish emir was everywhere: the same image that the national team had worn on T-shirts against South Korea a few months before now seemed to hang in every shop window and on every street corner. What had at first felt like a diplomatic flash of heat that would pass, like they always had in the past, had settled into something more attritional. I'd seen a huge banner with the same Emir Tamim image covered in signatures and words of adulation in the lobby of Al Sadd's stadium. The country seemed to be behind him.

But one thing stayed with me after talking to Xavi: the refrain that Qatar had no football culture, which I had been used to hearing. I had been guilty of acquiescing that refrain too; after all, Qatar was a tiny country and small crowds at matches were to be expected. But I had seen a deep and passionate football culture in every other country in the Middle East. Qatar had it too. You just had to want to find it.

I took a taxi back to a squat, nondescript building near the Aspire Tower. Deep inside a warren of corridors, offices and studios, I was led into a control room. Banks of screens lined the walls, with a Qatari producer at a control desk, calmly sliding faders and pushing brightly lit buttons. A huge window overlooked a studio preparing to go live. It had been made to look like a *majlis*, a square room with cushions on the floor for friends and family to meet in your home. For the first time in a while I thought of Yemen, their general secretary Hamid, and the qat-chewing sessions we had in his *majlis*. I wondered whether he had survived the appalling war and the nightly bombing raids by UAE and Saudi jets – built and supplied by the US and the UK – that had destroyed his country.

This was the set of *Al Majlis*, Qatar's version of *Match of the Day*, a football talk show which was also one of the most popular sports shows in the Middle East, even after the blockade. There was much to discuss after a particularly bad-tempered match. Al Rayyan, coached by Danish legend Michael Laudrup, versus Al Duhail, coached by future Algeria manager Djamel Belmadi. Belmadi was in the stands after getting a two-game touchline ban for ripping into the fourth official in the previous game. Duhail, which used to be called Lekh-wiya until they merged with El Jaish and changed their name, scored four times including two questionable penalties. But then, somehow, Al Rayyan fought back to 4–3. Sebastián Soria, the Uruguayan who was naturalised and played for the Qatar national team, scored twice. In the very last seconds, as Al Rayyan pushed for an equaliser, Duhail scored a fifth. It ended 5–3. When I came out of the stadium I saw a mob of maybe 50 young Qatari boys, perhaps ten years old, dressed in white *thobes* and massed behind metal crush barriers, throwing one rial notes at anyone in a Duhail shirt. But they were holding some back for the referee.

'Thank you referee, for the money, eh!' shouted one young Al Rayyan fan at the front.

So you think Duhail bribed the referee? I asked him.

'Money. Lekhwiya [Duhail's old name]. Victory,' he said, rubbing his wad of notes together.

You seem quite angry with the result, I said to his friend.

'Yes. Because the referee. He is the worst referee in the world. I think [he was paid] 20k [rials] for the match.'

Just then the referee and his assistants passed by. The boys began throwing notes in their direction and started shouting again.

'DUHAIL! MONEY! MONEY! ONE RIAL!'

The referee was also the topic of conversation in the studio. 'Everyone was tweeting, wait to see what they say on *Al Majlis*!' said Abdulaziz, the young producer on the show. His editor clicked his fingers and shouted camera instructions in Arabic in front of us. He was planning for a late night. There was never a planned end time for *Al Majlis*. They kept talking until they were done. 'We might not finish until two or three in the morning,' he said. The show attracted big names. Messi had been on for a rare half-an-hour interview. But things could also get heated. 'Sometimes, during the Champions League or Emir Cup this can last for 12 hours.'

The show's host was Khalid Jassem, a calmly spoken ringleader who never lost his cool as his guests around him lost their heads. He politely welcomed me and ushered me to the set, introducing me to the ten men, all but one wearing white *thobes*. They sat on white cushions placed next to each around the room, in front of overflowing bowls of fruit. They were the great and good of Qatari football, former players, coaches and newspaper editors.

'This is Humood Sultan, goalkeeper, from Bahrain. The best goalkeeper in the Gulf,' Khalid said. A friendly middle-aged man with huge hands got up and patted me on the back.

'And this is Adel al Mulla,' he said, introducing me to a former Qatar international striker who played in the 2000 Asian Cup in Lebanon. 'He was a professional player but he was always fighting, causing problems.' Everyone burst into laughter.

He didn't need to introduce that week's guest: Younis Mahmoud, the former captain of Iraq whom I had first met in Amman in 2007, just before they shocked Iraq, and the world, by winning the Asian Cup. He never got his move to Europe and played for ten years in Qatar. He'd just retired having played a record 148 times for his national team. He laughed as we embraced. 'Video!' The only thing he remembered of me was his teammates taking my top off and making me dance to Iraqi pop music on the team bus.

Suddenly, loud Arabic music started and the show's editor began to count down. 'Today's topic, the night will be full of things,' said Khalid before he walked to his camera position and the rest of the studio was cleared. The cameras rolled and the discussion crackled into life. The first penalty decision for Al Rayyan was dissected over and over again, from multiple TV angles. Humood, who'd seemed so friendly a few minutes ago, was now on fire, furious that the penalty had been given. Each guest was shouting over each other, gesticulating wildly with their arms. If it got too loud, Khalid would calmly intervene with a new question. But it was only a temporary respite as the arguments started again. 'They are angry with the *hakam*, the referee, because the first goal was not a penalty, and anyway it was offside,' whispered Abdulaziz, the producer, as we watched the show in the darkness of the control room, the studio lit in brilliant technicolour in front of us.

'He seems pretty upset by the decision. Is he always like this?' I asked.

'No, no, no,' replied Abdulaziz, before changing his mind. 'Yes. He is always like that *here*. You speak to him normally and he will be smiling. Only here is he like it.'

Humood was now off his cushion, standing in the middle of the set, trying to recreate the penalty decision. This had gone on for 30 minutes. There were still another seven goals to discuss just from this match. In the end the show lasted for four hours.

'When the referee makes a big mistake with a big club in Qatar, everyone wants to talk, you know. Everyone thinks their opinion is the right one,' said Khalid when we speak later. We were now in his large office a few doors down from *Al Majlis*'s studio. 'And that is what happens with my show. Everyone wants to talk. It takes time.' Khalid's role was to ask the questions and keep the peace. He said this was his 'gift from God. I know because anyone else, if he sits in my place, he cannot control nine people when they talk about football.'

The claims that the country didn't have a football culture baffled Khalid. He had one of the most popular TV talk shows in the Gulf. He had a million followers on Twitter. His show had been going out twice a week for 11 years. Long before gas money seriously changed Qatar, Khalid could remember the government giving everybody in the country a day off when Qatar played Brazil in the 1981 FIFA World Youth Championship, the precursor to today's FIFA U20 World Cup. Qatar won 3–2, with striker Khalid Salman scoring a hat-trick. They would make it to the final. They qualified for the 1984 and 1992 Olympics, getting to the quarter-finals in Barcelona. And on two occasions Qatar came within one game of qualifying for the World Cup, at Italia '90 and France '98. League games would regularly get 20,000 or more supporters. Big games and the Emir Cup final were still sell-outs today. 'We have football culture, our history. The Doha Stadium was the first in the GCC with real grass!' he said. Qataris were also realistic about what the country could achieve on the pitch. 'I'm not dreaming we will win the World Cup. I know that. But I'm dreaming we work hard for all teams in Qatar and the academy of Aspire gets a good team to play in 2022.'

This had been one of the big recent issues on the show. A few weeks ago Qatar lost 3–1 to Syria and were eliminated from qualification for Russia 2018. Billions of dollars had been invested in the Aspire Academy, and its Football Dreams project, which was finding and nurturing talent at every age level with the aim of building a competitive team for Qatar 2022. The Aspire Zone Foundation, the state-funded entity that officially owned Aspire, had even branched out into football club ownership, buying up Eupen in Belgium and then Cultural y Deportiva Leonesa in Spain, so that promising Aspire trainees could go to Europe and gain first-team experience. But the players were not ready for the full men's team yet and, to fill the gap, Qatar still relied on their tried and trusted trick of naturalising older professional players from Europe, Africa and South America, which had angered Qatari fans.

Qatar started some games with almost a full team of naturalised players. 'Anyone who gets a Qatar passport, we'll respect him,' said

Khalid. 'But we can talk about why are we taking players who are not quality? This is why the fans are angry.' The anger prompted the Qatar Football Association to consider phasing out naturalised players altogether so that young Qatari Aspire graduates could start instead. The national coach, Uruguayan Jorge Fossati, threatened to quit. 'If the federation wants to go another way, I'll respect its decision 100 per cent. And it'll be better for the Qatar national team to have another coach who supports that view.' Fossati quit a few months later and a new coach with a new direction was picked; Félix Sánchez, a Catalan coach who, like Xavi, had learned his trade at Barcelona's La Masia academy. 'The people who decide things here put him as the coach of the first national team and I think it is a really good decision,' Xavi had told me. 'He's a very good coach. He has experience. He worked in the youth teams in Barcelona. This is the way.' Immediately, fewer naturalised players were picked. The first team that played China in the final Russia 2018 qualification match contained eight Qataris who were born or raised in the country, with their football education coming via Aspire.

What the Qatar team would look like in 2022 has been frequently debated in Qatar. Although Aspire was preferable to naturalising seasoned pros from Brazil, many were players who had been discovered by the Football Dreams programme in Sudan, Nigeria, Egypt and beyond. They had been in Qatar since they were young kids so were as Qatari as anything else. Khalid pointed to the multicultural France team that won the World Cup in 1998, the US national team and British Olympians as examples of countries that have naturalised sportspeople. 'You know Mohamed Farah? He is Somalian, yes? But he got the British passport and got good results in the Olympiad,' said Khalid. Of course, it was far easier to get Qatari citizenship as a talented footballer than for an Indian bus driver or Nepali labourer who had worked in the country for 20 years. For them it was virtually impossible.

Khalid just wanted people to come to his country and see that what was written about it wasn't true. 'We have made mistakes,' he admitted. But there were changes coming. Workers were, he said, being treated better. They weren't being made to work in temperatures above 35°C any more. 'If I come and I see these people working in

45°C, I will call the police. They will come directly to stop this!' The Gulf blockade would pass, he said, as it was a conflict between brothers. Although a few days later Humood Sultan, the rambunctious Bahraini goalkeeping great and regular on *Al Majlis*, was reportedly arrested when he returned home for appearing on the show and giving material support to Qatar. He wasn't heard from for a few days, until he posted a video online filmed by his son denying he'd been arrested. 'The king is our king, may God prolong his life,' he said. 'Everything is fine.' But he never returned to the show.

It had been a long day and Khalid and I said goodbye. He suggested I speak to one of Qatar's greatest players, Khalid Salman, the man who scored a hat-trick against Brazil and who was responsible for a young Khalid Jassem getting an unexpected day off school 36 years ago. He'd often appear on *Al Majlis* too. As I left, Khalid still had a few calls to make to try and secure his next big-name guest. 'I'm really really trying to get Ronaldo,' he said. 'And Neymar.'

Khalid Salman was in his 50s now but in good shape, although he had to work hard at it. 'I'm keeping my fitness. We are the sportsmen,' he said, wearing a tracksuit and standing on the balcony of his seaside villa in the grounds of a luxury five-star hotel. He pointed towards the corniche, tracing out the 5km walk he did every day. 'Very quick, you get fat. When you see Maradona now . . .' he said, holding his stomach, and laughing.

He was a star from another era, from the 1970s to the 1990s, when Qatar wasn't exactly poor but was almost a completely different country altogether. He grew up in Al Sadd district, playing football on the streets. The president of the club saw him one day as he drove past and stopped his car. 'He called me over and asked me: "Who are you? Who is your father? You are a good player, you have to go to Al Sadd. Tomorrow you will go there and then tell them the president sent you,"' he recalled. It was 1976 and he was 14 years old. It was the start of a career that would see him play for Al Saad for nearly 25 years and win almost everything he could. He played 135 times for Qatar. As he talked about his career every anecdote was an incredible story largely unknown outside of the country, but which had become folklore in Qatari football. There was the time Al Sadd reached the final of the Asian Club Championship, the precursor to the Asian Champions League, against Iraq's Al Rasheed in 1989. Al Rasheed had been founded by Uday Hussein, who would force the country's best players – the whole national team, basically – to play for them. Al Rasheed won three titles in a row. When they lost, the players' heads were shaved. Torture or prison, sometimes both, were a possibility for particularly bad displays. They were deeply unpopular in Iraq. Khalid remembered meeting Uday during the first game in Baghdad. 'Uday and Qusay [his younger brother], we meet on the field,' he said. 'When you meet these people, you feel they have a lot of power. Everyone who comes to them, they are shaking. They were very afraid. They were very tough. And they came to win this competition. And we were afraid too. They had 40,000 people in Al Shabab [stadium].'

Perhaps it was the proximity to a megalomaniac madman, but the match didn't start well for Al Sadd. They were 3–0 down at half-time. 'Everyone from Al Saad was sitting in the dressing room at half-time. The coach said: "What do you want to do, you want to lose now? You have to fight,"' he recalled. 'We put our hands on each other, we have to play with one heart as normal. But we have to kill ourselves on the field. We are not playing for Al Sadd, but playing for Qatar. We have to fight like men. *Alhamdulillah,* first 15 minutes, I score, and after ten minutes we score the second goal: 3–2.' It at least gave them a chance and Khalid scored the only goal, a penalty, which won them the title on away goals back in Doha, despite it being the first day of Ramadan so every player had been fasting all day. Twenty thousand fans watched them lift the title.

It was Khalid's exploits for the national team that made his name. He scored twice against France at the 1984 Olympics. 'I was known for scoring goals against the big teams,' he said. But he was best known for arguably Qatar's greatest achievement in football, until they won the bid to host the 2022 World Cup. When they qualified for the 1981 FIFA World Youth Cup for the first time. Qatar was barely ten years old. 'When we arrived, everyone was asking, where is Qatar? What is Qatar? In 1981 nobody knew,' he said. But they found out quickly. Qatar, coached by Evaristo – the first Brazilian to ever play for Barcelona – beat Poland and drew with the US, setting up a quarter-final match against Brazil. No one expected Qatar, whoever they were, to go any further. 'I hadn't scored any goals. The manager came to me and said: "Khalid, you still have not scored one goal!" I felt really upset,' he recalled of Evaristo's unique motivational technique. 'I was putting on my shoes. I said to my manager: "I will say something between me and you. I will kill Brazil today." He said: "How?" I said: "I will score three goals." Until today, I don't know where these words came from or how I said these words to this gentleman.' Of course, Khalid Salman scored a hat-trick and Qatar won 3–2. 'I was crying after I scored that goal until the end of the game, until I got on the bus. I couldn't believe my promise that I will score three goals.' They dispatched England next, beating them 2–1, setting up a final against West Germany in Sydney. But any luck they had ran out. A vicious rainstorm flooded the pitch. In Qatar, Khalid told me, they never played in the rain. It hardly ever rained but, when it did, they stopped to protect the few football pitches they had. 'The water was coming strong and we didn't know how to play in the water. Normally the ball is fast. But the field is heavy. You have to know how to move the ball with the water.' He missed one open goal because the ball got stuck in a puddle. Qatar lost 4–0. But second place was more than anyone dreamed of. When he came home Khalid received a Mercedes and 200,000 rials from the emir, enough for him to get married.

Khalid never played in a World Cup again, at any level. They finished third when the top two teams qualified for Italia '90. And they went into their final qualification game against Saudi Arabia for a place at France '98 knowing victory would be enough. They lost 1–0. Qatar 2022 was more than just a home tournament for Khalid. It was a chance to right a wrong, even if it had to be vicariously. 'It was my bad luck that I never went to the World Cup, but the World Cup is coming to us!' he said. '*Alhamdulillah,* God will give us more life and I can see it.'

It was a football history that few had wanted to hear. But one goal here, one goal there, and Qatar's football reputation would have been very different. When Khalid was playing people came to the stadiums in big numbers too. But with wealth comes convenience. Most Qataris wanted to watch football on TV at home, he said. And there's the competition of the Premier League and La Liga. And computer games, of course, the bête noire of the old pro whether it is Qatar, Spain or Brazil. Most Qatari parents didn't want their sons playing football past 18, packing them off abroad to get an education instead. That left Aspire to make a team with what it could find, either here or abroad. 'We don't have the players now. This is the truth. But you don't need to make one good player. You need to be a team together, like we were before. The country has done everything, the stadiums, Aspire . . . Qatar is the number one for preparation. In five years the [World Cup] team will be 100 per cent different to what you see now.'

He had faith in the system, in Aspire, that it would deliver a team that could compete and, in his words, 'surprise people'. Although that looked far away right now. As the tournament approached it was tinged slightly with regret. He imagined what it would feel like when the tournament actually started. It already felt like Qatar had waited a lifetime for the World Cup to start, and there were still five years to go. 'I will feel sad and happy,' he said before I left. 'Sad because I wanted to be in this. But if God gives me the years, *inshallah*, I'll be a commentator.' That, he conceded cheerily, was the next best thing.

It was late at night, and cooler now. I'd come back to the Aspire Zone, back to the Khalifa International Stadium, which had just been totally renovated and reopened. It was the first 2022 World Cup stadium to be finished. In its shadow, on a floodlit training pitch, the final of a friendly tournament was taking place: Qatar Under-19s versus Croatia Under-19s. This was the future of the Qatar national team. The players here would be around 24 years old when the finals finally arrived, prime football-playing age. At least a handful of these players, with their teenage haircuts, braces and scrappy moustaches, would be in the squad when the World Cup started. The question was, which ones?

Sitting in shorts and a white Aspire T-shirt, on a plastic patio chair, Bora Milutinović watched from the sidelines. Bora held the joint record for the most teams managed at World Cup finals. He coached Mexico when they hosted in '86, took Costa Rica to Italia '90 with just two months' notice, Nigeria to the knockout stages at France '98 and China to their very first finals in 2002. But he was best known for taking charge of Team USA when they hosted in 1994, an event that had reinvigorated soccer in the US and perhaps even changed the direction of the global game. But none of that might have happened if it wasn't for the US overperforming, and reaching the knockout stage, in large part because of Bora's tough-love approach. He threatened to drop Alexei Lalas, who became a kind of stoner breakout star of the World Cup, if he didn't cut off his long ginger hair. 'Bora was hugely important to me because he had faith in me and he gave me opportunities, but he would test you in different ways,' Lalas told the *New York Times*. 'One day the assistant to Bora found me in my hotel room and he said: "I have a message from Bora. You need to cut your hair." I was pissed.' But Lalas complied. He said he still has the bag of hair somewhere.

Bora wasn't interested in coaching a sixth team to a finals. He was 73 now and could do without the stress. Instead he'd been hired as an advisor for Aspire and had the ear of the royal family. And all roads lead to 2022. 'It changes slowly, every day it gets better,' he said. As we spoke a steady stream of people from all over the world would stop to wish him well. He shook every hand with a smile, switching seamlessly between his native Serbian and Spanish, German and English. Every few minutes he would flip open a camcorder he'd brought with him, filming a few seconds of play, before putting it away again. 'Aspire. It's very important. You have so many young players they learn to play football. They learn so many things about football and about life here. They've made great progress.'

Qatar's main problem, according to Bora, was the maths. There was a pool of barely 300,000 citizens in total, made slightly wider by Aspire's worldwide talent hunt. Now the country had switched from obvious naturalisations of journeymen foreigners to something much more subtle, in part due to globalisation, a smaller world and shifting populations. A third of today's team had been born in West Africa. 'You have so many countries with players that have another nationality,' said Bora. 'Twenty years ago it was very difficult to take a player like this, 30 years ago impossible. But today is a different time.'

He'd first come to Qatar to coach Al Sadd back in 2004. As a footballing globalist, he was also an evangelist for their World Cup. He was now an official 2022 'Ambassador' for the tournament, as well as an advisor to Aspire. 'You need to give other people a chance to enjoy the World Cup,' he said when I asked him about the criticism surrounding 2022. 'Which country organises the best World Cup ever? What do you think? Germany. Nobody is like Germany. They organise good but you also need to give other countries a chance. For the people who live there, for the passion, for the region, for the religion, for the continent. Give them a chance to organise a World Cup. It will be perfect.'

With the final whistle approaching, Qatar's Under-19 team finally broke through Croatia's defence and scored the only goal of the game. 'They have three or four very good players with talents,' Bora said. 'Five years before it is difficult to know. But you never know what will happen in the future.' The team celebrated with a victory dance. I spoke to one of the players, who said he had been born in Nigeria, came to Qatar as a child, was spotted by Aspire and had moved up through their various national teams. But then I was angrily bundled away by a Qatari Football Association official before he could finish. He admonished me for asking questions about his player's journey to Qatar. 'Everyone is Qatari,' he said, pushing me off the pitch. Bora had seen enough and shook a last hand before going home. He wasn't too concerned about how the team was now. There was still time. 'To be ready, you need to be ready in 2022. Only this is important,' he said. 'One week before the World Cup you can say that your team is ready for the World Cup, not before.' The 2018 World Cup was behind them now. But there was a new coach in Félix Sánchez and they had already qualified for the 2019 Asian Cup. The problem was it was taking place in 16 months' time in the United Arab Emirates, a country that had banned Qataris from entering.

19

Return to Tehran

It was 12 years since I'd left Iran and everything, and nothing, had changed. Just like when I'd first stood here in 2006, it was an early spring which, in Tehran, is a time of contrast; snow was still thick on the peaks of the Alborz mountains that tower in the near distance north of the city, just before the Persian new year blossom arrived, when it's blazingly hot in the sun yet icy cold in the shade. Riot police massed alongside the wide boulevard behind the tall columns at the entrance with 'Azadi Stadium Complex' written in both English and Farsi. Perhaps it was the blue, cloudless sky, but the stadium's monochrome retro-concrete aesthetic looked more modern nearly two decades on. Around it, as with every match at the Azadi, a bustling city of industry had sprung up, one-mile deep. Hawkers brandishing contactless credit-card machines sold flags, scarves and baseball caps in red and blue.

Groups of men, only men, hung their flags from their car windows, playing Persian pop music, parking where they could on the nearby scrubland. They half ran towards the security barriers knowing that even with a ticket you weren't guaranteed a seat. Even though the stadium's official capacity these days was closer to 80,000, more than 100,000 people were expected today. The stadium was already three-quarters full, summoning a disorientating drone of horns, vuvuzelas and chants, as if a million bees had been released near the pitch. The pictures and videos from the stands were posted on Instagram and Telegram, or Twitter if they had a functioning VPN to bypass Iran's censors. The portraits of the imam and the ayatollah still watched over the pitch. The Tehran derby between the red of Persepolis and the blue of Esteghlal was to kick off in seven hours.

This was the biggest football match in the country and Persepolis had the chance to win the league against their biggest rivals. Persepolis has dominated the Persian Gulf Pro League this season and were 15 points clear. Esteghlal had virtually no chance of catching them. But they had the chance to ruin the party. Which was enough for today. I'd phoned the ex-Iran national team coach Afshin Ghotbi, who'd won the league as coach of Persepolis back in 2008, before I left. 'I took part in three derbies and I drew all three of them because everybody plays not to lose,' he told me. The pressure to win this game, he said, was immense. 'If you lose the game, regardless of what you win, even if you win the championship, you are defined by it.' Their current coach was none other than Branko Ivanković, who I had seen take the national team to the 2006 World Cup finals in Germany. That team were hounded by controversy and protests wherever they went thanks to the anti-Semitic speeches of then-president Mahmoud Ahmadinejad.

Since then we'd had the failed Green Movement, Iran's players making a stand in support of the protesters and Team Melli narrowly missing out on qualifying for the 2010 World Cup finals. We'd had the election of Barack Obama as president of the United States and the implementation of the Iran nuclear deal, designed to end Iran's pursuit of nuclear weapons in return for reintegration into the world economy. Ahmadinejad was gone, replaced as president by the nominally more reformist figure of Hassan Rouhani. And, just like in 2006, Iran was again preparing for a World Cup finals. They had qualified for Russia 2018 with ease thanks to a new generation of players including strikers Sardar Azmoun, Alireza Jahanbakhsh and Mehdi Taremi. Their captain was Masoud Shojaei, who scored Iran's only goal in that fateful 'green bracelet' World Cup qualifier against South Korea in 2009, and had survived the subsequent attempts to purge the team of those who had shown support for the Green Movement. Their coach now was Carlos Queiroz, hired the same year Ahmadinejad left office. They qualified with a transitional side for Brazil 2014 and were unlucky not to progress to the knockout stages.

But things hadn't really improved for ordinary people in Iran. The economy was still flatlining and Iran was devoting resources to a ruinously expensive war backing Bashar al Assad in Syria, as well as propping up Shia proxy groups in Yemen and Lebanon. Protests had broken out in Tehran the previous year partly around the issue of compulsory headscarves for women, and partially because of the cost of foreign adventures when domestic issues were so pressing. The Iranian rial had collapsed in value. And then Donald Trump was elected, Iran's nuclear deal was ripped up, and the country was headed towards another period of international isolation, cut off from the global financial system. The supreme leader was, of course, still in charge, unimpeachable.

I'd come back to Iran to watch the derby and speak to Queiroz but, when I got there, I found out he'd decided at the last minute to go to Russia for a meeting instead. As the hours ticked down towards kick-off the crowd became restless. A parade of entertainers were deployed; an old singer, a troupe of robot dancers sprayed silver and, most unusually, Tehran's chief of police was brought out to do a lap of honour. Several plastic bags full of liquid – I didn't get close enough to find out what liquid exactly, although I could guess – were thrown from the crowd and landed at his feet before his security bustled him down the tunnel. Then the atmosphere suddenly changed. Branko was brought out in front of the red half of the stadium. They chanted his name above the roar. He was adored. He'd won them the league last season, their first title in almost a decade. This season Persepolis had only lost one game and had effectively won the title in record time. They needed just a point today to confirm it. He ambled around in front of the crowd wearing a red training jacket, with 'Havadaran 12' printed on the back, soaking up the adulation. '*Havadaran*' means 'supporters' in Farsi, a tribute to the team's 12th man. And the number 12 is imbued with extra significance in Iran: Shia Muslims believe that a 12th and final Imam will reappear to redeem the world, much as Christians believe in the return of Jesus Christ.

Branko looked no different – perhaps a little greyer, maybe a little heavier – to the man I had met in 2006. Photographers fell over themselves to take pictures of him being received by the crowd as they chanted his name. He had been working in Iranian football for a

combined total of close to eight years, more than any foreign coach at
that point, successfully navigating the complex network of politics,
patronage and insane expectations that surrounded football in the
country. Winning helped to keep him here, of course. But so too did
the extreme chaotic love that poured down onto the pitch. Branko
seemed close to tears. Esteghlal also had a well-regarded foreign
coach, from Germany. Winfried Schäfer had been coach of Cameroon
at the 2002 World Cup, won the Africa Cup of Nations and spent
time coaching Al Ahli in the UAE, where he won the league. I'd interviewed him back in Dubai, in Al Ahli's dressing room, Schäfer wearing
nothing but a jockstrap. He was almost 70 now but he still had a
lion's mane of thick ivory-coloured hair on his head.

There was also a third special guest from abroad. Under the portraits of the imam and the ayatollah, a sign had been fixed between
the top and bottom tiers: 'Welcome Infantino'. FIFA president Gianni
Infantino was visiting Iran. The men's team had been the best in Asia
over the past four years, giving Iran some political clout within FIFA
and the Asian Football Confederation.

But there was one thing missing. As loud and as impressive as the
100,000-strong crowd was, there wasn't a single woman in
attendance – officially, anyway – due to a long-standing unofficial
stadium ban on female spectators. I had seen a large protest of women
outside the Azadi when I first arrived to watch Iran play Costa Rica
in 2006. But nothing had changed. Not in Iran anyway. Two months
previously Saudi Arabia, the other nation to ban women from football stadiums, had suddenly announced that women would finally be
allowed to attend matches. Later they announced the formation of the
first ever Saudi women's national football team. It was something
inconceivable a few years before but Saudi Arabia was undergoing a
cosmetic cultural revolution under its budding new autocrat-in-
waiting, crown prince Mohammed bin Salman. Hand in hand with
eye-catching reforms like lifting the ban on women driving, came a
crushing crackdown on any dissent inside and outside the Kingdom.
Activists had started to be rounded up and jailed. Dissidents abroad
were being targeted too. Even foreign politicians weren't immune. On
a visit to Riyadh, Lebanese prime minister Saad Hariri, who funded
Al Ansar and Al Nejmeh football clubs and was in his second spell as

prime minister since my trip to Lebanon in 2009, was effectively kid-napped and handed a resignation speech to be read out on Saudi TV. Hariri hadn't been sufficiently obedient to MbS or Saudi interest in facing down Iran by confronting their proxy in Lebanon, Hezbollah. So, the speech made clear, Hariri was to blame Hezbollah for his res-ignation. Hariri did what he was told and was allowed to leave for France two weeks later. A few hours after Hariri was 'kidnapped', 400 members of Saudi Arabia's elite were rounded up and imprisoned in the Ritz-Carlton Riyadh. Officially it was part of MbS's anti-corruption drive. The businessmen, government ministers and members of the royal family were forced to sign over billions of dollars of their assets to the state in return for their freedom. Several claimed they were tor-tured. But the move was closer to a purge, helping to weaken his rivals for power and send notice to anyone who planned to oppose him. Still, Iran was now the last country in the world that banned women from its stadiums.

Infantino, his distinctive bald pate clearly visible even from the side of the pitch, took his place up high in the VIP seats as the match finally started. I stood behind the goal and couldn't hear the referee's whistle over the noise, which, after nearly six hours, was almost too much to bear. As Afshin Ghotbi had predicted, the game was scrappy and disjointed. No one wanted to make a mistake. No one dared lose. And then, finally, there was a partial respite from the noise. Persepolis lost possession cheaply and Esteghlal attacked. A scramble in the six-yard box saw Iranian international defender Voria Ghafouri shoot against one post, and then another before it finally went in. The Persep-olis half of the stadium fell silent. On the other side of the stadium, the blue half was a riot of faraway noise and blue smoke. At the contact point where the two sets of supporters met, underneath the sign wel-coming Gianni Infantino, fights broke out as fans tore out plastic chairs and threw them at each other. As the 90th minute came and went, and injury time was coming to an end, bits of the Azadi were hewn off by Persepolis supporters and launched towards the pitch. But as it was perhaps 30 metres from the stand, over a running track, the rocks landed on the photographers behind the goal instead. A well-aimed smoke-bomb obscured the stand, meaning we couldn't tell what was coming. One piece of masonry missed my head by centimetres as rocks rained down all around us. We hid behind the advertising hoardings. Finally, the referee blew the whistle for full time. Esteghlal had won 1–0.

Persepolis's fans quickly emptied the stadium. The blue half of the stadium indeed celebrated as if they had won the league instead. They led an Iceland-style thunderclap whilst a terrified Winfried Schäfer, ivory mane poking out from the scrum of bodies that had surrounded him in congratulation, was taken on a terrifying lap of honour on the shoulders of an Esteghlal club official. He begged to be put down, but was ignored. Eventually, as the official tired, he begrudgingly complied, and Schäfer gingerly limped back across the pitch to the safety of the dressing room.

There would be no title for Persepolis today. But, as I left the stadium and checked my phone, I saw that there had been some trouble outside, via an anonymous activist account called @openstadiums that campaigned to end the stadium ban on women. Thirty-five young women and girls, some dressed as men and wearing fake beards, had been caught trying to get into the game. They had been corralled before kick-off into vans and taken to Vozara Detention Centre, a jail used to hold women for crimes against morality. There they awaited news of their fate, and news from the game. A kindly young soldier relayed the score to a room full of female prisoners, some wearing blue, some wearing red and some still wearing the fake beards they had arrived with. Half the room celebrated, whilst the other half mourned.

I'd very nearly not made it back to Tehran. Back in 2006, I was living in Dubai and took a punt on getting in after landing at Imam Khomeini International Airport. In hindsight this was a stupid risk to take given that journalists and dual-nationality Iranians were often arrested and accused of being spies. They would often become useful assets in international hostage diplomacy. An Australian colleague later told me that, on hearing about how I had got into Iran, he'd tried the same thing and was arrested, deported, and banned from returning. Before, I was young and dumb. Not to mention lucky. But I was a father now, and my daughter had Iranian blood. I was forever connected to this place one way or another. This time I had the means to do it properly, which meant months of negotiations with the Iranian ambassador in Belgrade, where I was living at the time. Dozens of letters were sent. I returned in the January snow three times for interviews as they weighed my request. But there was no news from Tehran, until a call came from the embassy on the morning my flight was due to leave. I threw a few things in a suitcase and just made it to the airport with 20 minutes to spare.

Having an Iranian press card had its benefits, but also its drawbacks. As a tourist in 2006 I had relative freedom to roam, but it was highly risky. As long as I wasn't caught doing any journalism I was fine. But if I crossed the wrong person it could mean a long stretch in prison. A press card gave some degree of protection, but it also meant I needed a government-approved minder, who would arrange my interviews, sit in on them and translate. My minder seemed like a nice person, trapped in a job that on the surface sounded quite cool, but when you drilled into it, was actually one of the reasons why Iran remained one of the least free places to be a journalist on earth. And it was clear they couldn't come with me to where I wanted to go next.

It was hard to find out exactly what had happened to the 35 women who had been arrested trying to get into the Tehran derby. I DM'd @openstadiums more out of hope than expectation. Yet I received a reply and agreed to meet the sender later that night. But first I had to give my minder the slip. I told them I was tired and needed some rest. They left me at the hotel, I waited half an hour, and headed for the Tehran Metro, making sure I wasn't followed and that my phone was off. 'Sara' and I had arranged to meet at a crossroads, at night, outside a metro station in northern Tehran. I didn't know what she looked like, or what her real name was. All I knew was the model of her car. It was a popular model in Tehran, I soon discovered, and it took me half an hour and several awkward misunderstandings with other drivers until I found her, parked around the corner.

Protest was dangerous in Iran. Human Rights Watch's most recent report on Iran said that the 'authorities in the security apparatus and Iran's judiciary continued to target journalists, online media activists, and human rights defenders in an ongoing crackdown, in blatant disregard of international and domestic legal standards.' But activists worked within whatever space they could find and Sara found hers in football. She had been running @openstadiums anonymously for the past five years, and was now at the forefront of highlighting the absurdities of the stadium ban. She had started campaigning against the ban long before. In fact, as we drove to find a quiet café nearby, we discovered that we had once been a few metres apart. Her first proper protest was the Iran–Costa Rica friendly at the Azadi in 2006. 'Me and two other guys, and groups of fans, we went there and demonstrated!' she said in disbelief when I told her it was the same Costa Rica game where I had seen women protesting outside. The protest, it turned out, didn't last much longer. The police put them all on a bus and dumped them in the middle of nowhere. When one enterprising protester somehow procured a minibus to take them back to the stadium, they were threatened with arrest, their cardboard placards were ripped up and they were forced to leave.

A few months later, in the final warm-up match before the 2006 finals, against Bosnia, they learned from their mistakes. This time they wrote their slogans on their headscarves, knowing that the police would never rip them off. 'It says, "I want half of my share of Azadi." Freedom,' she explained of the slogan once we had parked. She scrolled through her phone and her pictures from that time. The white headscarves with the red slogans; the Costa Rica game where we passed by; a picture of a soldier in fatigues aiming a kick at one woman protester; a banner that said: 'We don't want to be in *Offside*, we want to be in the stadium with our brothers', referencing Jafar Panahi's influential and prophetic 2006 film where a group of women and girls are arrested trying to get into the Azadi stadium to watch the Iran national team, dressed as boys. Panahi was arrested in 2010 and convicted of spreading propaganda against the Iranian regime. After a short spell in Evin prison, where Iran's political prisoners are held, he had been under house arrest and banned from leaving Iran.

We found a quiet hipster café that served cheesecake and tea. I was worried we looked too incongruous, but no one seemed to notice. The police at the Bosnia game, Sara continued, had been particularly aggressive. Mahmoud Ahmadinejad had actually announced an end to the ban on women entering football stadiums just before the game, but he had spoken out of turn. He was swiftly smacked down by the supreme leader who publicly said this would not happen. This meant that any protest wasn't just against Ahmadinejad, or the government, it was against the express wish of Iran's highest religious authority, a red line that should never be crossed. 'To them [the police] we went to the game against the will of the supreme leader. They were really harsh,' said Sara. 'One woman was beaten badly. She was wearing a chador [a black, all-enveloping outfit] but that was worse. They will normally say that we are non-hijabi, not good Muslims for going to this place. But they saw a woman with full chador and they were really angry.'

Within the activist community, Sara explained, sport had been seen as a frivolous issue and not one to really be taken seriously at all, not when there were bigger issues to deal with like the compulsory hijab and the entrenched legal imbalance of rights between men and women. Sara and a few dozen other women decided to change tact, and stay away from the stadiums, handing out leaflets in Azadi Square instead, whilst gathering evidence of the stadium bans to send to FIFA and the Asian Football Confederation. 'We sent so much evidence to the AFC,' she said. 'We sent them newspapers and sound and even went to the AFC to hand them over.' But nothing happened. And then most activism went dark after the crackdown that followed the failed Green Movement in 2009. Afterwards, the women decided that it was too dangerous. 'It's not worth the beatings and prison,' she said. 'It's better to go a little underground.' What followed was 'four years of silence'. It wasn't until 2013, with Ahmadinejad gone, Rouhani now in power and with FIFA president Sepp Blatter scheduled to visit Iran that Sara decided to start @openstadiums. 'I was completely alone. Tweeting these organisations, keeping my identity secret,' she said. 'You don't want to be discovered. Sometimes I get really afraid.' She had some early success. The account was noticed by Moya Dodd, a former Australia international player who was on FIFA's powerful Executive Committee. Dodd managed to raise the issue of Iran's stadium ban with Blatter, who in turn raised the issue privately and publicly after meeting with President Rouhani. What was once a minority issue was now mainstream. 'She [Sara] helped make the stadium ban a symbol of something much more: Iranian women's right to fully participate in society,' Dodd would later tell me.

In recent months more and more people had begun to speak out about the ban. One of the most high profile was Iranian captain Masoud Shojaei. A few months before, just after Iran had qualified unbeaten for Russia 2018 by beating Uzbekistan 2–0 at the Azadi, a reception was arranged at Hassan Rouhani's presidential palace. You can still find the video on YouTube; Rouhani, wearing a white turban and sitting on a chair trimmed with gold leaf, in front of two portraits of the imam and the ayatollah. The team, the new golden generation, sat in two rows in front of him. 'It was my wish to receive you here,' President Rouhani told the room, 'and, as the representative of the people, to congratulate you.' Carlos Queiroz was the first to approach the president and warmly shook his hand. The players rose and met the president, one by one, before, finally, the captain approached. Shojaei had played in two World Cups and was a regular for Greek side Panionios. He also had a reputation for being outspoken. He was part of Afshin Ghotbi's starting XI for that fateful World Cup qualifier where some of the players wore green wristbands in solidarity with protesters back home and had often spoken out on issues that affected ordinary Iranians, whether it was civil rights or the hidden issue of child sex abuse. He handed President Rouhani an Iranian team jersey signed by the whole squad, and began to speak.

Oddly, the video of the meeting abruptly cuts short and there was no audio. The official news agency later reported that Rouhani wished the players and coaches well on their journey to Russia. Outside a film crew was waiting to ask their captain about the meeting. 'Many, many women in Iran love to watch football matches played by men,' said Shojaei, looking like a film star as he talked directly into the camera. He had taken his moment with the president to raise the ongoing ban of women from Iranian football stadiums. 'If it is agreed to allow women in, a stadium should be built with the capacity of 200,000, because just as many women as men will be there.' Sara had spoken to Shojaei just after the Uzbekistan match. '"Tomorrow morning you will visit the president thanking you for the World Cup",' she recalled. 'We said: "Please Masoud, talk about the women's issue. No one else is going to do it." He went there. I opened my eyes and saw it. Masoud, thank you! He talked to the president, and on TV, [that] you have to let women inside.'

And then it was announced that Gianni Infantino would be coming for the Tehran derby. As Iran played very few high-profile friendlies at home, it was a rare match with international exposure to organise around. But, instead, 35 women were arrested. Sara contacted two female Iranian MPs who helped pressure for their release. 'The Islamic Republic is not a whole package of bad people,' she explained. 'If you are living in this country, you have to find some ways into the system.' The system was so complex that change was difficult. 'In Saudi one person decides. Here, we have so many people. So many ayatollahs. There is a president and cabinet. And the supreme leader.' The best-case scenario, she said, was to let women in step by step. 'But they have to start it!' Infantino's visit was a wasted opportunity. 'I saw Infantino laughing. It was like seeing the laugh of someone in the colosseum in Rome. He was sitting next to the communications minister, and it was like, you are such a disastrous man. His words go into thin air. Nothing happens.'

Are you hopeful the ban would be lifted? I asked her.

'Am I hopeful?' She took a few seconds to think about it. 'If I didn't have any hope I wouldn't continue this work.' She knew many of the women who had been arrested before the derby and suggested I call Farah.

There was, at least, one opportunity for Sara to see a game. She had started making tentative plans to travel to Russia for the World Cup, where she wouldn't be restricted and could finally buy her first ticket for a match. She was lucky she had the means, and also the opportunity. Sometimes even being a football player didn't exempt you. We talked about a new film that had just been released, *Cold Sweat*, that told the story of an Iranian player who had been banned from travelling to a tournament abroad by her husband. It was thought to be based on the true story of Niloofar Ardalan, then Iran's captain, whose husband banned her from travelling to Malaysia for a futsal tournament in 2015. The film had just won big at a local film festival but had effectively been banned from cinemas by hardliners for 'not being suitable for families'. Sara drove me back to my metro station. We passed Evin Prison, the notorious political prison where activists, especially female activists, are held and often tortured. 'You know what we call Evin?' she said as we glided by the dark complex nestled in front of the mountains. 'There are so many educated women – teachers, doctors, graduates – inside, we call it the "University of Evin".'

The derby had been a disaster for Persepolis fans, but it had been worse for Farah. She was one of the women who had been arrested and detained for trying to enter the Azadi stadium. 'All these years I would have loved to watch the game in the stadium and experience the atmosphere,' she said when we met. 'When you love the game you want to see the game and the players, close. Not at home.' We were sitting in a late-night café in central Tehran. Its retro design made it look like a bohemian 1960s tea house, untouched from the time of the shah. There was some discussion as to where we should meet without attracting attention. But after a few abortive attempts we finally agreed to meet in a place near my hotel so I at least didn't have to concoct an elaborate excuse to get away from my minder.

Farah was a student, and nervous. It was the first time she had been arrested although she would frequently laugh at the sheer absurdity of what she had just seen. 'They [the police] could not understand the love that was inside the hearts of these girls,' she said. 'They really think that these sorts of things belong to men. "You shouldn't be here. You shouldn't go to the stadium or love a club."' She had never seen Persepolis play live, a club she had supported since she was five. There had been a few attempts to watch the national team play. Last year's final World Cup qualifier against Syria was rumoured to be the first game women might be allowed into the Azadi. Farah even managed to buy some tickets, but in the end they were denied entry. 'It's very humiliating,' she said. 'I remember a guard said: "You can take the Syrian flag and get in." I'm Iranian. And I'm proud of it. Why should I change my flag? It's my country! They threatened to arrest me. I remember I started crying.' Only the Syrian women were allowed in.

Still, Farah thought the derby would be a huge event and, besides, Gianni Infantino would be in the crowd. She told her nervous friends the day before the game that there was no way anyone would be arrested with the FIFA president there. At some games women had tried to dress up as men to get past security, but Farah and her friends wanted to go as themselves. They would simply walk up to the gate with their tickets. There was, she explained, no actual law against women entering stadiums. It was just something that had been done once and had continued ever since. But at the stadium, her group was denied entry and told they would be arrested if they didn't leave. So they did, but they were followed by the *Gasht-e Ershad*, Iran's ultra-religious morality police. 'They surrounded our car and they were not nice,' she said of the moment she was arrested. 'They didn't touch us because they were religious and they didn't touch women. They just told us we should wait for the female guards to arrest us.' The situation deteriorated when the guards saw other fans taking pictures of the women. They were all taken to a holding cell where they met other women who had been caught, independently, trying to get in. Eventually four vans came to take them away to a nearby police station. 'We were terrified,' she said. One of the girls was just 13. 'It was just like *Offside*!'

Jail wasn't quite the place Farah thought it would be. For one, all 35 were put in the same room. Some were also allowed to keep their phones. A selfie that one of the women took went viral on Telegram. I'd later see a middle-aged man on the Tehran Metro looking intently at the photo on his phone, zooming in on the faces of each woman in turn. They all exchanged numbers and tips about what to do next time and, more importantly, how to more accurately act like a man to avoid detection. 'They were laughing all the time and talking about how to get in the next time. In front of the guards!' said Farah. 'What should they wear? What should they do? How should they walk to look like men?'

How do you pretend to walk like a man? I asked.

She leaned back, trying to give an impression of a man walking, chest puffed, like Marlon Brando's *Godfather*. 'You should put your legs apart from each other and walk like that,' she added. Manspreading seemed to be the key component.

The room was more or less split between Esteghlal and Persepolis fans and when the young soldier took pity on them and relayed the score, the room erupted. 'Half of us were screaming! It was very funny,' said Farah. Eventually, they were each brought to interrogation rooms and then processed. Their crime? Attempting to enter into a stadium illegally. 'Even though there is no such thing!' she quickly added. They each had their photo taken, and after six hours they were eventually released. Their story had, however, been heard around the world. Both the BBC and *New York Times* had reported on it. Gianni Infantino, meanwhile, had little to say and there would be no direct public mention of the stadium-ban issue, or the arrests, when he was in Iran. Infantino held a press conference, with no questions. He did, however, get animated when the issue of money came up. Iran, essentially, had a system where nothing was officially paid for domestic TV rights. 'When I hear for example that ... television, broadcasting rights are not awarded in an appropriate way, I am shocked,' he said, before urging that to change quickly. 'Otherwise it will be the last time I come here to praise Iranian football.' When a female journalist tried to ask Infantino about the stadium ban during a walk-and-talk later, he simply ignored her. 'When he came here. He didn't say anything! I don't trust him,' said Farah. 'It was very disappointing. They didn't care. They arrested us when he was inside. When he left Iran he said, yes, I've heard women were arrested. But when he was here he didn't say anything.' Another activist later told me they thought Infantino was so unimpressive that they must have 'accidentally hired the janitor'.

The arrests wouldn't stop Farah or others from attempting to enter the stadiums in future. Volleyball had been popular too until women were banned five years ago. But there was hope that would change. Basketball had just allowed women to return and Farah had recently been to a packed game where half the crowd were women, half men. One thing that would help, she thought, was more men speaking out, especially sportsmen. 'I saw girls in jail that were really anxious about the result of the game but none of the players [of Esteghlal or Persepolis] spoke about us,' she said. One exception was Masoud Shojaei. 'I remember the day he talked about it and we were so happy that the captain of the national team is talking about our issues,' she said of the moment Shojaei raised the stadium ban with President Rouhani. 'He is a really good guy, he always talks about the issues of society and cares about the people. If other players would support us, half of the country, it would make a difference.'

Persepolis was playing in an Asian Champions League match in a few days' time, but Farah wouldn't be trying to get into this one. She would wait, learn, and try again later. 'Going into the stadium comes out of my heart,' she said before we made sure no one was following us, and left in separate directions. 'I am doing this not just because it is a right we do not have but because I'd love to go to the stadium. I am willing to sacrifice and pay the price for it.'

I took the main highway south out of Tehran until I arrived at the Shahid Kazemi Stadium, on the city's outskirts. The newish Persepolis training ground was hard to get to if you didn't have a car but, inside, 300 furious Persepolis supporters had made it into the west stand, all shouting over each other in the direction of former Iranian international Afshin Peyrovani. He came on as a 75th minute substitute to shore up the defence in that famous 2–1 victory against the Great Satan at France '98. He was the technical director at Persepolis now, and stood in front of the angry crowd, a deep concrete ditch separating them, as he accepted the angry abuse. The cacophony of shouting was eventually whittled down to the loudest single voice. 'Forty million people couldn't sleep last night!' shouted the man, every man around him nodding in agreement. He began listing the team's defects. '[Midfielder] Mohsen Rabikhah failed in passing; [Full back] Hossein Mahini was unable to penetrate even once in the whole match!'

The fans were still angry at the derby day loss against Esteghlal, even though they were virtually guaranteed the title and were still 15 points clear of their nearest rival. Most were angry at the tactics and about coach Branko Ivanković leaving out some players, especially Mohsen Mosalman, an attacking midfielder and once the youngest goal scorer in Iranian league history who nonetheless hadn't quite lived up to his potential. As the shouting restarted Peyrovani lifted his hand to silence the crowd and began to speak.

'You guys are very important to us, that's why I came down to hear what you have to say; to listen to your opinions! Every one of you is entitled to his opinion. You may say what you think but the manager is the one who finally decides; the same manager who was responsible for the successes of last year and this year as well.

'You are right. Winning against Esteghlal tastes better, I agree! But I beg you to respect the team and the staff and each other. As a comrade, I beg you to be polite and respectable. No supporter was supposed to be here today but I asked them to let you in. Yesterday I cried for 49 minutes because I hate losing to Esteghlal. Please control your emotions and be decent.

'I sympathise with you all and I don't just say that to gain your appreciation. By coming here you showed us how important the team is for you! On Monday we're playing an Asian Champions League match and then again in the league. We *will* become the champions this year despite yesterday!'

His speech seemed to work, pacifying the crowd, even if there was grumbling at the back. 'I had a heart attack,' one fan told me when I asked why he was protesting when they were still 15 points clear at the top of the league. 'We prefer to be at the bottom of the league but beat Esteghlal at both derbies. Please tell Branko not to be so stubborn and to bring Mohsen Mosalman in.'

After a decade of trying to meet the insane expectations of Iranian football fans, Branko was used to this type of reaction. He sat at his office, painted red, deep inside the stadium far away from the protests. On his desk was a photo of his championship-winning side of last season. 'We will be confirmed champions five, six weeks before the end of the season; it's never been done before! But for our fans, the derby is as important as taking the championship. This is something they live the whole year for. So I am unsatisfied,' he said calmly, more of an explanation than a complaint. 'We are champions! We are not second. We are not third. We are champions. The fans are always right. Sometimes they complain. Some players, they move out of the club because of the fans. The fans cannot accept them. They cannot keep their emotions under control. It's a big pressure. It is not easy. We have 40 million fans.'

Working in Iranian football required incredible diplomatic skill. This was a space that wasn't quite a democracy, nor an ochlocracy, but something in between. In football, unlike in much of civil society, Iranians at least had some power to effect change, to freely speak their mind. The country's most popular TV programme was *Navad*, '90' in Farsi. In theory, *Navad* was a football talk show that interviewed all the big names in the Iranian game, but host Adel Ferdosipour would tackle bigger social issues too, especially corruption. It was estimated in one poll, shortly before the programme was taken off air by hardliners, that 51 per cent of Iranians had watched *Navad*.

Branko never spoke politics, only of the game, he said, but the nature of the job meant that he still found himself at the frontline of geopolitical events. He was assistant coach to Miroslav Blažević when the team played a World Cup qualifier against Iraq in Baghdad, in 2001. The Islamic Revolution, the Iran–Iraq War and then the First Gulf War meant it was the first time the two had played in Iraq in 25 years. The match, Branko said, was a wonderful moment, in front of a packed Al Shabab stadium. Blažević could be seen on the bench, next to Branko, smoking throughout the match. It passed peacefully even though Iran came from behind and won 2–1 thanks to goals from Ali Karimi and Ali Daei. It would be the last time Iran played in Iraq. The match took place four days before 9/11, and the world would change forever.

Iran missed out on the 2002 World Cup after losing a play-off against Ireland, Blažević was sacked and replaced by Branko. The road to Germany was pretty smooth, just 2 defeats in 12 matches, but things turned nasty in Pyongyang. Iran went 2–0 up against North Korea, prompting a rare show of spontaneous violence by the supporters, furious at the officiating by the Syrian referee who was pelted with bottles. When the match ended the Iranian players had to wait on the pitch for half an hour due to the violence in the stands. 'It was a big fight after we beat them 2–0. A lot of people, not just in the tribune, on the running track. They all ran onto the pitch and wanted to kill the referees,' he recalled. The crowd managed to break into the room where Branko was giving his post-match press conference. 'We had to find a safe place. They didn't control it,' he said. 'I don't know if they didn't want to control them or couldn't control them.'

And then came the election of President Ahmadinejad before the team left for the 2006 World Cup. Branko was left trying to minimise the political fallout from the protests that followed his team, whilst not alienating the president and the federation back in Iran. He knew what he could say and what he couldn't say. And how to sound like he was saying something outspoken or controversial when he wasn't, doing enough to keep the fans onside as an independent voice, but not enough to alienate Iran's multitude of 'ayatollahs', as Sara called them. It was an incredible skill I had seen in action first hand. Yet his biggest memory of the tournament, and regret, was an unfit Ali

Karimi. 'Karimi, his talent was like Messi,' he said. 'But three months before, for Bayern, he broke his ankle. He was not ready. And he was so nervous. People didn't understand. For three months he didn't have any good practice, just recovering. He was not fit. Our left-back broke his knee. Mahdavikia had a problem with his back. Hashemian, a problem with his leg. We were not ready.' The pressure, in the end, was just too much. 'It was difficult because Iranians love the national team incredibly,' he said. 'And it is not easy to isolate the players. It's not possible in Iran. They want to be with them. They [supporters] are coming to visit [the team hotel]. They have close friends, family. If you don't accept to see someone it is a disaster.'

Branko was fired but didn't burn his bridges. Which made it all the stranger that when he left the job, the next foreign coach was perhaps the least diplomatic choice the Iranian federation could have made. The combative Carlos Queiroz had been Sir Alex Ferguson's assistant at Manchester United and later coached Real Madrid and Portugal's national team. He had butted heads everywhere he went. When Iran called in 2011 he was available, and desperate. Back in 2010 he was coach of Portugal when an incident with a team from the national anti-doping body, the Autoridade Antidopagem de Portugal (ADoP), just before the 2010 World Cup finals, effectively ended his tenure. Queiroz had been angered by the anti-doping personnel arriving unannounced at an inopportune time. 'Mr Queiroz,' the Court of Arbitration for Sport wrote in a later judgement, 'uttered some very distasteful and sexually descriptive comments regarding the mother of the ADoP president.' Queiroz denied the charges but the doping body suspended him for six months. After some poor results, he was later fired. Iran was one of the few countries willing to take a chance on him. 'I spoke with him [Queiroz] and I recommended him to work here,' Branko claimed.

After time in the Chinese Super League, Saudi Arabia, UAE and three spells at Dinamo Zagreb, Branko returned to Iran to manage Persepolis. 'I know Iran, I know Iranian people, I know the Iranian mentality,' he said when I asked why had come back. He made a point of explaining how much the professional game had improved during his time in charge. Some players here were, he said, getting paid half a million US dollars a year, an almost unthinkable sum in Iran, and more than a lot of players might earn in most European leagues. 'The only problem,' Branko explained, 'is that they cannot accept competition between the players, inside the team. If I am not playing, I am dead. I am leaving the club, the national team. They do not accept competition for one place.'

That wasn't an outlook limited to Iranian players. Up until the derby the biggest scandal in Iranian football had been the ongoing feud between Branko and Queiroz. It all began with a seemingly harmless segment on *Navad*, which ran a campaign to find out who was the best foreign coach in Iranian history. 'I don't remember who was voted the best,' said Behnam Jafarzadeh, a football journalist I'd met in Tehran. 'But that was the start of the quarrel. It was a spark for the war.' Things deteriorated when several figures within the Iranian federation, according to Jafarzadeh, were furious with the way Queiroz spoke to them, and instigated a failed coup which, they had hoped, would end with Branko replacing him. Later Branko had complained that his Persepolis players were called up to a national team training camp in the UAE that he viewed as superfluous. Queiroz ranted to the press about Branko's disrespect and then expelled the players from the camp. 'The last two years we haven't spoken,' Branko said, sighing. 'He was very angry with me. So we've had no contact.' He was still magnanimous about the team Queiroz had built, and positive about their chances in Russia, even if he believed it was built on his foundations. The national team was, he believed, missing that little bit of magic. 'They just don't have a player like Karimi,' he said. 'This isn't a problem with Iran. It is a world problem. Look at Italy, they haven't got any. England? Who is the star in England?' He got up to start training and shook my hand. 'The last World Cup, Argentina should have been champions and this team beat Iran in the 90th minute only because Messi scores,' he said. 'Everything is possible.' The security had emptied the stadium. An hour later the hundreds of Persepolis supporters were still outside the ground, still complaining about the derby defeat.

Four days after the Tehran Derby, Persepolis were back at the Azadi Stadium for the Asian Champions League game against Al Wasl from the UAE. This time, there weren't any arrests of women trying to enter the stadium. The security was tighter. As I walked to the stadium

one police officer asked for ID. He wanted to make sure I wasn't from
the BBC, which had reported extensively on the women arrested at
the derby, and which the authorities thought was synonymous with
MI6. But the protests and the arrests did have some effect on the
domestic players. Before the game Persepolis midfielder Kamal Kamy-
abinia had come out in support of lifting the ban. 'It would be a very
great idea if women are allowed to come to the stadium,' he told me
at the pre-match press conference. 'I want the officials to take serious
measures to allow women to come to the stadium as they can come to
other stadiums, that would be very important.' Persepolis won 2–0
under leaden skies in front of 33,000 fans, a good crowd that still
seemed like a handful inside the vast bowl of the Azadi. Persepolis
would indeed win the league a few weeks later, with a 1–0 victory
against Padideh in the north-eastern city of Mashhad.

Women continued to try and enter Iran's stadiums, and continued
to get turned away or arrested. Some managed to get through. A picture went viral on Iranian Telegram of a group of women who
managed to sneak into the Azadi for the last home game of the season, dressed in red, wearing fake beards and holding up six fingers in
honour of a famous 6–0 rout of Esteghlal in 1973. 'I Google for different make-up [tutorials] and learn new ways and apply them to go
to the stadium,' one of the women explained afterwards. But then
attention had switched to the World Cup. Carlos Queiroz was now
enveloped in a new political controversy and had an important decision to make.

GRAZ, AUSTRIA, MARCH 2018

After all the stories and anecdotes I'd heard in Iran, Carlos Queiroz
came across in person as someone very different. It was a month after
I had been in Iran and we were sitting in a luxury hotel deep into the
hills of eastern Austria, around a 45-minute drive from Graz. I had
hoped to meet him in Tehran but it turned out that Iran was playing
rare pre-World Cup friendlies, against Tunisia and Algeria, at what
used to be called the Arnold Schwarzenegger Stadium. Queiroz, a big
man with a deep tan, leaned forward and started from the beginning,

describing the series of unfortunate events that had brought him to Iran in the first place. 'I still have nightmares when I think about what happened to me,' he said, his deeply set eyes shadowed and hard to read. He seemed more wounded than difficult.

Back in 2010 Queiroz was on the brink of losing what he freely admits was his dream job as coach of the Portugal national team. They had qualified for the 2010 finals but it had not been easy, and Queiroz had not gone without criticism. But these finals, to him, meant more than most and not just because it was the Portugal job. Queiroz had been born and raised in Mozambique, then a Portuguese colony. Taking his national team to Africa's first finals mattered to him. But that incident with a team from Portugal's anti-doping body left the threat of a career-ending suspension hanging over him. 'Some vicious documentations created at the time really put me in trouble,' he said, still clearly hurt by the incident. 'I was in the middle of the appeal when the phone rings.' It was the Iranian federation.

He'd received other calls, from several Asian national teams and also from Vasco da Gama in Brazil. But as soon as they heard about the pending judgement from CAS and the potential ban, they didn't call back. Iran, however, didn't seem to mind. 'They get back to me and said: "Look, with your name, the officials at the federation, independent of your position with CAS, are ready to offer the job,"' he recalled. 'When they told me this I thought, they deserve my respect and I should go there.' He watched Iran play Russia in Abu Dhabi a few weeks later. Iran won 1–0 thanks to an injury-time goal by Mohammad Reza Khalatbari. He'd seen enough potential. He took the job.

Despite being one of the best teams in Asia, Iran wasn't exactly a plum national team job. They had failed to qualify for the previous World Cup amid a chaotic political situation that had enveloped its players, as Afshin Ghotbi had told me, *mid-match*. The country was as politically and economically isolated as ever, not just by the US and Israel, but by the Gulf Arab countries too who had blockaded Qatar, in part, because of warmer relations between the two countries. Getting Queiroz, even a suspended Queiroz, was still a win. At a time when Queiroz thought the anti-doping incident would leave a 'shadow' on his career, the offer left a lasting impression. 'I went out from the Portuguese national team in a very bad and humiliating situation,' he said. 'They [the Iranian FA] told me: "Even if you are suspended you stay in the stands. And you run the team until the suspension is gone." This was very touching for me.' In the end Sir Alex Ferguson turned up for his CAS appeal to give a character witness. And whilst CAS ruled that his behaviour had been unacceptable, Queiroz won, the ban was dropped and the coast was clear for Brazil 2014 qualification. And that, as Queiroz said with glee, was 'when the battles started'.

Branko's 2006 team that included Karimi and Mahdavikia had more than a dozen players who had experience in top European leagues. But by the time Queiroz arrived in Tehran only two players were in Europe. One was Masoud Shojaei and he had been out injured for a year. And then there was the infrastructure. Iran has been under almost continuous international sanctions since 1979. 'The sanctions have consequences,' Queiroz explained. I'd long known how hard it was to attract any team to come to Iran to play a friendly, but the lack of money and materials to build professional facilities was still a shock. 'We trained with one pitch of 60 metres, one grass pitch built for the employees of the oil facility. It is a garden not a football pitch,' he said. A new training facility was built next to the Azadi, not quite to Queiroz's specifications, but as close as they could get under sanctions. The 'battles', as Queiroz called them, had seen him resign multiple times only to come back. He had fallen out with almost all the major figures in Iranian football, especially Branko, as the two regularly clashed over who should take precedence, club or country. The poor level of the Iranian league, according to Queiroz, compared to his national team preparations, was a theme he returned to again and again, a pointed dig at Branko. In fact, it was the reason for the majority of his rescinded resignations. But Queiroz had remained whilst others had fallen.

He was now the longest-serving Iranian national team coach in history and had managed, like Branko, to navigate Iran's complex bureaucratic structures to get things done, even as his temper sometimes got the better of him. Like the time Iran had to beat South Korea in Korea to qualify for Brazil 2014. The Koreans had complained about the conditions they faced when they had earlier played in Iran. It led to a war of words in the media, which culminated in South Korea's coach Choi Kang-hee telling the press that he would 'defeat Iran no matter what', and vowed to make sure that 'Coach Queiroz will be watching the Brazil World Cup on TV'. Queiroz responded by posing a picture of him wearing an image of a sad Choi pinned to his T-shirt. Iran won 1–0 and South Korea complained that Queiroz made an insulting hand gesture towards the bench after the game. 'I remember that game, we beat them with ten men,' he said. I ask about the T-shirt. 'I cannot deny that one!' he laughed. It was, for him, one of the highlights of the Iran job so far.

The 2014 World Cup was tough. 'It's really magic, almost a miracle what the boys, the players have been doing for the last seven years,' he said. 'The players and the places I've seen in my life, I've never witnessed players that deliver so much for one country and then receive so little.' Unusually, Queiroz wasn't fired and qualification for Russia was achieved at a canter, going 12 games without conceding a goal. But politics was never far away. Two of his best players were embroiled in a new scandal. Masoud Shojaei and his international teammate Ehsan Hajsafi both played for Greek Super League side Panionios, who had reached the qualification round of the Europa League. They were drawn against Israeli side Maccabi Tel Aviv. Ever since the revolution there had been an unofficial policy of sportsmen and women avoiding all contact with their Israeli counterparts during international competition.

The issue has come up before in wrestling, judo, swimming and boxing. At several Olympics too. But Shojaei and Hajsafi were now in a professional game, under contract with their Greek club. Avoiding the first game in Tel Aviv was easy enough. But the return in Greece saw the pair put under enormous pressure. They decided to play. 'Shojaei and Hajsafi have no place in Iran's national football team anymore because they crossed the country's red line,' Iran's deputy sports minister Mohammad Reza Davarzani said in a televised interview. 'To play with the representative of a loathsome regime, this is not acceptable for Iranian people.'

Both players were now targets. Especially Shojaei, who had already angered hardliners during the Green Movement match in 2009 against South Korea and for recently petitioning President Rouhani to allow women into Iran's stadiums. With Iran's spot at Russia 2018 already secured, Queiroz had a choice to make before the final two, essentially meaningless qualification matches. Go against powerful figures on principle, or relent, drop them both, and hope the problem went away. In the end Hajsafi took to Instagram to make a full apology. 'Deepest regrets and sincere apologies as the people of our country were rightly angered and correctly judged that the incident [playing against Maccabi Tel Aviv] should not have happened,' he wrote. It was enough for him to be included back in the squad. Masoud Shojaei, meanwhile, was dropped.

For seven months it looked like Shojaei would never play for Iran again. But Queiroz decided to pick him for the Austrian training camp. There were some who still wanted him banned for life for playing against an Israeli team. The head of the football federation, Mehdi Taj, was even called to court to explain why Shojaei was picked. 'Re-inviting Masoud Shojaei to play for the national soccer team shows that the soccer federation has not taken serious action on this issue,' Mohammad Ali Poormokhtar, a conservative member of Iran's parliament, told the country's official press agency. As ever there were different power centres to negotiate. On the one hand, the federation could not be seen to be banning players for political reasons as they could be suspended by FIFA. Elected representatives had their views, as did the clerical establishment. Each had powerful traditional media and social media to drum its point across. 'I was absolutely in control of my decisions and I always call with all freedom and authority the players that I want,' Queiroz said when I asked if there had ever been any pressure to ban Shojaei. 'My job was to read the situation, cool it down. Let the dust go down. When the dust was down it was easier to make things happen and solve the problem without hurting or offending or questioning anybody.' Neither had he blamed Shojaei for his absence, explaining how he 'cannot escape some duties and obligations' as captain. Queiroz, after all, was standing next to Shojaei when he made his plea to President Rouhani last year for women to be allowed into the stadiums. 'I was there and as long as you express your opinion with full respect, and education, I don't see anything wrong.'

Now it was all about getting the right squad together ahead of a group at Russia 2018 that, inevitably, meant that Queiroz would face his home country. And again, Iran had been handed perhaps the hardest group of the entire tournament: Morocco, arguably Africa's form team; Spain who, well, were Spain; and, of course, European Champions Portugal. 'Iran is in the best situation in this group, we have nothing to lose,' he says cheerily. 'Let's be honest, if I ask you: is Iran a candidate to win the World Cup?'

It takes a few moments for me to realise that he is asking for my opinion.

'Well, they could reach the knockout stage . . .' I offered instead.

'I'm asking, win the World Cup. With Brazil, with Argentina. Be honest. Be simple,' he replied, a little more aggressively now.

'Maybe not,' I agreed, before adding diplomatically, 'but I like the underdog . . .'

This was the wrong answer. 'I'll never accept that you call me an underdog!' he snapped back, and I was unable to read his eyes to find out whether it was totally in good humour or not. 'This is something I changed in Iran. We are not underdogs! Iran cannot win the World Cup. But they can win the Asian Cup. So this is part of one process.'

The next day, the former Arnold Schwarzenegger Stadium was a quarter filled with a small but noisy group of Iranian and Algerian fans. Masoud Shojaei was brought on as a second-half substitute, running himself into the ground as if making up for lost time. Iran won 2–1, but Queiroz was not happy. 'These two games against Tunisia and Algeria show we are far away and some people will not like what I am about to say but I don't care. As we say in Portuguese: "If you don't like it, eat less,"' he shouted to a near empty room of me and five Algerian journalists. 'The players, local players, are far away from the World Cup,' he added. He knew what the problem was. The national team wasn't being given the necessary respect it needed compared to the domestic league. 'So it is time for our federation, even the president of Persepolis who is, as far as I know, the sports minister, to make a decision. It is everything or nothing for us. The players must work and train with me.' It was, of course, a thinly veiled dig at Branko.

What can you change in such a short space of time? I asked him. The finals were a little over two months away.

'What is important for Iran? The local, domestic league, or the

World Cup?' he asked rhetorically. 'What do you expect against Morocco? A dance? A party? You expect that against Portugal and Spain those games are going to be rock and roll. It will not be an opera in the World Cup.' He left the stage angry. The battles were never over, even after you had won.

ATHENS, GREECE, APRIL 2018

There was a moment, late in 2017, when the World Cup felt impossibly far away from Masoud Shojaei. He was still technically playing for his Greek club Panionios, but their relationship had changed irrevocably after the controversies of the past few months. 'I had lost the national team and I was not in a good way,' he said. We were sitting overlooking the Mediterranean sea, in a café a few miles down the coast from the port of Piraeus. With all the heat that had surrounded Shojaei, it had been hard for us to meet. But after months of back and forth, and with a change in fortunes, we agreed to meet in Athens. It was an idyllic, quiet spring day. 'To be honest,' he said of the past few months, 'I was not fit, not in good shape. It was difficult to handle.' A year ago, his third appearance at a World Cup finals was not in doubt. He was the team captain and played in Europe. But a chance draw in last year's Europa League qualification against Maccabi Tel Aviv changed all that, and created a situation that was almost impossible to navigate. 'I decided only on game day to play,' he said . 'Both ways I lose. I play or don't play. I lose.'

Since making his World Cup debut at the 2006 finals in Germany, Shojaei had followed a well-worn path to European football. He left to play in La Liga for Osasuna, the same team as his former international teammate Javad Nekounam. He made 100 appearances before leaving Spain for Qatar and then, in 2016, arrived in Greece after signing for Panionios, in Athens. His first season was a revelation and Panionios spent a large stretch of it in second place. They fell away at the end but still reached the second qualification round of the Europa League. Shojaei signed a new contract, one of the biggest at the club, and the draw for the next round was made. After beating Slovenian club Gorica, Maccabi Tel Aviv would be next.

Iran's opaque power dynamics meant that it was sometimes hard to know where the line was. But not facing Israeli opponents was considered a very firm red line, even if it wasn't law. The club, meanwhile, were not happy. Shojaei was their biggest star and biggest investment ahead of a potentially lucrative run in the Europa League group stages. They also had the rules on their side. 'They were not a rich club. A good family club. They signed me and the other players. We were the top contracts in the team,' said Shojaei. He understood their predicament. 'You bring some players that want to help you and, imagine, the first game away they know that we [Shojaei and Hajsafi] couldn't travel.' The club begrudgingly accepted that, even after losing 1–0 in Tel Aviv. But they expected both players to be in the team for the return game in Greece. This too appeared to be problematic in Iran. 'I told them, it would be a big problem if I play,' Shojaei said. 'They were a little bit serious with me.' Shojaei didn't want to let down a club that had been kind to him since his arrival in Greece.

There was also the possibility that the Iranian federation might be punished over political interference if he didn't play. He was in an impossible position; ruin his relationship with his club and potentially jeopardise Iran's 2018 World Cup place or face the music back home. 'I tried to ask a few people from the federation to help me. It was difficult for them. It is not in the hands of the federation.' He called Queiroz too. In the end, Shojaei felt he had no choice and played the game. Maccabi Tel Aviv won 1-0.

'The next day was hell for me,' he recalled. 'But also I got some great feedback from the people who supported me from this time.' The incident was also, many fans believed, an accumulation of other things, namely Shojaei's outspoken support on numerous social issues. The Maccabi Tel Aviv game gave fuel to 'the people who didn't like [that] I spoke about women with the president'. This too had been controversial and was still fresh in the mind for some in Iran. 'As a football player, we don't play only in the stadium or on the pitch. We have more duties and more responsibilities,' explaining why he wanted to bring the issue up with the president after Iran had qualified for Russia 2018. 'Every time we go out [of the country] Iranian girls and women can come to the stadium. But in Iran? No? So what is the difference? I was searching for the answer.'

Shojaei only decided he was going to bring up the issue of the stadium ban on the morning of the meeting, and after consulting with his family. 'What can I ask? For money? For the bonus?' he said. 'I can ask for something more important. To do something for my people as the captain of the national team. Half of the country are women, you can help them.' He was nervous about the reaction he would get, but he found President Rouhani receptive. 'I said to the president the situation. And he was kind. He said: "We have a plan to do this."'

Still, after the Europa League knock out, Shojaei was dropped from the national team, a decision Queiroz had told me he took to protect his captain. And things were not going well with Panionios, who resented how the scandal had damaged the team's chances in Europe. But then, suddenly, everything changed. 'It went from 0 to 100.' AEK, one of Greece's biggest clubs, was challenging PAOK for their first title in 24 years and wanted to sign Shojaei. It was an easy decision to make. Almost straight away he was thrown into one of the most chaotic title races European football has ever seen. He was playing the night PAOK's Russian-Greek owner Ivan Savvidis stormed on to the pitch with a gun when PAOK were denied a last-minute winner against AEK for offside. 'I have never seen in my life, not even on YouTube or somewhere, that someone comes inside [the pitch] with a gun and with their bodyguards,' Shojaei said of that game. The day before we met, I had watched AEK beat Levadiakos at Athens's Olympic Stadium to clinch the title, although it would be a few weeks until it was official as PAOK had launched a legal challenge.

Just as important, discussions had begun about returning to the national team. Queiroz had flown to Athens to talk it through. 'Carlos. The people and Carlos,' he said when I asked who was responsible for bringing him back to the national team. 'Who had to make the decision to bring me back, finally? Yes or no? It was the coach. And then he said: "Yes." He could say no. No more problems for him. No more headaches.' When Shojaei arrived in Austria, it was an emotional moment. He described how he entered the dressing room, pulled on his national team jersey and took a moment for himself in the bathroom. He looked into the mirror with tears in his eyes. '"Thank God," I said. "You have to do your best, even better than before."'

A few weeks after we spoke, Shojaei was back in Tehran, sitting in President Rouhani's presidential office. Rouhani, wearing a white turban, was again sitting on a gold-trimmed chair. As before, the occasion was celebratory, a chance to wish the Iran national team luck before they departed for Russia. Queiroz had chosen his squad, which included Shojaei. 'Billions of people will watch your games as the representative of a great country with high culture and ancient history,' President Rouhani told the squad. 'Your high-quality football is one of the features that can promote our national pride and make Iran's name more famous.' Carlos Queiroz handed the president a red national team jersey with Rouhani's name and the number 12 on the back.

ST PETERSBURG, RUSSIA, JUNE 2018

Sara made it to Russia for the World Cup. We met in the café of her hotel for breakfast on the morning of Iran's first World Cup game against Morocco. She still wore her headscarf and clutched her bag, checking every once in a while as we spoke. Inside was her ticket for the match, the first time she'd ever been able to buy a ticket for any match before. 'I keep coming back and checking, checking, checking, it's like treasure to me,' she said, pulling out a long piece of card from a zip pocket and holding it carefully with two hands.

The tournament had begun the day before when Russia played Saudi Arabia in Moscow. Regionally Saudi Arabia had long been a football super power due to its extreme wealth and size. None of the same complaints about football culture levelled at other Gulf states could be levelled at Saudi Arabia. The league was well supported. The Riyadh–Jeddah derby between Al Hilal and Al Ittihad would regularly have 50,000-strong crowds. Violence wasn't uncommon at the Riyadh derby between Al Hilal and Al Nasr. Its teams regularly won the Asian Champions League. Only Japan has won more Asian Cups than the Saudi national team. And they were the only Middle Eastern team to reach the knockout stages of the World Cup. The problem was the power of money and the Saudi princes who owned the club. They often stopped players from getting experience abroad. So the new, open Saudi Arabia under MbS came up with a plan. A deal was struck with La Liga for a host of the best Saudi players to go on loan to Spanish clubs to get first-class experience in the run up to the finals.

Spanish scouts were sent to Saudi Arabia and nine players identified. The country's best talent, Salem al Dawsari, was picked by Villarreal. I spoke to him at their training ground shortly after he arrived on Spain's east coast, a little north of Valencia. He was quiet and polite, and seemed a little homesick. He hadn't yet found a local mosque he could pray at. 'I felt very happy and at the same time I felt sad too,' he replied when I asked how he felt when he heard a La Liga team had chosen him. 'I'm happy to join Villarreal and to work hard on my skills and talent that I have. But I am sad because I am leaving my other home, Al Hilal.' The hardest part was leaving his friends and family. 'But they believe in me and they know what I'm doing here.' In the end Al Dawsari made one appearance during the last game of the season, coming on as a second half substitute in a 2-2 draw against Real Madrid. Only two of the nine players managed to play any time at all. They all returned to Saudi Arabia to prepare for the finals. And lost 5–0 to Russia. Up in the crowd Gianni Infantino sat between Russian president Vladimir Putin and Mohammed bin Salman. Infantino could not hide his glee at being proximate to naked power.

Just as I had seen in Frankfurt back in 2006, tens of thousands of Iranians had descended on St Petersburg. There were some, like Sara, who had made the trip from Tehran but most here today had come from Iran's wider diaspora. As in 2006, the flag of the shah would be flown by some, and protests were planned too: on the issue of Iran's stadium ban but also a series of other grievances. All Iranians had been united in fury by Nike refusing to supply football boots to the national team just before the start of the finals, for fear of breaking US-led sanctions.

But today, Sara wasn't just an activist. She was a fan. 'I really wanted to enjoy it calmly,' she said ruefully. It was what she wanted more than anything, to be a normal fan in a sea of other fans, but life always intervened. 'This is a great opportunity to speak up and one of the things I really love to see is Iranian women wanting to watch the game. It is such a beautiful thing to witness.' Even so, Sara wasn't completely free, even 4,000km from Tehran. Government agents would be in the crowd, watching, taking photos, taking names. 'We want to do something, but there are so many officials from Iran so we have to be careful,' she said. 'It is really stressful, it is difficult when you are living in such conditions. Any move you make, you have to think, "Is this going to put myself or my family in danger?" You feel terrorised.' Later she would surreptitiously point to suspicious characters as they moved through the crowd; older men, on their own, smoking, circling groups of cheering young Iranians from a distance. Once you saw them, they seemed comically obvious. 'Going to prison is not something I want,' she said.

It had been a few months since the Tehran derby, Infantino's visit, and the controversy about Iran's captain Masoud Shojaei. Materially, not much had changed. Women were still barred, arrests were still taking place. FIFA had officially gone quiet. But @openstadiums had helped the issue gain a truly global audience. And there were allies in FIFA who were doing what they could to help, even as Infantino vacillated. Today's planned protest would have been outlawed by FIFA normally. And Russian police could surely be trusted to smash any signs of dissent at the slightest encouragement. But an internal battle had been won and the protest could go ahead. The early team news was in too. Masoud Shojaei was to start the game, joining a select club of players to have played in three finals. 'Masoud was incredible,' said Sara of her captain's support. 'We are really proud we have this kind of captain.'

It was a 1km-long walk, along a tree-lined boulevard, to the Gazprom Arena. It was full of song and drums and laughter. Thousands of Iranian women had joined the procession. Sara opened her arms wide and closed her eyes, as if bathing in a warm sun. Halfway there, next to a large fountain, Maryam Shojaei was holding a placard that read 'Shame on NIKE for forcing politics into sport'. She chanted 'Shame on Nike!' at everyone who passed by. Maryam was Masoud's sister and had been following the national team abroad, without Masoud's knowledge, and protesting anonymously where she could. She handed another placard to Sara: 'SUPPORT IRANIAN WOMEN TO ATTEND STADIUMS #NoBan4Women'.

'Shame!' the Iranian supporters shouted in support as they passed, stopping to have their pictures taken with the two. A group of four women holding the Iranian flag all wore black baseball caps with 'REAL WOMEN WATCH FOOTBALL' written on the front.

'Shame on Nike!' chanted Maryam. 'Shame on Trump!'

Russian police had gathered nearby. They looked on, but didn't intervene. 'I have my banner and I wish all the Iranian women were here today,' said Maryam, laying her sign on the floor briefly. 'I know how many texted me and are so envious I can go there. I have a banner for all of them.' Maryam's audience wasn't the international press, as such. Her message was aimed at FIFA. 'They are the only ones who can change this,' she said, as more and more men and women stopped to take pictures with the signs. 'We were so optimistic we could solve the issue, but not even President Rouhani can solve the issue. No, our audience is FIFA. That is the only organisation that could. It has to change this practice.'

As kick-off approached, the group split up and headed to their seats. Sara found her queue. 'Every time we went to demonstrate, it never happened,' she said, nervously, as we waited in the queue. 'Now football is going from two dimensions to three dimensions.' She had never got this far before. When it was her turn, she stepped forward, handed her ticket to the attendant, and waited. We both held our breath. This time, for the first time, her ticket worked. 'Wish me luck,' she said as she waved, turned and walked past security and into the stadium.

Over 60,000 supporters, split evenly between the two nations, watched what turned out to be an attritional game. Both teams had good chances, which they squandered, and there was a huge ovation for Masoud Shojaei when he limped off midway through the second half. The game looked like it was drifting towards a stalemate until, in the 95th minute, Morocco's Aziz Bouhaddouz diverted a swerving cross past his own goalkeeper. Carlos Queiroz and the entire Iranian bench invaded the pitch, until they were reluctantly persuaded by the match officials to return to the dugout and count down the final few seconds. It was the first Iranian World Cup victory since that famous win against the US at France '98, exactly 20 years before. The players made three laps of honour in front of their fans, who seemed reluctant to leave and waste this rare moment. Iran would be knocked out of the group stage, but not without a fight. Back in Tehran, women were allowed into the Azadi for the first time in decades to watch the match against Spain on a big screen, which Iran narrowly lost 1–0. They almost beat Portugal. Ronaldo had a penalty saved by Alireza

Beiranvand, who had run away from home as a teenager and slept rough in Tehran before being spotted by a coach. Ronaldo also somehow avoided a red card for elbowing Morteza Pouraliganji, even though it went to VAR. The night before, hundreds of Iranians held a noisy street party outside the Portuguese team hotel, with Ronaldo gesturing from his window to keep the noise down as he couldn't sleep. The match ended 1–1, and Iran was out. Queiroz was, of course, furious. 'You stop the game for VAR, there is an elbow. Elbow. Elbow is a red card in the rules, the rules doesn't say if it's Messi or Ronaldo,' he said after the game. He decided to stay as coach. The 2019 Asian Cup, hosted in the United Arab Emirates, was less than six months away. It was a chance to win a title and maybe, I thought, for him to get one up on Branko.

That was all to come, though. After the team had finally finished celebrating after the Morocco game, the Iranian fans poured into the concourses and celebrated in the fountain at the centre of the Gazprom Arena's vast park. Sara looked dazed. 'I don't know how to celebrate,' she said, trying to explain the feeling of watching her first World Cup match, and the first victory, end in the most dramatic fashion. 'I was shocked. It was something I had never experienced before. I need to go to more games.' She had a taste for it now.

20

The Road to Doha

Almoez Ali had four white-shirted Emirati defenders around him, but none of them could get anywhere close. As he burst down the left side of the penalty box, Ali opened his body and bent the ball around the diving goalkeeper's outstretched left hand. It ricocheted off the right-hand post into the back of the net. It was a moment of beauty, and a goal which put Qatar 2–0 up in their 2019 Asian Cup semi-final against the hosts, the United Arab Emirates. It was his eighth goal of the Asian Cup, a tournament in which Ali had become its breakout star. He was only 22 years old. In the moments after that goal, as he danced in front of the home fans, the tensions that had been simmering for months, years even, came to a head. Plastic bottles, sandals and shoes rained down around him. As George W. Bush discovered in 2008 when Iraqi journalist Muntadhar al Zaidi threw both his shoes at him during a press conference (shouting: 'This is a farewell kiss from the Iraqi people, you dog!'), shoe-throwing was a pretty grave insult in Arab culture. And Ali's goal had unleashed a torrent of anger.

The Gulf blockade, as it turned out, was not a short flash of fire that would burn out. Things did not go back to normal. It was just over 18 months since it had begun, and it had now settled into a stalemate. Qatar's economy hadn't collapsed. If anything it had diversified, bringing Qatar closer to Iran, not further apart. The construction of the World Cup hadn't been adversely affected and the government refused to implement any of the 13 demands that the coalition led by Saudi Arabia, the UAE and Bahrain had issued. And the coalition couldn't accept the humiliation of backing down without at least something to show for it. The only lever left was to try and win the information war. For 18 months, the UAE pumped out stories about the nefarious Qataris and their terrorist ways. The Qataris responded with stories about how it was being unfairly bullied. And so the anger built up, and shoes and the bottles flew.

The players were, at least, allowed to play. Qatari supporters had effectively been banned from travelling to the UAE. Besides, showing support or sympathy for Qatar was now a criminal offence, making the act of supporting the team in public all but impossible. But there had been one positive development over the past year. Qatar appeared to have found a team. When their Catalan coach took over, the national team had been relying on older naturalised players to try and compete. Instead Félix Sánchez started trusting the players that had been developed at the Aspire Academy. Suddenly the Qatar national team looked completely different. Almoez Ali was born in Sudan but came to Qatar when he was five. Winger Akram Afif was born in Doha and had Somali and Yemeni roots. Defender Bassam al Rawi was born in Baghdad but grew up in Qatar. They had all come through Aspire and were all in their early 20s. The captain Hassan al Haydos was the senior figure, at 31 years old, a one-club man having come through the youth team of Al Sadd. And they were tearing the tournament apart. In the group stage they didn't concede a goal, beating Lebanon 2–0, North Korea 6–0 (Ali scored four), before beating Saudi Arabia 2–0, a match Saudi fans had boycotted. Ali scored both goals then too. The team played, as Xavi had hoped, like a mini-Barcelona. They didn't stop when they were 2–0 up against the UAE either. They won 4–0, and would play in the final against either Japan or Carlos Queiroz's Iran. By full-time, there were no more shoes left to throw.

The blockade wasn't the only story of the Asian Cup. Yemen had somehow qualified for its first ever major tournament. It had been a tortuous few years for Yemeni football, and for Hamid, the genial general secretary of the Yemen Football Association, who I had chewed qat with and dreamed of the glowing future of football in the country. The last time we had spoken was in 2010. Yemen was due to host the Gulf Cup, in the port city of Aden and nearby Zinjibar. But there had been problems. A bomb had gone off in Aden, at the first division club Al Wahda – one of the clubs due to host the tournament. Hamid was summoned to a meeting in Beirut with the other Gulf FA chiefs. 'Don't worry, they have all confirmed their participation, the teams and the technical committees,' he cheerily told me on the phone when he returned to the capital Sana'a. 'The security is the responsibility of the state but football is making love and peace between people and we are sure that they will unite behind the tournament. Terrorists are in all the Arab countries. They will not affect it.'

After that bombing the situation got worse. In Aden, two senior British diplomats survived an assassination attempt whilst a French oil worker was murdered in a separate attack on the same day. Then came the attempted bombing of cargo planes destined for the US, using explosives stuffed into printer cartridges that had originated in Yemen. President Saleh himself promised that 30,000 troops would patrol the tournament and that US-trained anti-terrorist operatives would be in charge of guarding the teams, with extra security placed at hotels too. Hamid was satisfied, especially with the new stadiums he had secured. 'We have never had this before, this investment,' he said. 'We have two official stadiums to FIFA standard and new training fields. It's the first time in Yemen that the government has done this.'

Hamid believed this was finally a new dawn of Yemeni football. He was an optimist and believed football could even be a trump card to fight against Al Qaeda. 'They do not want love and peace; they are extremists and they don't represent the people,' he said. 'We want our people to know they are equal to other Gulf countries, and this will help development here in society and football. If they put their energies into football they won't put their energies into extremism.' The tournament went broadly without any major disasters, although Yemen lost all three games. But it was also one of President Saleh's last civil acts. The Arab Spring had arrived and he was ousted from power. But the battle for who controlled Yemen would destroy the country. Yemen were banned from hosting home games. By 2011 the stadium in Zinjibar was being used by the Yemeni army to land helicopters carrying weapons to fight Al Qaeda insurgents nearby. Forty-eight people, including 30 soldiers, were killed in a battle to control the stadium. Now the country was at war with itself, with the northern Houthi rebels, supported by Iran, vying for control with the government in Sana'a, backed by a UAE–Saudi coalition which had indiscriminately bombed civilian targets. The May 22 Stadium in Aden, which hosted the 2010 Gulf Cup final between Kuwait and

Saudi Arabia, was destroyed by coalition air strikes. The airport was terminally damaged.

When the Yemen national team played a World Cup qualifier in 2015 they had to be smuggled out of the country on a cargo ship leaving from Aden. They sailed for 13 hours to Djibouti (a photo of the team sleeping on the deck of the ship went viral on social media) and then flew to Qatar, where Hamid now lived. He'd survived the war that had killed as many as a quarter of a million people and didn't look like it was stopping any time soon. Incredibly, nine members of the squad still lived in Yemen, making their qualification for the 2019 Asian Cup all the more remarkable. But Hamid was in Qatar, so he wouldn't be at the tournament. 'Everything is destroyed,' he said sadly when we spoke on the phone. 'Nothing is left.' They lost all three games without scoring.

Carlos Queiroz, meanwhile, didn't get the ending he wanted either. Japan blew Iran away in the second-half of their semi-final and won 3–0. He quit after the game, at a press conference in Al Ain, in typically robust fashion, quoting Frank Sinatra's 'My Way' and shouting at the critics who he thought had made his life harder. 'In his last press conference he called a journalist a motherfucker!' said the Iranian journalist Behnam Jafarzadeh. 'He needs to be a little more diplomatic.'

In the final Qatar swept Japan away too, beating them 3–1 in the final at Zayed Sports City in Abu Dhabi. Almoez Ali was the tournament's top scorer. It was the only goal Qatar conceded in the whole tournament and marked an important moment in Asian football. Japan had won a record four titles and had, over the years, blazed a trail for Asian players competing at the highest level in European club football. On the other hand, Qatar didn't exist 50 years ago and they had never got past the quarter-finals of the Asian Cup before. Aspire had been the difference, and not just here. Six months before, at Russia 2018, two Aspire graduates became the first to play in a World Cup: Moussa Wagué for Senegal and Francis Uzoho for Nigeria.

FIFA president Gianni Infantino and the AFC's Bahraini president Sheikh Salman fixed their grins as they handed the trophy to captain Hassan al Haydos before the players celebrated winning a tournament under extraordinary political pressure. Pressure that wasn't going to let up anytime soon.

*

Gianni Infantino had been a fountain of new ideas since he was elected FIFA president. One of his first was expanding the World Cup to 48 teams, which was agreed for the 2026 finals, to be held in the US, Canada and Mexico. He would later make a startling pitch to the FIFA Council, the organisation's new ruling body that had replaced the Executive Committee, which had been tainted by the accusations of corruption connected to the 2018 and 2022 World Cup bids. He had been approached with a proposal for a revamped Club World Cup, expanded to include the biggest European clubs. It would be a direct challenge to UEFA's Champions League and would include a global version of UEFA's Nations League and rights to FIFA's vast and highly lucrative archive of intellectual property: videos, photos, computer games, the works. The figure was huge: $25 billion would be raised, far more than FIFA could have hoped to ask for. The current Club World Cup, according to the *New York Times*, was worth $100 million at best. But Infantino would not disclose to FIFA who was behind the deal due to a non-disclosure agreement. He wanted to push through an agreement at the FIFA Council anyway, claiming that there was a deadline before the deal would be withdrawn. UEFA's president Aleksander Čeferin, fearing a challenge to the supremacy of the Champions League, fiercely opposed the proposal, as did many of Europe's top club sides, at least in public. The council said they needed more time. Over the following months more details dripped out, including information about the role of SoftBank, the huge Japanese conglomerate, and the sovereign wealth funds of Saudi Arabia and the UAE. The three had combined to create the world's largest tech investment fund, worth $100 billion, called the Vision Fund: $45 billion had come from Saudi Arabia, and $15 billion from the UAE's sovereign wealth vehicle Mubadala. Mohamed bin Zayed was the chairman of Mubadala, Sheikh Mansour, the owner of Manchester City, its deputy chairman. Khaldoon al Mubarak, who runs Manchester City, was the CEO and managing director.

The full details of the deal remained opaque, but there was more. Infantino now wanted a 48-team World Cup in Qatar. This made little sense as it would be impossible for Qatar to host a 48-team World Cup at such short notice. So Infantino suggested that Qatar might consider sharing it with its neighbours. At the end of 2018, in Argentina, Gianni

Infantino addressed the leaders of the G20, the 20 largest economies in the world. MbS, who Infantino had smiled and joked with at the opening of the World Cup, was among them. After saying for years that sports and politics should be separate, Infantino gave a speech that claimed football could in fact be used to heal social and political divisions. 'Maybe, if football makes dreams come true, in 2022 we could also experience a World Cup in Qatar as well as, why not, some games in other countries of the Arabian Gulf. But this is another story, hopefully with a happy end. *Inshallah!*' he said. Later he told the *Guardian* that expanding and sharing the World Cup could help bring peace in the Gulf: 'if any discussion around the World Cup can help in any way whatsoever to make the situation evolve in that region, with regard to Saudi Arabia, it's a nice impact maybe.'

But facts on the ground were changing things. In October 2018, the dissident Saudi journalist Jamal Khashoggi had been lured to the Saudi consulate in Istanbul and brutally murdered. Khashoggi's journalism had been critical of MbS and countered the reformist narrative by highlighting growing authoritarianism and the jailing of anyone that disagreed with him, be they journalists, academics or feminist activists. Fearing for his life, Khashoggi fled to the United States where he wrote for the *Washington Post*. There, he was targeted by an online social media campaign, originating in Saudi Arabia, to intimidate and drown out opponents of MbS. Khashoggi called the pro-Saudi activists and bots his 'flies'. He had met and fallen in love with Hatice Cengiz, a Turkish graduate student. He had gone to the Saudi consulate to get a document so the two could be married. Cengiz waited outside but he never returned.

Inside the consulate, a 15-man assassination team was waiting. Khashoggi was beaten, strangled, drugged and then dismembered with a bone saw. The Saudi authorities furiously denied they were responsible but the sheer weight of evidence made that position untenable. They would eventually blame the killing on 'rogue' Saudi agents, who were closely linked to MbS's inner circle. Five low-ranked members of the hit squad were sentenced to death in a Saudi court (later commuted to lengthy jail terms) but those closest to MbS were cleared. No one has been executed for the crime. MbS himself would later take responsibility for Khashoggi's death, but denied he ordered it. The CIA later concluded he most likely ordered the killing.

This put Infantino in a difficult position. He was forced to stress that direct Saudi state funds would not be used to pay for any revamped Club World Cup. The FIFA Council eventually approved the new 24-team club tournament, with the first edition planned for 2021 (since postponed due to COVID), but a source I knew close to Qatar's organising committee said there was no way an expanded World Cup would happen. There was zero appetite to share the 2022 World Cup after everything that had happened. They would simply delay until the World Cup qualifiers began, which would make expansion impossible. As long as the decision rumbled on, time would eventually scupper Infantino's plans and, they cheekily added, Infantino's hopes for a Nobel Peace Prize.

The information war continued too. I'd been part of a *New York Times* investigation team that had uncovered how a little-known, London-based consultancy firm – whose founder has close links to the UAE's ruling elite – had been involved in a campaign to place negative stores in the British media, especially the BBC and the *Sunday Times*, designed to damage Qatar's chances of hosting the World Cup. But there was no killer blow. Even Donald Trump changed his mind. In July 2019, Emir Tamim was invited to the White House. The emir gave a speech making thinly veiled criticisms of Qatar's neighbours. 'Tamim, you've been a friend of mine for a long time, before I did this presidential thing, and we feel very comfortable with each other,' Trump said in the White House. They had just signed a $300 million weapons system contract. Qatar believed they had weathered the storm.

DOHA, STATE OF QATAR, DECEMBER 2019

It was for moments like these that the Khalifa International Stadium was built, and rebuilt. Tens of thousands of fans from across the world filled the stands at the centre of the Aspire complex. It was the semi-final of FIFA's Club World Cup. Today, it was the champions of South America against the champions of Asia: Flamengo from Brazil against Al Hilal of Saudi Arabia. The Club World Cup was, for most of its short life, a largely unloved inconvenience for European football, coming as it did in the middle of their season. Liverpool, who had won the Champions League earlier in the year, saw it as a benign inconvenience. Although not everyone felt the same. In South America, stretching back to the decades when the tournament was called the Intercontinental Cup, the Club World Cup was a chance to show the rich Europeans where the real talent in world football lay.

Flamengo had brought nearly 30,000 fans from the other side of the world. I'd flown with them from Rio to São Paulo to Doha, via Casablanca. When the team coach left for the Galeão airport thousands took a day off work to line the streets. Helicopters with TV cameras followed the cortège, beaming the images of the procession – known as the 'Aero-Fla' – live on prime-time TV. Thousands more waited at the airport itself, where a mini riot broke out when the coach glided past us and into the car park of the departure hall.

This tournament, though, had an even wider significance than usual. True, some of the biggest stars in world football would be here, like Liverpool's Mohamed Salah and Flamengo's striker Gabriel 'Gabigol' Barbosa. But also, after nearly ten years of speculation, lurid revelations, accusations of corruption, mistreatment, exploitation and geopolitical shenanigans, it was a chance for the world to finally see what a global football tournament in Qatar really looked like. How would Qatar handle thousands of boisterous fans? Would they be able to drink beer? What about gay fans? Would it be too hot? What about the thousands of workers from Asia reported to have died in the construction of the tournament's infrastructure? Qatar's huge bet on the World Cup was becoming a reality.

In the stands behind the goal, as the kick-off neared, the Raça Rubro-Negra had already been singing for an hour. Raça was the *torcida* – a kind of organised fan group comparable to ultras in Europe – of Flamengo and brought their own drums, flags, banners and songs thousands of miles with them. They had even written a song especially for the occasion, which I had heard sung incessantly in Rio and Doha, celebrating the time Flamengo beat Liverpool 3–0 in the 1981 Intercontinental Cup. Everyone assumed they would breeze past Al Hilal and into the final to face Liverpool.

I arrived nine hours early with Benfica, the capo of Raça, who was in charge of leading the songs in the stadiums. We had a pile of banners and a stack of paperwork as thick as a book. In global football fan culture, whether with ultras or *torcidas*, your banner was your identity. It was one of the reasons why rival groups often attempted to steal them. At Benfica's home on the outskirts of Rio, we had folded up three long banners, around 20 metres in length. Somehow, we had managed to fit them into a backpack which Benfica would carry to the other side of the world.

Actually getting them into the stadium was a different task altogether. FIFA had to approve each flag to make sure there were no political or racist symbols or words. Each had to be checked before entering, even if the Qatari police couldn't understand why you would go to the hassle of carrying such a thing from Brazil. After three lines of security, we were in, tying the banners to the front of the main stand with pieces of string. It was hard work, Benfica admonishing me constantly for working too slowly. But this was perhaps the most important ritual of being a fan, and being a member of Raça. You could be watching a match in the most corporate of corporate arenas, but if your flag was there, it didn't matter. A little piece of Rio was here, like the diplomatic mission of a foreign government. Once finished, we took our seats in the empty stadium, and waited eight hours for the start of the match.

Before the game, we watched Espérance from Tunisia, Africa's champions, play Al Sadd of Qatar. Espérance were well respected in the ultras scene and brought with them flares, perhaps the first time flares had been let off in a Qatari stadium, as well as a 'Fuck Fifa' banner. Their capo had snuck it into the ground by wrapping it around his body, under a baggy T-shirt. The police immediately sprang into action, wading in with batons to try and take the banner down. I was grabbed, dragged outside and threatened with arrest for filming it. They had never seen ultras before, nor did they have any idea how to deal with them. But I was released and allowed to watch Flamengo play Al Hilal.

Al Hilal was Saudi Arabia's most successful team. A year before, because of the blockade, there would have been doubts whether they would have travelled to Qatar to play. But they were here. There were even a few hundred Saudi fans with blue Hilal shirts on. It was a sign that the blockade was waning. The noise from the Flamengo *torcida* was incredible. They sang their Liverpool song.

> *In December 1981, you put the Englishmen in circles.*
> *3–0 against Liverpool, it left a mark in history.*
> *And in Rio there's no one like you, only Flamengo is world champion*
> *And now your people ask for the world again!*

They only stopped singing it, briefly, when Al Hilal took a shock lead in the 18th minute, the goal scored by Salem al Dawsari, the young Saudi player I had met in Spain. Benfica demanded his crowd sing louder. With their Brazilian-style drums keeping rhythm, the *torcida* urged Flamengo forward. They scored three without reply. Men wept. A woman repeatedly kissed a necklace with the face of Jesus on it. Flamengo won 3–1, and were in the final. Benfica stood on his chair and finally turned towards the pitch. 'Fuck you, Europe!' he shouted.

Qatar was almost ready. Most of the stadiums had been finished or were close to being finished. There was the lavish Museum of Islamic Art and the Arab Museum of Modern Art. A Fan Zone was being trialled where fans could go and drink subsidised beer in special areas far away from the city. Buses were laid on to take supporters a 20-minute drive to a soulless wide space that looked like an open-air Wetherspoons. A pint of beer would cost £15 in a hotel bar in Doha, but here it was a third of that. There was now a cheap and largely empty metro system that filled with football fans on matchday; ultras from Espérance, the *barras bravas* of Mexican side Monterrey and the *torcida* of Flamengo all drumming and singing in their own languages. Nervous security guards and policemen, unused to any public displays of anarchy, hung back, clearly under orders not to intervene in this unfamiliar dance. Flamengo fans dressed up in white *thobes*, red and white check headscarves and roamed the Potemkin-style 'old' city, which had been rebuilt from scratch, singing and dancing. 'Our way is a Brazilian way, samba, it's our way, a way of cheering,' said Benfica when I asked him about his *torcida*. The group, he explained, had been formed in 1977 with leftists ideals, a bulwark against the fascist military junta that ruled Brazil at the time. But over the years

Brazil's *torcidas* began to more resemble mafia clans. Murders were frequent. Benfica was part of a group of people trying to bring Raça back to its original ideals. 'Honestly I was already wondering how I would get the money to come to Doha but the Flamengo fan is capable of any sacrifice to realise this dream,' he said. The answer for Benfica was to get a loan. 'For Doha I have instalments to pay all the way to the end of next year.'

The final between Flamengo and Liverpool was the first time the Khalifa International Stadium had been full since it had been built. Liverpool fans had travelled from all across the Middle East, even from blockading nations. All of Flamengo's fans crowded into their usual spot, the stand behind one of the goals, with Benfica at the centre of it all. Immediately it was clear Liverpool were a different proposition to Al Hilal. They dominated possession but somehow Flamengo survived until half-time. As the game progressed in the second-half, Flamengo came back but it looked like it was all over when Liverpool were awarded a penalty in the dying minutes. A Flamengo supporter next to me kissed a picture of St Jude, Flamengo's patron saint, and prayed for divine intervention. VAR decided it wasn't a penalty after all. The game went to extra-time but Flamengo couldn't hold on. Brazilian international striker Roberto Firmino scored what would be the winner for Liverpool. The Liverpool fans were moderately happy with their new piece of silverware. Around me, children and adults were crying. Benfica and I waited for the celebrating players to leave the pitch before we cut down the banners and packed them away, ready for the long journey home.

The Qataris announced that the tournament had been a success. 'Our plans were previously theoretical and today they are being applied on the ground. Overall I think the Club World Cup has been a great success as a test event,' said Hassan Al Thawadi. 'There are three more years to go to learn, so I have no doubt that by 2022 we will be ready.' But there was someone I had to see before I left.

It had been four years since I'd first met Arman, but he hadn't aged a day. He was standing outside his labour camp on the road to Shahaniya and greeted me warmly. He waved me past the security guard at the front and started the tour of his home. There were wide paved roads with grass verges lined with identical rows of clean prefabricated huts. 'It's cold!' he said, surprised, rubbing his arms. It was, indeed, cold for Qatar standards: 18°C with a strong northerly wind.

I'd first met Arman as he was queuing for his flight from Hazrat Shahjalal International Airport outside Dhaka, the capital of Bangladesh. He was about to embark on a new life as a migrant worker in Qatar. Bangladesh was one of the biggest exporters of migrant workers to the Gulf. In fact, the remittances from migrant workers were now Bangladesh's biggest form of inward investment. The economy was utterly reliant on it. So much so that Bangladeshi workers were often treated the worst by Gulf states. Bangladesh was so reliant on the inflow of pay cheques from the Gulf that it turned a blind eye to most abuses, whether they were non-payment of wages in Dubai, the rash of deaths from working in the Gulf's incredible summer heat or the systemic sexual abuse of domestic staff in Saudi Arabia.

I had spent the previous two weeks hearing horrific stories from migrants who had managed to escape home. Others had been deported from the UAE or Saudi Arabia for daring to try and unionise. When they returned home they were treated as pariahs. Often their extended families had sold everything they owned to pay the agent and bribe the officials, who would smooth the worker's path to the Gulf, in the hope they would strike gold. Back home they were safe, but the family now had no income. Workers often felt guilty for returning. Suicide, I'd been told, was high.

Shariful Hasan, an investigative journalist who documented the treatment of his fellow countrymen and women abroad for the *Daily Prothom Alo*, told me that he would travel to the airport every Friday. Thousands more would be queuing to leave. It was also the time when the bodies of dead workers would be sent home. No one was counting the unnaturally large numbers of men dying in the Gulf – usually of heart complaints despite being in their 20s – so Shariful would keep count instead: ten bodies a week, 500 a year. Thousands since he had started counting. The airport was so full of migrant workers headed to the Gulf that a long queue snaked outside of its entrance. Inside, illiterate workers gestured to me to fill out their departure cards for them. I looked at their passports: short-term, one-month work visas for Qatar.

That was when I met Arman. He was ready to board a plane to Doha. A long line of workers stood wearing the same baseball hats and T-shirts, branded with the logo of the employment agency that had arranged their trip. There was a feeling of excitement. 'We are all excited, because we have jobs in Qatar!' said Arman cheerily. He was, he told me, a recent graduate but this was the only way for him to get a well-paid job on the Lusail site, the centrepiece of Qatar's 2022 World Cup development. 'I know this company. It is a big company, a big name in the construction game. So I am happy. We are happy we are joining this company.' And they were. Arman said he had been promised a wage of 2,200 Qatari riyals, around £450 a month. He would, he said, be there for a 'minimum' of five years. Arman was arriving just as Qatar, after years of criticism, appeared to be taking the abuse of the *kafala* system – which bound a worker to their employer – seriously. The government signed an agreement with the International Labor Organization which committed Qatar to passing laws that brought labour rights up to an international standard. The ILO would open an office in Doha and monitor the process.

Those five years were nearly up and Arman was still smiling. It hadn't been easy, he told me. Over the past four years we had stayed in contact by WhatsApp. He'd become something of a bellwether for me to understand how things were for the Gulf's vast underclass. How Qatar had coped with the blockade, how food had become scarce in the weeks that followed. How the huge hit, economically, had resulted in a slowdown at work that wasn't really reported to the outside world. He'd almost lost his job. But his company had also arranged for him to have an operation to fix a serious, and long-standing, medical issue he'd been carrying for years. His wages were low but he could send back enough to keep his family happy and to find a wife. He was also desperate to leave. The camp, he showed me, was orderly and clean. He lived with one other worker in an air-conditioned room. Food was served from a huge mess hall with different serving stations for the workers from India, Bangladesh, the Philippines and West Africa. 'Some people don't like our food. It's too spicy,' he told me as we sat down and ate a (mild) chicken biriyani. But for Arman Qatar was always a stopgap, a stepping stone to the West where you could earn real money and live a free life. Arman would often message me with emails he had been sent offering him jobs on construction sites in the US for huge corporations based in Houston or New York. He was thinking of applying but he was being asked to send hundreds of dollars to apply. The emails were all fakes. On top of all the other exploitative practices they faced, migrant workers were being targeted by scammers from Bangladesh and West Africa, posing as fake American employment agents offering fabulous jobs.

So he stayed, was promoted to foreman, and had come to terms with the alien conditions. 'I'm happy with the conditions and the work,' he said. 'The summer is too hot. Too hot. And it's good we have security but ...' Regardless of the conditions, this was still a camp, isolated from the rest of the country. It was almost impossible to leave it on your day off, especially in the summer. They lived a life completely separated from the glitzy seaside corniche. Arman was grateful for what he had. It could be much, much worse. The conditions here were much better than the camps I had seen down the road in Al Shahaniya, now heavily guarded and full of workers in the 'grey' economy; workers whose visas had expired but remained and could now be exploited outside of the system. But he wanted a normal life, with a family and kids. 'I hope I can see you one day away from here,' he said. He had a few leads about a job in Belgium. When I took a picture of the mess hall with my camera, four security guards arrived to stop me from taking any more. I was being watched by the network of CCTV cameras around the camp. I wasn't sure if they were designed to keep people like me out, or workers like Arman in.

There were very few public spaces where workers could gather on their days off. There was the mosque of course, or the Church of Our Lady of the Rosary, a vast Tower of Babel complex that held mass for dozens of different countries and denominations. A board by the entrance listed mass times for various denominations and languages: Lebanese Maronites, Sri Lankan Tamils, Indian Catholics, Christians from Nigeria, Ghana and Egypt. I spoke to Christian workers from Nigeria and Ghana who were mainly hired as security guards. They were recent arrivals and had no problems with late payment, just low payment and a feeling that, as Africans, they were at the bottom of Qatar's racial hierarchy. But here, in the church, they felt like equals. It was as much a social space as a religious one.

And there was also cricket. A few minutes' walk from the church, on a patch of sand between a school and a six-lane highway, a cricket tournament was taking place between four teams of Indian workers from the same electrical engineering company. Each team had a different coloured flag: grey, blue, red or green. A nearby table had a heavy, gold-coloured trophy that was supposed to be for the company's annual tug-of-war competition but someone had mislaid the cricket trophy and this was all they could find at short notice. By 2022 Qatar will have spent at least $200 billion on football. Yet ironically cricket was the country's most popular sport. It was the true game of the street, with hundreds of games played on patches of sand like this throughout Doha every Friday.

I spoke to the players – storekeepers, engineers, labourers, drivers – next to a makeshift manual scoreboard. We watched the games unfold in front of us, a round-robin six-over tournament, with a ten-over final. It was cool and overcast, thick grey clouds hanging in the sky. A fierce wind blew the sand into our faces, turning everything sepia. Everyone had the same story. Most were from Kerala. Life was hard, of that there was no doubt. But they were proud of their work and didn't want to be seen as charity cases or victims. There was a genuine joy and camaraderie as the tournament progressed, something that was often lost when speaking to migrant workers in the Gulf, who were far away from their wives and families. Juice and chocolate biscuits were shared and passed around. 'It's not easy for these guys, they have tough lives away from home,' said Sajman, one of the foremen from the company who'd driven them there. No one could find the numbered slates for the scoreboard so they used a cricket scoring app on one of the players' mobile phones instead. 'Every Friday we come here. We have one day off. It's their only entertainment. We play here and for one or two hours we are somewhere else.' The tournament came down to the last ball between the grey and the blue team. We all stood in silence, the cold wind blasting sand into our eyes. The batsman for the grey team connected, and smashed the ball long and high. The 50 men started celebrating before it had landed. There was no boundary but Sajman declared it was a six.

Postscript

ANTALYA, REPUBLIC OF TURKEY, OCTOBER, 2020

Except for the buzzing sound of late afternoon heat, the Titanic Stadium was silent and empty. I wasn't sure if I'd turned up at the right stadium until a large coach arrived through the mirage rising from the tarmac. It swung into the empty car park, carrying two-dozen players wearing maroon tracksuits. The Qatar national team filed out silently and into the stadium. It had been less than ten months since I'd watched Liverpool win the Club World Cup in Doha, a dress rehearsal for what a tournament in Qatar might look like. It mostly went to plan. The Metro was working. There was no crowd trouble aside from a few boisterous Tunisian ultras. The final in the Khalifa International Stadium was sold out, the biggest crowd in Qatari history. And then COVID-19 struck and the world changed.

Suddenly foreign travel was impossible. The world had been endless to me before. Now my world was very small. Even watching a football match live seemed like a crazy possibility. Government lockdowns and movement restrictions had made international football almost impossible to arrange. Millions of people died. We went from a collective world to an atomised existence. The world still turned, and there was still a World Cup to get ready for. But was a World Cup, or indeed any tournament where large numbers of people crossed borders for a collective experience among thousands of strangers, ever going to take place again? It felt like a relic from a bygone era.

This was to be Qatar's first game in nearly 11 months, since the global pandemic started. Very few countries were open to guests, except Turkey. This stretch of southern Mediterranean coastline had been turned into a kind of training theme park for football clubs. Training pitches and stadiums had been built all along the coast, with attendant hotels, catering for professional football teams all across Europe who would come for warm-weather training camps from Russia, Serbia, Germany and Bulgaria. It had been a lucrative business but COVID had destroyed tourism, on which Turkey heavily relied. So they kept the training camps open. It was the only place Qatar and Ghana could play each other in a friendly. 'We are really exciting to play for Qatar, we have a tough match,' said Hassan al Haydos, the captain, as we stood by the pitch. He couldn't stop smiling through the whitest teeth I had ever seen. 'It was really difficult to stop suddenly everything. It was a strange moment. But thank God we got through this.'

Hassan had built a gym in his house to try and keep in shape but the pandemic checked the national team's progress. They had won the Asian Cup, for the first time, in the UAE. They were then invited to play in the Copa America, where they were drawn in the same group as Argentina. Most people thought they would be smashed, but they fought back from 2–0 down to draw against Paraguay and only lost to a single, 86th-minute goal against Colombia. They were still in the game against Argentina until a late Lionel Messi goal. 'I think we still have the desire,' Hassan said, but today was the first chance to see if they could get back to where they were. 'We are trying step by step to get back.' After spending $200 billion on a tournament, spending 15 years on a global talent search and surviving a geopolitical crisis, the biggest threat to Qatar 2022 had come from Wuhan.

It had been 15 years since I first visited Qatar in 2005 and met Manfred Hoener (who died of a heart attack at the age of 79 in March 2021). In those 15 years football had provided me a window of understanding into a diverse and vibrant region. But it was also much more than that. The Middle East had become a genuine financial power in the global game. And football had afforded a voice to those who had no other. It had provided a space to breathe where none other existed. It had provoked both fear and admiration in dictators and presidents alike. It had fuelled at least one revolution and provided heroes and villains in other uprisings. The powerful wanted to hold the game close, whether it was Hosni Mubarak or the royal family of Abu Dhabi. To understand football in the Middle East was to understand, at least partially, the Middle East itself. Many of the people I had met – the fans, the officials and the players – would play their own roles in the future direction of their countries. Some big, some small.

In Iran, women were still struggling for the right to enter the stadium. After the World Cup in Russia things went back to the way they were. Until the death of the 'Blue Girl'. In 2019, Sahar Khodayari, a 29-year-old fan of Esteghlal, was arrested for dressing as a man and trying to sneak into the Azadi to watch her team play Al Ain in the Asian Champions League. She was charged with not wearing a hijab, as there is no law officially banning women from football matches, and spent several days in prison. After her last court case, fearing she would receive a six-month jail sentence, she set herself on fire. In the aftermath, Iranians denounced a system that would allow something like this to happen. The legendary former midfielder Ali Karimi urged all fans to boycott the stadiums until women were allowed to return. Under pressure, the authorities relented and a few weeks later women were let into the Azadi to watch a World Cup qualifier against Cambodia. The 4,000 women chanted 'Blue Girl, Blue Girl!', named after the colour of Esteghlal's jersey. Iran won 14–0.

The relaxation of the ban was temporary, though, and Iran's qualification for Qatar 2022 continued to be dominated by the issue. Activists felt that the government was hiding behind COVID restrictions to avoid reform. Eventually, 2,000 women were allowed into the Azadi to watch Iran qualify for Qatar 2022 by beating Iraq 1–0. But @openstadiums wasn't happy, saying ordinary women couldn't buy tickets and that the 2,000 were handpicked VIPs. When Robert Malley, US special envoy for Iran, tweeted how happy he was to see women in the stadium, @openstadiums replied: 'Fighting for human rights is really difficult when officials get manipulated this easy . . .'. 'Sara' is still fighting. Branko, meanwhile, left Iran on a high, moving to Qatar after winning Persepolis's third title in a row. And Carlos Queiroz? He took the Egypt national team job and got them to the final of the 2022 Africa Cup of Nations. During the semi-final he got sent off for screaming at the referee and had to be dragged off the pitch. He was given a two-match ban and had to watch Senegal beat Egypt in the final from the stands. His contract was terminated by mutual consent. 'He is like José Mourinho,' said the Iranian journalist Behnam Jafarzadeh. 'He wants to poke people in the eye, and if they become annoyed, he thinks he is doing them a favour.' Truly, the battles never end.

The former saviour of Beitar Jerusalem, Guma Aguiar, meanwhile, was never seen again. In June 2012, as legal cases mounted against him and his mental health deteriorated, he jumped into his speedboat in the Florida Keys and disappeared. His boat, the *T.T. Zion*, was found drifting and empty. Aguiar was gone, his phone and wallet were found on board. At first it seemed like a clear case of suicide, a troubled young man about to lose everything taking his final stand. One coastguard suggested that the abrupt change of speed and the broken tow bar indicated that Aguiar might have been thrown overboard. In the Gulf Stream, his body would be taken north and never seen again. In fact, few involved in the case truly expected a body to be found, but not because of the speed of the Gulf Stream. Some believed Guma Aguiar might have faked his death.

Guma's wife Jamie and his mother Ellen quickly embarked on a costly legal battle over Guma's remaining assets. 'There's certainly enough evidence that one could deduce that he's still alive,' explained Jamie Aguiar's lawyer Bill Scherer, sitting in his smart conference room in Florida, speaking to me on Skype back in 2013. 'It would be a nice chapter in a mystery novel ... He could have been thrown out [of the boat], drowned and his body swept north and never found. Or he could have stayed in, it drifted to shore, he jumped out the boat and was picked up by someone who was waiting for him. It could have been either or.' If Guma Aguiar was alive, where could he possibly go? One theory was the Netherlands. According to Scherer, around the time of his disappearance Aguiar's (unnamed) best friend and business partner upped sticks and moved to Amsterdam. 'The sister and the brother-in-law are in Amsterdam and trying to avoid our process so we can take a deposition and ask them, on oath, whether they know where he is,' said Scherer. 'Amsterdam is a place he used to like to go ... We learned Guma loved Amsterdam. For obvious reasons ...'

There was also, according to Scherer, the case of Guma's missing clothes. 'Socks, shoes, custom-fitted clothing all removed [from his house in Israel]. Personal items. Things that he would want to have if he was still alive,' he said. 'They [whoever removed the clothes] got in without any evidence of forced entry but they cut out all the internal video surveillance. And they would only know how to do that if they knew the setup.' But after three years, there was no sign of Guma. His wife and mother eventually called a truce and agreed to declare him officially dead, after accidentally falling overboard and drowning, in 2015. His body was never found.

The responsibility for funding Beitar Jerusalem had returned to Arcadi Gaydamak, who made one last attempt at changing the attitudes on the terraces of the Teddy Stadium by sanctioning the signing of two Chechen Muslim players. La Familia were furious. When one of the players scored his first goal for the club, La Familia turned their backs en masse. Arcadi's time at Beitar was coming to an end. He sold the club a few months later but his legal troubles were about to take a turn for the worse. Gaydamak had been found guilty in his long-running 'Angolagate' court case in France. He was later acquitted but then sentenced to three years in prison for tax evasion, and released with a tag after just a year inside. 'I was never a football fan, I always said that,' he said in the documentary *Forever Pure* when asked why he had bought Beitar. 'Beitar had more fans than all the other clubs in Israel combined. And this is why it is a very interesting propaganda tool. It has a huge influence on Israeli society.'

Beitar was sold to businessman Eli Tabib, whose attempts to tame La Familia didn't go well either. The group would protest in his neighbourhood. In 2015 he was shot outside his Tel Aviv home. 'True, it was an attempted assassination. Soccer is bankrupt. I need to sit down and think hard about whether to stay in the world of soccer and whether to remain in Israel at all or return to the United States.' He stayed on and in 2018 vowed to rename the club Beitar 'Trump' Jerusalem in honour of the US president. In the same year he sold the club to a young cryptocurrency entrepreneur, Moshe Hogeg. He too quickly fell foul of La Familia, receiving death threats when the club signed Ali Mohamed, a striker from Niger, even though he was a Christian. 'After countless inquiries and checks regarding the identity

of the player Ali, we hereby announce we have no problem whatsoever with this player, since he is a devout Christian,' La Familia wrote
in a statement on their Facebook page. 'But we do have a problem
with his name. We will make sure that his name is changed so that the
name Mohamed is not heard at Teddy Stadium.' Ali Mohamed never
did change his name. It was a small victory.

But then came the strangest act of all. An Emirati businessman
made an offer to buy Beitar. The UAE and Israel had just normalised
diplomatic relations – the so-called 'Abraham Accords'. As flights
began between Tel Aviv, Abu Dhabi and Dubai, something I thought I
would never see, the purchase was seen by some as a symbolic attempt
to seal the deal. La Familia raged. But the purchase didn't happen. An
Israeli investigation found that most of the sheikh's supposed fortune
was in non-tradable bonds connected to Venezuela's bankrupt government, which were, essentially, worthless. It reminded me of
Sulaiman al Fahim, the face of the Manchester City takeover in 2008.
He hadn't fared too well either. He was sentenced to five years prison
in the UAE for taking £5 million from his wife's account to fund his
purchase of Portsmouth.

Manchester City, meanwhile, have become one of Europe's most
successful and powerful clubs. Since the takeover in 2008 City had
won six Premier League titles, two FA Cups and six League Cups.
A new ownership structure was created called City Football Group
which bought stakes in football clubs around the world. CFC now
owned or part-owned football clubs in Japan, Australia, the US,
Spain, Uruguay, China, India, France and Belgium. Although officially a private purchase by Sheikh Mansour, in reality the resources
of the state were put to the club's disposal, from the key figures
who run Abu Dhabi's government and economy also being put in
charge of running the club, to the huge sponsorship deals with
UAE-owned entities, often run by members of Sheikh Mansour's
own family. They had created a new hybrid form of ownership that
projected Abu Dhabi's name out to the world and minimised the
negative publicity that came from the UAE's appalling human
rights record. They had also accidently discovered a useful ancil-
lary benefit: by delivering success to a starved, underappreciated
club, and by leveraging football's innate tribalism, football

supporters would rally behind the owner regardless of what he, the board or the UAE did. Why pay for armies of troll farms to sell your message about the war in Yemen or the poor treatment of migrant workers when tribal football fans will do it, with much more credibility, for free?

The royal family's activities were also impossible to regulate. In late 2018 an investigation by German magazine *Der Spiegel* appeared to show how Manchester City's ownership had allegedly gone to extraordinary lengths to circumvent UEFA rules to pump large amounts of cash into the club, much of it officially off the books so that it appeared to comply with Financial Fair Play. FFP was a system of economic governance brought into football by UEFA designed to curb debt and profligate, unsustainable spending by the likes of City in the first place. The documents came from Football Leaks, a trove of documents obtained by the Portuguese hacker Rui Pinto. The details appeared to be damning, and UEFA banned the club from the Champions League for two seasons. But the club assembled an expensive army of lawyers, took UEFA to the Court of Arbitration for Sport and won. Many of the claims, CAS would later say, were time barred.

Manchester City, alongside Qatar-owned PSG in France, had perfected such a successful model that in 2021 they were followed by the Public Investment Fund (PIF), Saudi Arabia's sovereign wealth fund, chaired by Mohammed bin Salman, who finally succeeded in buying 80 per cent of Newcastle United. There were grave misgivings about the purchase within the Premier League. Not least because of Saudi Arabia's abysmal human rights record and MbS's own alleged complicity in ordering the dismemberment of Jamal Khashoggi, whose fiancée campaigned hard against the deal. 'The world powers, especially in the West, remained silent about the crime and they didn't hold him [MbS] accountable. And we see the result of the silence. To buy this football club and no one can stop him,' Hatice Cengiz told me when we spoke on a video call. She had been inundated with abuse after tweeting a statement opposing the takeover, from a mixture of Saudi nationalists, bots and Geordie supporters. 'He [MBS] sends a message that he can buy whatever he wants. That is why I felt I had to speak out,' she said.

The Premier League delayed approving the purchase. And although no official reason was given for the delay, Saudi Arabia was at the time busy boycotting Qatar. One weapon was the mass pirating of Qatar-funded sports broadcaster beIN's foreign sports rights using a Saudi-based entity called beoutQ. Despite pressure from the UK Conservative government, desperate for Saudi inward investment after Brexit, the English Premier League resisted. It would not have been a good look allowing an owner connected to the Saudi state, which was at the time stealing their product, to own an English club. But a year later they relented, assured that a Newcastle United majority-owned by a sovereign wealth fund, chaired by the crown prince, and with a board full of government ministers, would not be controlled by the state. To date, the Premier League have never made public what legal assurances they were given. The deal was made by the same fixer who worked behind the scenes on the Manchester City purchase, Amanda Staveley.

Newcastle United supporters celebrated outside St James' Park, delirious to see the back of previous owner Mike Ashley. Some carried Saudi flags or wore Arabic dress. The vast majority of Newcastle fans approved of the deal – a survey by the Newcastle United Supporters Trust found that 96.7 per cent of the 3,000 fans they asked backed the takeover – whilst deflecting any criticism as jealousy or hypocrisy. In the weeks after the purchase, I was reminded of one of Hatice Cengiz's emotional Twitter posts, calling on Newcastle United to oppose the takeover, and the incredible abuse she received afterwards – a mixture of whataboutery and Saudi state talking points – from people who said they were Newcastle United fans. One tweet in particular stood out for me: 'You do realise we do want the Saudi Takeover to happen your letters are irrelevant and not helpful Muhammad bin Salman will be considered a fucking legend on Tyneside after this.' The post ended with a Saudi flag emoji. It was sportswashing in real time. MbS had already won. There was now a new power in world football.

In Egypt the ultras were outlawed in 2015 and branded terrorists. The Ahlawy burned their banner in 2018 and deleted their Facebook account. It had been too dangerous to continue under the repression of Abdel Fattah el Sisi. The ultras melted back into their lives, but no one gave Amr up. In fact, he embarked on the extraordinary final act. He was chosen as secretary general of CAF, although to the outside world it wasn't that much of a surprise. His father was Mustapha

Fahmy, who was secretary general of CAF for nearly three decades. His grandfather Mourad was CAF's first secretary general and a former government minister.

But Amr brought with him a new set of priorities, a moral absolutism that is commonly found in the ultras scene. He wanted to stamp out corruption and wrongdoing whilst modernising the game. He approached the job as a fan and not a businessman or a bureaucrat. VAR was introduced, referees were fired and a system of central payments introduced for transparency. Soon he was rubbing powerful people up the wrong way, including his new boss, CAF president Ahmad Ahmad. Amr was deeply suspicious of what he saw as an artificially inflated sportswear contract. He began collecting evidence. There were allegations that Ahmad misappropriated funds to send African FA chiefs from Muslim countries on a pilgrimage to Mecca. He started putting together a dossier of testimonies from women who alleged they were sexual harassed by Ahmad.

Just as Amr was about to blow the whistle, he found out he was suffering from a brain tumour. He took a leave of absence and undertook a course of chemo. It was a touch and go but, a year later, the tumour was in remission and he was back at work. He felt that he had limited time, and that allies of the president would try to quash the allegations and then remove him. Amr sent the dossier of sexual harassment testimonies to FIFA's ethics committee in Zurich. At the same time, through a trusted lieutenant from the Ahlawy, he began leaking the documents to the press. It was all there: emails, contracts, the entire paper trail. As he feared, Amr was sacked.

The story still made it into the international press. The corruption allegations were so severe that Ahmad was arrested and questioned in France before being released without charge, although an investigation is ongoing. Meanwhile, FIFA president Gianni Infantino took the unusual step of appointing his general secretary Fatma Samoura as a 'General Delegate for Africa', effectively putting her in temporary charge of CAF whilst an ethics investigation was opened into Ahmad's conduct. Ahmad clung on but Amr wasn't satisfied. He decided that, if he wanted to really clean up African football, he needed the top job. So he announced that he would run for CAF President in the 2021 elections.

'My campaign will focus on pro-Africa, pro-football and anti-corruption,' he told the BBC.

But it wasn't to be. In February 2020, Amr Fahmy died. He was survived by his wife and his three-month-old daughter. Banners were raised to honour him across Europe, the revolutionary ultra who had built an army on the terraces before taking that black-and-white moral absolutism inherent in ultra culture into one of football's most powerful jobs. Ahmad Ahmad was banned from standing as president. Amr had got his man.

In Yemen, football was still being destroyed. In December 2021 Saudi jets hit the same stadium in Sana'a I'd visited back in 2007.

The rebel players had mixed fortunes. In Libya, Walid el Kahtroushi retired in relative obscurity a few years after fighting for the rebels and playing in the 2012 Africa Cup of Nations. A second civil war broke out in 2014 that lasted six years and took as many as 15,000 lives. In Syria, the revolution was all but crushed. Abdul Basset al Saroot evaded assassination but his story mirrored the trajectory of Syria's conflict. He became more religious as Islamist groups rose to prominence in the fighting. He was accused of joining ISIS, which he denied, although he conceded they were an effective fighting force against Bashar al Assad. He died in 2019, in a Turkish hospital, after being shot in a firefight with pro-government forces. At the time, he was a senior commander for Jaish al Izza, the 'Army of Glory', affiliated with the Turkish-backed Free Syrian Army. He was 27 years old. Hakeem al Araibi, the young Bahraini player who was tortured and escaped to Australia, found himself in jail in November 2018 when he decided to go on honeymoon in Thailand. Bahrain had requested a 'Red Notice' through Interpol, in effect an international arrest warrant, and he was taken into custody in Bangkok.

After intense pressure FIFA eventually wrote to the Thai government, two months after Hakeem's arrest, asking for him to be released. The 'Red Notice' had been raised 19 days before he travelled, and after he had bought his ticket, suggesting Hakeem may have been watched. The Bahrain government insisted he would get a fair trial. 'Had Al Araibi remained in Bahrain, he would also have had the chance to appeal alongside his co-accused,' a spokesperson told the *Guardian*, even though there was ample evidence he was playing football at the time the crime he was accused of was committed. Others I had spoken to were also being persecuted. Nabeel Rajab, the human rights activist, had been in jail since 2017. In 2018 he was sentenced to five years in prison for tweeting criticism of the Bahraini government.

Sheikh Salman made no public comment about Hakeem. When asked about the case, all the AFC would say was that it was 'working with many stakeholders, including FIFA and the FA of Thailand, on this matter. While this work is on-going we will make no further comment.' Eventually, after 72 days in prison, Hakeem was released and took the first flight to Melbourne.

'Melbourne is the best city in my life. I can't live without it,' said Hakeem when we talked on the phone. It was three years after he had almost been deported to Bahrain. 'When I was in Thailand I missed Melbourne too much. I explained to the people, Thai people, how the sky was too close to the earth. It has such clean air.' He had a good life now. He still played football in the Victoria State League but he knew he would never fulfil his potential, partly because he still felt the psychological effects of what had happened to him. 'I remember, as soon as the plane arrived in Thailand they took me from inside the plane, 20 police, like a movie.' The prison, he said, was one small room. 'Fifty people were sleeping together. Your body size was your space. You go to the toilet, no wall. They watch you. They keep us in the room for 18 hours. No food. Only water.'

He knew what would happen to him if he was sent back. 'They would 100 per cent torture me. All I was thinking of was my wife on her own in Melbourne.' He had no contact with the outside world until former Australian international Craig Foster took up his case, and turned up with a letter from Hakeem's wife. 'He gave me some freedom when I read my wife's message. He said he will support me in FIFA. He gave me hope,' he said. Eventually the pressure worked and Hakeem was released. He was now an Australian citizen, a father, and spoke good English. But he was still scared of leaving the country. He missed his mother. His brother, the activist, had died shortly after spending eight years in prison. 'Something in my mind is always in Bahrain. I think they still want to take revenge on me. Sometimes I see cars around my house. I sometimes think they want to kill me,' he said. 'One thing happened in my job, I was stuck in the lift for ten minutes. I was thinking, it's Bahrain, they are trying to kill me.' He has therapy and medication but the best medicine is his work. He works as a coach for Football Victoria, visiting schools and helping recently arrived refugee kids. 'I like to see kids smile when I tell them my story,' he said. 'And to show them how different their life can be between then and now.'

The Qatari team came out into the lobby of the Titanic Stadium one by one. The coach Félix Sánchez spoke to each player individually. There was no shouting or screaming. This, give or take a few players, would be most of the team that played in the opening game of the World Cup, with Almoez Ali as the focal point in attack. The team lined up in the centre of the Titanic Stadium pitch, the sky streaked gold and blue as the sun set and the Qatari national anthem played.

It was still incredible to me that the country I had visited over 15 years before was about to host a World Cup finals. At times it looked inevitable that the World Cup would be taken away from Qatar. It had won the bid, fought a regional cold war, built a competitive team from scratch and navigated the intense, legitimate criticisms that had followed it for a dozen years. The most damaging had been its treatment of migrant workers. In theory much had changed. New reforms had been promised in 2017 that would abolish *kafala*, allowing workers to change jobs and leave the country without their boss's permission. A new standardised minimum wage was introduced. Agent fees would be banned. Worker accommodation improved, even if it was more out of political expediency than anything else. 'The reform process came out of a political crisis not a human rights crisis,' explained Nicholas McGeehan, a human rights activist who has been campaigning against the injustices of *kafala* for two decades. 'It was the Saudi–Emirati aggression that led Qatar to be isolated and in need of friends everywhere and that was when the ILO was brought in. On paper that reform process looks good.'

On paper. But, as ever, how these new laws were implemented meant that little changed on the ground for many workers. They were still appallingly paid. They were still treated as a disposable underclass. 'The situation is not significantly better than in 2004 or 2010. Which is to say there have been some impressive legal reforms. But if you are a worker on the ground now you wouldn't recognise any significant difference in your treatment from ten years ago,' said McGeehan. The problem, he believed, was that *kafala* was incredibly popular with Qatari citizens as it kept a tight control on its migrant population. 'In many cases the employers see these workers as property, chattel. And people they are free to employ or dispose of at their whim.'

The country was ready, but what would happen after the World Cup? As the magnifying glass of scrutiny moved elsewhere? Would the reforms stay in place? 'Others might be more optimistic but we needed legal reform to be implemented and take hold to demonstrate to the local and the business population that loosening these bonds could be beneficial to Qatari society and its economy. And that hasn't happened,' said McGeehan. 'If that couldn't be done under this spotlight, and there can be no brighter and harsher spotlight than a World Cup, what hope is there of reform when the spotlight is gone? The legacy of the World Cup won't be the transformation of labour rights in the region, but the fact hundreds of thousands of people were brought in, many of them suffering dreadful harms and abuses. And this system has persisted.'

But, barring a nuclear war or an even deadlier pandemic, Qatar 2022 was happening. In November 2021 Joe Biden beat Donald Trump in the US presidential elections. And two weeks before Biden's inauguration, the leaders of Qatar, Saudi Arabia, UAE, Bahrain and Egypt met in the Saudi town of Al Ula and ended the blockade. Qatar's land border with Saudi Arabia was opened and flights resumed. Qatar had not agreed to any of the 13 demands made by the coalition.

Back in Antalya, the match began between Qatar and Ghana, and was played in near silence, with no fans. Qatar lost 5–1.

Acknowledgements

This book, as much as it's about football in the Middle East, is also about luck and the enduring kindness of humans. Over the past 17 years I have been blessed with fortune and the goodwill of strangers. The list is endless and largely anonymous: the Syrian border guard who took pity on me when I had no visa; the taxi driver in Israel who drove me to the Egypt border when my card stopped working; the football fans whom I befriended when stranded outside football stadiums in Jordan, Egypt, Bahrain or Yemen. The young men who shielded me under gunfire in Port Said, or protected me on the streets of Cairo as the revolution fell apart. The photographers I've worked with who have saved me from the beatings I sometimes deserved. The families in the West Bank and Gaza and Lebanon that invited me into their homes for dinner. I only have fragments of names and places, sometimes just a photo. Many of these experiences I have not written about. I have kept those memories to myself. But they are always with me and will stay there for the rest of my life.

This was my first book and it changed the direction my life would go in. I'm thankful to my publisher, Ebury, for republishing *When Friday Comes*, especially Andrew Goodfellow and Robyn Drury, as well as Howard Watson. And also to my agent Rebecca Winfield, who took a punt on me after reading the first three chapters 17 years ago. We've been together ever since. The book would not have existed at all if it wasn't first picked up by Iain MacGregor at Mainstream and then by James Corbett at deCoubertin. I met James whilst being lightly interrogated in a holding pen at Tel Aviv airport. The two of us were on our way to report in the West Bank, which had raised suspicions among the Israeli border guards. He was reading the first edition of *When Friday Comes* and vowed, when we were both eventually let out, to publish an updated edition. What were the chances of that?

Much of the travel that was needed for this book has been paid for through various commissions from magazines, newspapers and radio stations, which enabled me to meet the people that make up the spirit of this book. A huge thank you to everyone at *Delayed Gratification*; Andrew Das at the *New York Times*; Richard Padula at the BBC World Service; Alex Chick at the Bleacher Report; John Sinnott and Ben Wyatt at CNN; Jonathan Wilson at the *Blizzard*; Gavin Hamilton at *World Soccer*. I'd also like to thank Matthew Lowing at Bloomsbury, for letting me use some material about Qatar and the UAE from *The Billionaires Club*, and Will Tidey at the Bleacher Report, who commissioned my original story about the Tehran derby. An abridged version of Amr's story also appears in *1312: Among the Ultras*, also published by Ebury.

The sheer volume of people I have met over nearly two decades is too long to list here. But for this new edition I'd also like to thank everyone from the Ahlawy who I can't mention by name; Rafael de Moura Machado for his help and excellent company in Qatar and Brazil; Sayed Alwadaei for his help with connecting me to Bahraini sportsmen and activists; Reza Nazar for his guidance and Iranian translations; Merhdad Masoudi for his help getting me into Iran; in Turkey, Bora İşyar for his always brilliant editing advice; and Randa Saidi for looking after my most precious human whilst I wrote. Thanks also to Maher Mezahi, Ali Khaled, Morad Dakhil, Bassil Mik dadi and Uri Levy. Apologies to anyone I have shamefully forgotten to mention. Tell me and I'll buy you a drink.

I'd like to thank my family, my mum and dad, sister Laura and Robbie for digging through dozens of boxes to find all my old note-books, USB sticks and negatives. And most importantly Mitra Nazar and my daughter Mila, for whom everything is for. I love you.

Index

423